FamilyFun
VACATION GUIDE
New England

By Deborah Geigis Berry and the
experts at FamilyFun Magazine

DISNEP
EDITIONS
New York

FamilyFun
VACATION GUIDE
New England

Editorial Director
Lois Spritzer

Design & Production
IMPRESS, INC.
Hans Teensma
Pam Glaven
Katie Craig
Lisa Newman
James McDonald
Katie Winger

Disney Editions and *FamilyFun*

Book Editors
Alexandra Kennedy
Wendy Lefkon
Lisa Stiepock

Research Editor
Beth Honeyman

Contributing Editors
Jon Adolph
Rani Arbo
Duryan Bhagat
Jodi Butler
Jaqueline Cappuccio
Deanna Cook
Tony Cuen
Ann Hallock
Jessica Hinds
Martha Jenkins
Heather Johnson
Rich Mintzer
Jody Revenson
David Sokol
Deborah Way

Copy Editors
Diane Hodges
Jenny Langsam
Monica Mayper
Jill Newman

Editorial Assistants
Laura Gomes
Jean Graham

Production
Janet Castiglione
Sue Cole

This book is dedicated to our *FamilyFun* readers, and contributors, and to traveling families everywhere.

WRITER
Deborah Geigis Berry is a contributing editor at *FamilyFun* magazine and frequently appears on national television to discuss family travel topics. She lives in Windsor, Connecticut, with her husband, Bryan, daughter Acadia, and son Hudson.

Illustrations by **Kandy Littrell**

For information address Disney Editions, 114 Fifth Avenue, New York, New York 10011-5690.

Printed in the United States of America

First Edition

Library of Congress Cataloging-in-Publication Data on file
ISBN 0-7868-5304-2

Visit www.disneyeditions.com

CONTENTS

Dear Parents,

A FRIEND OF MINE—a dad—said something recently that rang true to me. "A great childhood," he said, thinking aloud, "is really made up of a thousand small good moments." His comment prompted me to step back and take stock of what those moments might be for my own two young sons. What will be their happiest memories? Topping the list in my mind are the simple but extraordinary pleasures we've had traveling together: the hermit crabs we discovered at a Maine beach, the afternoon spent playing catch on the Mall in Washington, the thrill of a first flight, a first train ride, a first hike to a mountaintop.

As parents, we all work incredibly hard to find the time and money to take our children on vacation. We want to show them the remarkably varied American landscape and intro-duce them to its many cultures and histories. We want to get away from jobs, homework, and household chores long enough to enjoy one another's company uninterrupted. And most of all, we want to have fun.

The editors at *FamilyFun* and I take great pride in this book and others in the series. They are a culmination of ten years worth of gathering for our readers' the best vacation advice out there. Traveling with children is an art—and our charge is to help with your deci-sions every step of the way so that you can make the most of every minute of your time away.

Alexandra Kennedy

Alexandra Kennedy
Editorial Director,
FamilyFun magazine

How to Use This Guide

ELCOME TO THE world of *FamilyFun* magazine's new travel guide series. In our effort to present you with the finest in vacation options, we called on the best experts we know: our hardy group of writers. All are parents who travel with their kids, and all live and work in the area(s) about which they're writing. These are the people who can tell you where to find that teddy bear shop that isn't in the main mall, which restaurant has the best milk shakes, which museum will invite your toddler to roll up his sleeves and create art, and which theme park will give your preteen a good return on the price of admission. With all their recommendations comes the endorsement of their kids: our traveling children have been our best critics.

Since all of the guides in this series cover more than one state, we have divided them into easy-to-use sections. So here's a guide to the guide.

READY, SET, GO!—is a mini-encyclopedia of handy facts, practical advice, what to do/where to go/when to go/how to travel: in other words, all you need to know about planning a successful family vacation.

INTRODUCTION—will give you an overview of the states being covered in this guidebook. Read it—it will whet your appetite, and perhaps give you some new ideas for family activities.

CHAPTERS—States and chapters are presented in geographical order. Chapters represent the regions we think your family will enjoy most. We have omitted those places that we feel would not be family-friendly or are too expensive for what you get in return. We also make note of attractions that appeal only to a certain age range.

FamilyFun has given each entry a rating—stars (★) that range from one to four—to guide you to our favorites. Remember, however, that this guidebook contains nothing that we do not recommend—it's just that we liked some things better than others. We've also assigned a dollar sign rating ($)—in high season for a family of four, also ranging from one to four. Check the price range at the start of each chapter as the key changes. We hope that this will help you to decide whether a hotel, restaurant, or attraction will fit in with your budget.

Typically, we start each chapter with an introduction, followed by *FamilyFun*'s Must-See List of up to ten things to try to do while visiting. We've divided attractions into two categories: "Cultural Attractions" (museums, historic sites, and so on) and "Just for Fun" (water parks, zoos, aquariums, roller coasters, and the like). Wherever possible, we've included Website information.

What more can we say? We hope that this guide helps you to fashion the best possible vacation for your family, one that is a pleasure in the planning, a delight in the doing, and one that will leave every member of your clan with memories that will last a lifetime—or at least until ninth grade.

Bon Voyage!

New England

A NEW ENGLAND vacation can encompass anything your family wants it to, from mountains and seashores to theme parks and natural retreats. It also can span centuries of history. With so much to see and do, however, you need a plan of action—exactly what this book provides. No matter how short or long your stay, we'll help you get the most out of your trip, with tips on both time-honored attractions and out-of-the-way places. We'll also help you choose that "home away from home" and recommend eateries that serve up traditional Yankee fare yet know how to cater to kids.

History buffs will find plenty to do here: walk Boston's Freedom Trail, reenact the Boston Tea Party, and hearken back to earlier eras at Plimoth Plantation and Old Sturbridge Village, both in Massachusetts, or at Old York Historic Sites in Maine. Learn about exotic sea creatures at some of the nation's best aquariums, and explore North America's largest display of dinosaur tracks at Dinosaur State Park, home to 500 immense imprints. Museumgoers can choose from exhibits on science and art, antique cars and

trolleys, and farming and maple sugaring. Good news for young travelers: hands-on opportunities abound.

Some of the region's most awesome attractions come courtesy of Mother Nature, who blessed Maine with 3,478 miles of coastline and carved the Old Man of the Mountain in New Hampshire's Franconia Notch State Park. Nature enthusiasts can embark on virtually every outdoor adventure imaginable. In winter, there's skiing, snow tubing, ice-skating, and horse-drawn sleigh rides. In spring and fall, consider hiking and biking, canoeing, and kayaking, and, for the more daring, white-water rafting. And in summer, oh, those glorious beaches. Every New England state except Vermont boasts its share of shoreline and seafaring opportunities. (In the Green Mountain State, you can take to the water on literally hundreds of lakes and streams and thousands of miles of river.) The region also lays claim to three popular island getaways: Block Island, Martha's Vineyard, and Nantucket.

Baseball fans are in their glory at one-of-a-kind Fenway Park. Those willing to venture farther afield can watch farm teams at play in minor-league games throughout the region. Water and theme parks provide chills and thrills, and working farms foster a new appreciation of rural life.

In between activities, of course, you'll need a place to bunk down and rest assured, we've got you covered. New England offers accommodations to suit every style, so we've included recommendations on everything from country inns and chain hotels to cottages, condos, and grand resorts. Campers are in luck, with literally thousands of options and as few or as many amenities as your family desires. Variety is the order of the day in dining choices, too. In fact, in many New England restaurants, parents can sample regional specialties, such as lobster in the rough, while kids dine on old standbys of pizza, hamburgers, and chicken nuggets.

NOTE: The New England region is filled with decidedly seasonal destinations. Many attractions, inns, and restaurants close at some point. **Be absolutely sure to phone ahead to avoid disappointment.** And now it's time to…

Let the family fun begin!

Pack up and get going.
You're on vacation!

Ready, Set, Go!

JUST TEN YEARS AGO, *FamilyFun* was a fledgling magazine, and the family travel "industry"—now a booming, $100 billion annual trade—was as much a newcomer as we were. In a way, you could say we have grown up together.

FamilyFun was one of the first national magazines to actively research and publicize travel ideas for families with school-age children (a fun job, we must add). Over the last decade, as the numbers of traveling families increased, so did the business of family travel. These days, there are more resources, opportunities, and means for the vacationing family than ever before —which, in turn, gives *FamilyFun* the chance to be an even more valuable clearinghouse of ideas for you.

Through the years, we have been privileged to work with veteran travel writers and editors who have gone around the world with their kids. We've also taken time to listen to our readers—insightful, creative families from across the United States—and to note (and sometimes publish) their stories, recommendations, and tips on traveling as a family. A combination of those two wisdoms is what awaits you on the following pages.

Although it may not be readily apparent, a lot of trial and error underlies these pages. Each destination, before it reaches this book, undergoes a rigorous investigation, and not all make the grade.

We know that family vacations are a big investment, and we know that's why you're here. You're hoping to sidestep the pitfalls of experimentation and to locate destinations that will be a real hit with your family. Congratulations! You've come to the right place.

FIRST STEPS

At the outset, organizing a family vacation can seem as daunting as landing a probe on Mars. Better to stay home and watch the Discovery Channel, you think—maybe toast a few marshmallows in the fireplace.

The truth is that planning an adventurous vacation can be fun, especially if you prepare for it in advance and involve your kids. The onerous part is remembering all the things you have to think about.

That's where we come in. This introductory chapter covers family travel from A to Z, from deciding where to go, to getting there and making the most of your vacation. Some of this may seem like old news to you, but we want to make sure you don't forget a thing.

How much do we spend?

Chances are, you already know approximately what you have to spend on a vacation—and you've already got a modus operandi when it comes to money matters. Maybe you're a family that carefully figures a budget, then finds a vacation to fit it. Or maybe you're the type to set your heart on a once-in-a-lifetime trip, then scrimp and save until you can make it happen.

HAVE MODEM, WILL TRAVEL

For information on how to research and book travel plans on the Web, turn to page 31.

Determine the type of trip you will take. Before you even start your planning, take a moment to consider: what kind of trip are you taking? Are you splurging on a dream vacation, or conserving on a semi-annual getaway? What aspects of this trip are most important to you?

Budget carefully. Once you know what those broad parameters are, the next step is to think through your vacation budget in detail—if not at the outset of planning, then at an opportune point along the way. When you know what you have to spend, you'll make quicker and less stressful decisions en route and you'll be able to pay the bills without a grimace once you get home. You'll find lots of budget-saving tips in this introductory chapter.

When can we go?

Scheduling your vacation well can make a big difference in everyone's experience of the trip.

Consider each individual. Most likely, tight school and work schedules will decide when you travel — but if possible, aim for a time slot that allows everyone to relax. For instance, an action-packed road trip sounds exciting, but it might be just the wrong medicine for a parent who's squeezing it into a packed work schedule. End-of-summer trips may be tough for kids with back-to-school anxieties, and midyear trips that snatch kids from school sometimes cause more trouble than they're worth.

Where do we go?

In this book (and the others in this travel series), you'll find scores of winning family destinations. By all means, though, don't stop here. Doing your own research is half the fun, and these days, you have a wealth of resources at your disposal.

Make a list of destinations. What hot spots intrigue your clan? What adventures would you like to try? Draw up a big list, and don't worry about coming up with too many ideas—you can return to this list year after year. Here are a few trails you can follow: relatives, friends, and coworkers (who love to report on their own successful trips), a professional travel agent, local chambers of commerce and state tourism boards, and magazines, the Internet (see page 34 for some good family travel sites), and local hotels and outfitters in the geographic areas you're interested in.

Evaluate your family. A good vacation has to accommodate *everyone* in the family, no matter what their ages, limitations, or interests. While no destination will make everyone happy all the time, you should search vigilantly for those that offer a niche for each family member.

Involve your kids. The more involved your kids are in planning—especially during these early, brainstorming stages — the more likely they are to work to make the trip a success.

Experiment wisely. While experimentation can add spice to a trip, too much may overwhelm your kids (and you). If your child has her heart set on horseback riding, for example, make sure she tries it out at home before you put down a deposit on a dude ranch vacation.

Check the season. Be informed about travel conditions for the time of your trip and make sure you're not heading for trouble (hurricane season in Florida, for example, or black-fly season in the Adirondacks). This is especially important if you're cashing in on off-season deals.

Local Flavor on the Cheap

Don't wait till you arrive at your destination to investigate opportunities for local fun—research a few in advance:

♦ Check out a regional festival or agricultural fair. For fairs in the western U.S., visit www.fairs net.org and for festivals nationwide, visit www.festivals.com

♦ Explore a college campus (which may offer green space, bike paths, museums, observatories, and more). To find a list, go to a general Internet search engine like www.yahoo.com, click on education, and search for colleges by state. Then, call the school's information office for a map and a roster of special events.

♦ Visit a farmers' market. For a list of markets around the U.S., log on to www.ams.usda.gov/ farmersmarkets/

♦ Take in an air show (they're usually free at military bases). For a list of air shows by region, see www.airshows.org

♦ Find a local nature center or Audubon preserve.

Schedule appropriately. How much time do you need to give this particular destination its due? You don't want to feel like you're rushing through things—but neither do you want to run out of activities that will interest your kids.

Should we have an itinerary?

Drawing up a travel itinerary, whether it's rough or detailed, will ensure that you travel wisely, hit the hot spots, and give everyone in your group a say in what you'll see.

Include something for everyone. No doubt, each member of your family will have his or her own list of must-sees. If a unanimous vote on itinerary stops is out of the question, ask everyone to write down top choices, then create a schedule that guarantees each person at least one or two favorites. If your children span a wide age range, remind them that there will be some patient standing by while siblings (and Mom and Dad) have their moments in the sun.

Involve the kids (again). Once you've got the basic stops down, kids can help research destinations, plan driving routes, locate pit stops, and help plan rainy-day alternatives.

Make a plan, then break it. Don't let your preplanned schedule get in the way of spontaneous delights. What if your kids want to ride that water slide for an extra three hours? One fun moment in hand is usually worth at least two on the itinerary.

Beat the crowds. Remember to head for popular attractions first thing in the morning or in late afternoon and early evening. Save the middle of the day for poolside fun or activities that take you off the beaten path and away from crowds.

Travel in tune with your family's natural rhythms. Preschoolers tend to be at their best early in the day—a good time for structured activities. Many teens, on the other hand, are pictures of grogginess before noon. Adapt your itinerary to suit ingrained family habits—including your usual meal and nap times—and you'll have smoother sailing. When visiting very popular destinations, take the time to find out in advance when their slowest periods are.

Train Your Own Tour Guides

Guided tours at historic sites and museums are often a snooze (or too sophisticated) for young kids. Instead, create your own tour—have each family member study up on a different attraction by writing or calling for brochures, surfing the Web, and visiting the library. Then, when you arrive, you'll have an expert guide on board.

GETTING THERE

As we all know, the experience of taking kids from point A to point B runs the gamut from uneventful (read: bliss) to miserable. Knowing the ins and outs of your travel options will speed you toward a sane trip.

FamilyFun READER'S TIP

Hire Some Junior Travel Agents

When we were planning a summer trip to Louisiana, I overheard one of my kids tell another that they were going to have to do everything Mom and Dad wanted to do. That's when I decided that each family member would get to plan a full day of our trip. I purchased a regional travel guide and told everyone they had $200 for one day's activities, meals, and accommodations, so they would have to budget (a useful exercise for my 10- and 12-year olds). Every night, any money left over from that day was given to the next planner. I am proud to say that everything went well, and the kids proclaimed it the best vacation ever!

Cindy Long, Spring, Texas

15

By Plane

PROS: It's fast. And if you land a good deal, air travel can actually be affordable.

CONS: If you don't land a good deal, air travel can be prohibitively expensive, especially for a big family. Other pitfalls include flight delays, mounting claustrophobia on long trips, and strict baggage restrictions.

Look for deals. Traveling in off-peak season and taking off-peak flights (very early or very late in the day) may save you money; flying midweek and staying over Saturday night almost always will. You may also wish to research deals at different airports (for instance, T. F. Green Airport in Providence, Rhode Island, often offers cheaper fares than Boston's Logan Airport 45 minutes away). Also, remember that most sale tickets have a cutoff date—you'll have to book two, three, or four weeks ahead of your departure date to get the deal.

Consider using an agent. Booking your own airline reservations on the Web is a cinch these days (see pages 35 and 36), but there are still advantages to using a professional travel agent who knows your family's needs. First of all, for the $10 or $20 per-ticket surcharge you may pay, you'll save Web-surfing time, and you'll be spared the stress of baby-sitting the fickle airline market. Also,

an agent may be able to suggest a Plan B (such as using a smaller airport to get a better deal)—something the Web search engines can't do for you. Try to get a good agent recommendation through friends, coworkers, or relatives; if you need further help, the American Society of Travel Agents (703-739-2782, www.astanet.com) provides a list of members, as well as brochures on travel topics (including one on how to choose a travel agent).

By Car

PROS: Road trips are the cheapest way to get from here to there, and they can also be real adventures. In addition, the car is familiar territory for your kids, so they'll feel right at home (for better or worse) during the trip. And, of course, a road trip affords you priceless flexibility.

CONS: You're in for major advance planning, from making sure your car is in good condition to scheduling regular rest stops and having a dependable cache of road snacks, games, and other diversions. Even with those, the hours of close confinement may quickly erode your family's wanderlust.

Get a good map. If you belong to AAA, request a free "TripTik" map. Otherwise, you can map your route and download printed driving directions on Websites like www.mapquest.com, www.freetrip.com, and www.mapsonus.com

WHEN YOU BOOK

♦ Try first for a nonstop flight. If that's not available, fly "direct," which means you'll stop at least once but won't switch planes.

♦ Book flights that depart early in the day, if possible. If your flight is delayed, you—and the airline—will have time to make other arrangements.

♦ Specify your ticketing preferences, whether paper or electronic.

♦ Check to see if a meal will be served in flight. If so, order meals your kids like. Many airlines offer kids' meals or a vegetarian choice that may be pasta. If not, plan accordingly.

♦ Ask for the seats you'd like, whether they're a window, an aisle, or the bulkhead for legroom.

PACKING TIPS

♦ Stuff your carry-on for every contingency. Pack all medications, extra clothes for little kids, diapers, baby food, formula, wet wipes, and snacks (they'll also help kids swallow to relieve ear pressure).

♦ Have each child carry a small backpack with travel toys, a light sweatshirt, and a pair of socks for the flight.

ON THE DAY OF YOUR TRIP

♦ Call ahead to check for delays.

♦ Have all photo IDs within easy reach (not necessary for kids under age 18 traveling with their parents on domestic flights; on most international flights, even infants will need a passport).

♦ If you have heavy bags, check your luggage first and then park.

♦ If you are early for the flight or run into long delays, don't go straight to the gate. Instead, meander through the airport's diversions: windows onto the runways, children's play areas (many major airports now have these), Web access computers, and, of course, stores where kids can find a treat to tide them over.

♦ Carry on extra bottled water. It's easy to get dehydrated on a plane, and the drink service may be slow in reaching you.

ON THE PLANE

♦ Ask if your child can view the cockpit (the best time may be after the flight is over).

♦ Secure pillows and blankets for family members who may want to nap.

♦ Take breaks from sitting; occasionally walk the aisles and switch seats.

FLYING FEARS

Most children are fearless fliers—and those who are afraid often can trace their concerns to adults who unintentionally transmit their own fears. If you need help answering your children's questions, you can ask them on-line at www.wic-kid.com

FamilyFun TIP

Bookworms

When you're on the road, there's nothing like a good story to pass the time. For night drives, audio books can be a lifesaver. Try borrowing or renting one from your local library, or visit www.storytapes.com, the Website for Village StoryTapes (800-238-8273). You can either rent or purchase from their excellent selection; three- to four-week tape rentals cost $6 to $17 (for *Harry Potter IV*); to buy, tapes cost $12 to $60.

Be prepared for emergencies, large and small. It goes without saying that your car should be in prime working order before you depart. You should have supplies for road emergencies on board, as well as a good first-aid kit (see page 33 for a list of what to include), and, if you have one, bring a cell phone.

Keep things orderly. We all know what happens to our cars within minutes of the time the kids buckle in; on long road trips, expect the chaos to rise by a factor of ten. In an effort to keep things in check, bring containers to hold trash and toys; pack the children's luggage so it's easiest to reach; divvy up the back-seat space so kids know where their boundaries are; and go over basic behavior rules before you leave.

Drive in time with your family's rhythm. Night driving offers less traffic and a chance that young kids will sleep (you can let them ride in their pj's). Alternatively, an early start may avoid late-afternoon, kid-cranky hours. When possible, go with your family's natural flow.

Help prevent motion sickness. Have frequent, small meals during your trip (symptoms are more likely to occur on an empty stomach). Over-the-counter medications such as Dramamine, as well as ginger ale, ginger tea, or ginger candy also can help, but once symptoms begin, it's usually too late for oral medications. Make sure the car is well ventilated, and have sickness-prone travelers take a window seat, which offers

WEATHER WATCHERS Before you leave, assign forecaster duties to one of your kids. Using the Internet, he or she can research and predict the type of weather you'll encounter (and advise everyone on what to pack). Try www.weather.com

fresh air and a view of the road. If a child feels nauseated, have him look straight in front of the car or focus attention on the horizon. If your child becomes carsick, stop the car to give him a break from the motion; having him lie down with his head perfectly still also may help.

By Train

PROS: First of all, trains are just plain cool, for kids and adults alike. Second, there's room to explore, and everyone can kick back and enjoy the view. And third, if you are headed to a major metropolitan area with a good public transit system, you'll avoid the expenses and hassles of city driving and parking.

CONS: There's only one national passenger rail service, Amtrak, and at press time its future was in question. Also, Amtrak's limited network may not be convenient to your destination (ask about connector trains and rental car agencies when you call). In some regions of the United States, Amtrak's city-to-city service rivals car, bus, and plane travel for efficiency; on cross-country hauls, this is not the case. If you're investing in a long train trip, you're in it more for the experience of train travel.

Inquire about special deals. Children ages 2 to 15 usually ride for half fare when accompanied by an adult who pays full fare. Each adult can bring two children at this discounted rate. Amtrak also offers

A Road Trip Survival Kit

A BAG OF TRICKS

♦ mini-puzzles with a backboard
♦ video games, cassette or CD player (with headphones)
♦ paper, pens, pencils, markers
♦ travel versions of board games
♦ stuffed animals
♦ Etch A Sketch
♦ colored pipe cleaners
♦ deck of cards
♦ cookie sheet (a good lap tray)
♦ word puzzles
♦ small action figures or dolls
♦ stickers
♦ Trivial Pursuit cards
♦ cotton string (for cat's cradle games)

A COOLER OF SNACKS

Bring lots of drinks and a cache of snacks like granola bars, trail mix, grapes, carrot sticks, roll-up sandwiches, fruit leather, and popcorn.

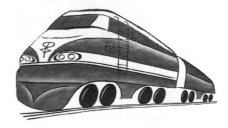

Keeping 'Em Busy: 60-Second Solutions

SQUABBLE SOLUTIONS

Give your kids 25 cents in pennies at the start of the trip. Each time they fight or whine, charge them a penny. Offer a reward, such as doubling or tripling their money, if they haven't lost a cent during the ride.

WAGER AND WIN

Kids are natural wagerers—they love to bet how much, how long, how far, how many. If you're in a bind for a moment's entertainment, ask them to guess the number of French fries on your plate or to estimate how many steps it will take to walk to your airport gate. The key here is to be able to verify the guesses—you'll need to wear a watch with a second hand and carry a calculator.

CREATIVE COMPETITION

Kids love challenges. Need to get rid of the trash in the car? See who can smash the trash into the smallest paper ball, then toss it in the wastepaper bag. Want quiet time? Hold a five-minute silence contest. Need to get through errands in a hurry? Challenge your kids to a race against time. You may feel that your motives are transparent, but your kids won't care.

special seasonal rates, other family deals, and Web-only deals.

How to find them. Amtrak's Website, www.amtrak.com, provides information on fares, schedules, reservations, routes and services, station locations, and special offers. You can also call Amtrak at 800-872-7245 for information and reservations. When you book, ask if there is a full-service dining car and ask whether you can reserve a block of seats for your family.

Consider a sleeper car. For overnight trips, sleep-in-your-seat fares are the cheapest, but first-class bedrooms are much more comfortable.

Arrive early. If your train seats are unassigned, get to the station early for the best chance of eveyone's sitting together. You can even have one parent run ahead to grab a group of seats while the other shepherds children and luggage to the platform.

By RV

PROS: It's a home away from home, which means you can eat, sleep, and use the indoor plumbing (as everyone will agree, one of the finest features of RV travel) whenever you want. In an RV, you are free to explore with independence, self-sufficiency, and freedom—three assets that can be priceless when you're traveling with kids.

CONS: It's a home away from home,

Patchwork Pillows

I am 10 years old, and every year my family goes camping. I collect patches from each place we visit, including the Grand Canyon, Yellowstone and Yosemite National Parks; San Francisco; Las Vegas; and, most recently, Santa Fe, New Mexico. I put all the patches I've collected during each year on separate pillows. I keep the pillows on my bed to remind me of our great trips.

Alex Smythe, Tucson, Arizona

which means you face dishes, cooking, and maintenance (generators, water pumps, waste tanks, and the engine, for starters). In addition, RV rentals are not cheap, although they can compare favorably to the cost of a week's lodging, food, and travel (especially for big families).

What they cost. Expect to pay rental fees between $500 and $1,500 per week, depending on location, model, and time of year you'll be traveling, and the luxury factor (RVs can get pretty posh). Gasoline costs will be high, but you'll save considerably on food and accommodations (campground fees average $20 to $40 per night).

How to find them. Rental information is available through auto clubs and through Go RVing (888-GO-RVING, ask for the free video and literature; www.gorving.com). Cruise America (800- 327-7799) offers 150 rental centers across the United States and Canada. The RV America Website (www.rvamerica.

com) has listings of dealers, clubs, and resources.

Be a savvy renter. Choose an RV that's big enough for your family, but know that many campgrounds only permit vehicles less than 30 feet long. Before you rent, ask how many people fit comfortably in the RV, what powers the appliances, how much insurance is required, and whether supplies such as linens and kitchen utensils are included in the rental price. Get a demonstration of how to work everything in the vehicle, read the manual, practice a little ahead of time, and you'll be ready to take the plunge.

By Bus

PROS: The major advantages of bus travel are that it's cheap, that it spares you the stress of driving, and that tickets usually can be purchased on the day of your trip, at the station. **CONS:** Unfortunately, traveling by bus often takes longer than by car. What's more, bus travel offers little opportunity for diversion for your

Thinking of Skipping School?

children. And since you're sitting close to other passengers, many lively family games are off-limits (some buses offer a TV movie; ask when you call).

How to find them: Greyhound Lines (800-229-9424) offers service across the United States. In the Northeast, between New Hampshire and Washington, D.C., Peter Pan Bus Lines (800-237-8747) is another option. Both have Websites, www.greyhound.com and www.peterpanbus.com, complete with fare and schedule information. To locate smaller local or regional bus lines, try the local Yellow Pages or the department of travel and tourism in the region you'll be visiting.

By Rental Car

PROS: This isn't exactly a pro, but if you've flown or trained into an area without a safe and dependable public transport system, you'll need a rental to get around. Plus, a rental car is cost-efficient for families (as opposed to solo travelers). Best of all, you won't be putting miles on your own car—and if you rent a minivan, you can have drink-cup slots and elbowroom for every single kid.

CONS: None, really, save the expense and a list of rental and insurance decisions that can be as daunting as a Starbucks menu.

How to find them: Your travel agent can book a car for you, but if you want to do it yourself, you'll find all the major agencies in the 800 directory.

Compare costs. Whether you shop on-line or over the phone, compare costs for as many companies as you can (no one company has the best deals in every city or state). In general, weeklong and weekend rentals are a better deal than per-day rentals. In your research, you may wish to inquire about companies' service records, especially if you're going with a local budget chain.

Ask about discounts. Membership in AAA or other associations, credit cards, entertainment book coupons, and package-deal reservations may net you bargains: ask about potential discounts when you make your reservation.

Ask about services and charges. Rental car companies put a lot of information in fine print. So, before you pay (and before you drive away), ask lots of questions. What are the mileage and one-way drop fees? Is there a fee for early or late car returns? Should you bring the car back with an empty gas tank or a full one to get the best refueling price? Does the company offer 24-hour breakdown service? Do the cars have air-conditioning, a jack, and a spare tire? Is there a fee for extra drivers (married couples are often exempt,

but you should check). Are car seats available at no extra charge? (Even if the answer is yes, your own car seat may be cleaner, and, because it's familiar, more comfortable for your child.)

Pay only for the insurance you need. The car, and any damage to it, will be your responsibility for the duration of your trip. Before you purchase insurance from the rental agency, check to see whether your own auto or liability insurance provides adequate coverage. Some credit card agreements may also include rental protection; call the customer service

---

FamilyFun READER'S TIP - - - - - - - - - - - - - - - - - -

Tabletop Scrapbook

Here's a fun project my family has long enjoyed while traveling. After we have mapped out our vacation, my kids, and now grandchildren, use a laundry pen to draw our route on a cotton tablecloth. We pack up the cloth along with colored markers, and while on the road, family members take turns marking the name of towns and rivers and noting funny signs. When we stop for picnic lunches, we not only use the cloth but also continue adding drawings of sights we've seen and things we've done. After the trip is over, we have a memory-filled tablecloth to use for years to come.

Janet Askew, Adair, Iowa

number on the back of your card to inquire.

WHERE TO STAY

Where you tuck your kids in at night depends entirely on your family's traveling style and budget—and, of course, on what's available in the area to which you're traveling. There are so many options—hotels, motels, inns, cottages, cabins, condominiums, resorts, time-shares, campgrounds—it can be hard to know where to start.

Lists of local accommodations can be found through tourism boards, the Web, travel books, and the 800 numbers or published directories of major franchises. However, finding the places that really go the extra mile for families isn't easy. This book—and other family travel publications—will be your best bets, as will the time-tested recommendations of friends and acquaintances. Always, always ask your own questions as well: see our checklist on page 25 for some basics.

Hotels, Motels & Lodges

From generic chains, to mom-and-pop operations bursting with character, to ritzy palaces, this category really runs the gamut. If you don't have a dependable recommendation (from a friend, trusted travel agent, or guidebook like this one), you may wish to place your trust in the major chains (budget or no) where you at least know what you're getting.

How to find them: Most major chains can be found in the 800 directory (as well as on the Web) and can provide a list of property locations. Alternatively, you can contact regional travel bureaus or consult a national rating system, such as those in Mobil Travel Guides (available in bookstores or the on-line store at www.mobil.com) or the Automobile Association of America (call your local AAA office to order regional TourBook guides).

PICKY EATERS? If you have picky eaters in the family (or if you suspect a child may not enjoy the food at a certain restaurant), feed them ahead of time—and let them enjoy an appetizer or dessert during your meal.

Inns, B&Bs, and Farm Stays

These have traditionally been the domain of honeymooning couples and retirees. Increasingly, though, they are accommodating a growing family travel market. There are certainly gems out there for your discovery—but do your research rigorously (speak with the owner, if possible) to find out whether kids are *truly* welcome at the destination of your choice. The last thing you want to be doing on vacation is shushing your kids and shooing them away from pricey antiques. Look for inns and B&Bs attached to a working farm— these tend to be more kid-friendly, with animals to watch and feed and plenty of outdoor play space.

How to find them: Try travel magazines, regional chambers of commerce, and two excellent Websites, www.bedandbreakfast.com and www.bbgetaways.com

Condos and Cottages

These are ideal if your group is staying put for the length of your vacation, since they offer room to spread out and cook your own meals. When you book, ask about amenities: does the condo come with linens, pots and pans, a television, phone, dishwasher, and washer/dryer? Are there extra tax and/or booking fees? If you rent directly from the owner, be even more rigorous in your questioning. Is there

WHAT TO ASK BEFORE YOU BOOK

1 **ACCOMMODATIONS:** What rooms (or condos or cabins) are available? How many beds are there and what size are they? Are the rooms nonsmoking? What amenities are included (laundry, phone, cable TV, refrigerator, balcony, coffee service, cots, cribs, minibar)? Are the rooms located in the main building? What specific views are available? Is there a charge for kids staying in the same room with parents? Are there family packages? Can guests upgrade rooms upon arrival?

2 **DINING:** Are there dining facilities on the property? If so, are there restrictions for kids? What are some menu items, and what does the average meal cost? Is there a kids' menu? Is there a complimentary breakfast offered? Are there snack and/or drink machines? If there are no dining facilities on-site, is there a family restaurant nearby?

3 **RECREATION:** What recreational facilities are available (game rooms, pool, tennis courts, equipment rental, and so on)? At what hours are they available? Are there additional charges for their use? Are there age or time restrictions for any recreation? What recreational options are available in the nearby community (movie theater, minigolf, bowling, and the like)?

a cancellation policy if the place is not up to your standards?

How to find them: The Internet has made it easy to connect potential renters with homeowners and rental brokers. Unfortunately, that means there are literally thousands of sites to sift through. Luckily, most sites offer very detailed information on properties, so you can actually make an informed decision on-line to pursue a place.

For starters, here are the Website addresses for a number of national and international vacation rental clearinghouses: www.eLeisure Link.com (888-801-8808); Barclay

----

Family Hostels

A CHEAP SLEEP

If you think hostels are the exclusive domain of students and backpackers, think again: many of the neatest have private family rooms that can be reserved in advance. Some also offer special programs, such as historic walking tours, natural history programs, and sports activities. Hostels in the Hostelling International/ American Youth Hostels system are as varied as their locations and include registered historic buildings, lighthouses, and a former dude ranch. For the latest edition of *Hostelling Experience North America*, call *202-783-6161* or visit www.hiayh.org

International Group (800-845-6636; www.bar clayweb.com); and 10,000 Vacation Rentals, Inc. (888-369-7245; www. 10kvacationrentals.com).

To rent directly from a property owner, try Vacation Rentals by Owner at www.vrbo.com You also can locate condos and cottages by inquiring at local tourism bureaus, local realtors (especially for seaside properties), and major resorts, which often keep lists of rentals on property or nearby.

Campgrounds

These range from the extremely rustic—grassy knolls with fabulous views to the luxurious—complexes with video games, sports areas, and fax and modem hookups.

Depending on where and how you prefer to camp, you'll have your pick of sites in state or national parks, national forests, or private campgrounds. (See "Happy Campers," pages 38-39.)

When you book a site, inquire: What are the nightly fees? Does the campground accept reservations? If no, how early should you arrive in order to claim a site? Is there a pool or lake? Lifeguards? Equipment rentals? Laundry facilities, rest rooms, and hot showers? A grocery store nearby? Remember that campgrounds near major tourist attractions fill up early, so make reservations in advance (choice spots in some national parks, for example, fill up months ahead).

How to find them: In addition to the campgrounds recommended in this book, you can find lists of camp-grounds on the Internet: check out About.com's camping section at www.camping.about.com, www.camping-usa.com, and the National Association of RV Parks & Camp-grounds at www.gocampingamerica.com For campgrounds in national parks, visit www.nps.gov and state. For a national directory of KOA campgrounds, visit www.koa kamp grounds.com

Resorts

A resort vacation is a big invest-ment, and up-front research is essen-tial to ensure you get your money's worth. When you are making inquir-ies, don't be shy about taking up the resort staff's time with questions. Be sure to grill them with the entire housing quiz on page 25. Ask, too, about programming for kids and families. If there is a children's pro-

---

FamilyFun TIP

Walk it through

When you're booking a room or condo over the phone, ask the reser-vation specialist to "walk" you through the place, virtually, from the front door to the balcony view (if there is one!). They may think you're going over-board — but you'll really know what you're getting.

---

gram, what days and times does it run? Is it canceled if not enough kids sign up? What is the ratio of counselors to children? What are the age divisions? What activities does the program offer? What are the facilities? What, if any, is the additional cost? Are there games, programs, or organized recreation especially for families? Baby-sitting services? Assistance for kids who get sick? What are the terms for these? If the resort is "all-inclusive," find out

---

FamilyFun READER'S TIP

Invent a Travel Kit

When our family flies, I make travel kits for my two sons, Noah, 8, and Paul, 4. I fill old wipes boxes with a variety of treats: chocolate kisses, fruit snacks, a sealed envelope with a love note inside, stickers, and a small wrapped package such as a pencil sharpener, pencils, and a blank book (I staple together scratch paper). I write the boys' names on the front with a perma-nent marker, and then, in flight, they decorate the boxes with stickers. The trick is not to give them the travel kits until we're on the plane. After they exhaust their supply of goodies inside, they can refill it with things they collect during the trip.

Kathy Detzer, White River Junction, Vermont

Travel Insurance

It's not for everyone, but some travelers like to invest in this just-in-case insurance. Cancellation policies cover losses if you can't make your trip due to illness or a death in the family (you may wish to consider this if you have to put down a hefty deposit or prepay for your vacation in full). Medical policies provide for some emergency procedures. You can buy travel insurance from a specialty broker (see below), from your travel agent, or directly from an insurance company. Do not buy insurance from the tour operator or cruise line you will be traveling with.

Travel Guard International
(800-826-1300; www.travel-guard.com)

CSA Travel Protection
(www.csatravelprotection.com)

Travel Assistance International (800-821-2828; www.travelassistance.com)

Access America (866-807-3982; www.accessamerica.com)

exactly what is covered. If you will be taking advantage of the services included in the price, it may mean a good deal for your family; if not, you might be better off elsewhere.

How to find them: Travel magazines, travel agents, and family travel Websites (see page 34) will all be able to offer recommendations on family resorts. Also, the Globe Pequot Press (www.globepequot. com) has two good resource books: *100 Best Family Resorts in North America* and *100 Best All-Inclusive Resorts of the World.*

SAVING MONEY

A great vacation balances moments of extravagance with activities that are as enjoyable as they are affordable. The key, then, is to find painless ways to cut costs so that you can feel good about indulging. Here's a host of secrets from budget-savvy travelers.

Stock up at home. Specialty items, such as sunscreen, film, batteries, over-the-counter medications, and first-aid supplies can be outrageously expensive in vacation spots. Buy them in bulk at home and bring them with you.

Travel off-peak. Whether it's a ski resort town in the summertime, or Yosemite National Park in the spring, or the Adirondacks in the winter, off-peak travel is one of the best ways to save, as long as you're primed to enjoy the unique flavor of an off-season trip. Rates for travel and lodging are often slashed considerably—and you can enjoy a different perspective (and fewer crowds) at the destination of your choice.

Don't delay. The sooner you begin planning and booking your vacation (six months to a year or more in advance is not too early), the more deals will be available to you.

Shop around. This is the cardinal rule of vacation planning. Take time to compare prices for every service that you'll be buying, from airfares, hotels, and rental cars to tickets for attractions.

Ask for discounts. Don't be shy about asking for discounts. Call ahead to the attractions that you plan to visit and ask where one finds discount coupons. When making

Guided Tours

WHEN DO YOU NEED ONE?

For certain types of specialty travel (technically challenging outdoor adventures, for example), an expert guide is a necessary aid for a safe and enjoyable trip. In addition, using a local guide for day trips (say, fishing or snowmobiling) can be a wonderful way to connect with local lore and culture in the region you're visiting. In general, however, guided tours (especially group tours that include full itineraries and meals) tend to be pricey, tightly scheduled, and lacking the freedom most families value highly.

----

hotel reservations, ask if discounts are available—if not on the room alone, then on a package that may include the room and tickets to a nearby attraction. Coupons are also available on-line: a good place to start is the coupon link at www.about.com

STRAP A SHOE BAG to the back of the front seat and stuff it with your small kid-entertainment supplies: crayons and coloring books; kids' magazines; craft supplies, such as pipe cleaners, markers, glue sticks, and construction paper; songbooks; paper doll kits; a deck of cards; and a cassette player with story tapes. And don't forget a Frisbee, jump rope, and chalk (to draw hopscotch grids) for rest stops.

Make Your Own Postcards

While traveling by car or plane, my kids entertain themselves by creating their own postcards. Before the trip, I buy blank, prestamped postcards from the post office. Once we are under way, the kids draw pictures on the cards — usually of things they have done on vacation or are looking forward to doing. We address the cards to relatives and friends and drop them in the mail, making sure we send a few home for our own travel journal. This activity has been so successful, we now give friends travel kits of the prestamped cards and crayons as a bon voyage gift.

Lynette Smith, Lake Mills, Wisconsin

Look at package deals. At first blush, packages can seem outrageously expensive. But before you pass them up, compare them carefully to what you'd pay if you bought all the pieces of your vacation separately. Rates for airfare, lodging, and car rentals can be substantially lower when purchased together, especially for popular destinations. Contact your travel agent for information or research deals from travel clubs like AAA (call your local chapter or visit www.aaa.com), American Express Travel Services (800-346-3607; www.americanexpress.com), and from tour agencies affiliated with major airlines.

Use member benefits. Membership in an auto club, professional organization, or Entertainment book club may score you discounts on travel bills—ask before you book. Your credit card company, as well, may offer free services, such as collision-damage and travel-accident insurance, if you use the card to pay for travel expenses (call to request a copy of the company's travel benefits policy). If you travel regularly, the savings you'd garner from Web-saver clubs like www.bestfares.com can be well worth the $50 to $70 annual fee.

Tickets to attractions. Buying tickets to attractions in advance through an association or organization or at the hotel desk often will save you money. Equally important, you'll avoid the ticket line itself. On-line, try www.citypass.com for discount tickets in major metropolitan areas.

Keep your distance. Unless on-site housing offers necessary convenience for your family, consider lodging that's outside the major tourist area or city you're visiting. An extra 15 minutes of travel can considerably reduce lodging expenses, especially if you're staying more than a few days.

Check out kids' deals. Look for hotel deals where kids eat and/or stay free with their parents.

Consider cooking. Dining out is certainly part of the vacation experience, but three meals per person, per day add up quickly. Cooking your own meals can save you lots of money, even if you factor in the expense of a room with a kitchenette. In a regular hotel room, you can probably manage breakfast and/or lunch with a well-stocked cooler.

Pack your own minibar. Those high-priced hotel minibars are magnets for kids. Make a list of your kids' favorite treats, then purchase them in bulk as individually wrapped items. Pack a selection in a separate box or bag that can double as the designated minibar once you arrive at the hotel.

Let's do lunch. If you have a yen to try a particular fancy restaurant, head there during lunch. The atmosphere will be the same, and the menu will be similar, but smaller lunchtime portions will be accompanied by lower prices.

Revel in free fun. Remember the birthday when your child spent more time playing with the wrapping paper than with the actual toy? Vacations are filled with similar, low-cost but memorable moments, including hours at the beach, hiking trails, parks, and playgrounds. If you're in a new area, scan the local paper for listings, or call a local travel bureau or chamber of commerce for ideas.

Be savvy about souvenirs. Decide ahead of time how much you're willing to spend on souvenirs. Depending on the age of your kids, give each child his or her own spending money (they'll be stingier with their own funds than they are with yours). As an added incentive, let them keep a portion of any money they don't spend.

USING THE WEB

With the advent of the World Wide Web, individuals now have access to all the tools that travel agents use (and then some). The trick is to know how to use them well.

PROS: Researching travel ideas on the Web may draw in your kids more readily than a guidebook would.

Packing With—And For—Kids

Like so much of your family vacation, packing is a balancing act—in this case between including everything you need and making sure you can actually lift your bags. No matter where you're headed, this checklist should cover most of the essentials.

Give the kids a role. Every child has favorite outfits as well as clothing that he or she won't wear (and that you shouldn't bother packing). Young children can select the clothes they'd like to bring and set them aside for you. Older kids can do much of their own packing, especially if you help them write up a checklist of their own.

Don't worry about wrinkles. Like aging, this happens even with the best of precautions. Suggest some folding methods, but don't insist on your kids' finessing this. One surprisingly effective technique for kids is simply to roll everything up.

Make each child responsible for his or her own luggage. A backpack and a soft-sided suitcase for each child will do the trick. Let your kids decorate their bags with stencils and stickers — and remember to attach a name tag.

Separate toiletries in sealed, waterproof bags. Lids on toiletries often pop off or open during travel.

Take precautions in case of lost luggage. If you're flying to your vacation destination, pack at least one complete outfit for each family member in each suitcase. That way, if a piece of luggage is lost, everyone still has a change of clothes. Also, pack medications, eyeglasses, and contact lens solution in carry-ons.

Clothing

Include an outfit for each day of the week, plus extra shirts or blouses in case of spills. If your children are younger, encourage them to choose brightly colored outfits that will make them easier to spot in the crowd.

♦ Comfortable shoes or sneakers
♦ Socks and undergarments
♦ Sleepwear
♦ Light jackets, sweaters, or sweatshirts for cool weather
♦ Bathing suits
♦ Sandals or slip-on shoes for the pool
♦ Hats or sun visors
♦ Rain gear, including umbrellas

Toiletries

♦ Toothbrushes, toothpaste, dental floss, and mouthwash
♦ Deodorant
♦ Combs, brushes, hair accessories, blow-dryer
♦ Soap
♦ Shampoo and conditioner
♦ Shaving gear
♦ Feminine-hygiene items

- Lotions
- Cosmetics
- Nail care kit
- Tweezers
- Cotton balls and/or swabs
- Antibacterial gel for hand washing
- Sunscreens and lip balm
- Insect repellent

Miscellaneous "must-haves"
- Essential papers: identification for adults, health insurance cards, tickets, traveler's checks
- Wallet and/or purse, including cash and credit cards
- Car and house keys (with duplicate set packed in a different bag)
- Eyeglasses and/or contact lenses, plus lens cleaner
- Medications
- Watch
- Camera and film (pack film in your carry-on bag)
- Tote bag or book bag for day use
- Books and magazines for kids and adults
- Toys, playing cards, small games
- Flashlight
- Extra batteries
- Large plastic bags for laundry
- Small plastic bags
- Disposable wipes
- First-aid kit
- Travel alarm
- Sewing kit

Keep Your First-Aid Kit Handy

There's no such thing as a vacation from minor injuries and ailments, so a well-stocked first-aid kit is essential to have on hand. You can buy a prepackaged kit or make your own by packing the following items in an old lunch box:

- Adhesive bandages in various sizes, adhesive tape, and gauze pads
- Antacid
- Antibacterial gel for washing hands without water
- Antibacterial ointment
- Antidiarrheal medicine
- Antihistamine or allergy medicine
- Antiseptic
- Antiseptic soap
- Pain relief medicine—for children and adults
- Cotton balls and/or swabs
- Cough medicine and/or throat lozenges
- Motion sickness medicine
- Fingernail clippers
- First-aid book or manual
- Ipecac
- Moleskin for blisters
- Ointment for insect bites and sunburn
- Premoistened towelettes
- Thermometer
- Tissues
- Tweezers and needle

FamilyFun TIP

The Internet Travel Bible

If you're serious about researching (and especially booking) travel plans yourself, consult *Online Travel* by Ed Perkins (Microsoft Press, $19.95). This paperback tome is an invaluable resource on getting the best deals available and navigating the benefits and pitfalls of today's travel market, both on- and off-line.

Plus, when it comes time to book reservations, the Web can be a treasure trove of bargains—if you know how to hunt for them (see "The Internet Travel Bible" above). Why is that so? In essence, the Internet allows travel service providers to change their bargain pricing structures and unload unsold seats and rooms at a moment's notice. Of course, agents are still out to make as much money as they can—but you often can reap the benefits of their last-minute sales. In fact, many of these sales are available only on-line.

CONS: Keeping tabs on the travel market on-line can be extremely time-consuming if you are determined to find the best deal possible. In addition, since Web search engines can't read your mind and ask you questions, they can't ferret out all your options—just the ones that fall within the parameters you specify. So if you aren't a savvy searcher, you might miss the best deals (or the best destinations) even after hours of research.

Family travel Websites. It's a challenge to locate truly family-friendly sites among the hundreds available. For researching travel ideas and gathering travel tips, here are some of the best sites. Try our own Website too—www.familyfun.com—it too has a lot of travel ideas.

♦ www.vacationtogether.com is a searchable database of family vacation ideas, reprinted from various publications (including *FamilyFun* magazine). You'll also find packing checklists and links to reservation sites here.

♦ www.travelwithkids.about.com is a terrific clearinghouse for family vacation ideas, package deals, current bargains, lists of accommodations, packing checklists, travel tips and games, downloadable maps, and more.

♦ www.thefamilytravelfiles.com is a well-organized family travel Website that showcases a range of trip ideas and offers a free travel e-zine.

♦ www.familytravelforum.com is a monthly on-line newsletter specializing in well-screened links to family-friendly accommodations, airfare deals, seasonal events, and more.

General travel sites. In addition to family-specific sites such as the ones listed above, there are literally thousands of useful Websites that can help you plan and book your vacation. They are too numerous to list here! We have included many of our favorites throughout this chapter; in addition to those, here are a few you may find useful.

♦ www.officialtravelinfo.com lists contacts for travel and tourism bureaus worldwide (you can search the United States by state).

♦ www.fodors.com, www.frommers. com, and www.nationalgeographic. com are sites related to travel magazines. Often, they'll post selections from current issues, as well as other travel-related articles.

♦ www.travel library.com (a wide range of travel topics, travelogues, and destination information) and www. about.com (a general site with good travel links) are sites that can lead you to travel information that you may (or may not!) be looking for.

Book your own airline reservations. Using the same databases as travel agents use, the leading travel sites have made booking your own flight as simple as typing in when you'd like to leave, when you'd like to return, your origin and destination, and airline choice. They kick back a list of flights that most closely match

Broker a Hotel Deal

Great deals at major hotels usually turn up off-season or at the last minute, but here's another tactic families can try: work with a hotel consolidator (also called a hotel broker or discounter).

Consolidators work by securing blocks of hotel rooms at wholesale prices, then reselling them at rates that are—in theory, at least—lower than the published "rack" rate. Some consolidators will only reserve your room; you pay the hotel directly. Others require a prepaid voucher that you present to the hotel upon arrival. Many consolidators claim savings of 10 to 50 percent (some even more), but as with any bargain, it pays to know what you're getting into.

SOME TIPS:
- Ask about service charges. Is there a user fee for the consolidator?
- Are there financial penalties for trip cancellation or rescheduling?
- Compare rates. The consolidator may not beat a hotel's special offers.

With those caveats, try:
Quikbook: Good selection and easy to use, with hotels in 33 cities. Call 800-789-9887 or see www.quikbook.com
Central Reservation Service: Lists hotel deals in ten major cities. Call 800-555-7555 or visit www.roomconnec tion.com

Gumshoe Games

The detectives in your group will just love these tests of their sleuthing ability.

Secret highway messages: Pass out the pencils and paper, and keep your eyes peeled for official road signs. Each time you spot one, write down the first letter. When you've passed five to seven signs—and have five to seven letters—you're ready to crack the code. Here's how: each letter stands for a word. So the letters D, S, C, S, and A could stand for the secret message "Drive slowly, construction starts ahead." Of course, others in your family may interpret it as "Dad, stop, candy store ahead."

Two truths and one lie: The first person makes three statements about himself or herself. Two are true; the other is a lie. For example, you could say, "I had a dog named Puddles. My sister cut off my hair once when I was asleep. I won the school spelling bee when I was in third grade." Everybody then holds up one, two, or three fingers to show which statement they think is the lie. Reveal the answer and let the next person fib away.

your specifications and then let you choose the flights you want. After confirming your choices, you pay with a credit card, print your itinerary, and either receive your paper tickets in the mail or, more likely, pick up your tickets when you check in at the airport. **NOTE:** Some people prefer paper tickets because if a flight is missed or cancelled an e-ticket may not be exchangable at a different airline's counter.

Our favorite flight sites are Expedia (www.expedia.com), Travelocity (www.travelocity.com), and Trip. com (www.trip.com). Don't assume that all offer the same flights or the same prices; the important thing is to shop around, even among these sites.

Before you pay for your tickets, you should double-check with two other sources. First, look at your chosen airline's home site to see if they offer extra miles for booking flights on-line, or special, unadvertised Web deals. And call your travel agent, tell her the flight you're interested in, and see if she can beat the price. Lastly, be sure you're aware of the taxes, airport surcharges, and possible site use fees that may be added to your ticket price.

For more information about airlines, airports, and on-line reservations, go to www.iecc.com/airline/. Also, check out Ed Perkins' *Online Travel* (Microsoft Press, $19.95). To find out more about frequent flier mile programs, visit www.frequent flier.com

Book hotel and rental car reservations. In general, hotel and rental car reservations work the same way that airfare reservations do. The Web is an excellent source of hotel deals (especially for vacation packages, if you're a savvy shopper); rental car companies, on the other hand, generally offer little in the way of discounts above what you can get at the desk.

FREE ATLAS

Best Western offers free road atlases with Best Western sites: call 800-528-1234.

Sign up for e-mail newsletters. If you find a good travel Website that offers a free newsletter, it doesn't hurt to sign up—you may receive timely notice of travel deals that you otherwise would miss. Just be sure that you save any information on how to cancel the subscription in case you want to opt out.

Are Internet travel arrangements foolproof? No, unfortunately. The Internet is prime territory for scams, although you can guard against most of them with a few protective strategies. First, deal with major sites (like the ones listed in this book) or directly with brand-name company sites (like Avis or Holiday Inn) whenever possible. When you're transmitting your credit card information, make sure your connection is secure (your browser should tell you when one has been established). Also, you should double-check to see that the service provider's Website has a secure server. (Look for a locked padlock in the corner of your browser's window or "https"—the "s" stands for "secure"—in the URL.) If a site doesn't seem completely aboveboard, it may not be. Finally, when in doubt, back out. As long as you don't give a company your credit card number, they can't charge you anything.

FamilyFun READER'S TIP

A Colorful Road Game

This homemade road game is a big hit with my 4-year-old son, Tommy. I clip cards out of colored construction paper and print a different letter of the alphabet on each. During a car ride, each of us picks a card and searches for an object or a structure that matches the color and begins with the letter on our card. For example, a player with a *B* on a yellow card might spot a school bus. Since we began playing this game, my son tends to remember many more details about our travels. Instead of hearing, "Are we there yet?" we hear, "Oh no, I haven't found mine yet!"

Susan Robins, Cottage Grove, Oregon

Happy Campers

If your family's idea of a vacation involves nightly campfires, sleeping bags, and potential wildlife sightings near (or in!) your living space, check out these great resources for tent and RV camping.

The Trailer Life Directory provides travelers with a list of several thousand campgrounds and RV parks throughout the United States and Canada. Each location is rated on a three-step scale that assesses the park's facilities, cleanliness, and overall appeal; ratings are updated on an annual basis. You can register at www.tl directory.com to search the directory for free or order your own copy for the road on-line or at bookstores.

Woodall's campground directories also rate a large number of parks—more than 14,000 locations throughout the United States and Canada are scored on their facilities and recreation. You can purchase a directory which covers the entire area, or shorter versions of the guide are available for the western and eastern regions. Woodall's also publishes a directory exclusively for tent campers. Again, you can register to access campground listings for free at www. woodalls.com, but the on-line directory does not include Woodall's convenient rating system. The complete directories can be purchased at Woodall's Website or bookstores.

There's no centralized reservation system for every campsite within the **National Park system**, so your best bet is to contact each individual park. Campground reservations here usually must be made several months in advance since the sites are so popular, so don't count on finding a space unless you've planned ahead. Contact information for the National Parks can be found at their Website, www. nps.gov Policies for state parks also vary from place to place, so you'll have to contact individual campgrounds for camping information.

Veteran car campers recognize **KOA Kampgrounds** by their familiar yellow, red, and black signs. KOAs allow your family to rough it while enjoying many of the amenities of home. Novice campers will be thrilled to have access to hot showers, flush toilets, laundry facilities, and convenience stores. All KOA locations have both tent and RV sites, and some even have cabins that your family can rent. If you plan to stay multiple nights at one or more KOA Kampgrounds, consider purchasing a Value Kard. You'll get a 10 percent discount on your registration fees and a free copy of the KOA directory (you'll still pay for shipping). You can also research KOA locations for free at www.koakamp-grounds.com or purchase your own directory on-line or by calling 406-248-7444.

If you're looking for campgrounds where your family can pitch a tent in peace and quiet, check out *The Best in Tent Camping* series (published by Menasha Ridge Press). The books detail the best in scenic, tent-only sites without all of the bells and whistles.

One key to a great camping trip is remembering all of your supplies. If your family is RV or car camping, you can usually purchase any forgotten items on the road. However, if you're traveling far off the beaten path, you'll need to be careful to double-check your belongings.

Here's a checklist of supplies to make your camping experience go smoothly. If you're renting an RV, be aware that you may be able to rent your bedding and cooking supplies for an additional fee and save the trouble of bringing your own.

- Tent(s) and tent stakes
- Plastic ground cloth/tarp
- Sleeping bags (or bedding, for an RV)
- Sleeping pads
- Camp stove (with extra fuel)
- Pots, plastic dishes, mugs, and utensils
- Water bottle or canteen
- Lantern and/or candles
- Bottle and/or can openers
- Sharp knife (parents should hold on to this)
- Plethora of plastic/trash bags
- Dish soap (preferably biodegradable)
- Stocked coolers
- Water (or a portable filter or purifying tablets)
- Waterproof matches or lighter(s)
- Flashlights (and extra batteries)
- Bandanna (for use as a head covering, pot holder, and napkin)
- Trowel
- Folding saw
- First-aid kit, medications
- Sunscreen
- Insect repellent
- Toilet paper
- Day packs
- Child carriers (for little ones)
- Compass and area map
- Clothing (make sure to pack many layers)
- Two pairs of shoes (in case one gets wet)
- A hat
- Sunglasses
- Toiletries (try to take only necessary items)
- Camera
- Binoculars
- Kid supplies (toys, books, favorite stuffed animal)

Maine

LICENSE PLATES proudly declare that Maine is "Vacationland"—and with good reason. Our most northeastern state boasts some 2,000 miles of lakes and streams, 3,478 miles of coastline, a mile-high mountain (Katahdin), the nation's second-most-visited national park (Acadia), and approximately 30,000 moose.

The southern Maine coastline is strung with wildly popular family beach towns, complete with lobster shacks, lighthouses, and white-sand beaches. Maine is the place for you and your kids to try white-

Western Lakes
and Mountains

Down East Maine

Midcoast Maine

Portland Area

Southern
Maine

water rafting, fly-fishing, or even rock climbing (log on to www.maineguides.com for a list of guides).

And if your family wants to truly get away from it all, Maine also has remote waterfront camps where you can rent a cottage without a phone or TV and spend your days fishing, hiking, or canoeing in peace and quiet.

Explore what locals refer to as the real Maine, the peaceful areas that aren't overrun with tourists. Get off busy Route 1, the road most travelers take along the coast, and head down one of Maine's scenic peninsu-

las to watch the sunset. Spend time at a nature refuge, go to the beach, eat a lobster—it doesn't get much better than this.

ATTRACTIONS

$	under $10
$$	$10 - $20
$$$	$20 - $30
$$$$	$30 +

HOTELS/MOTELS/CAMPGROUNDS

$	under $100
$$	$100 - $200
$$$	$200 - $300
$$$$	$300 +

**RESTAURANTS
(PER ADULT ENTREE)**

$	under $10
$$	$10 - $20
$$$	$20 - $30
$$$$	$30 +

***FAMILYFUN* RATED**

★	Fine
★★	Good
★★★	Very Good
★★★★	*FamilyFun* Recommended

From Kittery to Old Orchard Beach, southern Maine's coastal towns are full of classic summer pleasures, including seaside amusement parks and dockside lobster bakes.

Southern Maine

SOUTHERN MAINE'S COASTAL towns are similar in some ways, yet each is distinctive. All boast lovely, white-sand beaches; lots of family-oriented amenities; and many fun things for kids to do. In fact, the area is such a blast for children, many families never bother to venture north toward Portland and points beyond. In a way, you can't blame them. This part of Maine is the fun zone, packed with everything a family could want in a vacation: top-rated water parks, picturesque lighthouses, miniature-golf courses, mouthwatering ice cream, kid-friendly hotels and restaurants, and the opportunity for adventure.

Because each town in the region has its own personality, you can choose the one that suits your style and wallet or meander up the coast, playing for a bit in each one before moving on. Here's a brief guide to get you oriented.

Kittery, the gateway to Maine, is one of New England's best places to go bargain shopping. But it's also a historic treasure, with magnificent forts for your family to explore.

THE FamilyFun LIST

MUST-SEE MUST-SEE

The Goldenrod (page 54)

The Seashore Trolley Museum (page 46)

Wells National Estuarine Reserve at Laudholm Farm (page 48)

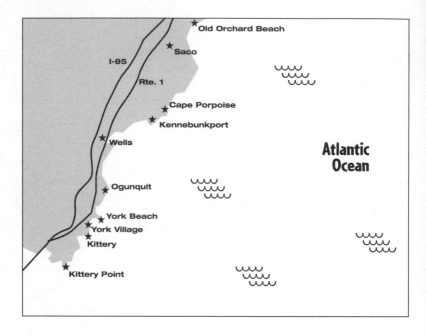

York is composed of York, York Village, York Beach, and Cape Neddick. Together, they're a haven for history lovers (see Old York Historic Sites at right) and for beach lovers, who can choose from several sandy wonderlands. One of the best places in Southern Maine— The Goldenrod, purveyor of made-before-your-eyes taffy—is here, and your kids will enjoy horseback riding on Mount Agamenticus.

Ogunquit is a recreational feast, home to a three-and-a-half-mile-long beach; Perkins Cove, a little fishing area where you can nibble seafood by the dock and go whale-watching; and Marginal Way, a mile-and-a-quarter seaside walking path with spectacular ocean views. If you're traveling on a budget, play in Ogunquit for the day and stay overnight in Wells.

Unpretentious, welcoming, and affordable, Wells has the best dough-nut shop in the area, a family-oriented beach, pick-your-own fruit farms, and beautiful places for kids and parents to hike.

With its gorgeous concentration of historic inns and bed-and-breakfast inns, Kennebunkport is a town fit for a president. (George and Barbara Bush have a summer retreat here.) In the picture-postcard-perfect downtown, families can board lobster boats, eat hamburgers by the Kennebunk River, and shop for cool souvenirs. Some of the area's most beautiful beaches, and one of Maine's most fun museums, The Seashore Trolley Museum, are here.

Old Orchard Beach is a carnival where everyone's invited. About a third of the visitors are French Canadian, and you'll see signs in French all over town exclaiming *bienvenue*. Both Canadians and Americans come here to enjoy the town's famous seven-mile-long beach, array of oceanfront motels, and countless seaside amusements.

Nearby **Saco** is the envy of its neighbors: it has two of the best theme parks in the area. Families from all over the state come to ride the water slides at Aquaboggan and get their thrills on the wooden roller coaster at the well-manicured Funtown Splashtown.

CULTURAL ADVENTURES

Old York Historic Sites ★★/$$
Tour York Village and get a taste of life in one of New England's earliest settlements. On select summer afternoons, the Old York Historical Society takes you back to colonial times through themed programs geared to families (and, sometimes, exclusively to kids). Depending on the schedule, you might meet the schoolmaster in the Old School House, make a basket, or try candle dipping. Kids who aren't afraid of the dark also enjoy evening candle-

DREAMY DRIVE-INS

For generations, families have spent summer nights under the stars, watching movies on a big screen. In New England, the tradition is still going strong. Here are some favorite family drive-ins:

MAINE: Bridgton Drive-in *(Rte. 302, Bridgton; 207/647-8666)*; Skowhegan Drive-in *(Rte. 201, Skowhegan; 207/474-9277)*.

MASSACHUSETTS: Mendon Drive-in *(Rte. 16, Mendon; 508/473-4958)*; Tri-Town Drive-in *(3 Youngs Rd., Rte. 13, Fitchburg; 978/345-5062)*; Wellfleet Drive-In *(Rte. 6, Wellfleet, Cape Cod; 800/696-3532; 508/349-7176)*.

CONNECTICUT: Mansfield Drive-in *(Junction of Rtes. 31 and 32, Manchester; 860/423-4441)*; Pleasant Valley Drive-in *(Rte. 181 off Rte. 44, Barkhamsted; 860/379-6102)*; Southington Twin Drive-in Theatre *(Meriden Waterbury Tpke. and Rte. 322; 860/628-2205)*.

RHODE ISLAND: Rustic Drive-in *(Rte. 146, North Smithfield; 401/769-7601)*. See "Last Picture Show," page 338.

NEW HAMPSHIRE: Weirs Drive-in Theater *(Rte. 3, Weirs Beach; 603/366-4723)*.

light tours of the Old Gaol (the British term for jail), featuring costumed performers in the role of prisoners. Buy tickets right there at Jefferds' Tavern. *Rte. 1A, York Village; (207) 363-4974;* www.oldyork.org

 The Seashore Trolley Museum
★★★★/$$

If you plan to visit this outstanding museum, you're on the right track— it's one of the best attractions in the region. The highlight for kids is riding a vintage trolley down four miles of track. As the trolley rolls by 320 acres of wooded countryside, the enthusiastic conductors (many of them grandparents) share tales of the trolley era. Kids can even sign up to be a motorman and take the helm of the 20-ton trolley, an achievement marked with a diploma and souvenir photo. The exhibits feature dozens of restored 19th- and early-20th-century trolleys and mass transit vehicles. You can picnic on the grounds and pick up a trolley-themed gift in the store. On select summer nights, the museum also hosts ice cream and sunset rides.

195 Log Cabin Rd., Kennebunkport; (207) 967-2800; www.trolleymuseum.org

JUST FOR FUN

Aquaboggan
★★/$$$

Splash-happy families will thoroughly enjoy this water park with its wave pool, big swimming pool, three curvy water slides, bumper boats, and tube adventures. When you're ready to dry off a bit, try the miniature-golf course or race cars. *Rte. 1, Saco; (207) 282-3112.*

Funtown Splashtown U.S.A.
★★/$$$$

This roadside amusement park is home to a wooden roller coaster, Excalibur, along with miniature golf, batting cages, arcades, and classics such as bumper cars and spinning teacups. Its small water park has nine water slides and a kiddie pool (but if it's water you primarily want, our vote is Water Country in Portsmouth, New Hampshire). *Rte. 1, Saco; (800) 878-2900; (207) 284-5139;* www.funtownsplashtown usa.com

Ghostly Tours
★★/$

Light your lantern and follow the narrator to York's historic graveyard on these popular hour-long tours. You'll hear ghost stories and witch tales and learn about such local legends as Handkerchief Moody, a minister who always wore a black handkerchief around his face. The stories aren't all that scary. **NOTE:** Kids ages 8 and up who aren't afraid of the dark will probably be fine. *250 York St., York Village; (207) 363-0000.*

Mount Agamenticus
★★/Free
Head up a winding back road to this 580-foot-high mountain, where, from the summit on clear days, you can see Mount Washington and sweeping ocean views. Bring your mountain bike or try horseback riding, corral rides, scenic trail rides, and private lessons are offered. Riders are advised to call ahead for hours and reservations. *Mountain Rd., off Rte. 1, York; (207) 363-1040.*

Palace Playland
★★/$$
For many kids, there's no better reason to come to Old Orchard Beach. This seaside amusement park is packed with every video game, carnival ride, fast-food joint, and kiddie amusement you can imagine. Highlights for kids are the Liquid Lightning water slide, 75-foot-high Ferris wheel, Galaxy roller coaster (with a 50-foot drop), and hand-carved carousel. Plus there's a humongous pinball and video arcade that bills itself as the largest in New England. *1 Old Orchard St.,*

Rest Stop

For a break from Old Orchard's crowds and kitsch, head to **Ferry Beach**, a 100-plus-acre natural area. Pick a color-coded trail and wander by a Tupelo swamp, dunes, or a bog, while learning about native wildlife. The preserve has a sand beach and peaceful picnic areas with grills. *Rte. 9, Saco; (207) 283-0067.*

Old Orchard Beach; (207) 934-2001; www.palaceplayland.com

Pirate's Cove ★★★/$
If Old Orchard Beach's attractions are not thrilling enough for you, pick up a putter and have a go at this 36-hole themed course, which challenges you to shoot your way through mountain caves, over footbridges, and under waterfalls. For an extra challenge, take your cue from the pirates and wear an eye patch. *70 First St., Old Orchard Beach; (207) 934-5086.* (There's another Maine location on *Rte. 3, Salisbury Cove, Bar Harbor; 207/288-2133.*)

Rachel Carson Wildlife Refuge
★★★/Free
Named for the world-renowned ecologist, the mile-long Rachel Carson trail is an ideal place for families to explore an environment that's fairly uncommon in Maine: the salt marsh. Pick up a trail guide at the

visitors' center, and set off on a journey past rivers, streams, and wildlife in this 5,000-acre preserve. *321 Port Rd., Wells; (207) 646-9226.*

Spiller's Farm ★/$

This small, family-owned farm invites you to pick apples and pumpkins, and, of course, tour the farm. Your kids can watch the Hereford beef cows being fed and maybe even see some wild turkeys. *1123 Branch Rd., Wells; (207) 985-2575.*

Wells National Estuarine Reserve at Laudholm Farm ★★★/$

This 1,600-acre natural gem offers seven miles of hiking trails that wind past old fields, woodlands, wetlands, salt marshes, and a barrier beach. You can learn more about the ecologically rich environment in the nature center and through hands-on programs designed for families and kids (for a small additional fee). Depending on the schedule, you might go fishing in the marsh with a net (known as seining), make casts of animal tracks, take a nocturnal wildlife walk, or learn about the constellations at a star party. There are special, half-day, Just for Kids pro-

grams, too. This is a beautiful spot for a picnic. *342 Laudholm Farm Rd., Wells; (207) 646-1555.*

BUNKING DOWN

Anchorage Inn ★★/$$

Across the street from Long Sands Beach, this inn is a good spot for families on a budget. Nothing fancy, it has basic rooms (with ocean or garden views), outdoor and indoor pools, and an on-site restaurant. *Rte. 1A, York Beach; (207) 363-5112.*

Beachmere Inn ★★★★/$$

This grand Victorian resort has been run by the same family for generations, and the owners excel at making guests feel welcome. The inn crowns a hill with a sweeping view of Ogunquit Beach and sits directly on the scenic path known as Marginal Way. It also has its own little beaches for guests to enjoy. The best bet for families is to stay in the freestanding unit known as Beachmere South or to rent rooms in one of the cottages; both have kitchenettes. *Beachmere Pl., Ogunquit; (207) 646-2021;* www.beachmereinn.com

USED DURING WORLD WAR I and World War II, **Fort Foster** has several small public beaches, a playground, picnic areas, barbecue grills, and views of Whaleback Lighthouse. *Pocahontas Rd., Kittery, Maine; (207) 439-2182.*

Cabot Cove Cottages
★★/$$

In this laid-back lodge, families stay in rustic, knotty-pine cottages with kitchenettes that have a lived-in look and views of the pretty tidal cove. The lodge furnishes rowboats and a canoe, plus there are picnic tables, swings, and a barbecue pit. The beach is a short walk away. *7 S. Main St., Kennebunkport; (800) 962-5424; (207) 967-5424; www.cabotcove cottages.com*

The Dockside Guest Quarters
★★★/$$

This family-owned lodge is a good choice if you crave peace and quiet and don't mind driving out of the way to get it. You'll stay on a private peninsula bordering York Harbor and the Atlantic Ocean. Multiunit buildings contain standard rooms and suites with private decks and water views. Although there are no organized activities, families can play on the beach, rent a boat, join a game of croquet, or go fishing. *Harris Island Rd., York; (800) 270-1977; (207) 363-2868; www.dock sidegq.com*

The Dunes ★★★★/$$

One of the prettiest spots in Ogunquit, this 12-acre, secluded waterfront retreat is a family's dream. You can borrow boats and paddle across the Ogunquit River to the beach (in low tide, you can simply walk across), play croquet

FamilyFun TIP

Thar She Blows

The personable crew of the 40-foot vessel *Deborah Ann (Perkins Cove, Ogunquit; 207/361-9501)* offers smaller, more personalized journeys than those on higher-speed vessels (these take four and a half hours).

and shuffleboard, relax by the garden, and play on the swing set. You can rent guest rooms (cable TV, refrigerators), suites (full kitchens, cable TV, fireplaces, ocean views), or cottages (full kitchen, cable TV, ocean and tidal river views, fireplaces). *Rte. 1, Ogunquit, (207) 646 2612.*

Elmwood Resort Hotel
★★/$$

For a more reasonably priced alternative to Kennebunkport and Ogunquit, try staying in Wells, which is just as friendly. The large modern units in this hotel have full kitchenettes, plus there's a big indoor pool, outdoor pool, and playground. *Rte. 1, Wells; (800) 697-8566; (207) 646-1038; www.elmwood-resort.com*

Garrison Suites Motel and Cottages ★★★/$

With a view of the Rachel Carson Wildlife Reserve and the Atlantic Ocean, this location is hard to beat, especially for the price. Families can stay in a motel room with two double beds or opt for a suite with a large living room, private bedroom, sleep sofa, and full kitchen. There's lots of room for kids to run around, and the Stritch family will make you feel welcome. *1099 Post Rd., Wells; (800) 646-3497; (207) 646-3497; www.garrisonsuites.com*

Idlease & Shorelands Guest Resort ★★★/$$

This place is ideal if you and your kids want a relaxed retreat in a posh, upscale town. You can choose from clean, contemporary cottages and two-bedroom apartments, all set on spacious grounds with pretty gardens, picnic tables, and outdoor

Lobstering with Captain Tom

Did you know a mother lobster can carry tens of thousands of eggs? Or that lobsters have greenish blood? You'll learn all kinds of fun facts about the clawed critters on a 50-minute lobster boat trip with the knowledgeable Captain Tom Farnon. Aboard a 25-foot skiff, you'll cruise to and from York Harbor, watching Captain Tom pull up traps. Kids can handle the sea creatures as Farnon, a former educator, patiently answers their questions. *Town Dock #2, York; (207) 363-3234.*

grills. You can gather with other families around the big outdoor pool, and there are swings, horseshoes, shuffleboard, bikes to borrow, a video library, and laundry facilities. The beach is a short walk away. Unlike other places that merely accept children, this one caters to them through and through. *Rte. 9, Kennebunkport; (800) 99-BEACH; (207) 985-4460.*

Maine Stay Inn & Cottages ★★★/$$$

From the outside, the Italian-style house with its white columns, wraparound porch and cupola, looks too fancy to open its doors to children. Not so. Carol and Lindsay Copeland, parents of two daughters, welcome young visitors. Families typically stay in the English-style cottage rooms (equipped with kitchens and working fireplaces) behind the main house. You don't even have to walk up to the main house for breakfast; the staff will deliver it in a basket directly to your door. To amuse kids, there's a wooden climbing structure and croquet set. *34 Maine St., Kennebunkport; (800) 950-2117; (207) 967-2117; www.mainestay inn.com*

The Meadowmere Resort ★★★/$$

With two beautiful pools, a scrumptious, complimentary breakfast, spacious rooms (some with kitchenettes), a game room and laundry

Counting the Miles

Last summer, we set out on our first big road trip. To get us through the first long day of driving (500 miles), I strung a long string with a marble-size bead for every 25 miles we would travel. Every fourth bead was a white bead. As we completed each 25 miles, the children moved a bead to the other end of the string. Our children could visualize how far we had to go by how many beads were left. After 100 miles, the white bead was moved, signaling a treat from Mom's Bag. Every day, our kids stayed occupied counting the beads, comparing how far we had come to how far we had to go. Our first grader added the 25's and informed us often of our progress.

Jane Rice, Maple Grove, Minnesota

room, a barbecue area, and easy access to the trolley, this place is a winner for families. It's also a short bike ride to Perkins Cove. *Main St. (Rte. 1), Ogunquit; (800) 633-8718; (207) 646-9661.*

The Old Colonial ★★/$$

The Davis family welcomes you to this recently remodeled beachfront motel with a large outdoor pool and an extensive video library. Rooms have cable TV and refrigerators; efficiencies have kitchens and cookware. It's a short walk to Palace Playland. *61 W. Grand Ave., Old Orchard Beach; (888) 225-5989.*

Pink Blossoms Family Resort ★★★/$$

This appealing retreat offers meticulously kept, pastel-colored studios, duplexes, and suites for families, with kitchenettes, cable TV, and dining areas. There's a pretty outdoor pool

and a tennis court. Nearby, the resort maintains eight town houses, each with a large deck and gas grill. *154 Shore Rd., Ogunquit; (800) 228 PINK; (207) 646-7397.*

The Rhumb Line ★★/$$

Billed as Kennebunk's affordable, year-round resort, the Rhumb Line is the kind of place where you'll all feel at home. Kids can run around on the four-acre property, there are indoor and outdoor heated pools, and on select summer nights, the staff prepares lobster feasts under the gazebo out back. Continental breakfast is included in the rate. The Rhumb Line is on the trolley line. *Ocean Ave., Kennebunkport; (800) 33-RHUMB.*

Royal Anchor Resort ★★/$$

Located a mile from Old Orchard Beach, this is a fine place for those who enjoy the rambunctious pier, but appreciate time away from the action, too. The well-kept motel sits on its own private, 400-foot stretch of beach. Continental breakfast is served daily, and families can enjoy tennis, a heated pool, basketball, and a kids' play area. *201 E. Grand Ave., Old Orchard Beach; (800) 934-4521; www.royalanchor.com*

Seacastles Resort ★★★/$$

Located on a pretty side street, this resort offers studio units and suites with kitchen facilities for families, plus a heated indoor pool. If you're bringing the extended family, this is a good (though pricey) place because of the deluxe suites and penthouse apartments. There are extra charges for kids ages 2 and up. *104 Shore Rd., Ogunquit; (888) 926-8732; (207) 646-6055.*

Seafarer Motel ★★/$$

This well-run motel isn't as flashy as its neighbors, but the prices are right, the rooms are clean, and it has large indoor and outdoor pools. *Rte. 1, Ogunquit; (207) 646-4040.*

Seagull Motor Inn ★★/$

Situated on 11 acres overlooking a salt marsh and the Atlantic Ocean (you need to drive or take the town trolley to actually get to the beach), this value-priced motel offers clean rooms and pine-paneled cottages with and without kitchens. The cottages are close together, so you won't

have a lot of privacy, but there's a lovely, huge yard where children can play, plus shuffleboard and basketball courts, and a large outdoor pool. *Rte. 1, Wells; (207) 646-5164.*

Sea View ★★★/$$

This beachfront motel on West Grand Avenue is a nice choice for families. It features two-bedroom suites with kitchenettes, as well as standard rooms, a gas grill by the outdoor pool, and direct access to the beach. *65 W. Grand Ave., Old Orchard Beach; (800) 541-8439; (207) 934-4180.*

GOOD EATS

Alisson's ★★/$$$

Named for the owner's daughter, this family restaurant is a comfortable place to bring kids. They get crayons, take-home sippy cups, a children's menu (including jumbo hot dogs and fish-and-chips), plus TLC from the friendly staff. The general menu includes burgers, seafood, nachos, and cold-cut sandwiches. You can also get a "beach box" to go, containing a sandwich, chips, a cookie, and a drink. *5 Dock Sq., Kennebunkport; (207) 967-4841.*

Barnacle Billy's ★★★/$$

For 40 years, families have wandered to Ogunquit's Perkins Cove and plunked themselves on the deck for a seafood dinner—and a superb view of lobster skiffs, soaring seagulls, and sailboats. Billy sometimes plucks a lobster from the tank and lets kids hold it. He dishes up hamburgers and other kid favorites, too. *Perkins Cove, Ogunquit; (207) 646-5575.*

Billy's Chowder House
★★★/$$

Some locals say the chowder here is the area's best. You can test it for yourself, along with dozens of other seafood, steak, chicken, and Italian entrées. The kids' menu includes children's sundaes. *Lobster Landing, Wells; (207) 646-7558.*

Bob's Clam Hut ★★★/$-$$

After you've had your fill of shopping at the outlets, sit down to great seafood at this appealing restaurant, where papier-mâché fish dangle from the ceiling. If you believe the funny painting on the wall, even the *Gilligan's Island* crew has enjoyed Bob's legendary clams. Kids will love the free activity books and the Ben & Jerry's ice cream counter. *Rte. 1, Kittery; (207) 439-4233.*

Cap'n Simeon's Galley
★★★/$$

Treat yourself to seafood and a view of two local lighthouses at this waterfront spot in Maine's oldest community. Kids get crayons and a coloring mat menu listing all of their favorites. *Rte. 103, Pepperrell Cove, Kittery Point; (207) 439-3655.*

Chauncey Creek Lobster Pier
★★★★/$$

The creekside view makes this one of the best places to try lobster in the rough. To supplement your lobster and seafood feast, the Spinney family lets you bring in any food or drinks not sold on the premises. Pick a bright-colored picnic table along the cove, unpack your cooler, and enjoy; there's also an enclosed area for inclement weather. *Chauncey Creek Rd., Kittery Point; (207) 439-1030.*

Congdon's Doughnuts
★★★/$

Send your diet packing and head to this local landmark for doughnuts that are absolutely mouthwatering. Choose from a selection that includes sugared, buttercrunch blueberry, and chocolate chocolate. If you'd prefer a sit-down meal, opt for the family-oriented dining room, where friendly waitresses bring mouse-shaped pancakes and hot dogs for the kids and scrumptious omelettes and sandwiches for the

adults. *1090 Post Rd., Wells; (207) 646-4219.* Congdon's also operates a bakery in Ogunquit, next to the Leavit Theater.

Fisherman's Catch
★★★★/$-$$

Enjoy a view of the dunes while you dine on clam chowder, lobster, and scallops at this fun, affordable restaurant. Need a paper towel? Reach for the grinning lobsters, which dangle over the picnic tables; rolls of towels are handily ready to be pulled from their claws. Kids' meals range from fish-and-chips to hot dogs and come with a freeze pop as a treat. *Wells Harbor, Wells; (207) 646-8780.*

Flo's Takeout ★★/$

Some families love hot dogs so much, they're willing to wait and wait and wait. And that can be the case if you don't arrive at 11 A.M. sharp outside this small, nondescript shack. Know exactly what you want (order your dogs with special sauce) before it's your turn (help can be a bit brusque here). The payoff? Delicious, steamed Schultz's dogs that you can enjoy at a picnic table

with other frankfurter fans. *Rte. 1, Cape Neddick; no phone.*

The Goldenrod
MUST-SEE FamilyFun MUST-SEE ★★★★/$

Don't leave southern Maine without stopping at this landmark, which since 1896 has made a type of saltwater taffy known as Goldenrod Kisses. The place is so charming, you may feel as if you're on a movie set, but rest assured, this is the real thing. Just ask your kids, who will delight in watching as the sweet gobs are stretched and formed (180 pieces per minute). Other kid pleasers: shopping for penny candy, choosing from 135 flavors of homemade ice cream at the antique marble soda fountain, and enjoying home cooking by the stone fireplace in the dining room. Kids will have a hard time choosing—waffles, hamburgers, PB&J, and tuna are all here. *York Beach; (207) 363-2621.*

Huot's ★★/$-$$

To experience the quiet side of Old Orchard Beach, head to Camp Ellis, the southern end of the seven-mile-long beach. In this peaceful fishing

THE GOLDENROD makes 12 flavors of their saltwater taffy, including cinnamon, molasses, and vanilla. If you're stuck with a craving, they'll ship you some by mail. Check out their Website at www.thegoldenrod.com or phone them at (207) 363-2621 for more info.

village, you can walk along a break-water, watch the sunset, and get a good meal at this local favorite. Squeeze into the wooden booths and enjoy clam chowder, haddock sandwiches, and kids' staples. *Camp Ellis Beach, Saco; (207) 282-1642.*

Joseph's by the Sea
★★/$$

In an area chock-full of deep-fried fast-food takeout stops, this is a refreshing choice for families willing to spend a bit more to enjoy a meal by the water. Kids can order chicken fingers and hot dogs; parents can dine on charred salmon and pepper-crusted filet mignon. *55 West Grand Ave., Old Orchard Beach; (207) 934-5044.*

The special trade-mark of **Flo's Hot Dogs** is a mixture of mayonnaise and hot sauce.

La Stalla Pizzeria
★★/$$

In a sea of seafood restaurants, it's comforting to know there's a family-focused pizza place. Crayons, color-ing sheets, a friendly staff, and affordably priced meals make this a great destination. Along with the classic pies, you can sample the Aegean, spanakopita, and chicken Caesar. There's a long list of subma-rine sandwiches, too. *38 Woodbridge Rd., York; (207) 363-1718.*

Lobster Barn ★★/$$
Under this "barn" roof, you'll find the full range of seafood fare, plus a kids'

menu that includes hamburgers, cheeseburgers, and chicken fingers. On warm days, you can eat at the casual, outside facility, Lobster in the Rough. *Rte. 1, York; (800) 341-4549; (207) 363-4721.*

The Lobster Pot ★★/$$
This restaurant doesn't have a water view or much atmos-phere, but it's a good choice for families with kids. The dining area is roomy, and though the fare is heavy on seafood, you can also order sandwiches, chicken Parmesan, and classic kids' favorites. *62 Mills Rd., Cape Porpoise; (207) 967-4607.*

Lobster Shack
★★★/$

Since 1947 families have ordered clams and lobster rolls from this unpretentious restaurant by the drawbridge in Perkins Cove. Sit on a bench and watch the boats and gulls sail in the harbor; indoor and outdoor tables are available. *Perkins Cove, Ogunquit; (207) 646-2941.*

Maine Diner
★★★/$-$$

This popular family spot has won many awards for its lobster pie, and it dishes out dozens of other scrumptious meals as well. From homemade crab cakes and chili skins to blueberry pancakes and pulled

BBQ pork, the place has something for even the most finicky eaters. There's a kids' menu, and an awesome array of homemade desserts, including a New England favorite, Indian pudding. *Rte. 1, Wells; (207) 646-4441.*

Nunan's Lobster Hut
★★★/$$

If you're lobster maniacs, take your place at a long wooden table in this narrow shack of a restaurant, and dig in. Besides lobster salad, lobster stew, and boiled lobster, you'll find burgers, hot dogs, PB&J, and homemade blueberry pie. *Rte. 9, Cape Porpoise; (207) 967-4362.*

Ogunquit Lobster Pound
★★★/$$

Pick a lobster from the tank, find a table by the shady pines, and relax while you wait for your order. Kids can run around in the wooded grove, and the staff will gladly cut and crack open the lobsters so they're easier for little fingers to manage. There's a kids' menu with chicken nuggets, hot dogs, and pizza, too. *Rte. 1, Ogunquit; (207) 646-2516.*

Rapid Ray's ★/$

For a quick, affordable meal that's tastier than typical fast food, look to this local landmark. For nearly 50 years, the Camire family has kept customers coming back with its signature hot dogs, burgers, and fries. *179 Main St., Saco; (207) 282-1847.*

Vinny's East Coast Grille
★★★/$$

Dubbing the family room "the kids' room," this restaurant gives families a place of their own. Here you'll find all the comforts of home—posters, butterflies hanging from the ceiling, stuffed animals, and TVs playing family movies. Don't be surprised if your favorite cartoon characters show up with free balloons for the kids. Menu items are equally family-friendly: chicken nuggets, pizza, and burgers for kids, and seafood pesto, chicken Alfredo, and prime rib for Mom and Dad. *Rte. 1, North, Ogunquit; (207) 646-5115.*

Warren's Lobster House
★★★/$$

Just across the Piscataqua River from Portsmouth, New Hampshire, this dining landmark (est. 1940) treats families to a salad bar with more than 50 offerings, a kids' menu with all the standard goodies, and lobster and beef feasts for Mom and Dad. Patrons with boats can dock outside (no charge) while dining, and antsy kids can inspect the collection of sailor's knots or search for souvenirs in the on-site gift shop. *Rte. 1, Kittery; (207) 439-1630.*

The Wayfarer ★★★/$$

Slip into one of the cozy, old-fashioned booths and enjoy a great meal in this scenic fishing village, just two miles from downtown Kennebunkport. Kids can dine on hot dogs and downsized roast steak. Parents can dip into shrimp scampi, chicken piccata, and haddock hacienda. *Pier Rd., Cape Porpoise; (207) 967-8961.*

Souvenir Hunting

Perkins Cove Candy

Satisfy your sweet tooth at this family-owned shop with melt-in-your-mouth fudge, chocolate turtles, taffy, and nostalgia candylike coconut watermelon slices. *Perkins Cove, Ogunquit; (207) 646-7243.*

Lighthouse Depot

Billed as the world's largest lighthouse gift and collectible store, this emporium features thousands of themed gifts, from lighthouse magnets and mugs to blankets and collectible figurines. *Rte. 1, Wells; (800) 758-1444.*

FamilyFun TIP

Shop Till You Drop

One of New England's premiere bargain-shopping destinations, Kittery's long strip of outlet malls contains dozens of family favorites. **Yummies Candy & Nuts**, **Hanna Andersson**, and **OshKosh B'Gosh** are just a few of the hot spots for young shoppers. For more information (and a list of stores and discount coupons), call *(888) KITTERY.*

River Place Toys and Games

Don't let the name fool you. Yes, you'll find educational toys, story books, and stuffed animals at this boutique. But it's also the place for gorgeous women's clothing and jewelry. *250 York St., York Village; (207) 351-3266.*

Kids on the *Lucky Catch* lobster cruise don rubber gloves to haul up crabs and starfish that land in the traps.

Portland Area

IN A STATE devoted to outdoor pursuits and laid-back living, it's no surprise that Maine's largest city isn't your typical urban metropolis. Sure, there are glass office buildings, fancy galleries, coffeehouses, and first-rate museums, but Portland's location on Casco Bay opens the door to nautical adventures that kids love. At the busy wharf, families can board a lobster boat, cruise to the island home of legendary Arctic explorer, Admiral Robert E. Peary, or watch fishermen unload their catch at the Portland Fish Exchange.

Many Portland-area activities are designed to bring your family closer to nature. Casco Bay has hundreds of scenic islands to explore by boat, kayak, and bike. Cycling the East Promenade Bike Path, which winds past the harbor, is a fun, low-cost activity. Just a short drive away, in Cape Elizabeth, you'll find some of the area's prettiest beaches and lighthouses.

MUST-SEE

THE FamilyFun LIST

MUST-SEE

Children's Museum of Maine
(page 60)

***Lucky Catch* Lobster Cruise**
(page 63)

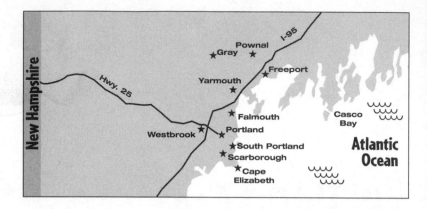

In casual Portland, even cultural institutions have a relaxed dress code and easygoing manner toward kids. The Children's Museum of Maine rolls out the red carpet for families, as does the Portland Museum of Art. On Friday night, the state's largest art museum hosts special workshops for families, and admission is free.

It's especially fun to explore the city's Victorian and contemporary neighborhoods on foot. You'll love wandering through the Old Port Exchange, a five-block district of old warehouses reborn as fashionable restaurants, boutiques, and specialty shops (including one of New England's best kite stores; see Souvenir Hunting on page 69). It's also home to the city's lively farmers' market, where you can find everything from just-picked apples to fresh-baked chocolate-chip cookies.

Of course, when it comes to shopping, there's no place like Freeport. Just north of Portland, this town boasts more than 150 outlets, including the famed L.L. Bean and L.L. Bean Kids. A few minutes away from the downtown commercial district, you can camp and hike by the bay, and eat succulent lobster on the edge of a scenic pier. One of the state's best family-oriented inns, the Isaac Randall House, also makes its home in Freeport. It's worth a trip just to sleep in the red caboose.

CULTURAL ADVENTURES

Children's Museum of Maine ★★★/$$

With three floors of exhibits to entertain and educate children, you could easily spend the entire afternoon here. Kids can fly in a space shuttle; visit an animal hospital; wander into a giant, inflatable whale; and mosey through "Our Town" to run errands at a kids' bank and supermarket. They can even get into the local scene by pulling traps off a lobster boat. *142 Free St., Portland; (207) 828-1234;* www.childrensmuseumofme.org

Maine Narrow Gauge Railroad Museum ★★/$$

Take a short-but-scenic train ride along the Eastern Prom, which offers beautiful harbor views. Your kids will delight in riding the narrow-gauge rail cars, which were used between 1870 and 1940 because their smaller size made them cheaper to build and run. Kids can venture back to the caboose and learn about a bygone era from friendly, costumed volunteers. Though the train ride is the highlight for kids, you may want to spend a few minutes inside the museum, checking out Maine's only narrow-gauge parlor car (1901) and other models. Christmas train rides are held in December. *58 Fore St., Portland; (207) 828-0814;* www.mngrr.org

Portland Museum of Art ★★/$

Maine's largest art museum is the place to be on Friday night, when admission is free, and the halls are filled with families. The Maine masterpieces by local artists Winslow Homer, Andrew Wyeth, and Edward Hopper will fuel your excitement about vacationing on the coast. *7 Congress Square, Portland; (207) 775-6148;* www.portlandmuseum.org

Southworth Planetarium ★★/$$

Even on a foggy night, you can see the stars at this educational facility run by the University of Southern Maine. Parents can select age-appropriate shows for their child (during ABCs of the Sky, for example, preschoolers learn a celestial-themed alphabet), attend a family show about the constellations, or see a laser light show with music from the Grateful Dead and the Beatles. Arrive

---

FamilyFun READER'S TIP -

WIndow Box Organizer

In the past on family road trips, I've found that keeping books and games organized and within reach (instead of under the seats) was a challenge for my boys, Joshua, 6, and Brooks, 4. I finally figured out the perfect solution: I purchased a plastic window planter and cut two parallel slits through the bottom of one end. I threaded the middle seat belt through the slits, so the box stays safely attached to the backseat. I even attached battery-operated lights (the kind you clip to books) on both sides of the box so the boys each have a lamp for reading. Best of all, the box keeps them on their own sides of the car, reducing the fight factor tremendously.

Angela Ruder, San Antonio, Texas

a bit early, so you'll have time to taste "astronaut ice cream" in the gift shop and watch shuttle launches and NASA space probes in the interactive computer area. *96 Falmouth St., Portland; (207) 780-4249;* www.usm. maine.edu/planet/

JUST FOR FUN

Bradbury Mountain State Park ★★★/$

Hike just a quarter mile to the summit of Bradbury Mountain and you'll be rewarded with a gorgeous view of Casco Bay and New Hampshire's White Mountains. Also within the park are a playground, softball fields, and a camping area (extra charge). *Rte. 9, Pownal (six miles from Freeport); (207) 688-4712.*

Desert of Maine ★★/$$

No, you're not hallucinating. That is, indeed, a desert just two and a half miles from Freeport's factory outlets. More than 11,000 years ago,

a glacier slid over the area, leaving behind sand mineral deposits that eventually formed this 40-acre geological curiosity: a real desert complete with dunes. You and your kids can explore the dunes on a guided tram ride, join a gemstone hunt, make jewelry, and view vials of multicolored sand from around the world. There's also an adjacent campground. *95 Desert Rd., Freeport; (207) 865-6962;* www.desertofmaine.com

Eagle Island ★★★/$$$$

You'll feel like explorers yourselves as you pack lunch rations, hop on a boat, and head to Eagle Island, the summer home of Admiral Robert E. Peary. Before you go, make sure you tell your children of his crowning achievement: in 1909, he became the first American to reach the North Pole. On the 80-minute trip to the admiral's isolated retreat, you'll spot osprey and the silver bobbing heads of seals. Once at the island bluffs, you'll tour his home, which hasn't changed much since he lived there from 1912 to 1920. (Even his children's toys are on display.) Rangers will be happy to tell you of Peary's adventures and guide you to scenic walking trails. The entire outing takes about four hours and is available via the **Coast Watch & Guiding Light Navigation Company** *on Long Wharf in Portland (207/774-6498)* and **Atlantic Seals Cruise**, which departs from *the South Freeport Wharf (207/865-6112).*

Gilsland Farm ★★/Free

For a peaceful hike past rolling fields and a salt marsh, stop at this 60-acre retreat, the headquarters for the Maine Audubon Society. The farm also periodically hosts family-oriented programs. Call to see if anything is going on when you'll be visiting. *118 Rte. 1, Falmouth; (207) 781-2330.*

Joker's ★★/$$

Don't wait for a rainy day to visit Joker's. This noisy, indoor fun park has more than 150 video games, amusements, and climbing structures where kids and adults alike can blow off steam. Navigate "ball crawls" and "web elevators" in the three-story A-Maze-Ing Playhouse, play laser tag, ride a go-cart, join a game of spaceball (volleyball on a trampoline), and munch on nachos at the 420-seat food court. A miniature-golf course is right outside, too. There's no admission; each activity is priced separately. *510 Warren Ave., Portland; (207) 878-5800.*

MUST-SEE Lucky Catch
FamilyFun ★★★★/$$$

MUST-SEE Ninety percent of America's lobsters are caught off the Maine coast, and you can help snare some on this working lobster boat. During a 90-minute, hands-on adventure around Casco Bay,

Captain Tom Martin equips you with rubber gloves and aprons, and teaches you to bait, set, and haul traps. Learn to measure lobsters to see if they're "keepahs," handle starfish and other creatures that land in the traps, and maybe even steer the boat by historic lighthouses and Civil War forts. You don't just watch and listen, you get your hands wet. *170 Commercial St., Portland; (207) 233-2026;* www.luckycatch.com

> Watch the **Portland Sea Dogs**, the farm team for baseball's Florida Marlins, take on opponents at Hadlock Stadium in Portland. (800) 936-DOGS.

Mackworth Island
★★/Free

Just a ten-minute drive north of Portland, you can walk the perimeter of this small, pleasant island and enjoy dramatic views of the city and the bay. *Rte. 1, Falmouth.*

Maine Wildlife Park
★★/$

Wild about animals? Head to this 200-acre facility and visit the orphaned or injured wildlife that are under the care of volunteers. Depending on when you visit, you'll meet moose, bobcats, ravens, and turkey vultures, many of which are recovering here before they're released back into the wild. Others are permanent residents because they can't survive on their own. Don't forget your hiking boots and a picnic lunch. This spot offers nature trails and scenic picnic areas. Call ahead for program times. *Rte. 26, Gray; (207) 657-4977.*

Scarborough Marsh Nature Center ★★★/$

Paddle along Maine's largest salt marsh, and you could meet egrets, herons, and glossy ibises. Rent a canoe and explore the 3,000-acre marsh on your own, or sign on for a canoe tour down the Dunstan River, led by a friendly naturalist. Sunrise, full-moon, and midday tours are available. If you're not into canoeing, the staff at this Maine Audubon Nature center offers nature programs for children during the summer. Depending on when you visit, the lineup might include everything from a bug hunt to nature games. Courses are available for kids ages 3 to 11; most classes last from one to two hours; preregistration is essential. Open May through Labor Day only. *Pine Point Rd., Scarborough; (207) 883-5100.*

Wolfe's Neck Farm ★★/Free

Home to pigs, goats, cows, horses, and chickens, this 650-acre organic farm along Casco Bay invites families to feed and pet the animals. This nonprofit farm (run by the Wolfe's Neck Farm Foundation), whose organic meats are sold in stores and at the Portland Public Market, also features hiking trails, walking tours, and special seasonal programs. The farm operates an adjacent campground (extra fee), with some sites on the bay. If possible, visit in spring, when you'll get to meet farm babies. *10 Burnett Rd., Freeport; (207) 865-4363;* www.wolfesneckfarm.com

BUNKING DOWN

AmeriSuites ★★/$$

Here's another good bet for families who like the all-suites approach. Though it's chock-full of business types during the week, families rule the roost on weekends. Located on a quiet hill near the Maine Mall, the hotel offers a VCR with Nintendo in each unit, plus an indoor pool and complimentary continental breakfast. There's no on-site restaurant. *303 Sable Oaks Dr., South Portland; (800) 833-1516; (207) 775-3900;* www.amerisuites.com

Comfort Suites ★★/$$

If you want enough room to stretch out, this is the place to do it. Each spacious suite in this property, built in 1999, has a refrigerator, coffeemaker, and microwave. You can also enjoy the indoor pool and complimentary continental breakfast. *500 Rte. 1, Freeport; (877) 865-9300;* www.freeportcomfortsuites.com

Embassy Suites ★★/$$

If staying 500 yards from the airport attracts rather than repels you, consider staying here. Every suite has a private bedroom and TV for parents, plus, for kids, a living area with pullout sofa; there's also a microwave, refrigerator, and second TV. The space comes in handy, particularly when kids want to watch *Barney* movies on their VCR. The property also has a large indoor pool. A daily breakfast buffet is complimentary at the on-site bistro, Cafe Stroudwater, and children dine free at lunch and dinner when parents purchase meals. *1050 Westbrook St., Portland; (207) 775-2200; www. embassysuites.com*

Freeport Inn
★/$$

Freeport is known for its bargains, and this is one of its better lodging deals. At this roadside motel (adjacent to Route 1 and I-95) about three miles from downtown Freeport, you can get a comfortable, affordable room or suite with a color TV. (TIP: If you have a lot of luggage, ask for a first-floor room, as the property has no elevator.) The spacious grounds have a safe play area, and you can bring a pet. A bonus: proximity to the Freeport Café (see Good Eats), a local landmark where folks line up out the door for the homemade muffins. *Rte. 1, S. Freeport; (800) 99-VALUE; (207) 865-3106.*

Holiday Inn Portland West
★★/$$

One of the best lodges for families in the area, this country-themed property gives free toys to kids on check-in, features a big outdoor swimming pool and indoor hot tub, and (as is true at other Holiday Inns) provides free meals for kids when an adult orders an entrée. It's just a few minutes to downtown Portland. *81 Riverside St., Portland; (800) HOL-IDAY; (207) 774-5601; www.bass hotel.com/holiday-inn*

Inn by the Sea Crescent Beach
★★★/$$$

Just minutes away from bustling Portland, this first-class inn has a

L.L. Adventures

If you've always wanted to try sea kayaking, orienteering, snowshoeing, or fly-fishing as a family, but didn't know where to start, turn to the pros at the **L.L. Bean Outdoor Discovery School.** For years, the experts at L.L. Bean have helped kids and parents feel confident through a series of popular Parent & Child classes that range from a couple of hours (archery) to overnight adventures (fly-fishing weekend). The programs are led by kid-friendly instructors who make learning fun. (Play "pizza tag" as you learn to cross-country ski.) The Freeport-based school also offers kids-only adventure camps. Reserve well in advance for classes. *Freeport; (888) 552-3261.*

supremely beautiful beachfront setting, a private entrance to Crescent Beach State Park, a pool and shuffleboard court, and luxurious accommodations. The best bets for families are the one-bedroom garden suites in the main house (full kitchen, two TVs with VCR) or the garden cottages (two-bedroom, first-floor suites with a full kitchen and two TVs with cable). With advance notice (but no extra charge), you can also bring the family pet. *40 Bowery Beach Rd., Cape Elizabeth; (800) 888-4287; (207) 799-3134.*

Isaac Randall House ★★/$$

This Federal-style house was built in 1823 for Isaac Randall and his bride, Betsy. They lived here for 50 years and raised eight children. The current managers of this bed-and-breakfast inn, Cynthia and John Wallet, have four girls and love hearing the pitter-patter of little feet. They warmly welcome families and pets, too. By far the most fun place to sleep is the restored caboose car—it's behind the house and is equipped with phone, TV, and bunks for the kids. The main inn boasts creative options as well. (The aqua room features a king-size bed and two twins nestled in the wall within a sleeping nook.) The price includes snacks (there's always ice cream in the fridge) and a hearty breakfast. The six-acre property has a playground and a pond for skating. *10 Independence Dr., Freeport; (207) 865-9295.* **NOTE:** For tips on other family-oriented B&Bs in the area, call *(800) 853-2727.*

FamilyFun TIP

Fish Tale

Hold your nose, pull on your sweaters, and head for the **Portland Fish Exchange** for an inside look at the fish industry. Before the fish ends up on your plate at a Portland area restaurant, it probably arrives at this busy dock and goes to auction. Every week, fishermen unload half a million pounds of haddock, redfish, flatfish, and more. Show up early in the morning and you can see how they sort the vast ocean harvest. For exact times, call first. *6 Portland Fish Pier, Portland; (207) 773-0017;* www.portlandfish exchange.com

GOOD EATS

Cole Farms ★★/$

After you visit the Maine Wildlife Park, stop here for great-tasting comfort food (meat loaf, homemade pies, roast turkey), and lots of TLC for the kids. *Rte. 100, Gray; (207) 657-4714.*

Freeport Café ★★★/$

Who better to create the kids' menu than kids themselves? That's the case here, where local students came up with such wonders as Goldilocks

Porridge with Fruit, Luscious Lasagna, and Perfect Pizza on an English muffin. (Different groups of children devise the menu each year, so items may vary.) With a scrumptious assortment of home-cooked breakfasts, soups, and sandwiches, parents will also have a culinary field day. Many of the waitresses are Moms who make kids feel at home with crayons and coloring sheets. *Rte. 1, S. Freeport; (800) 99-VALUE; (207) 865-3106.*

Fresh Market Pasta
★★/$

If your kids like pasta, they'll be in heaven at this casual, affordable spot in the historic Old Port Exchange. At the counter, order big, inexpensive bowls of homemade pasta of the day with your favorite sauce, then find a table in the spacious dining area and enjoy. Fresh Market Pasta offers kids' portions and colossal chocolate-chip cookies. *43 Exchange St., Portland; (207) 773-7146.*

The Governor's ★★/$

This Maine-based chain typifies the phrase "family restaurant." The kids' menu is filled with mac 'n' cheese, pizza, and "oodles of noodles"; the prices are low; and no one cares if you spill juice on the floor. Best of all, a train runs along a track on the upper wall just under the ceiling. Crayons and sippy cups are part of the package. *Adjacent to the Best Western, 700 Main St., South Portland;*

Go Global

Where in the world should you go next? For inspiration, look to **Eartha, the world's largest rotating globe** (nearly 130 feet around and some 5,600 pounds), in the DeLorme Map Company's lobby. The adjacent map store has an exceptional array of aerial maps, travel guides, travel software, and children's books. *Two DeLorme Dr., Yarmouth; (800) 642-0970; (207) 846-7100.*

(207) 773-2177. There are several other locations throughout the state.

Haraseeket Lunch and Lobster
★★★/$$

Relax by South Freeport's scenic harbor at this local favorite, known for exceptional lobster, clams, and scallops (as well as burgers, BLTs, and grilled cheese sandwiches). Watching the lobstermen unload their traps is as much a treat as the fare. *Main St., South Freeport; (207) 865-4888; (207) 865-3535.*

Margarita's
★★★/$$

Attention, amigos: for delicious Mexican food in a festive atmosphere, head to this friendly spot. Keeping kids happy is a top priority with servers, who give children Wikki Stix to bend and menu mats to color. They deliver the meals pronto, too. Two Portland locations: *11 Brown St. (207/774-9398)* and *242 St. John St. (207/874-6444)*, with many others throughout Maine, New Hampshire, and Connecticut.

Portland Public Market
★★/$-$$

This festive, enclosed market offers wares from more than two dozen locally owned businesses. Choices include pastries, produce, cheese, seafood, and pies and cookies straight from the oven. Grab a snack, hang out at a table on the second floor, and watch the action below. *Preble St. and Cumberland Ave., Portland; (207) 228-2000.*

Two Lights Lobster Shack
★★★★/$-$$

Chow down on fried seafood, hot dogs, and burgers at a picnic table just a stone's throw away from the mighty Atlantic. Families have been coming to this first-rate lobster "shack" since the 1920s to watch the waves crash against the rocks, see boats pull into Portland Harbor,

and, of course, eat lobster in the rough. There's also an indoor dining room decorated with old milk bottles, antique tools, and license plates. If you clean your plate, try the homemade "whoopy" pies for dessert. *219 Two Lights Rd., Cape Elizabeth; (207) 767-5835.*

Village Café ★★/$$

The Reali family has been running this local favorite for more than 60 years. Their specialty: making you feel at home while the aroma of homemade pizza, lasagna, steak, and seafood wafts through the large, cozy dining rooms. Kids can color their place mats, which double as children's menus. *112 Newberry St., Portland; (207) 772-5320.*

SOUVENIR HUNTING

The Creative Resource Center

Are you and your kids crafty? This nonprofit emporium is the place to pick up a treasure trove of dowels, poster board, Styrofoam, and more—for a song. Why not give each of your children a dollar, have them fill up a basket of these recyclables (donated by local businesses, including L.L. Bean), and see who can make the coolest creature? *1103 Forest Ave., Portland; (207) 797-9543.*

L.L. Kids

In a town with nearly 200 outlets, L.L. Kids stands out. This 17,000-square-

EVERY LOBSTERMAN'S buoys have a unique color scheme, different from all other fishermen in the state. How many of these patterns can you and your family find during your trip?

foot retail entertainment complex, adjacent to the famed L.L. Bean flagship store, features a two-story waterfall, trout pool, electronic climbing wall, interactive mountain bike test ride, a discovery trail, and oh, yeah, clothes. During summer, the place gets as crowded as a theme park, so It's best to visit at off times. *8 Nathan Nye St., Freeport; (800) 341-4341.*

Northern Sky Toyz
In the historic, five-block entertainment district of Portland known as the Old Port Exchange, you'll find this store, which stocks an exceptional line of kites, yo-yos, and juggling supplies. *388 Fore St.; (207) 828-0911.*

The Maine Bear Factory
A takeoff on the Vermont Teddy Bear Company, this shop invites kids to design their own bear and watch it being stuffed, sewn, and brushed on the spot. With rates starting at about $30, this is a pricey, but memorable, splurge. *294 Rte. 1, S. Freeport; (207) 865 0600.*

Wilbur's of Maine Chocolate Confections
The theme here is Maine, with sweets shaped like lobsters, wolves, and moose. Or try the chocolate pizza, blueberry jelly beans, and enormous chocolate-chip cookies. *32 Independence Dr., Freeport; (888) 762-5787.*

Whether you hitch a ride on a lobster boat *(page 74)*, learn to kayak *(page 79)*, or take a pirate cruise *(page 80)*, boating is the best way to explore middle Maine's craggy coast.

Midcoast Maine

THE COASTAL AREA FROM Brunswick to Stockton Springs is generally considered midcoast Maine, an area where the shoreline juts out with dozens of peninsulas. Each contains coves and crags, which are filled with forts, lighthouses, beaches, and fishing villages that young visitors love to explore. To start your midcoast adventure, get off busy Route 1 at Brunswick and head toward the water.

At the southern tip of the Harpswell Peninsula is Bailey Island, where you can stay overnight at a working lobster marina and watch fishermen haul in their catch. The Phippsburg Peninsula is home to inviting, kid-oriented bed-and-breakfast inns, as well as Maine's spectacular Popham Beach. Every summer, thousands of families travel down the Boothbay Peninsula to

Boothbay Harbor for cruises, children's festivals, and clambakes. On the Pemaquid Peninsula, you can see one of New England's most spectacular lighthouses and watch the Atlantic pound against the rocky coast.

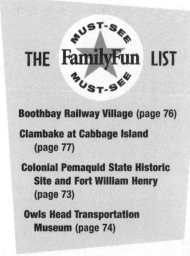

THE FamilyFun LIST

MUST-SEE · MUST-SEE

Boothbay Railway Village (page 76)

Clambake at Cabbage Island (page 77)

Colonial Pemaquid State Historic Site and Fort William Henry (page 73)

Owls Head Transportation Museum (page 74)

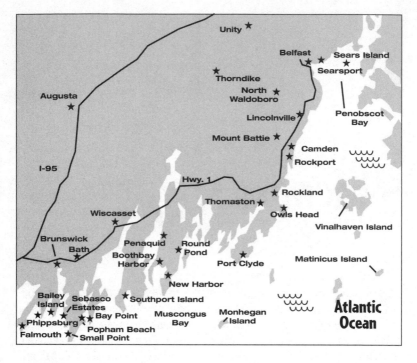

The islands off these peninsulas are full of surprises as well. Ten miles out to sea, on Monhegan Island, families who love to hike will encounter a deep, dark spruce forest that seems right out of a fairy tale. Those who ferry 12 miles over to undeveloped Vinalhaven Island can spend the afternoon swimming in tree-rimmed granite quarries.

Back on the mainland, rejoin Route 1 in Rockland, Maine's windjammer capital, and meander north along the coast. The gritty seaport town of Rockland (which claims to land more lobsters than anywhere else in the world) entices families to hop aboard a ferry, sailboat, or

historic windjammer for an adventure at sea. The *Timberwind* offers family trips for kids ages 5 and older about six times annually. *(Contact the Maine Windjammer Association, 800/807-WIND.)*

Classy Camden has a picture-perfect harbor and beautiful Mount Battie, where you can see glistening patches of ocean while you hike. Farther north, in the low-key coastal community of Belfast, you and your kids can get an inexpensive takeout lunch and watch the sailboats glide along Penobscot Bay from a picnic spot at Heritage State Park.

If you come in September, make sure to attend the Common Ground

Country Fair, one of the state's best family celebrations. Held in Unity, the environmentally friendly fair features organically grown food, a kids' activity area, fiddlers and dancers, a storytelling festival, and, of course, plenty of farm animals.

CULTURAL ADVENTURES

 **Colonial Pemaquid State Historic Site and Fort William Henry ★★★/$**

The Pemaquid Peninsula has a magnificent lighthouse; a crescent-shape, white-sand beach (Pemaquid Beach Park); a round stone fort (Fort Henry); and the remains of a 1620s settlement. When you visit Colonial Pemaquid, don't expect Plimoth Plantation. There aren't any costumed interpreters or, for that matter, buildings to tour. Instead, you'll see the excavated foundations of early Pemaquid structures, appealingly laid out by Penobscot Bay. Though there isn't a lot to explore outside, you can have fun touring the adjacent fort and the Colonial Pemaquid Museum, where you'll learn about 17th-century life. On a scavenger hunt, kids can search the museum for common items of that period, such as lead musket balls, thumb scrapers, and clay pipes. At just $4 for a family of four to explore

the museum, site, and fort, this is one of Maine's great vacation bargains. *Rte. 130, Pemaquid; (207) 677-2423; www.state.me.us/doc/prks lnds/pemaquid.htm*

Farnsworth Art Museum and Wyeth Center ★★/$$

With more than 8,000 art objects from Colonial days to the present, this exceptional museum can be a bit daunting for children. That's why the staff offers Family Sundays once a month. These interactive, creative sessions are linked to a current exhibit. For example, inspired by Elizabeth Noyes' collage works, a family might craft its own collage of memorable photos. In June 2000, the museum opened a new education center, where patrons can learn about three generations of the artistic Wyeth family through a computer database containing on-line programs geared to kids ages 10 and older. There are three computer terminals in the center. *16 Museum St., Rockland; (207) 596-6457.*

Lobster Lore

Learn everything you wanted to know about lobsters and then some on a two-hour tour on the *Lively Lady II*, led by Captain Alan Philbrick, a former biology teacher and lobster fisherman. As you sail past lighthouses and weather-beaten islands, you can watch the captain haul traps, listen to lobster lore, and handle the creatures in the on-board touch tank. *Bayview Landing, Camden; (207) 236-6672.*

Maine Maritime Museum ★★/$

Maine's 400-year-old shipbuilding legacy comes alive at this museum, set on the banks of the Kennebec River. The extensive complex includes the Percy & Small Shipyard, where you can learn how multi-masted schooners are constructed; a lobster exhibit, where you can touch the animals and watch volunteers prepare lobster meat in a canning room; and a dock where you can tour the historic fishing schooner *Sherman Zwicker*, or hop aboard one of the museum's excursion boats. For kids, however, the place to be is the children's play area, where they can play in a giant sandbox ship and climb up to the crow's nest to look for pirates. *243 Washington St., Bath; (207) 443-1316; www.bathmaine.com*

MUST-SEE FamilyFun MUST-SEE Owls Head Transportation Museum ★★★★/$$

On select weekends, you can see a World War I Fokker ("Red Baron") triplane sail through the sky over this wonderful museum, which is dedicated to the pre-1930 age of transportation. You also can ride in a Model T Ford and try to keep your balance on an antique bicycle. On a regular basis, families can see one of the world's best collections of pioneering aircraft, ground vehicles, and engines, including the world's first Ford Mustang and the largest motorcycle ever produced (the Scripps-Booth Bi Autogo). With a children's park and picnic area, a 60-acre park, and the festive atmosphere of the colorful air shows, this is a definite for kids. *Rte. 73, Owls Head; (207) 594-4418;* www.ohtm.org

Peary MacMillan Arctic Museum ★★/Free

If you've been to Eagle Island to learn about Admiral Robert E. Peary, the first explorer to reach the North Pole, and you want to learn more, visit this free museum on the Bowdoin College Campus. (Peary was a Bowdoin graduate.) A huge, soapstone polar bear greets you at the front door, inviting you to investigate Arctic objects. You'll find Peary's North Pole sled and goggles, mounted polar bears, hawks, and other Arctic animals. High-tech it isn't, but it just may whet your children's appetites for adventure travel. *Hubbard Hall, Bowdoin College, Brunswick; (207) 725-3416;* aca medic.bowdoin.edu/arcticmuseum

Penobscot Marine Museum ★★/$$

For a taste of what it was like to be a captain on the high seas in the 1800s, visit this historic village and its 13 buildings, many of which are former sea captains' homes. In the portrait gallery, you'll meet plenty of sea captains with long, bushy sideburns. Plus, you'll get to hoist sails, play old-fashioned games like skiddle (the precursor to pinball), even try on sailors' clothes. Call for a schedule. *Rte. 1, Searsport; (207) 548-2529;* www.penobscotmarine museum.org/

Shore Village Museum ★★/Free

Lighthouse fanatics will find a colossal collection of working foghorns, flashing lights, search-and-rescue gear, bells, and boats at this museum. The large gift shop has many lighthouse souvenirs. *104 Limerock St., Rockland; (207) 594-0311;* www.light house.cc/shorevillage/

Just for Fun

Belfast & Moosehead Lake Railroad ★★/$$$

From the sharp blast of the whistle to the rhythmic chug-a-chug, you and your kids will enjoy riding this 1913 Swedish steam locomotive through Maine's countryside. Before the ride begins, you can watch the engineers turn the engine on an Armstrong turntable. The scenic rides sometimes feature skits and singing. Trains depart from Unity to Burnham Junction (two hours) and Belfast to Waldo (90 minutes, round-trip). In Belfast, you can also sign up for a Rail-Sail combo, which includes the train ride and a 90-minute boat trip on Penobscot Bay. The railroad also runs themed Halloween and Christmas trains. *One Depot Sq., Unity; (800) 392-5500.*

Betselma ★★/$$$

Captain Les Bex enjoys taking families on one- and two-hour cruises through Penobscot Bay on his 30-passenger powerboat. Depending on the length of your journey, you

André the Seal Statue

In 1961, Rockport resident Harry Goodridge found an abandoned seal pup in the harbor. The animal went on to win the hearts of American children as the star of Lew Dietz's book *A Seal Called André,* and of the 1994 movie about André's rise from his sad beginnings to his place as a legend among mammals. Though André died in 1986, his memory lives on at this marble statue (unveiled by André himself in 1978) in Rockport's Marine Park.

may see dolphins, seals, lighthouses, and nesting osprey. *Camden Public Landing, Camden; (207) 236-4446; www.betselma.com*

Boothbay Railway Village ★★★/$$

At this sweet, historic village, families can board a narrow-gauge steam train (the rails are just two feet apart) and take a mile-and-a-half journey through the woods and under a covered bridge. After the ride, you can inspect the shiny collection of more than 60 antique vehicles (from Stanley Steamers to Packard Limos), and stroll through the village to see the sheep, one-room schoolhouse, and the toy shop. The train buffs who work here are wonderful with kids and host several family events throughout the year. There's a playground and picnic areas, so you

could spend the afternoon here, too. *Rte. 27, Boothbay; (207) 633-4727; www.railwayvillage.org*

Bryant Museum ★★/Free

If you like Barbie dolls, this unique museum is worth a stop. More than 300 Barbies from different eras are on display. There's also a doll circus (featuring dozens of dolls enjoying a spin on a mini Ferris wheel and a merry-go-round), hurdy-gurdies, player pianos, and antique cars. *Rte. 220, Thorndike; (207) 568-3665.*

Camden Hills State Park ★★/$

For a knockout panoramic view of the coast, take the toll road up the 900-foot-high Mount Battie. You'll feel like a giant when you look down at Camden Harbor and see the tiny sailboats below. The steep trail to the top of this mountain is a bit much for kids, but the 6,500-acre

MONHEGAN ISLAND

IF YOU'RE SERIOUS about hiking, consider taking the hour-long ferry trip to this rocky island, ten miles off the coast. A haven for artists (including Rockwell Kent), Monhegan has a lighthouse and 17 miles of hiking trails that wind through deep spruce forests and along spectacular cliffs. You'll feel as if you wandered into a fairy tale as you hike along the Cathedral Woods Trail, so

named because the branches of tall, slender trees are interlaced in Gothic arches. Wear sturdy hiking boots and make sure to bring sweaters and rain gear. Several boat companies can get you to this wilderness island, including **Monhegan Thomaston Boat Line** *(Port Clyde; 207/372-8848)* and **Balmy Days Cruises** *(Pier 8, Commercial St., Boothbay Harbor; 207/633-2284).*

park has plenty of other trails that are appropriate for children. *Rte. 1, Camden; (207) 236-3109.*

Camden Snow Bowl ★★/$

If your family likes to stick together, crunch up on a wooden toboggan for a free-spirited ride down this popular toboggan chute. The toboggan championships are festive affairs, and you're welcome to join the fun. You can ski and snow-tube here, too. In summer, you can hike or go mountain biking on the ski trails. *Camden; (207) 236-3438; www.camdensnowbowl.com*

Clambake at Cabbage Island ★★★/$$$$

Parents and kids alike rave about the cruise on the *Argo* to Cabbage Island, where kids can hike, explore a lighthouse, fish off the dock, and feast on an original Down East clambake. The chefs cook lobsters and clams in seaweed, cover them with tarpaulins and rocks for flavor, and serve them with corn, potatoes, and blueberry cake. The adventure lasts about three hours, and it's a blast. *Pier 6 from Fisherman's Wharf, Boothbay Harbor; (207) 633-7200.*

Kelmscott Farm ★★★/$$

It's a bit off the beaten track, but worth the drive to see 18 species of rare livestock breeds, including curly-haired Cotswold sheep (they look like they need their bangs cut),

Gloucestershire Old Spots pigs, and Kerry cattle. The nonprofit farm, dedicated to the conservation of endangered livestock, offers tours and wagon rides, as well as excellent education programs. Animal births and birthdays are celebrated with great fanfare here. *Rte. 52, Lincolnville; (207) 763-4088; www.kelmscott.org*

Marine Resources Aquarium ★★/$

It's worth a trip to this small, well-run aquarium just to touch the live shark. In a separate 20-foot touch tank, you can also feel the spiny skin of a sea urchin, and watch a moon snail pull in its gooey foot. The octagonal building also is home to Larry, a 20-pound lobster that likes to show off his mammoth claws; red sea anemones; purple sun stars; striped bass; and more. This is an unusual opportunity to get a close look at some of the fish that may show up on your dinner plate. *McKown Point Rd., W. Boothbay Harbor; (207) 633-9559.*

Popham Beach State Park ★★★/$

Only the thick-skinned and, of course, kids, swim in these frigid waters. But the three beaches here are spectacularly beautiful. The park also has picnic tables and bathhouses. *Off Rte. 209 in Phippsburg; Maine Bureau of Parks and Recreation, (207) 287-3821.*

Romar Bowling Lanes
★★/$$
Your kids will have fun to spare at this eight-lane, candlepin bowling alley. Situated in what looks like an old-time log cabin, the alley (with a snack bar, video games, and pool tables) has been entertaining families since 1929. *On the Byway, Boothbay Harbor; (207) 633-5721.*

Sears Island
★★★/Free
Accessible from Searsport via a causeway, Maine's second-largest uninhabited island is a paradise for hikers and cyclists. As you make your way around the five-mile perimeter, you'll enjoy gorgeous views of neighboring islands and encounter some of the local wildlife.

BUNKING DOWN

Blackberry Inn
★★/$$
Though this vibrantly colored Victorian Painted Lady is geared primarily toward hosting adults, it has a magnificent carriage house that's perfect for families. Parents can sleep in a four-poster bed; there's a separate bedroom for the kids, and an inviting eating and living area. Cyndi and Jim Ostrowski are excellent hosts and happy to point out the area's best kid activities, restaurants, and bike routes. Cyndi even delivers homemade breakfast to the car-

riage house each day so you can take it easy. *82 Elm St., Camden; (800) 388-6000; (207) 236-6060;* www. blackberryinn.com

Brown's Wharf
Motel & Marina ★★★/$$
A gargantuan statue of a fisherman clad in a yellow-slicker welcomes you to this family-owned hotel, located on a bustling marina. Spring for a motel room with a deck, and you can watch the boats sail in and out. Kids can order chicken fingers and other favorites at the on-site seafood restaurant, and have fun calling grandma from the authentic red London telephone booth. If the motel had a pool, we'd like it even more. *Atlantic Ave., Boothbay Harbor; (800) 334-8110.*

Camden Riverhouse Hotel
★★★/$$
Details make the difference when it comes to making families feel welcome, and this excellent hotel (part of the Best Western franchise) knows how to please. Surrounded by cheery sunflowers and gardens, this property feels private and quiet, but it's just a short walk over the little foot-

bridge to Camden's terrific shops and restaurants. In a sunny sitting room, you can eat an exceptional, complimentary continental breakfast. *11 Tannery La., Camden; (800) 755-RIVER.*

Country Inn
★★★/$$

This appealing inn is one of the Camden area's best places to stay if you're traveling with children. The newly remodeled suites, decorated with quilts, are cheery and spacious. Plus, there's a big indoor/outdoor pool with a sliding roof, a playground in the big backyard, complimentary continental breakfast, and afternoon tea. *Rte. 1, Camden; (207) 236-2725.*

Edgewater Farm B&B
★★★★/$$

This phenomenal bed-and-breakfast redefines the term. Sure, the restored 1800 farmhouse has beds (lots of them) and delicious breakfasts, but the extras are what make this spot exceptional. There's a large indoor pool for guests, family suites where everyone can spread out comfortably, a game room with Ping-Pong, and a spacious sunroom. Plus, Bill and Carol Emerson are avid gardeners, and four acres of fruit trees, flowers, and herbs (used in the cooking) surround the property. You're close to several beaches here, but you won't want to leave. *Rte. 209, Small Point; (207) 389-1322.*

Glenmoor by the Sea
★★★/$$$

Just one and a half miles south of Lincolnville Beach, this lodge has clean, modern rooms and one- and two-bedroom cottages that work well for families. (They have air-conditioning, TV, and telephones.) There's a large outdoor pool, a tennis court, and a scenic path to the Glenmoor's private shorefront. Go ahead, sleep in. The owners deliver continental breakfast to your room (anytime between 7:45 and 9 A.M.). *Rte. 1, Camden; (800) 430-3541; (207) 236-3166; www.glenmoor bythesea.com*

Lobster Village ★★★/$$

If your family just can't get enough lobster, you may want to stay in a studio apartment on Mackerel Cove,

Maine Event

Maine Sport Outfitters offers several **kayaking trips** just for families, including excursions on the St. George River and Megunticook Lake. The four-hour trips, tailored to your children's pace, are an ideal way for them to learn to paddle. If you're ready to dive into the sport, you can take a seven-hour family clinic and even sign on for a three-day adventure. The outfitter also rents bike equipment and can help you chart a safe, **scenic** cycling route. *Box 956, Rockport; (800) 772-0826; (207) 236-8797; www.mainesport.com*

directly above a working fishing marina. Children's author Maureen Babicki runs a restaurant and bed-and-breakfast from which you can watch the workings of an authentic fishing village. The apartment has a wood stove, pullout couch, and double bed, plus a refrigerator stocked with breakfast items (no extra charge), and a TV/VCR with Maine-themed videotapes. With windows on three sides overlooking the harbor, the chance to watch lobstermen at work is a trip. Keep in mind, however, that the fellows rise extremely early to go to work and, because you're close to their boats, you might, too. Beneath the apartment, there's a seafood restaurant with a patio. Want to learn more

It's the *Ruth*

Strap on your eye patch and peg leg—it's time for a ride on the *Ruth*, a popular **pirate cruise** that departs twice weekly from the dock at the Sebasco Harbor Resort. On the journey, you'll stop at an island and search for buried treasure. (Every child gets a reward; the booty may include coupons for free ice cream.) The *Ruth* also offers lobster boat cruises and trips to Eagle Island, the home of Admiral Robert E. Peary. *Rte. 217, Sebasco Estates; (207) 389-1161.*

about lobstering? The marina is dotted with signs featuring the village mascot, Lucius the Lobster, who loves to share fun facts explained on the signs. For an even more meaningful experience, read Babicki's book, *Island Fisherman.* Set at Lobster Village, it's the story of Danny, a boy who learns the ropes of the lobstering profession from his grandpa. *Mackerel Cove, Bailey Island; (207) 833-6656.*

Ocean Gate ★★★/$$

Just a two-mile drive from Boothbay Harbor, this waterfront resort on Southport Island seems a world away. Families come to this 85-acre wooded retreat to escape the crowds, unwind, and enjoy fun activities. You can play tennis, go boating, and swim in the huge outdoor pool. Some of the buildings look a bit dated, but they're clean and equipped with all the comforts of home. A wonderful buffet breakfast, which you can eat outside on a spacious patio, is included in the price. *Rte. 27, Southport Island; (800) 221-5924;* www.oceangateinn.com

Rocktide Inn ★★★/$$

Right on Boothbay Harbor, this is a prime spot to watch the boat action and enjoy some convenient amenities. The inn has an indoor pool, complimentary breakfast buffet, and, in summer, the Rocktide Trolley shuttles guests into town. In the main dining room, a choo-choo

Nature's Clowns

The **Hardy Boat Cruises** gets our seal of approval. The one-hour tour takes you to meet slippery seals that ham it up by playing and swimming just a few yards from the boat. You can't help cracking up when they start carousing on the rocks. *Rte. 32, Shaw's Fish and Lobster Wharf, New Harbor; (800) 2-PUF-FIN.* **Cap'n Fish Boat Cruises** *(Pier 1, Boothbay Harbor; 800/636-3244)* also offers a 75-minute narrated seal watch. www.hardyboat.com

train runs on a track along the ceiling, delighting kids as they dig into their franks and burgers. *35 Atlantic Ave., Boothbay Harbor; (800) 762-8433.*

Samoset Resort
★★★/$$$

Though the Samoset is chiefly known for its outstanding 18-hole golf course on the ocean, it's a fine family resort as well. During the summer and school vacations, the Samoset offers an assortment of activities (family bingo, movie nights, and magic acts), children's programs (the summer Sam-o-camp lets kids play wacky games and make cool crafts with their peers), and even kids' fitness classes. The first-class amenities include indoor and outdoor pools, a terrific playground with a mini climbing wall and sand scoopers, and tennis courts. The Samoset's concierge staff can help you arrange child care and activities on and off the resort. Baby-sitting is also available in the fitness center. *220 Warrenton St., Rockland; (800) 341-1650.*

Sebasco Harbor Resort
★★★/$$-$$$

This 550-acre family resort offers dozens of activities, restaurants, and special programs—all just a few steps from your door. The fun includes pirate adventures aboard the *Ruth* (see page 80), lobster bakes on the lawn, family days at the beach, softball games, arts-and-crafts classes, candlepin bowling in the old-time alley, canoeing on Wah-Tuh Lake, tennis, mountain biking, and kids' programs in several age groups. Families can stay in basic cottages or inn rooms that, though not particularly fancy, have all the modern conveniences. Many parents like the feeling of security here; the self-contained property is a safe place for kids to explore with their new friends. *Rte. 217, Sebasco Estates; (800) 225-3819;* www.sebasco.com

Small Point B&B ★★/$$

Jan and David Tingle and their daughters, Lindsay and Katie, love hosting families in their coastal farmhouse. In fact, the girls thoroughly enjoy playing with young visitors and are very sweet about sharing their toys. Though the property is small (you'll need to rent two rooms for a family of four), it's ideally located near Popham Beach, one of Maine's best sandy playlands. The Tingles know all the great places to take kids on the peninsula and are happy to direct you to them. David and Jan were once a charter captain and chef team, and Jan continues to dish up delicious breakfasts that will keep you full for the day's adventures. *312 Small Point Rd., Phippsburg; (207) 389-1716.*

Spruce Point Inn
★★★/$$

This gorgeous resort at the end of a private peninsula offers children's programs in July and August, run by local educators. At the Lighthouse Camp, kids spend five hours each day swimming, taking nature walks, and making crafts, while parents can enjoy tennis, boating, or taking the shuttle over to the golf club. Spruce Point also offers Kids Night Out, an evening activity program (there's a fee) that frees up parents to dine privately. There's a playground, an oceanside saltwater pool, and a variety of deluxe accommodations, from standard guest rooms to cottages. This isn't a family resort in the way Sebasco Harbor (see page 81) is, but rather a place where parents can enjoy a deluxe vacation, knowing their kids are in good hands. *Box 237, Boothbay Harbor; (800) 553-0289.*

Strawberry Hill Motor Inn
★★/$$

Located on pretty Glen Cove, this pleasant motel is just three and a half miles from both Rockland and Camden, and it has everything you and your kids might need: a heated outdoor pool, easy access to the shore, and clean, smoke-free rooms. *886 Commercial St., Rockport; (800) 589-4009.*

GOOD EATS

Anchor Inn Restaurant
★★★/$$

There's no doubt that kids are appreciated here: the proof is hanging on the walls, in the form of their crayon masterpieces. Kids can get cheezaroni and hot diggity dogs, while parents can order Portuguese mussels and beef tenderloin. The location on Round Pond is a winner. *Round Pond Harbor; (207) 529-5584.*

Beale Street BBQ ★★/$-$$

While Mom and Dad feast on ribs and jambalaya, kids can color their menu and sip a Shirley Temple. This hip, amiable spot dishes up barbecue-pulled chicken, grilled hot dogs, and other classic favorites for the little ones. *215 Water St., Bath; (207) 442-9514.*

The Brown Bag ★★/$$

Stop here for delicious, pecan sticky buns and an appealing selection of creative breakfasts (Toad N' Hole is grilled, homemade bread with an egg center) and healthy sandwiches. Order takeout, or eat in the pleasant, casual dining room. *606 Main St., Rockland; (207) 596-6372.*

Cappy's Chowder House ★★/$-$$

This loud, crowded place can be a mob scene, but the staff enjoys kids and supplies them with activity sheets, crayons, balloons, and, of course, their favorite grub (all served with curly fries). Pop into the bakery for scrumptious cookies and sweets. *Main St., Camden; (207) 236-2254.*

The osprey dives into the water to catch fish. It searches for food from 30 to 100 feet above and plummets into the water feet first.

Dave's Restaurant ★★/$$

When you're done exploring Owls Head Lighthouse, head to this friendly restaurant for seafood, hot dogs, pizza, hamburgers, and other kids' classics. After coloring at the table, kids can test their swing in the batting cage out back. *Rte. 1, Thomaston; (207) 594-5424.*

Ebb Tide ★★/$$

Follow the candy-striped awning to this little gem for humongous pieces of fresh-baked peach shortcake. The quarters are tight, but the portions are right. You'll find buttermilk pancakes, hot dogs, and hamburgers,

too. *43 Commercial St., Boothbay Harbor; (207) 633-5692.*

Ernie's Drive-In ★★/$

Also on Bath Road, this is another good family spot for southern fried chicken, grilled hot dogs, lobster rolls, and double cheeseburgers. The prices are somewhat higher than at Fat Boy's. *Bath Rd., Brunswick; (207) 729-9439.*

Fat Boy Drive-in ★★/$$

Families come here not for the food, but for the fun. Pull into the parking lot, flick on your lights, and order a Canadian BLT, cheeseburgers, 20-ounce frappés, and onion rings. Then turn on the radio, and enjoy the nostalgia along with everyone from Bowdoin College students to airline pilots. (The drive-in is right across from the local airfield.) *Bath Rd., Brunswick; (207) 729-9431.*

Great Impasta ★★/$$$

This cheery Italian restaurant greets children with crayons and treats them to kid-size portions of manicotti, lasagna, salad, and ice cream. *42 Maine St., Brunswick; (207) 729-5858.*

Jordan's Restaurant ★★/$$

Local families come to this unpretentious restaurant for creamy chowder and stews, seafood, and ice cream treats. The friendly staff gives kids crayons, coloring books, and storybooks containing a kids' menu. Children can order from cleverly named selections such as the Pirate Chest (clams) or Bugs Bunny Burgers (hamburgers). On a sunny day, you can eat outside on the deck. *Maine St., Searsport; (207) 548-2555.*

Kennebec Tavern ★★/$$$

Located on the banks of the Kennebec River, this casual restaurant dishes up everything from deli sandwiches to seafood dinners in a comfortable atmosphere. Kids will find hamburgers, pasta, and other staples on the menu. On warm days, you can dine outside. *119 Commercial St., Bath; (207) 442-9636.*

FamilyFun TIP

Cowabunga!

Break out the milk; you're about to see some big Oreo cookies. Drive along Russell Road in Rockport to **Aldemere Farm**, and you'll spot a herd of Belted Galloways feasting in the field. These adorable black cows have a white creamy middle (a wide girdle of white encircles their midsection), hence the nickname, **"Oreo cookie" cows**. Their distinctive appearance translates into darling souvenirs. In nearby shops, you'll find the Belted Galloways on mugs, T-shirts, and aprons.

Moody's Diner
★★★/$$

Got a hankering for comfort food? Head to this family-owned diner whenever the urge strikes—it's open round the clock—and feast on old favorites like meat loaf and sweet cream pies. Kids get coloring books and crayons, plus a menu with lots of choices. *Rte. 1, Waldoboro; (207) 832-7468.*

Red's Eats
★★/$$

You'd be hard-pressed to find better hot dogs (or lobster rolls). Grab a kids' Yummy Meal complete with a dog, dinosaur fries, drink, lollipop, and toy. Then find a picnic bench and enjoy. *Water St., Wiscasset; (207) 882-6128.*

Sarah's ★★★/$$

This restaurant spoils kids with treats and tempts them with a lengthy list of family favorites, from Mexican pizza and roasted franks, to lobster whaleboats and spaghetti with garlic bread. Enjoy the delicious, homemade fare inside or on the dock overlooking the Wiscasset Bridge. *Main St., Wiscasset; (207) 882-7504.*

Sea Basket
★★★/$-$$

Skip the fancy restaurants and stop at this takeout restaurant on Route 1 for delicious fried seafood. You'll find clams and scallops, lobster rolls, and a clean, wholesome atmosphere. *Rte. 1, south of Wiscasset; (207) 882-6581.*

Sea Dog Brewing Co.
★★/$$
At this comfortable brew pub, your family can play with board games while you wait for your meals. The kids' fare includes soft pretzels, baby Barney burgers, and Dini's Beanies and Weenies. You'll find the Sea Dog at: *43 Mechanic St., Camden, (207) 236-6863; 26 Front St., Bangor, (207) 947-8004; and 215 Foreside Rd., Falmouth, (207) 781 0988.*

Souvenir Hunting

Granite Hall Store
This old general store carries hobbyhorses, homemade fudge, and the traditional penny candy in large glass jars. There's also an ice-cream takeout window where you can order Maine Black Bear and other Gifford's flavors. *Rte. 32, Round Pond; (207) 529-5864.*

Grasshopper Shop
You'll be enchanted by the range of novelty gifts here, from bubblemakers and noisemakers to ladybug-patterned boots to bathtub toys. The picnic table in the corner gives kids a place to try out the toys. *400 Main St., Rockland; (207) 596-6156.*

Mackerel Sky Studio
The craggy beauty of the midcoast has long inspired artists to draw and paint, and you and the kids can do likewise at this studio/retail store. Depending on when you visit, the possibilities may include modeling clay sculptures, tie-dyeing a T-shirt, painting a colorful canvas, or creating pictures with rubber stamps. Little artists pay an hourly studio fee, plus a fee for the project. *18 Todd Ave., Boothbay Harbor; (207) 633-7686.*

Orne's Candy Shop
They've been making fudge here for a century, and they've gotten pretty good at it. Drop by for a sample. *11 Commercial St., Boothbay Harbor; (207) 633-2695.*

Owl & Turtle Bookshop
Find Robert McCloskey's *Blueberries for Sal* and *One Morning in Maine*, plus dozens of other children's books by Maine authors at this exceptional bookstore. There's lots for Mom and Dad to read, too. *8 Bayview St., Camden; (800) 876-4769.*

Planet Kids
This planet is home to a huge selection of toys, including Thomas the Tank Engine trains, hot-colored yo-yos, nature activity kits, and a cache of cuddly stuffed animals. *10 Main St., Camden; (207) 236-9022.*

The dramatic-looking Bass Harbor Head Lighthouse marks the southernmost tip of Mount Desert Island— and Acadia National Park.

Down East Maine

W HEN FAMILIES CROSS the bridge over the Penobscot River into the stretch known as Down East Maine, they enter a geographic area of unparalleled beauty. Granted, the entire Maine coast is gorgeous, but, somehow, even more so here. Settlers of the Blue Hill and Deer Isle peninsulas must have felt the same way, for they named two of the towns Sunshine and Sunset. Fans of children's author and local resident Robert McCloskey will recognize Blueberry Hill from his classic books, *Blueberries for Sal* and *One Morning in Maine*. On a summer visit here, you can enjoy the same simple pleasures as Sal, taking nature walks and kerplunking fresh-picked blueberries into a tin bucket.

Beyond East Penobscot Bay lies Down East's big draw: Acadia National Park. Though it's one of the nation's smaller parks, Acadia welcomes three million visitors annually to explore its wonders on Mount Desert Island and beyond (see "15 Ways To Have Fun with Kids at Acadia" on page 91). Established in 1916, this 40,000-acre paradise invites you to watch the Atlantic

THE **FamilyFun** LIST

MUST-SEE
MUST-SEE

Acadia National Park (page 89)

Diver Ed's Dive-in Theater (page 89)

Timber Tina's Great Maine Lumberjack Show (page 89)

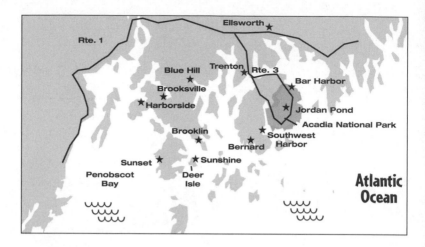

crash against colossal granite rocks, see the only fjord on America's east coast, and stand atop Cadillac Mountain, the highest point on the Atlantic coast north of Brazil.

Though the area is crowded in the summer, you can escape the masses by staying on the eastern lobe of Mount Desert Island. Or, if you prefer, you can join the throngs in popular Bar Harbor, a beautiful, collegial town packed with family restaurants, accommodations, and activities, all amid an unbeatable setting. Whether you're snacking on homemade fudge from a local candy shop, wandering at low tide onto Bar Island, or enjoying a concert on the green, Acadia's beauty surrounds you. Shopkeepers add to the area's appeal, pulling out all the stops to make your vacation fun. (Any town that dishes out lobster ice cream, earns our thumbs-up.) The **Bar Harbor Chamber of Commerce** (93

Cottage St.; 800/288-5103; 207/288-5103) can supply maps and lodging information.

Though few families build in time to explore Washington County, the coastal area north of Acadia, it's worth a trip if you love to camp, fish, and hike, and can do without some conveniences.

CULTURAL ADVENTURES

George B. Dorr Museum of Natural History at College of the Atlantic
★★/$

This small museum may be just the ticket on a rainy day. Students at this ecologically minded college created the exhibits, which include mounted bears and foxes, whale skeletons, an observation tank filled with sea creatures, and hands-on nature activities. In summer, staff members offer kid-oriented programs. *Rte. 3, Bar Harbor; (207) 288-5015;* www.coamuseum.org

JUST FOR FUN

Acadia National Park
FamilyFun ★★★★/$$

There are dozens and dozens of ways for families to have fun in the dramatic cliffs, forests, and beaches of Acadia. See page 91 for our top 15. *Mount Desert Island, (207) 288-3338;* www.nps.gov/acad/home.htm

Diver Ed's
FamilyFun Dive-in Theater
★★★★/$$$

If you splurge on one boat trip in Maine, make it this one. Ed Monat is not only an accomplished diver, but a kid-loving comedian. This College of the Atlantic graduate personally greets everyone aboard his 49-passenger boat, the *Seal*, then invites kids to help him don his wet suit and push him overboard as he begins his underwater explorations to catch sea creatures in Frenchman Bay. Carrying a video camera, Ed chronicles his aqueous adventures, which are broadcast in real time on an onboard movie screen. "Have you ever seen anyone swallow a sea urchin?" Ed says, as he stuffs the creature into his mouth to a chorus of groans. Throughout the two-and-a-half-hour trip, Ed mesmerizes children with fun facts about sea cucumbers, lobsters, and sea stars, and other specimens, all of which he invites children to hold before they are safely returned to sea. *Cruise departs from the Bar Harbor Pier, Bar Harbor; 207-288-DIVE.*

The Great Maine
FamilyFun Lumberjack Show
★★★/$

Sure, Timber Tina's, as they call this show, is a tad touristy, but that doesn't matter to kids. They happily jam the

Kayaking 101

Each year, more families are settling into kayaks in Bar Harbor to get close-up views of Acadia's islands, rocky coast, and sea life. If your kids are at least 8, they can experience the excitement on a half-day family tour conducted by **Coastal Kayaking Company.** Registered Maine Guides teach the basics of using large, stable, two-person kayaks (equipped with foot-controlled rudders) before you paddle away in search of harbor seals and osprey. The guides are kid-oriented, tailoring the pace to children's (and parents') abilities. The two-and-a-half-hour Sunset Tour is also a lot of fun. *48 Cottage St., Bar Harbor; (207) 288-9605.*

bleachers in the outdoor arena to see lumberjacks demonstrate under-hand chopping, ax-throwing, and speed-climbing up tall poles during this 75-minute show. At intermission, kids can try crosscut sawing, and win a free souvenir "wood cookie," which the lumberjacks will gladly autograph. Kids can also sign up for logrolling lessons (competitors stand on a red cedar log in the water and try to knock their opponent off balance). *Bar Harbor Road, Ellsworth; (207) 667-0067; www.mainelumberjack.com*

Isle au Haut
★★★/$$$

For a real Down East adventure, take a boat ride to Isle au Haut (eye-la-ho), an untouched, isolated island that few tourists see. Your reward for making the one-hour trip to Duck Harbor is a series of hiking trails that provides exquisite views of the bay and Mount Desert Island. Prepare for the primitive: there are no amenities on Isle au Haut (there are portable toilets). You must pack everything in, and that means car-rying all essentials when you hike. For many, that's a small price to pay to soak up such natural glory. The Isle au Haut company on Deer Isle runs several ferryboats daily. For a schedule and directions to Ferry Landing, call *(207) 367-5193.*

Mount Desert Oceanarium, Southwest Harbor
★★/$$

Although it's not the four-star New England Aquarium, this education center will still have your kids enjoying handling sea potatoes, starfish, and horseshoe crabs. Through interactive exhibits, kids can learn secrets about seafood, sail boats in a tank, and hear whale songs. *172 Clark Point Rd., Southwest Harbor; (207) 244-7330.*

Mount Desert Oceanarium/Lobster Hatchery
★★/$$

Geared to children ages 10 and up who can sit through a slightly scholarly explanation of lobster developments (crayons and coloring supplies are provided for those who want to skip the talk), this facility welcomes families to the hatchery to see egg-bearing lobsters and babies in various stages of development. Depending on when you come, you might also meet seals in the outdoor pool, and, in the Maine Lobster Museum, kids can climb aboard a lobster boat and hear fun facts about sea life. The oceanarium/hatchery is

---

FamilyFun TIP

A Faster Whale Watch
Bar Harbor Whale Watch Company *(1 West St. [next to pier]; 800/508-1499; 207/288-2386)* offers two-and-a-half- to three-hour cruises aboard the jet-powered catamaran *Friendship V.*

15 WAYS TO HAVE FUN WITH KIDS AT ACADIA

WITH 40,000 ACRES OF soaring granite cliffs, dense evergreen forests, sand and cobblestone beaches, and an abundance of wildlife, Acadia National Park is a paradise for nature-loving families. To whet your appetite for adventure, head for the **Hull's Cove visitors' center** *(207/ 288-4932)* and watch the inspiring 15-minute film. Then take your pick from the following outings.

1. Drive the Park Loop Road. This 20-mile toll road on the east side of Mount Desert Island introduces your family to some of Acadia's greatest hits. You'll pass Thunder Hole, where the tides thunder through a narrow granite channel when the conditions are right, glacier-carved Jordan Pond, and 1,530-foot-tall Cadillac Mountain.

2. Take a hike. Kids love meandering down the Ship Harbor Nature Trail *(off Route 102A on the western part of Mount Desert Island)*, an easy 1.3-mile path that winds past spruce forests and along a salt marsh. At nearby Wonderland, families can stroll past pretty pines and relax on large flat rocks that overlook the craggy shore.

3. Meet a ranger. In summer, several ranger programs cater to families. During "Mountain Mysteries," children ages 5 to 12 and their parents accompany a ranger up one of Acadia's mountains to learn its secrets *(207/288-5262)*. "Islands Edge" takes families on a journey through the park's coastal forests and rocky shores *(207/288-5262)*.

4. Hit the beach. Break out your buckets and shovels and build sand castles out of the coarse-grained sand at Sand Beach, Acadia's only sand beach. The water is chilly for swimming (temperatures rarely rise above 55 degrees), but you'll still see determined kids splashing in the surf. Echo Lake, on the western side of Mount Desert Island, is a bit warmer. Lifeguards patrol both spots from May until October.

5. Cycle the carriage roads. For two-wheeled fun, plan a family bike trip on the park's scenic carriage roads, which are off-limits to cars (for bike rentals, call Bar Harbor Bike Shop at 207/288-3886). The Eagle Lake and Jordan Pond loops are especially popular with families (at the latter, you can break for lunch at the scenic Jordan Pond House).

continued on next page

The gravel carriage roads can be hilly, so take your time and bring lots of water.

6. Enjoy a nature cruise. Diver Ed's Dive-in Theater (see page 89) offers top hands-on cruises for kids. Whale watches (see page 90) are also popular. Another possibility is the two-hour ranger-led Frenchman Bay Nature Cruise *(207/288-3322)*, where kids can search for eagles, osprey, harbor seals, and porpoises.

7. Find tidepooling treasures. You never know what creatures will wash up a low tide at Seawall. Children frequently discover green crabs, mussels, and periwinkles.

8. Become a Junior Ranger. Pick up a Junior Ranger activity booklet at the visitors' center, complete a ranger-led program or two, and your young naturalist can earn an official Junior Ranger pin.

9. Take a horse-drawn carriage ride. Tired of hiking and biking? Let hearty Percheron and Belgian draft horses do the work as you enjoy the park from an open carriage. *Call* **Wildwood Stables** *(207/276-3622)*.

10. Camp out. Mount Desert Island features 17 campgrounds, including three run by the National Park Service. Blackwoods Campground *(off Route 3 five miles south of Bar Harbor)* and Seawall Campground *(four miles west of Southwest Harbor)* have rest rooms, cold water (no showers), picnic tables, and outdoor amphitheaters. *Call (800) 365-2267.* Mt. Desert Campground *(Route 198, Somesville; 207 244-3710)* is a clean, family-owned campground with some waterfront sites along Somes Sound. Duck Harbor Campground, located on pristine Isle au Haut, can only be reached by ferryboat. There is a special-use permit fee, and you must submit a written application to reserve one of the sites. *Call (207) 288-3338.*

11. Watch the sunrise. For the first view of the morning sun in America, drive up to the top of Cadillac Mountain and join the group of locals who routinely rise before dawn to watch this special spectacle. You'll be rewarded with awesome views of the rays glowing over the Porcupine Islands.

12. Meet Mother Nature. Learning about the park's 160 bird species and dozens of marine and land mammals is fun at the Nature Center, where kids can join a scavenger hunt. At the nearby Abbe Museum at Sieur de Monts Spring, families can crawl into an authentic wigwam, examine Native American artifacts, and wander down an interpretive trail. The new (September 2001) Bar Harbor branch of the Abbe Museum has a discovery room where children can learn about Maine's Native Americans by weaving and exploring the children's library; *26 Mount Desert Street (Route 3), Bar Harbor; (207) 288-3519.*

13. Take a break. Many area restaurants will pack lunches to go. Tote yours to Pretty Marsh, on the west coast of Mount Desert Island, for a break from the crowds and views of the islands in western bay.

14. Lighten up. Built in 1858, Bass Harbor Head Lighthouse, at the rocky southernmost tip of Mount Desert Island on Route 102A, is one of the most photographed in Maine. You'll see why when you arrive at this beautiful spot on scenic Bass Harbor.

15. Get misty. At Schoodic Point, on Acadia's Schoodic Peninsula, you'll feel the ocean spray as the Atlantic relentlessly slams into the shore. Because the point isn't protected by barrier islands, the ocean's force is fast, furious, and unforgettable. Though an hour away from Bar Harbor on Route 186, a trip to Schoodic Peninsula is worth the effort. It's less crowded here, so your family can freely explore the six-mile park road, hiking trails, and scenic vistas. During your visit, it's also fun to browse in the shops in the nearby resort town of Winter Harbor.

located on 20 wooded acres and has a scenic walking path that you can take (for an extra charge) past the neighboring salt marsh. Money-saving combination tickets to the two Mount Desert oceanariums are available. *Rte. 3, Bar Harbor; (207) 288-5005.*

Pirate's Cove
★★★/$

This 36-hole golf course replicates the one at Old Orchard Beach (see page 47). *Rte. 3, Salisbury Cove, Bar Harbor; (207) 288-2133; www.piratescove.net*

BUNKING DOWN

Acadia Inn
★★★/$$

This well-kept motel, owned by the same folks who run the swanky Bar Harbor Inn, has a big outdoor pool and a playground. Kids can borrow board games at the front desk, and complimentary continental breakfast is served each morning. *98 Eden St., Bar Harbor; (800) 638-3636; (207) 288-3500.*

Atlantic Oakes By-the-Sea
★★★/$$$

Acadia's free shuttle, the *Island Explorer*, stops here dozens of times daily, making it an ideal location if you plan a lot of local sight-seeing. This waterfront resort has 150 oceanview rooms, indoor and out-

Sailing Along

Your family can take a relaxing, two-hour sunset cruise on the *Margaret Todd*, the first four-masted schooner to sail New England waters in half a century. As the 151-foot, historic windjammer meanders by the islands of Frenchman's Bay, listen to the live music, sip a soda, check out the gorgeous Maine coast, and watch the sun set into the silvery sea. *Purchase tickets at the Bar Harbor Inn Pier or at 27 Main St., Bar Harbor; (207) 288-4585.*

- - - - - - - - - - - - - - - - - - - -

door pools, tennis courts, and a pebble beach. Instead of heading into town for breakfast, you can spring for a hot or cold buffet at the hotel and eat it on the sunny back patio. Some units have kitchenettes. *Rte. 3, Bar Harbor; (207) 288-5801; (800) 33-MAINE.* **NOTE:** The same management operates two nearby properties, the **Bayview** (which rents gorgeous, but pricey, town homes to families) and the **Atlantic Eyrie Lodge** (a hilltop hotel with a pool overlooking Frenchman's Bay).

Bar Harbor Motel
★★★/$$

This motel is a good base camp for families visiting Acadia National Park; you can access trails right from the property. Besides hiking, you can splash in the enormous outdoor pool, monkey around at the playground, and stroll through the 14-acre grounds. Choose between standard rooms and two-bedroom family units. *100 Eden St., Bar Harbor; (207) 288-3453.*

Colonial Travelodge
★★/$$

If you want to save quite a bit on lodging, consider staying in Ellsworth, 20 miles from Bar Harbor. At this family-oriented motel, you can rent standard rooms, family suites with kitchenettes, or even Sleepy Bear's Den, a themed guest room with kid-size chairs and a VCR. There's an indoor pool and complimentary continental breakfast, too. The setting on a busy main strip isn't particularly scenic, but if you're going to play all day in Acadia anyway, who cares? *321 High St., Ellsworth; (207) 667-5548;* www.acadia.net/colonial

Goose Cove Lodge
★★★★/$$$$

For 50 years, this first-class lodge has beckoned travelers to the remote Deer Isle peninsula. You can stay in suites, rooms, or private cabins scattered across 21 acres of coastal forest. The lodge offers a range of activities for families, including cycling adventures, astronomy programs, lobster boat trips, kayak seminars, and special children's outings. On most nights in high season, children dine separately from their parents, enjoying kids' cuisine and a fun-packed activity program. Families eat together at breakfast and on Friday nights, when everyone feasts on lobster at the beach. There are no TVs or telephones in the rooms. *Deer Isle, Sunset; (207) 348-2508; www.goosccovclodge.com*

Harbor View Motel & Cottages
★★/$-$$
A short walk to the village of Southwest Harbor, this family-oriented motel has 20 units (nine with decks that overlook the busy fishing harbor), an efficiency apartment, and seven cottages (some sleeping up to six). *Corner of Main Street and Lawler Lane, Southwest Harbor; (207) 244-5031 or (800) 538-6463.*

Hiram Blake Camp
★★★★/$$$$
Though this camp is situated off the beaten track on the northern end of East Penobscot Bay, families book cabins here years in advance. And because so many return each year, it's tough to get a spot. What's the big deal? The camp blends setting with simplicity. Founded in 1916 by Hiram Blake, the facility has been managed by his family ever since.

Here, you can watch the vivid sunsets, row boats along the scenic shore, and generally enjoy each other's company. The gray, weathered cottages have a living room with a wood-burning stove, a kitchen, and a porch. Breakfast and dinner are served in the main dining room. Your pet is welcome, too. *Harborside; (207) 326-4951.*

Holiday Inn Sunspree
★★★/$$
If you're in the mood to splurge, head to this resort hotel on Frenchman's Bay. Designed so your family can have a fun vacation right on the premises, the property has refrigerators in every room, tennis courts, a heated pool, a shoreline jogging path, and several restau-

Upward Ho!

If your kids enjoy indoor climbing gyms, give them a taste of the real, outdoor thing. Atlantic Climbing School offers half-day rock-climbing trips on some of Acadia's gentler, family-friendly slopes. With the help of an experienced guide, even beginners can quickly master safe climbing techniques. Guides will customize trips to suit your family's needs, skill, and comfort level. Shoes, equipment, and transportation are included in the price. *24 Cottage St., Bar Harbor; (207) 288-2521.*

rants. There's a kids' club in summer, and the *Friendship V* whale-watching cruise leaves from the resort's back dock. *123 Eden St., Bar Harbor; (800) HOLIDAY;* www.basshotels.com/holiday-inn/

Morgan House
★★/$$

Since one of your hosts, Richard Rechholtz, is a park ranger, your family will get the inside scoop on where to hike and bike in Acadia. This gray 1903 Victorian home, on a quiet side street in downtown Bar Harbor, has a Master Suite (ideal for a family of four) with a queen-size canopy bed, pullout couch, and collection of antique hats on the wall. You know you're in the right place when you walk up the staircase lined with smiling teddy bears. Breakfast is included in the rate. *15 High St., Bar Harbor; (207) 288-4325;* www.barharbormorganhouse.com

Oakland House
★★★★/$$$$

It takes a bit of effort to journey to this peaceful seaside retreat on the pastoral Blue Hill Peninisula, but your reward is a vacation spot where your family can embrace life's simple pleasures without the distraction of televisions or phones. Choose one of 15 cabins (equipped with full baths, kitchens, and living rooms with fireplaces) in the woods or along the water's edge, and spend your days combing tidal pools for sea

stars, mussels, and periwinkles, swimming on the lakefront beach, hiking, or reading by the fire. Founded in 1889, Oakland House has been run for generations by the same family, and your host Jim Littlefield is the founder's great-grandson. During the peak summer season, the all-inclusive rate comes with gourmet breakfast and dinner (families even have their own special dining room, which makes it easy for kids to meet other young guests), plus there's a lobster bake. *435 Herrick Rd., Brooksville; (800) 359-RELAX; (207) 359-8521;* www.oaklandhouse.com

GOOD EATS

Eat-A-Pita ★★/$

At this pleasant café, you can order delicious chocolate-chip pancakes made from scratch, bagel sandwiches, chocolate caramel brownies, or creative salads. If you're going on a picnic, stop here for pita sandwiches. *326 Main St., Southwest Harbor; (207) 244-4344.*

F.W. Thurston Co.
★★★★/$$

Located on Bass Harbor, on the quiet southwest tip of Mount Desert Island, this is the spot to go for lobster in the rough in a serene setting. As you eat lobster and steamed mussels (or hot dogs), feast your eyes on the fishing boats and lobster traps laced with colorful buoys. If you can, come for the sunset. *Steamboat Wharf Rd., Bernard; (207) 244-7600.*

Jordan Pond House
★★★★/$-$$

For nearly a century, it's been a tradition to take tea on the lawn at Jordan Pond and munch on colossal, fresh-baked popovers. Thousands of families continue that tradition each year by trekking here, in the middle of Acadia National Park, for good eats and incredible views of the twin peaks known as the Bubbles. (You can cycle or hike directly to the restaurant by following the carriage roads through the park.) Enjoy the customary tea, or order from the lunch or dinner menu; indoor seating is also available. *Jordan Pond; (207) 276-3316.*

Jordans Restaurant
★★/$

For blueberry pancakes, head to this kid-friendly spot in downtown Bar Harbor. Kids get crayons and sippy cups, and though there's no kids' menu as such, the chef can dish out half portions to suit smaller palates. The spot is open for breakfast and lunch. *80 Cottage St., Bar Harbor; (207) 288-3586.*

Maine Street Restaurant
★★/$$

No matter what sort of mood your kids are in, you'll feel comfortable at this casual, roomy restaurant. Kids

Not Roughing It

It's an experience all right: outdoor adventures all day long, gourmet meals for dinner, and down comforters at night. Based in a lodge on Eggemoggin Reach, a secluded natural paradise on Penobscot Bay, **Maine Coast Experience** caters to travelers who want their activities and meals planned for them as one package deal.

You can try kayaking, lobstering, whale-watching, or cycling with other guests, then congregate for gourmet meals in Eggemoggin Lodge's light-filled dining room. There's a game room with a pool table and big-screen TVs, and kids have free use of bikes.

This kind of pampering, as you'd expect, comes at a price. If you can afford it, though, you may enjoy leaving the question "What can we do?" to someone else. You can stay for the night or the week. *Brooklin; (888) 559-5057; (207) 359-5057;* www.mainecoast experience.com can color at the table while you wait for piled-high plates of homemade spaghetti and meatballs, lasagna, or seafood. *297 Main St., Bar Harbor; (207) 288-3585.*

124 Cottage St. ★★/$$

For fancier fare, head to this cozy local favorite. The food is creative and elegant (try the Bombay chicken with curry sauce, apples, and cashews), and owner Ed Ciampa knows how to make families feel at home. He'll gladly let your children play with his own son's toys while they're waiting for their meals. The kids' menu includes baked pasta marinara. *124 Cottage St., Bar Harbor; (207) 288-4383.*

The Riverside Café ★★/$

Leave Ellsworth's main commercial strip and head downtown for this popular café, where they know how to cater to kids. Your children will get a sliced apple or crackers when they sit down, along with crayons; their drawings may even end up on the wall. You'll find everything from nachos and eggwiches to BLTs and fruit yogurt smoothies. Save room for the homemade pie. *151 Main St., Ellsworth; (207) 667-7220.*

SOUVENIR HUNTING

Acadia Shops

This top-notch retailer features hundreds of Maine-made crafts and Jordan Pond paraphernalia (popover pans, the famous jam, hand-painted creamers), as well as educational toys, books, games, and activity kits for children. The kites are fabulous. *85 Main St., Bar Harbor; (207) 288-5600.*

The Christmas Spirit

No matter what time of year, you'll quickly get into the holiday spirit at this festive shop, run by Pete and Beverly Bono. The walls are filled with thousands of handmade orna-

---

FamilyFun READER'S TIP

Scenic Views

I am always trying to make car travel more fun for my kids and easier on me. One idea that has worked very well is a picture scavenger hunt. I cut pictures out of old picture books, magazines, and catalogs and paste them on a piece of poster board. Then I punch holes in the two top corners of the poster, tie a piece of elastic between them, and hang the poster from the back of the front seat. Each time they see one of the items—an airplane, tractor, bicycle, or horse, for example—they place a sticker on that picture. My kids love this game so much that it entertained them throughout a recent 13-hour trip.

Lisa Reynolds, San Antonio, Texas

ments and crafts fashioned by local artisans. Many can be personalized right on the spot. Pick one as a souvenir and watch the staff ink on everyone's name. *80 Main St., Bar Harbor; (800) 242-2913.*

Nervous Nellie's Jams and Jellies

You can practically smell the home-cooked jam from the road. Anne Greacen uses fresh, local fruit to make wild Maine blueberry preserves (and a dozen other flavors) in a small steam kettle. You can watch and smell the process in her tiny, white clapboard jelly kitchen. You can also sample the products in the café, which serves tea, scones, and homemade jam. Set by the water in the picturesque hamlet of Deer Isle, the jam factory is also home to Ann's husband, artist Peter Beerists, who makes kid-pleasing, whimsical sculptures from found objects—a big red lobster and a fish playing checkers, a Dalmatian dressed in a fireman's helmet, and a pistol-toting dinosaur all set for a showdown, to name a few. The couple doesn't mind at all if you bring a picnic and enjoy the views from the apple orchard. *598 Sunshine Rd., Deer Isle; (800) 777-6845.*

Treasure Island

Find kites, beach toys, bug huts, and train sets here. *100 Main St., Ellsworth; (800) 243-7970.*

Yes, kids, you can see moose at
Moosehead Lake. In fact, you are likely to.

Western Lakes and Mountains

LTHOUGH MANY FAMILIES flock to Maine's coastal communities, there's a whole chunk of the state—colossal chunk —that you and your kids will enjoy exploring, where you typically won't have to put up with the crowds, traffic, and expense of the seashore. Maine's Western Lakes and Mountains, the Kennebec Valley (home of Augusta, the state capital, and the white-water rafting mecca, the Forks), and the Moosehead Lake and Katahdin regions in northern Maine, give families the chance to turn an ordinary vacation into an adventure. In the wildly beautiful 202,064-acre Baxter State Park, for example, you'll stand a good chance of meeting a moose and seeing dozens of other kinds of wildlife as you hike trails beneath the shadow of Maine's tallest peak, Mount Katahdin.

By and large, western and northern Maine are places to make your own adventure, and some of them don't even require money. Unbelievably, you can go rockhounding for free at several quarries in the Oxford Hills, searching for tourmaline, quartz, amethyst, and other once-buried treasures. It only costs a few dollars to rent a canoe and glide across Rangeley Lake or swim in

THE FamilyFun LIST

MUST-SEE MUST-SEE

Maine Discovery Museum
(page 103)

Norlands Living History Center
(page 104)

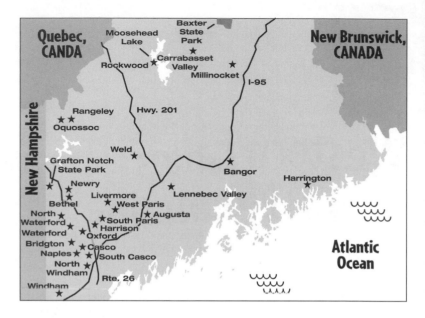

popular Lake Sebago. In Bethel, families who love to hike need only stop at the **Evans Notch visitors' center** *(18 Mayville Rd.; 207/824-2143)* for free information on kid-appropriate trails in the White Mountains.

If you want to get even more adventurous, you can try white-water rafting in the Forks (many outfitters offer trips for children ages 8 and older), llama trekking and dog-sledding near Bethel, moose-watching and snowmobiling at Moosehead Lake, and, of course, skiing and snow-boarding at some of New England's friendliest mountains (see "Fun Family Ski Resorts" on pages 108–109). While just a few years ago some of these activities were reserved exclusively for die-hard adventurers, today, many reputable outfitters

offer family packages that cater to children. Often, they include instruction geared to kids, and kid-size gear, homecooked meals, and a safe, warm place to sleep, so you don't need to sacrifice the comforts of home.

Though this underrated region is geared to nature lovers, it's worth making a city stop. Augusta is a treasure, home to the nation's oldest wooden fort, a popular children's museum, and the Main State Museum, where your family can learn about Maine's colorful heritage.

Lastly, in an area known for its majestic lakes, it's a must to pack a lunch, rent a boat, and have fun zipping through the water. There are dozens of outfitters who rent motor-boats, pontoon boats, jet skis, and the like.

CULTURAL ADVENTURES

Children's Discovery Museum
★★/$

At this museum, kids can dress up in costumes, stage a videotaped play, and watch themselves on TV; climb on real construction equipment; meet Stuffee, a lovable, colossal doll with removable organs; learn about the ecology of the Kennebec River in the nature studies room; and visit the post office, grocery store, and communications center. If you and your kids are into crafts, there's also a recycling shop, where you can buy corks, oatmeal boxes, coffee cans, and more. *265 Water St., Augusta; (207) 622-2209.*

Maine Discovery Museum
★★★★/$$

It's a long way to Bangor, but the payoff is this outstanding three-story children's museum in a historic downtown building. You can hear stories in a room designed to resemble a ballpark (subsidized by novelist, baseball fan, and Bangor resident Stephen King and his wife, Tabitha), record songs in a soundproof booth at a recording studio, crawl through a giant intestine, stamp your passport as you visit (through video and hands-on displays) the *Goodnight Moon* room and Zuckerman's Barn

Llama Trekking

Meet Mocha, Amadeus, Jack, and the rest of the llama pack at the **Telemark Inn**, a century-old wilderness lodge that offers summer llama treks and other animal adventures. After an orientation, naturalist Steve Crone assigns a faithful llama to each member of your family, and the exotic beasts carry your packs (you don't ride the animals) on a hike through the White Mountain National Forest.

You can choose a one-day hike, or a three-day (or more) adventure package that combines hiking, llama trekking, and camping out. Crone shares kids' fascination with animals and enjoys pointing out beaver dams and other natural wonders.

In winter, Crone also offers **dogjoring**, a sport that's a cross between Nordic skiing and dogsledding. The skier is attached to one of Crone's Siberian huskies (or to your pet dog, if she's hearty enough) by a towline. You then trek behind the dog and, together, gleefully glide down the trail. Dogsledding, horse-drawn sleigh rides, and horseback riding can also be arranged. *R.F.D. 2, Box 800, Bethel; (207) 836-2703.*

of E. B. White's *Charlotte's Web*, and work on delightfully messy projects with a real artist in the Art Studio. *74 Main St., Bangor; (207) 947-5596.*

Maine State Museum
★★★/Free

Tucked away in the state library, this museum features three floors of fascinating exhibits about Maine's natural and industrial history. There's an old-time feel here, with few of the hands-on interactive stations that you find at newer museums. Even so, the museum is no less fascinating than its high-tech counterparts. Through dozens of exhibits and dio-ramas, kids can learn about lumbering, quarrying, lobstering, and shipbuilding. For most, however, the natural history area is tops; they can meet moose, black bears, and other native creatures in settings so lifelike, you'll almost forget you're indoors. *State St., Augusta; (207) 287-2301.*

Norlands Living History Center
★★★★/$$$-$$$$

This is a fine place to stop in at, but what makes it special is its family programming. One of the most unique ways for children to learn about 18th- and 19th-century rural life is to sign on for a family live-in at this year-round educational center. Formerly home of the Washburns, a prominent political family in the 1800s, the 455-acre estate invites families to experience firsthand the New England farmer's creed, "Use it, wear it out, make it do, or do without." Although dates of live-ins vary, one typical arrangement is for families with children ages 6 and up to spend two days and nights role-playing members of a farm family. Under the supervision of a staff member, participants complete farm chores (there's a 6:30 A.M. wake-up call), prepare meals using old recipes, play period games, and attend school; there's also a small amount of leisure time. No, it's not glamorous—instead of a modern bathroom, participants use a cham-

Design Your Own Adventure

Whether you want to take a snowmobile tour, go on a wildlife safari in an all-terrain vehicle, or try kayaking or fly-fishing, **Sun Valley Sports** will make it happen. The family-oriented guides enjoy teaching children about the magic of the outdoors on half- and full-day trips. You provide yourselves—they'll supply the snacks, equipment, and know-how. If you prefer, you can just rent equipment and head out on your own. *129 Sunday River Rd., Bethel; (207) 824-7533.*

Down by the Riverside

Compared to the Saco, the Androscoggin River is an undiscovered gem—and an excellent place if you want to have a paddling adventure. **Bethel Outdoor Adventures and Campground,** run by Pattie and Jeff Parsons and their four children, offers guided trips on this pretty river. (There's no white water, so it's ideal for beginners.) *121 Mayville Rd., Bethel; (207) 824-4224.*

ber pot—but it's a chance for adventurous families who love history to live it, not just learn it. The rate includes lodging, all meals, snacks, and activities. Many themed festivals, such as the summer Strawberry Festival and an autumn Civil War Festival, are held annually. If you're stopping in the summer, you can also take a guided tour of the property (tours not offered during the school year). *290 Norlands Rd., Livermore; (207) 897-4366.*

Old Fort Western
★★/$

New England's oldest surviving wood fort was built in 1754 and is as busy as ever. Costumed interpreters welcome kids to tour the 16-room garrison house, which was used as a fort, trading post, and lodge. You might end up pitching in with domestic duties or helping out in the store. The National Historic Landmark holds many family-oriented events, including hosting military encampments, old-time Fourth of July celebrations, and period crafts demonstrations. *16 Cony St., Augusta; (207) 626-2385;* www.old fortwestern.org

JUST FOR FUN

Baxter State Park
★★★★/$

For adventurous families, visiting Baxter State Park is the high point of a trip to Maine. The 202,064-acre wilderness area surrounds the 5,267-foot-high Mount Katahdin. Although most parents and kids don't scale the mountain, they enjoy shorter hikes teeming with wildlife, plant life, and amazing views. The park was a gift from Maine's former governor, Percival B. Baxter, who wanted the land to remain undeveloped forever. True to his wish, Baxter State Park is a wilderness area in every respect. You tote in your own water (water in the park is untreated), first-aid supplies, and snacks, and the nearest convenience store is several miles from the park entrance. Come prepared to see pretty waterfalls (Little Abol Falls trail), moose strolling around a pond (the Sandy Stream Trail), and dozens of exotic wildflowers (Daicey Pond Nature Trail). To get oriented, stop at the visitors' center by the Togue Pond Gatehouse for a hiking map and assistance in choosing a route. There are ten campgrounds in the park, some of which have tent sites, cabins, lean-tos, and bunkhouses. To reserve a spot, write or visit **Park Headquarters**, *64 Balsam Dr., Millinocket, ME 04462* (you cannot reserve sites by phone). For other information, call *(207) 723-5140.*

Beech Hill Farm
Bison Ranch ★★/$

Want to come nose to nose with an American icon? Spend an hour at this working ranch. Your family can hop on a hay wagon, see a herd of about 30 buffalo grazing in the field, learn fun facts about the shaggy breed (bison meat has fewer calories than chicken), and get a closer look when they approach the wagon to snack on apples. You'll also meet Belgian draft horses and goats, and you can buy buffalo souvenirs (including buffalo meat) in the trading post. *630 Valley Rd., Waterford; (207) 583-2515.*

Big Adventure Center
★★/$$$

Don't let the rain dampen your spirits. Instead, head for this indoor recreation center with a climbing wall that kids as young as 3 can learn to scale and a laser tag game popular with teenagers. (Players step into a dimly lit, fogged area and negotiate barriers, platforms, and other obstacles.) There's also a video-game room and, for when the weather

clears, an outdoor 18-hole miniature-golf course. *Corner of Airport Rd. and Rte. 2, Bethel; (207) 824-0929;* www.bigadventure.com

Carousel Horse Farm
★★/$$

This horse farm offers pony rides, trail rides, and wagon rides over 100 miles of trails. On the ice-cream ride, kids board the wagon and venture down the hill to Pears Ice Cream for a cone. *69 Leach Hill Rd., Casco; (207) 627-4471.*

Carter's Farm ★★/$$

No matter what time of year you travel, Dave and Anne Carter and their three daughters can help your family enjoy a low-cost vacation in the Western Lakes. In warm weather, they can outfit you with canoes and kayaks for adventures on the Androscoggin River. In the winter, they welcome families at their cross-country ski centers in Oxford and

Bethel. Families can stay in the modern ski lodge, a remote cabin with gaslights, or a cozy bed-and-breakfast with pine paneling. *420 Main St./Rte. 26, Oxford; (207) 539-4848.*

Grafton Notch State Park
★★★/$

The scenic drive to this pristine hiking area will whet your appetite for the splendor to come. The park is a beautiful place to spend the day, particularly in autumn when the leaves turn brilliant shades. Start your outing at Step Falls (south of the park entrance off Route 26), where you can slither down rock slides into cool rushing water. Then continue on to Screw Auger Falls for a picnic and Moose Cove for a quarter-mile nature walk. It can be tricky to find the trailheads, so get a free map of the Upper Androscoggin Valley at the Bethel Area Chamber of Commerce, *30 Cross St; (207) 824-2282.*

Mountain View Sports Park
★/$$

On your way to Sunday River or Sugarloaf, stop by this 14-acre park for some winter tubing fun. Tubers take a lift up an 85-foot hill and glide down a 100-foot-long run.

Maine has a good many places that bear the names of international locales. You'll find **Paris**, **Norway**, **Mexico**, **Sweden**, and even **China**. The Lynchville signpost (junctions of Routes 5 and 35 in Oxford) pays homage to this legacy. Its black-and-white arrows point the way to Maine's foreign-named hamlets.

Kids ages 3 to 7 can ride with an adult in a one-person tube for no extra charge, or your whole clan can board a family tube. *Rte. 26, Oxford; (207) 539-2454.*

Mutiny Brook Stables
★/$

This 800-acre farm offers one-hour trail rides for parents and kids ages 7 and up. The slow, scenic rides through the woods afford pretty mountain views. Stop by in the spring and see the foals. *177 Sweeden Rd., S. Waterford; (207) 583-6650.*

Naples Seaplane Service
★★/$$$

Sebago Lake is so huge that the only way to see it all is to fly over it. This seaplane fits six travelers and makes a 25-mile loop over the lake in a trip that lasts about 15 minutes. *Naples Village Dock, Naples; (207) 693-5138.*

Seacoast Fun Park
★★/$

At this popular recreational center, families can board go-carts and negotiate hairpin turns on a hilly track (there are height restrictions; call ahead to check), and play miniature golf on a big, nautical-themed course complete with lobsters and fishing boats. If you dare, you can even brave Skycoaster, a free-fall

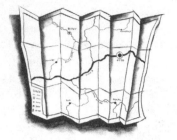

attraction where the brave-hearted don a hang-gliding harness and drop 100 feet toward the ground. In the winter, the park transforms into the Seacoast Snow Park, offering snow-boarding, tubing, and ice-skating. There is no admission fee at this ten-acre park; you pay for each attraction separately. *Rte. 302, Windham; (207) 892-5952.* A second facility, in Trenton, has a water slide, but no Skycoaster.

Sebago Lake State Park
★★/Free
After hiking on scenic nature trails, you can relax on a pleasant beach equipped with bathhouses and staffed (in season) with lifeguards.

FUN FAMILY SKI RESORTS

Sugarloaf
Fans of this resort don't mind traveling off the beaten path (it's two hours west of Bangor) for exceptional activities and a village filled with more than 20 restaurants, shops, and a grocery store. Besides downhill skiing and snowboarding, families can enjoy cross-country skiing, ice-skating, sleigh rides, the Turbo Tubing Park, movie nights, and snowshoe safaris.

There are 1,400 skiable acres, including New England's only lift service above tree-line; 126 trails and glades (24 percent beginner, 20 percent intermediate, 38 percent advanced, 10 percent glades); 14 lifts, including two superquads; and 92 percent snowmaking coverage. Family facilities include child care for ages 6 months to 2½ years; clinics for 3 to 12; and Learn-to-Ski and Learn-to-Ride programs for adults.

Lodging options include the **Grand Summit Resort Hotel,** the **Sugarloaf Inn,** and 7,800 on-mountain beds in town houses within walking distance of trails or chairs.

In summer, try fishing in the stocked 12-acre trout pond, mountain biking on 50 miles of trails, taking a twilight moose cruise, or signing up for golf camp. Sugarloaf's summer outdoor adventure camps for children are exceptional. These day camps feature archery, fishing, wall climbing, and hiking, and teach children environmental awareness. *R.R. 1, Carrabassett Valley; (207) 237-2000; (207) 237-6808 (snow phone); (800) THE-LOAF;* www.sugarloaf.com

Rangers offer many interpretive programs, from guided hikes to nature activities (June 20 to Labor Day). *Rte. 302, between Naples and Casco; (207) 693-6613.*

BUNKING DOWN

Aimhi Lodge ★★★★/$$$$
Nestled at the tip of a back road, on the edge of Little Sebago Lake, this family resort will seem familiar even if you've never been there before.

And it probably is: it's been on the cover of the L.L. Bean catalog. A Maine tradition since 1919, this rustic retreat has been run by the same family all these years. It has a rambling main lodge with a stone fireplace, and cottages so close to the lake you can nearly dip your toe in from the front porch. With names like Naughty Pine, Hoot Owl, and Northern Lights, these humble homes (which are modern on the inside) are a family's base for a week of old-fashioned fun. There are more than 20

Sunday River
Sunday River has eight connected peaks with acclaimed children's programs, family activities, and an array of restaurants and on-mountain lodging. The resort boasts 6,000 beds in 700 condominium units; two full-service, slope-side hotels: the **Grand Summit** and the **Jordan Grand**; a ski lodge, and a dorm.

There are 660 skiable acres; 127 trails (25 percent beginner, 35 percent intermediate, 40 percent advanced); 18 lifts, including four high-speed quads; and 92 percent snowmaking coverage. Family facilities: Tiny Turn programs for 3-year-olds; Mogul Munchkins for children 4 to 6; Mogul Meisters for kids 7 to 12; Perfect Turn clinics for skiers over age 12; Maine Handicapped Skiing programs. Learn-to-Ski or Learn-to-Ride programs use the

Guaranteed Learning Method: your money back if you don't learn the sport. At the after-dark White Cap Fun Center: a lighted tubing park, a lighted half-pipe for snowboarders, a lighted skating rink, snowshoeing, snowmobile tours, and a video-game arcade. The **Sunday River Inn and Cross Country Center** *(207/824-2410)* is nearby.

From June to early October, cyclists can go mountain biking at the Sunday River Mountain Bike Park, which offers lift service and 60 miles of terrain. If you'd rather tour on foot, check out the trails at the hiking center. Prices for individual activities vary widely. In the summer, kids ages 5 to 12 can join the fun at Camp Sunday River for a day or a week. *Off Rte. 2, Newry; (800) 543-2-SKI; (207) 824-3000; www.sundayriver.com*

rustic cottages (one, two, and three rooms), all with screened lakeside porches and private docks. The activities are endless—boating, waterskiing, swimming (the lake is about 70 degrees in summer), fishing, tennis, and sailing, plus weekly lobster bakes and chuck-wagon lunches. Family-style meals are served in the main lodge; children under 3 dine together under the supervision of a counselor, so parents can relax. Because many families return to the Aimhi year after year, the cottages are booked well in advance. *N. Windham; (207) 892-6538;* www.aimhilodge.com

Bethel Inn & Country Club
★★★/$$$

Despite the name, this is no exclusive country club. Families will feel right at home at this rambling, yellow wooden inn. What's more, you'll find lots to do on the 29 miles of groomed cross-country ski trails, championship golf course, and hiking trails, and in the lake, pool, and game rooms. In the summer, the inn hosts Camp Songo (on a daily or weekly basis). Families of four typically stay in one of the 60 rooms or suites in the inn, or in a two-bedroom town house (there

According to local records, **Paul Bunyan** was born in Bangor, Maine, on February 12, 1834. Townsfolk salute the mythic hero with a 31-foot-tall statue. Sporting a red-and-black-checked lumberman's shirt, the fiberglass woodsman never tires of posing for snapshots. *Main St., Bangor.*

are 40 of these). All activities, plus breakfast and dinner, are included in the price (there are no extra greens fees). *On the common, Bethel; (207) 824-2175.*

Big Moose Inn & Cabins
★★/$-$$

If you plan on hiking in Baxter State Park, you may find it cozier and more comfortable to stay here than to camp out in the park. You can rent a campsite, cabin, or simple guest room and, since you're just eight miles from the park, head there during the day. With two freshwater lakes, the inn is an ideal place to swim, canoe, and fish. *Millinocket Lake, Millinocket; (207) 723-8391.*

The Birches Resort
★★★★/$$$$

It takes an effort to get to this 11,000-acre rustic retreat in northern Maine (it's a four-hour drive from Portland), but the payoff is a chance to play in a wilderness fast disappearing from the American landscape. Families can rent one of 15 hand-built cottages (they have one to three bedrooms), built in 1935 when the place was exclusively a sporting camp. Situated along 40-mile-long Moosehead Lake, the rustic cottages have hot and cold running water, electricity, cooking and bath facilities, and a woodstove or fireplace. Spend your time relaxing on the front porch, hiking or cycling on the property's 36 miles of trails, rent a canoe, kayak, or motorboat, or join a moose safari (a guided boat trip where you may sight one of the big brown guys). For those who crave more adventure, the resort's on-site outfitter, Wilderness Expeditions (see at right), offers guided white-water rafting trips and other guided outdoor activities. Included in the rate are three meals daily; you can also prepare meals in your cabin. The Birches also rents yurts and cabin tents (a less expensive, though still not cheap, option). *The Birches Rd., Rockwood; (800) 825-WILD.*

FamilyFun TIP

Camp Wilderness

Wilderness Expeditions, a top-notch outfitter run by the folks at The Birches Resort on Moosehead Lake, offers a four-day **Family Adventures Camp** that includes sea kayaking, hiking, white-water rafting, mountain biking, and windsurfing with a Registered Maine Guide. The evening program includes storytelling by the campfire, and sing-alongs. Lodging, meals, and equipment are included in the price. In the winter, you can sign on for snowmobiling and snowshoeing excursions. *The Birches Rd., Rockwood; (800) 825-WILD.*

Chapman Inn
★★★/$$

There's nothing stuffy about this bed-and-breakfast and its picture-perfect location. You'll find a laid-back game room, private saunas, and even a family suite. Depending on the season, your hosts serve cocoa and cookies in the afternoon. Awesome breakfasts are included in the room rate. *On the village common, Bethel; (207) 824-2657; www.chapmaninn.com*

Grant's Kennebago Camps
★★★/$$$$

If you hear the call of the wild and you don't mind living without

phones or televisions for a few days, this is your kind of place. Founded 100 years ago, this rustic, 18-cabin camp used to attract mostly fishermen. Now it also attracts families, drawn to its serene location on Kennebago Lake. There aren't any organized activities, but you can hike, swim, canoe, and watch for moose on the lake. Delicious meals are served in the lodge. **NOTE:** You must travel nine miles on a gravel road to reach this camp, so make sure you bring the essentials. *Box 786, Rangeley; (800) 633-4815.*

Hunter Cove Cabins ★★/$$

Looking to keep it simple? Rent one of the eight rustic cabins on a sheltered cove on Rangeley Lake and spend the week canoeing, swimming, and boating. You won't have to live without creature comforts: the cabins have satellite TVs and VCRs, as well as kitchens and screened-in porches. *Mingo Loop, Rangeley; (207) 864-3383.*

Kawanhee Inn ★★★/$

They don't make them like this anymore. At this vacation gem, rent one of the 1930s cabins (equipped with stone fireplaces and kitchens) around Webb Lake and spend your days kayaking, canoeing, rockhounding, hiking on exceptional trails, and even panning for gold on the nearby Swift River. You can cook in your cabin or dine in the main lodge. *Rte. 142; Weld; (207) 585-2000.*

The Maine Houses ★★/$$

If you're planning a family reunion or traveling with extended family, this is the way to go. The company rents out houses in Bryant Pond, 14 miles from the Sunday River Ski Resort. With no on-site manager, they operate like self-service inns. You do the housework and haul out the trash; the staff provides the dishwashing liquid and the trash bags. The Maine House (accommodates 29 people), directly on Lake Christopher, has a large recreation room, a huge yard with 200 feet of lake frontage, a boat dock equipped with canoes and sports equipment (free for guests to use), a steam room,

eight bedrooms, a color TV, and a VCR. Two other houses, the Maine Mountain View House (24 people) and the Maine Farm House (33 people), are just a short walk away. *For reservations, call (800) 646-8737.*

Migis Lodge ★★/$$$$

One of the priciest area resorts, the Migis appeals to families who think it's worth it to spend quite a bit more to vacation in the lap of luxury. The cottages on Sebago Lake look like they're straight out of a home-design catalog—fieldstone fireplaces, gleaming woodwork, and porches, to name just a few amenities. Kids' activities include a Zoo Program, and a supervised evening of activities that also lets Mom and Dad dine alone while the kids chow down together. Otherwise little ones under age 5 eat with their parents in the family dining room. *Box 40, South Casco; (207) 655-4524;* www.migis.com

Point Sebago Resort ★★/$$-$$$$

With its economical prices, this resort campground is a good option for families seeking an affordable vacation at Lake Sebago. Set on 800 acres, including nearly a mile of beach, the resort offers supervised kids' programs and a variety of lodging options: campsites, trailers, park homes with the feel of an RV, and resort cottages similar to mobile homes. In summer, the resort features various themed activity weekends, from swinging 1950s and 1960s to Pirates of Sebago. Families can rent boats, play tennis, horseshoes, and miniature golf (there's also an 18-hole championship golf course). Kids can also attend their own evening programs. The food in the Lakeview Restaurant isn't going to win any prizes, but the staff does its best to keep kids happy, and that counts for something. *Box 712, Casco; (800) 530-1555.*

Rangeley Inn ★★/$

This historic inn is the place to stay if you want the best of both worlds: outdoor adventures by day and a civilized setting, in the town center, at night. Located on the shore of Haley Pond, the property offers three lodging choices. You can stay in the 35-room inn, a 15-room motor lodge, or one of two cabins. The fancy dining room serves SpaghettiOs for kids, and the helpful staff is happy to assist you in arranging outdoor adventures, from gold panning and moose-watching to mountain biking and snowmobiling. This inn attracts a diverse crowd, from seniors on bus trips to parents with young kids. *51 Main St., Rangeley; (800) MOMENTS; (207) 864-3341.*

Senator Inn & Spa
★★★/$$$

With its capital location, this Best Western hotel does attract its share of politicians, but it's also a great place for families. Kids get free

adventure kits at check-in and there's an appealing wooden playground and nature trail in the back of the property. The indoor pool is also a winner. You can stay in a standard room or rent a cowboy-style cabin; these sleep two comfortably. *Western Ave. at I-95, Augusta; (877) 772-2224; (207) 622-5904.*

Sunday River Inn ★★★/$

This cozy, family-oriented inn is the antithesis of the big neighboring ski resorts—and the perfect place for you to enjoy an old-fashioned winter vacation. Families typically stay in dorm rooms with a shared bath (the less expensive option) or a family room with a private bath. Buffet-style meals are served in the informal dining room. Kids can relax by the large, fieldstone fireplace and play a board game with other young guests. The inn's 25-mile network of cross-county ski trails is exceptional, and you can rent kid-size equipment (along with pull sleds for babies and snowshoes) in the on-site shop. There's also a skating rink, and a two-hour kids' program on winter

weekends, where little ones can play animal bingo and make snow sculptures. Rates include breakfast and dinner. Open Thanksgiving through April 1. *23 Skiway Rd., Newry; (207) 824-2410.*

Tarry-A-While Resort
★★★/$$

Since the 1890s, families have been coming to this kid-friendly retreat to hear the call of the loon and to relax with a puzzle on the front porch. If that's your cup of tea, you'll have a marvelous time. Located on scenic Highland Lake, this simple retreat invites you to spend your days on the sandy beach, canoe, kayak, and play croquet. Families typically stay in one of the rustic cottages (no phone or TV) and enjoy a delicious breakfast buffet in the Tarry-A-While Restaurant. Kids will find all of their favorites on the menu at lunch and dinner, and the kitchen gladly honors requests for healthful substitutions (vegetables instead of fries). *Highland Rd., Bridgton; (207) 647-2522.*

The Telemark Inn
★★★/$$$

Set two and one half miles off the nearest back road and surrounded by national forest, this rustic lodge is the place to try animal adventures (see page 103) and other sports. In the winter, for example, you can rent snowshoes and try Telemark skiing just for the day. You can also opt for a winter package, including meals and overnights, in an Adirondack-style lodge with a huge, mineral-stone fireplace. *R.F.D. 2, Box 800, Bethel; (207) 836-2703.*

Twin Pine Camps ★★★/$$

This is a convenient, comfortable place to stay if you plan on hiking at Baxter State Park during the day. Each cabin has a full kitchen and bath and comfortable furnishings; some have a fireplace or woodstove. From your home away from home, you'll have a view of Mount Katahdin. For recreation there's a pool table and heated indoor pool. *Millinocket Lake, Millinocket; (800) 766-7238; (207) 723-5523.*

FamilyFun READER'S TIP -

Tic-Tac-Tine

While my sister Barb and I and our seven kids were waiting for dinner at a restaurant recently, my nephew Josh, age 9, surprised me with a game he invented using dinner utensils and sugar packets. He set up forks, spoons, and knives in the traditional tic-tac-toe grid and gave me the choice of being the *X*'s (regular sugar packets) or *O*'s (artificial sweetener packets).

Soon everyone at the table was pairing off to play, and it was a fun way for us to pass the time before our meal arrived.

Theresa Jung, Cincinnati, Ohio

GOOD EATS

Breau's Pizza & Subs ★/$
Your kids will think that the talking wastebasket is reason enough to come to this restaurant. ("Hello, welcome to Breau's. So you feel like a nut? How about a maple-nut ice cream?") Besides, with a long list of subs, pizza, pita pockets, and ice-cream concoctions, you can be sure that everyone in your family will find something to like. *Rte. 2, Bethel; (207) 824-3192; (207) 824-4711.*

Chunky's Cinema Pub ★★/$$
Here's a new and improved twist on the days of the drive-in movie. At Chunky's, instead of watching a movie from your car, you can lean back in a Lincoln Town Car seat, order your favorite food, and enjoy a first-run flick—inside this unique theater/restaurant. Kids' menu items include the Kevin Bacon Burger, Love Me Tenders, and Babe in the City (roast pork on a roll). The bonus: better sound and no traffic jams or long lines at the concession. *North Windham Shopping Center, Windham; (207) 892-4777.*

Denny's Classic Diner ★★★/$$
Slick back your hair, pull on your poodle skirt, and doo-wop your way over to Classic Denny's (a spin-off of the grand-slam breakfast chain) for 1950s food in a spotless diner. Sit at the counter for a strawberry malt or slip into a sparkling red vinyl booth for a burger and fries. You can play the jukebox for free, and kids get an activity book, crayons, and toys to amuse them. *11 Civic Center Dr., Augusta; (207) 623-1290.*

The Gingerbread House ★★/$-$$
True to its name, this is one of the sweetest dining spots in the Rangeley Lakes. You can sit at the ice-cream bar and order an old-fashioned ice-cream soda, or sit down in the dining room for brunch or dinner. (You'll find everything from corn dogs and grilled cheese to hickory-planked salmon and crab cakes.) There's even a short nature trail out back, where you can walk off the banana chocolate crepes. *Rte. 4, Oquossoc; (207) 864-3602.*

Loon's Nest ★★/$$
Having too much fun on the boat to break for lunch? Just float on over to the Kezar Lake Marina, dock by the restaurant, and enjoy a scrumptious seafood dinner on the lakeside deck. Dig in to fried clams and fish-and-chips and be sure to save room for yummy Gifford's ice cream. *Kezar Lake Marina at the Narrows, Lovell; (207) 925-1911.*

Olde Mill Tavern ★★/$-$$
Over the years, this building has taken turns playing host to a play-

house, public hall for chicken raffles, basketball stadium, roller rink, and lumber store. No matter what its form, however, it's always been a local hot spot—and remains one today. Kids will have fun looking at the Ricker plow and farm tools hanging from the rafters, and digging into PB&J and French-bread pizza. *Main St., Harrison; (207) 583-4992.*

Pat's Pizza ★★★/$$
Founded in the college town of Orono in 1953, the restaurant's specialty is thin-crust pizza that's so addictive you'll want to eat here several times during your vacation. Good thing Pat's has restaurants at about 15 locations in Maine; you can eat your way around the state.

Dog Days of Winter
Liz Como and Andy Chakomakos are hooked on huskies and love sharing their know-how on **dogsled trips**. On a half-day adventure (geared to kids ages 8 and up), your family will head for the hills, learn how to harness the dogs, and settle back in the basket of the sled (two people can usually fit in the basket) for an exhilarating ride. If you're up for it, you can even ride on the back of the sled with the musher. On your journey, you'll learn how huskies are trained and why they love to pull. You'll also get plenty of loving licks from the happy pack. *Box 1105, Lovell; (207) 928-2026.*

At each location, you can choose from a dizzying list of toppings, from hot dogs to jalapeños, while your kids are kept busy with crayons and activity books. You can find Pat's in Windham *(Rte. 302, Roosevelt Trail; 207/892-1700)*; Augusta *(292 State St., 207/623-1748)*; and Bethel *(Box 127; 207/824-3637)*, and other regions throughout the state.

The River Restaurant ★★/$$
When you're in rock-hounding country, head to this former schoolhouse for a satisfying meal with a little style. Kids will find all of their favorites on the menu, while parents can dig in to beef Stroganoff and prime rib. *Rte. 26 at Snow Falls, West Paris; (207) 674-3800.*

Sunday River Brewing Co. ★★/$-$$
Colorful pennants adorn this pleasant brew pub, just down the street from Sunday River Ski Resort. It's also one of the best places in town for a burger, barbecue, and steak bombs (shaved steak, salami, pepper Jack cheese, green peppers, and onions on a roll). *Rte. 2, Bethel; (207) 824-4-ALE.*

Tut's General Store and Restaurant ★★/$$
This general store has been providing local families with all the essentials since the 1860s. In the general-store section, kids will find

stuffed animals and their favorite candy. In the dining area, the whole family can enjoy buttermilk pancakes, burgers, pizza, and root beer floats. The prices are so reasonable, you'll think the clock stopped 20 years ago. *Rte. 35, North Waterford; (800) 281-4437; (207) 583-4447.*

SOUVENIR HUNTING

Mt. Mann Jewelers

The best part of this store is what's under it—a crystal cave. To adults it may seem more like a couple of low-lit rooms filled with shelves containing mica and other rocks and minerals. But to kids, it's a veritable gold mine. For a few bucks, they can take a bucket, search the cave for glittering specimens, and then identify their treasures with the help of a chart. Owner Jim Mann is a self-taught rock hound and excellent jeweler who enjoys sharing his know-how with kids. *57 Main St., Bethel; (207) 824-3030.*

Perham's of West Paris

At this combination shop and museum, your little rock hounds will find a vast collection of rocks and minerals for sale and on display, plus rock tumblers, picks, and kids' geology books. There's also a scale model of a feldspar quarry and plenty of jewelry for Mom—or Dad. *Rte. 26, West Paris; (800) 371-GEMS; (207) 674-2341.*

Pooh Corner Farm

This country floral shop is a great place to buy pumpkins in the fall and Winnie the Pooh paraphernalia all year long. Plus, you get to meet the company mascots: Piglet the real pig and Eeyore the real donkey. *Bog Rd., Bethel; (207) 836-FARM.*

The Toy Shop

You'll find American Girl dolls, science toys, Legos, Brio trains, and more at this well-stocked shop with two locations: *Philbrook Pl., Bethel (207/824-TOYS),* and *Market Square, South Paris (207/743-TOYS).*

New Hampshire

A VACATION IN THE Granite State promises nothing less than the best. Here, you'll find New England's tallest mountains (the craggy Whites) and the 6,440-acre Franconia Notch State Park, where Mother Nature carved the 40-foot-high Old Man of the Mountain. The region's largest concentration of family attractions and an undying commitment to fun conspire to make New Hampshire a vacation venue that will make you want to return again and again.

For outdoor fun, New Hampshire is a clear front-runner. The state boasts 86 named

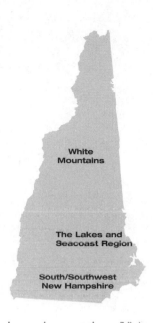

White
Mountains

The Lakes and
Seacoast Region

South/Southwest
New Hampshire

peaks and more than 30 fami-ly-friendly ski resorts (see "Fun Family Ski Resorts" on page 137). There are 1,300 lakes (the largest is 28-mile-long Lake Winnipesaukee), and 40,000 miles of rivers and streams, creating a paradise for swimmers, boaters, fishermen, and water-skiers. More than 80 percent of the state is covered in forest, so you're never far from a beautiful hike. New Hampshire even tweaks out 18 miles of shoreline along the Atlantic, so families can have fun in the sun at Rye, Wallis Sands, and Hampton beaches. If you'd rather play indoors, you can visit two fine children's museums, a plane-tarium, and plenty of shopping outlets.

ATTRACTIONS
$	under $10
$$	$10 - $20
$$$	$20 - $30
$$$$	$30 +

HOTELS/MOTELS/CAMPGROUNDS
$	under $100
$$	$100 - $200
$$$	$200 - $300
$$$$	$300 +

RESTAURANTS
$	under $10
$$	$10 - $20
$$$	$20 - $30
$$$$	$30 +

FAMILYFUN RATED
★	Fine
★★	Good
★★★	Very Good
★★★★	FamilyFun Recommended

The naturally formed, 40-foot-high Old Man of the Mountain is Franconia Notch's icon, but kids might get an even bigger kick out of the park's aerial tramway.

White Mountains

NEW ENGLAND'S TALLEST peaks emerge from the landscape in this 1,200-square-mile region in north-central New Hampshire. Tiny roadside cabins dot the lawns of area motor courts, and waterfalls bubble through 782,000 acres of forest. But the kid appeal here is not the natural beauty but the just-for-fun places to visit. At Santa's Village, for example, kids can feed real reindeer and walk through a lollipop forest. In Story Land, you can climb into giant footwear and visit with the Old Woman Who Lives in the Shoe. Six rail lines, from steam models to coal-fired pufferbellies, can take you chug-chugging through the region. The Old Man of the Mountain surveys it all from above.

Major attractions clamor for your attention, inviting kids to

THE FamilyFun LIST

MUST-SEE · MUST-SEE

Clark's Trading Post (page 124)

Franconia Notch State Park (page 125)

Mount Washington Auto Road (page 127)

Mount Washington Cog Railway (page 127)

Polly's Pancake Parlor (page 141)

Story Land (page 129)

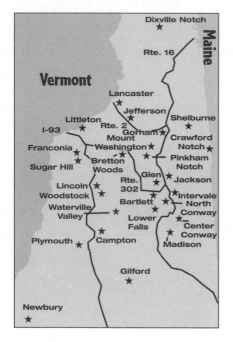

tain House in Jackson, and the Balsams Resort in Dixville Notch.

No matter where you bunk down, the high point of your White Mountains vacation is bound to be a trip to Mount Washington, which you can explore by foot, rail, or car (see page 127).

Closer to the ground, in the 782,000-acre White Mountain National Forest, you'll find 1,200 miles of hiking trails, more than 100 scenic waterfalls, and 23 dramatic notches—including the standouts Franconia, Pinkham, and Crawford. You could spend all day hopping between scenic trails along the Kancamagus National Scenic Byway (Route 112), a route that's almost 35 miles long and connects the east and west sides of the range. At popular Lower Falls, you can slither down the natural water slides in the Swift River. For trail maps and information on kid-friendly hikes, stop at the WMNF Saco Station on the Kancamagus highway in Conway *(603/447-5448)*. Another great resource is the Appalachian Mountain Club, which operates eight high "huts" along the Appalachian Trail where hikers can stay. These rustic lodges have bunk rooms, shared bathrooms, and cold running water; two of them—Zealand Falls and Lonesome Lake—are relatively accessible for families; all provide children's programming. For information, call *(603) 466-2727* or log on to www.outdoors.org

explore granite caves, head to the top of New England's tallest peak, and watch trained bears play basketball in exchange for ice cream.

Vacationers have headed north to the White Mountains for centuries. Inspired by landscape paintings and essays by writers such as Nathaniel Hawthorne, the first summer tourists arrived in the cool mountains in the 1800s. To accommodate them, local entrepreneurs built a carriage road, a cog railway to the top of Mount Washington, and grand hotels that catered to wealthy families. Three of these luxury lodges still welcome vacationers today: the Mount Washington Hotel in Bretton Woods, the less fancy Eagle Moun-

If you opt for a winter vacation, you can choose from nine downhill ski resorts and nine cross-country ski centers, all within a 90-minute drive of one another.

Cultural Adventures

Hartmann Model Railroad and Toy Museum ★★/$

Kids love watching trains wind through tunnels, over bridges, and past miniature train stations and buildings here. The hobby shop is the perfect place to get your own layout on track. *Rtes. 302/16, Intervale; (603) 356-9922*; www.hartmannrr.com

Heritage New Hampshire ★★★/$

Why read about moments in New Hampshire history when you can relive them instead? This multisensory museum, created by the folks from Story Land (see page 129), takes you through a series of dioramas that re-create the sights and sounds of New Hampshire's bygone days. Your adventure spans 350 years, starting in 1634 with a stormy crossing from England. Once you arrive in the New World, you get to explore pioneers' cabins, meet George Washington at a Revolutionary War–era rally complete with fireworks, and ride in

BACKSEAT BEDLAM

In the privacy of your own car, you can laugh as loud as you want or shout out the answers to questions. So don't hold back when you play this game — laugh, yell, or sing your hearts out.

BUZZ is a team effort to try to reach 100 without making a mistake. Take turns counting, beginning with one. Every time you get to a number that's divisible by seven (7, 14, 21, . . .) or has a seven in it (17), say "Buzz" instead of the number. If one person forgets to say "Buzz," everyone has to start over. If this is too hard, say "Buzz" for every number divisible by 5. If you want a real challenge, try Fuzz Buzz. Say "Fuzz" for every number with a three in it or that's divisible by three, and "Buzz" for every number with a seven in it or that's divisible by seven.

a simulated train through Crawford Notch. The exhibits are indoors, so this is a good pick for a rainy day. *Rte. 16, Glen; (603) 383-4186;* www.heritagenh.com

JUST FOR FUN

Appalachian Mountain Club
★★★★/$$
Founded in 1876, this nonprofit environmental organization offers many family programs, from rock-climbing adventures to beginner backpacking trips. It also is the place to turn for some of the area's most distinctive lodging (see page 130). For a schedule of programs, call *(603) 466-2727* or log on to www.out doors.org. Before you undertake a family hike, stop at AMC head-quarters for advice on the best trails for little feet. *Rte. 16, Pinkham Notch; (603) 466-2727;* www.outdoors.org

Clark's Trading Post
FamilyFun ★★★★/$$

MUST-SEE
MUST-SEE

Operated by the Clark family since 1928, the "post" is a meticulously maintained antique village. Here you can buy a hand-dipped ice-cream cone at the Peppermint Saloon, dip your own candles, explore museums of Americana, hop on a water bumper boat, and wander upside down through Merlin's Mystical Mansion. The real reason your kids will want to visit, however, is the bear show. Live ted-

dies shoot hoops, ride on swings, and catch baseballs. Filled with corny jokes (when the bears get a headache, they take bear aspirin), the half-hour shows are a blast. The other highlight is the steam-powered White Mountain Central Railroad. What starts as an ordinary train ride becomes an attempt to flee the legendary Wolf-man, who's been known to boil kids for dinner. The theatrics are probably too much for preschoolers, but older kids have a field day following the conductor's rules for banishing this bad guy: squint your left eye, point to the perpetrator, and shout, "Scram, you old goat!" The range of Wolfman souvenirs available in the gift shop testifies to his popularity. *Rte. 3, Lincoln; (603) 745-8913;* www.clarkstradingpost.com

Conway Scenic Railroad
★★★/$$$$
Of the three excursions offered by this company, the best bet for kids is the 55-minute trip aboard the

Blazing Trails

If you and your kids have always wanted to try a new sport together, **Great Glen Trails** is a great place to learn a number of them—although seasoned athletes will have a great time, too. Surrounded by Mount Washington and the Presidential Range, this 1,110-acre all-season recreational area offers equipment rentals, including children's bike trailers and pull sleds. Instructors can help your family master the 25 miles of groomed trails, or learn to snowshoe, mountain bike, canoe, kayak, and fish. The base lodge has an appealing restaurant that dishes up chili and other favorites, and there's child care, too. In winter, you can ride above the tree line on the Mount Washington Auto Road in a specially designed van, and then drive, snowshoe, or cross-country ski down. *Rte. 16, Pinkham Notch, Gorham; (603) 466-2333;* www.mt-wash ington.com/ggt/index.html

Valley Train, which makes an 11 mile journey through farmlands to Conway, the Moat Brook, and the Saco and Swift rivers. *North Conway; (800) 232-5251; (603) 356-5251;* www.conwayscenic.com

Crawford Notch State Park
★★★★/$$

The history of this 6,000-acre state park may give you the willies, but it's an interesting and hauntingly beautiful stop. Back in 1826, it was home to an inn, operated by the Willey family. One day, a horrible rainstorm pelted the notch, causing an avalanche. The Willey family ran outside to escape danger. Instead, they and two employees were killed by debris. Ironically, the inn, which no longer stands, was spared. To this day, the Willey House Memorial (home to park headquarters) provides a sense of the unpredictable power of the White Mountains. The

path is also an excellent spot for a picnic and hike; ask a ranger for a list of kid-friendly trails. *Rte. 302, Hart's Location; (603) 374-2272.*

Franconia Notch State Park
FamilyFun
★★★★/$$-$$$$

You may already know that this 6,440-acre park as the home of the famous, 40-foot-high profile of the Old Man of the Mountain. But there's a lot more to do here than gaze upon his craggy visage and snap his portrait. Located between the towering Franconia and Kinsman mountain ranges, the park also invites families to take a hike, swim amid the mountains at **Echo Lake**, visit the dramatic, natural gorge known as the Flume (see below), and ride the **Cannon Mountain Aerial Tramway** to the 4,200-foot-high summit. Once there, you can walk along the **Panoramic Rim Trail** and climb an observation tower. Back at the base, you'll find the free **New England Ski Museum.** Bikers can try the eight-mile-long bike path, but be forewarned that some sections are steep. *Rte. 3, Franconia; (603) 823-5563.*

A Hiking Hand

Hike around Mount Washington in style with a **walking stick** your child can design herself. All she'll need is a dry (not green) fallen branch from a hardwood tree, such as maple, ash, or hickory, acrylic paints, and twine.

When you're looking for a stick, the key is to find one that feels comfortable to your child. Generally, it should be about the same height as a ski pole—a little higher than her waist—and easy to grip.

Once you've got the right one, peel away the bark. If it still feels rough, smooth it with some fine sandpaper. Then, your child can paint on bold patterns—or, try putting different colors on paper plates and rolling the stick in them to create a swirled effect. For a personalized touch, she can use twine to tie on feathers and pinecones, or other treasures found along the trail.

Flume Gorge ★★★/$

Part of sensational Franconia Notch State Park, the 800-foot-long Flume just screams "natural wonder." You can take a bus from the visitors' center to within 500 feet of the gorge, then follow the walkway to inspect it at close range. You'll also get an up-close view of glacial boulders, Avalanche Falls, and a 40-foot-deep glacial basin known as the Pool. The Flume and Pool walking loop stretches about two miles and is steep in places. Most folks take about an hour and 15 minutes to complete it; even most 3- and 4-year-olds can handle it. The visitors' center provides a rock-solid orientation film. *Rte. 3, Franconia; (603) 745-8391.*

Fun Family Ski Resorts

For all-season information on Attitash Bear Peak, Black Mountain, Bretton Woods, Cranmore Mountain, Jackson, King Pine, Mountain Club on Loon, and Waterville Valley ski resorts, see pages 137–140.

Ham Ice Arena ★★/$

If rain puts you in a jam, head to Ham. The arena offers year-round public ice-skating and skate rentals; there's also a snack bar. *87 W. Main St., Conway; (603) 447-5886.*

Hobo Railroad ★★/$

Climb aboard a vintage railcar for an 80-minute ride along the Pemigewasset River. Be sure to visit the ice-cream car during your diesel-powered journey, or, better yet, treat yourselves to a Hobo picnic lunch. You'll get a sandwich, chips, a drink, and cookie—in a sack that's tied to a stick, hobo-style. *Rte. 112, Lincoln; (603) 745-2125;* www.hoborr.com

Lost River Reservation
★★★/$

Not for the fainthearted (and best for kids 7 and older), this attraction involves climbing up and down more than 1,000 steps on a three-quarter-mile journey through Lost River Gorge. Those who make the effort will be rewarded with the chance to squeeze through about ten caves and rock ledges, formed when glaciers ruled the world. Along the way, you'll negotiate the Lemon Squeezer, Hall of Ships, and Bear Crawl. If cave-crawling holds no appeal, you can bypass the caves and stick to the boardwalk. There's also a place to pan for minerals, for an added fee. *Rte. 112, N. Woodstock; (603) 745-8031.*

Mount Washington Auto Road
FamilyFun MUST-SEE MUST-SEE ★★★★/$$

Open since 1861, the nation's first tourist attraction invites families to drive (slowly, of course) up an eight-mile auto road to New England's highest point. On your journey, you can listen to a cassette filled with driving tips and fascinating facts about the fabled peak, where 231 mph winds were clocked in 1934.

The peak is the site of the world's worst weather and is overcast more than 300 days a year; during your visit, it's common to encounter foggy conditions, a significant drop in temperature, or a sudden change in weather patterns. Though the driver's eyes will be glued to the sometimes narrow, winding road, young passengers will enjoy breathtaking vistas as the car travels above tree line toward the clouds. On top of the mountain lies mile-high Mount Washington State Park, where you can (weather permitting) take in a view of four states, Canada, and the Atlantic, buy souvenirs, and wander through the Mount Washington Observatory Museum. If you prefer, you can take an escorted van ride to the top. In the winter, you can brave the road in an all-terrain snow coach. Admission to the Auto Road includes a bumper sticker proclaiming that your car climbed Mount Washington. *Rte. 16, Gorham; (603) 466-3988;* www.mountwashington.com/autoroad/

Mount Washington Cog Railway
FamilyFun MUST-SEE MUST-SEE ★★★★/$$$$

The price is steep, but, then again, so is the trip. You can nearly hear the coal-fired train mutter, "I think I can, I think I can," as the cog huffs and puffs to the 6,288-foot summit of Mount Washington. A tourist attraction since 1869, the determined rail line uses one ton of coal and nearly 1,000 gallons of water during each excursion. The three-hour round-trip journey may be a bit much for very young children, but most families are fascinated by the chance to chug up one of the world's steepest tracks and travel above the clouds. At the base lodge, you can watch a movie about this incredible architectural feat, grab some lunch, and explore vintage trains, such as the original coal-fired Peppersass, the first to make its way up the mountain. *Rte. 302, Bretton Woods; (800) 922-8825; (603) 278-5404;* www.thecog.com

Nestlenook Farm
★★★/$-$$$
In winter, this 65-acre farm looks positively idyllic. Red-cheeked skaters glide across Emerald Lake under white, vintage bridges. Horse-drawn Austrian sleighs whisk riders along the Ellis River, stopping along the way so kids can pet the reindeer. When the chill sets in, you can warm up by the bonfire and snack on popcorn dispensed from an antique wagon. If your family wants to spend the night, you can bunk down at nearby Luxury Mountain Getaways (see page 133). *Dinsmore Rd., Jackson Village; (800) 659-9443.*

Pirate's Cove Adventure Golf
★★★/$$
One of the largest of several area miniature-golf courses, this one challenges children with two courses (36

holes total) lined with caves, cascading waterfalls, and dastardly pirates. *Rte. 16, North Conway; (603) 356-8807;* www.piratescove.net

Polar Caves
★★/$
Since 1922, this attraction has enticed children to explore cool (in every way) granite caves formed during the glacial age. Once havens for rumrunners and fugitives on the Underground Railroad, the caves are connected by wooden walkways that allow children to choose easy or challenging routes. On your adventure, you can search for Pharoah's Profile, squeeze through Fat Man's Misery, and negotiate the Lemon Squeeze. You can feed fallow deer here and stop at the Maple Sugar Museum, too. *Rte. 25, Plymouth; (603) 536-1888.*

Santa's Village
★★★/$$
Bah, humbug, if you don't believe in Santa. He's waiting to meet you, even in the heat of summer, at this 50-year-old theme park. Geared to young kids and nostalgic parents, Santa's Village offers the chance to feed real reindeer, receive a diploma from Elf University, and visit Santa's summer home. The park is also home to 12 rides, from Santa's Skyway Sleigh to the Yule Log Flume (geared largely to kids ages 2 to 8). There are picnic and play areas, plus polar-themed jamborees and crafts

workshops for your little elves. As at Story Land, if you buy a ticket at 3 P.M. or later, you can return for a free day during the current season. *Rte. 2, Jefferson; (603) 586-4445;* www.santasvillage.com

The Stables at the Farm by the River ★★★★/$-$$$$

Take the reins at these stables and you'll enjoy beautiful mountain views and scenic trails by the Saco River. Depending on the season, you can ride ponies, donkeys, or draft or saddle horses. In the fall, join wagon rides; in the winter, sleigh rides. *2555 West Side Rd., North Conway; (603) 356-4855.*

★ Story Land
FamilyFun ★★★★/$$

Aside from Mount Washington, this is probably the region's main attraction—and deservedly so. At the 35-acre, meticulously maintained park, young children get to meet Cinderella and ride in her pumpkin coach, greet the Old Woman who Lives in a Shoe, and pose for a picture with Humpty Dumpty. There's plenty for older children, too, including Dr. Geyser's Remarkable Raft Ride, the Bamboo Chutes raft ride, and the Polar Coaster. After you've tried the 16 themed rides, you can play in a water-spray park, travel overseas at A Child's Visit to Other Lands, and take in a show. Story Land wins extra accolades for its reasonable food

prices and generous admissions policy: buy your ticket at 3 P.M. or later and come back any day in the current season for free. *Rte. 16, Glen; (603) 383-4186;* www.storylandnh.com

Whale's Tale Water Park ★★/$$$

Splash-happy kids revel in this watery playground, equipped with a giant wave pool, speed slides, tube rides, and a video arcade. For toddlers, there's Whale Harbor, an activity pool with fountains and slides. Although not nearly as large or up to date as Water Country (see page 155), this place will do the trick for kids who want to get wet in the White Mountains. *Rte. 3, Lincoln; (603) 745-8810.*

FamilyFun TIP

Paddling the Saco

With its typically calm water and riverbanks dotted with campsites, the Saco River is an ideal spot for family canoe trips. **Saco Bound**, a popular outfitter, provides maps for self-guided trips, basic paddling guidelines, a shuttle service, and canoe rentals. The seven-mile journey from headquarters to the Pig Farm is especially popular with families who enjoy stopping at beaches along the way to swim and picnic. The outfitter can also arrange a trip along the Kennebec River at the Forks in Maine. *Rte. 302, Center Conway; (800) 677-7238; (603) 447-2177;* www.sacobound.com

BUNKING DOWN

AMC Huts
★★★★/$$$

If you're looking for a special over-night experience, why not shoot for the sky? The Appalachian Mountain Club operates eight huts high in the mountains that have heavenly views. The huts are scattered across the White Mountains about a day's hike apart and can only be reached on foot. The dorm-style lodging isn't fancy, but the experience is a blast. It gives you the chance to meet hikers from all over the world and break bread together at long, family-style tables filled with home-cooked food. Blankets and pillows are supplied, though you'll need to bring sheets, as well as snacks and water for your hikes. Lonesome Lake and Zealand Falls are most accessible for children, and all eight huts offer children's programming. Reservations are strongly suggested. The price reflects a nonmember rate that includes breakfast and dinner for two adults and two children. Because members qualify for a lodging discount, you may want to consider joining the organization. *(603) 466-2727;* www.outdoors.org

The Balsams Grand Resort Hotel
★★★★/$$$$

Expect to hear a collective gasp when you drive down the steep dip into Dixville Notch and spy this palace on Lake Gloriette. Since 1866, this colossal, French Provincial–style resort has wooed visitors to the state's Great North Woods, directly north of the White Mountains. One of New Hampshire's last remaining "grand hotels," the 215-room resort has provided the royal treatment for luminaries such as Ronald Reagan—and you'll get it, too. Service is paramount, and a staff of up to 400 will cater to your every whim. (If there's a downside to all the attention, it's the guidelines for tipping. These are rather involved, as you'll see when you read the guest handbook.) Considering that it's a historic showpiece, the Balsams is nevertheless very family-friendly. It offers adjoining rooms, children's programs for kids ages 3 to 12, and a children's menu in the fancy dining room. (There's a dress code at dinner, but kids seem to enjoy the chance to put on the Ritz.) Activities include swimming in the outdoor pool and in Lake Gloriette, golf, cross-country skiing on a 60-mile groomed trail network, Alpine ski-

ing at the Balsams Wilderness Ski Area, boating, tennis, snowmobiling, nature programs, bocce, jogging, fishing, and even moviegoing in the resort's 250-seat theater. *Rte. 26, Dixville Notch; (800) 255-0600;* www.thebalsams.com

Buttonwood Inn ★★★/$$

A couple of rooms at this 1800s farmhouse-turned-B&B can accommodate three or four; a two-room family suite fits up to five. There's a large outdoor pool, swings, a family room with a VCR, and a big yard where kids can blow off steam. Infants or children over age 6 are most likely to fit in here. *Mount Surprise Rd., Bartlett; (800) 258-2625; (603) 356-2625.*

Comfort Inn & Suites ★★★/$$

This property offers 82 rooms and suites (with microwaves and refrigerators), an indoor pool, complimentary continental breakfast, and free HBO. What kids like most, however, is the model train that chugs around the lobby. Set back from the street, the hotel is next to the Hobo Railroad and Hobo Hills Adventure Golf Course. *Rte. 112, Lincoln; (888) 589-8112;* www.comfortinn.com

Cranmore Mountain Lodge ★★★/$-$$

This lodge scored with Babe Ruth when he stayed here 50 years ago, and it covers all the bases with families,

POLAR EXPRESS

Each December, the Believe in Books Literacy Foundation re-creates the magical night chronicled in Chris Van Allsburg's picture book, *The Polar Express*. Families board the train in North Conway, then head for the North Pole. There, you are greeted by elves and led to a warming room, where you'll hear the Caldecott Award–winning tale and get to visit with Santa. The round-trip takes about two and a half hours. This fund-raising event is so popular that its sponsors sell tickets via a mail-in lottery system ($$-$$$$). Non-refundable processing fees must be paid several months in advance. It's worth it, though, especially when you see the look of wonder in your child's eyes. *For information, call the Polar Express Information Hotline at (603) 447-3100;* www.polarexpress.org

131

too. The laid-back complex faces the dramatic Presidential Range and includes a country inn, a barn with four guest rooms, and a 40-bed hostel. You and your kids can use the indoor/outdoor heated pool, visit the farm animals, and enjoy mountain biking, fishing, and cross-country skiing. *80 Kearsarge St., North Conway; (800) 526-5502.*

Eagle Mountain House
★★/$$

You'll feel as if you stepped back in time when you visit this historic inn, which has been welcoming travelers since 1879. There's a 280-foot wraparound veranda, the period lobby has an antique phone booth, and the guest rooms have old-fashioned appeal. (They are, however, equipped with cable televisions.) At certain times, such as school vacations, there are kids' programs with

special dinners, movies, and fun and games. There's a game room with a pool table, and building blocks for younger kids. In winter, families can ski out the door onto Jackson's excellent Nordic trail network, or sled and tube. In summer, kids love swimming at Jackson Falls or in the heated outdoor pool. During certain periods, children under 12 eat and stay free. *Carter Notch Rd., Jackson; (800) 966-5779; (603) 383-9111;* www.eaglemt.com

Joe Dodge Lodge
★★/$

Located at AMC headquarters, this rustic lodge offers AMC programs, but, unlike the organization's high huts, is accessible by car. You can reserve family rooms and sign kids up for nature programs that will earn them a Junior Naturalist badge. Lovely trails are just outside your

Taste-testers

While traveling, my husband and I grew tired of our children's requests to visit the same old fast-food places for the latest kids'-meal prize. So we instituted the no-fast-food rule: when our family hits the road on vacation, we only stop at restaurants we can't visit back home. In other words, no nationally franchised restaurants or fast-food joints. The idea is to find some regional flavor. The rule has the added benefit of taking us off the beaten path a bit. As it gets closer to lunch or dinner, we look for one-of-a-kind diners, rib joints, custard shops, and the like. Thanks to this rule, we have eaten Indian fry bread in the Badlands, great sloppy ribs in Tennessee, sensational seafood in South Carolina, and more. Dylan, age 7, and Ryan, 10, enjoy being on the lookout for the quirkiest place and don't even miss the "prize inside" scene.

Lisa Tepp, Milwaukee, Wisconsin

door. The price category listed here reflects the nonmember rate for a private room; meal plans are available. *Rte. 16, Pinkham Notch; (603) 466-2727.*

Luxury Mountain Getaways
★★★/$$-$$$$

This company rents out beautiful town houses, suites, penthouses, and vacation homes to families who want to pamper themselves during their visit to the White Mountains. Many of the units come equipped with gas-log fireplaces, 35-inch televisions, and whirlpool baths. The Nordic properties (particularly Nordic Village and Nordic Highlands) are especially kid-friendly, with a playground, two heated outdoor pools, a heated indoor pool, and a game room. The higher up the rental units, the better the views (and, as you would expect, the higher the prices). *Rte. 16, Jackson; (800) 472-5207;* www.nestlenook.com

Mill House Inn ★★/$$

Offering 96 spacious rooms and suites, this popular hotel has indoor and outdoor heated pools and tennis courts. It's also attached, via enclosed walkway, to the Millfront Marketplace, home to the excellent Innisfree Bookshop and several restaurants. *Rte. 112, Lincoln; (800) 654-6183.*

Mount Washington Hotel & Resort
★★★★/$$$$

Built in 1902 against the backdrop of Mount Washington, this grand hotel is one of only a few remaining from the era when well-heeled families came to cool off in the White Mountains for the summer. The resort is full of charming touches, from the 900-foot wraparound porch to the octagonal dining room adorned with stained-glass windows to the uniformed elevator operator who will whisk you to your floor. Feel free to explore the Gold Room, site of the 1944 Bretton Woods Monetary Conference, which established the World Bank. Though you need to dress up at dinner (Dad needs to wear a jacket), most kids seem to enjoy this formality. The National Historic Landmark hotel opened for the winter season for the first time in 2000. There are indoor and outdoor pools, tennis courts, a patio-level floor of stores where you can buy ice cream and sweets, and a 62-mile trail system for cross-country skiing and snowshoeing. For kids ages 5 to 12, there's a Kids Kamp (extra fee), where they make crafts and enjoy nature programs. You can also stay at the economical sister property, the Bretton Woods Motor Inn, and use the Mount Washington Hotel's facilities for free. **HINT:** If you're on the Modified

A male **moose's antlers** average between four and five feet in width.

American Plan, we suggest eating all your meals in the Mount Washington Hotel. The family restaurants included on the plan are much less impressive, and you don't save money anyway. *Rte. 302, Bretton Woods; (603) 278-3300;* www.mt washington.com

The New England Inn and Resort
★★★/$$-$$$

Located on the picturesque Intervale Resort Loop, this nine-acre inn has welcomed visitors for more than 150 years. Contemporary cottage suites contain a living room with fireplace, a loft for sleeping, and a private, king-size bedroom. The Mount Washington Valley cross-country trail system runs through the resort, plus there's a big outdoor swimming pool, an adjacent children's wading pool, and tennis courts. Tuckerman's Tavern, a casual restaurant on site, serves burritos, burgers, quesadillas, and nachos. *Rte. 16A, Intervale; (800) 826-3466; (603) 356-5541;* www.newengland inn.com

FamilyFun SNACK

Good for You

Make rocket fuel for your kids with a mix of dried apples, pineapples, cranberries, mangoes, cherries, banana chips, and raisins. One cup fulfills two of the recommended five minimum daily servings of fruits and veggies.

The Old Field House
★★★/$$

Whether you want old and comfy or new and contemporary, you'll find it here. Families can get a standard room with two double beds or opt for a deluxe suite in a country lodge complete with fireplace, dining area, kitchen, and pretty breakfast room. (Complimentary breakfast includes muffins, cereals, and fruit.) There's a game room and cozy Fireside Room, where you can play checkers by the fire. Families who like modern town houses can stay at the adjacent Farm, in fully equipped condos that accommodate up to eight guests. The Mt. Washington Valley Ski Touring Network is right outside the door, plus there are two outdoor pools, and on-site laundry facilities. *Rte. 16A (Intervale Resort Loop), Intervale; (800) 444-9245; (603) 356-5478;* www.oldfieldhouse.com

Philbrook Farm Inn
★★★/$$-$$$

At this historic, unpretentious inn (circa 1861) on the Maine border, you can meet the fifth generation of Philbrooks to welcome travelers to the Androscoggin River Valley. You can stay in the main inn (rooms are small, so families of four will probably need two rooms) or in one of the old-time cottages, with claw-footed tubs and screened-in porches. There's no television, air-conditioning, or phones, but there's plenty to do: hiking, swimming in the outdoor pool, playing pool in the game room, cross-country skiing and snowshoeing, and downhill skiing at nearby Maine ski resorts. Dinner and breakfast (included) are provided in the dining room. *881 North Rd., Shelburne; (603) 466-3831.*

Purity Springs Resort
★★★/$$$$

Run by the Hoyt Family for nearly 100 years, this 1,000-acre resort is a nice spot for families who want to escape North Conway's traffic tangle. You can swim, boat, canoe, or fish in 150-acre Purity Lake; take a dip in the indoor pool; and join planned activities in the Clubhouse. In winter, there's cross-country skiing, snowshoeing, and, up the street, Alpine skiing at King Pine Ski Area (owned by the same family). The rate includes meals; the number of meals served per day depends on the season. *Rte. 153, E. Madison; (800) 373-3754.*

The Red Jacket Mountain View
★★★★/$$-$$$

Set on Sunset Hill alongside Route 16, this resort provides a classy but comfortable family vacation. In peak periods, there are Mountain Magic activity programs for children ages 4 and up. Depending on the season, you can enjoy sledding on the hill out front, swimming in indoor and outdoor pools, sleigh rides, and themed programs from poolside

cookouts to wacky Olympics. There's also a playhouse and a game room with video arcade. The rooms are spacious, especially if you opt for a loft (parents get a king-size bed, and kids get an upstairs loft room with two twins) or a two-bedroom town house. Story Land and other packages are offered. *Rte. 16, North Conway; (800) R-JACKET;* www.red jacketresorts.com

Storybook Inn
★★/$$

Much larger than it appears from the street, this 100-acre resort motel includes several buildings with family-size rooms, heated outdoor and indoor pools, a playground, wooded picnic areas, and a game room. It's also very convenient to Story Land. *Rtes. 16 and 302, Glen; (603) 383-6800.*

Whitney's Inn
★★★/$$-$$$

Based near Black Mountain Ski Area, this 1840s-era inn offers several lodging options (inn rooms, suites, cottages) and delicious meals (including children's favorites) by the fireplace in the dining room. Activities include hiking, cross-country and downhill skiing, sledding, sleigh rides, lawn games, and swimming in the outdoor pool or private pond. There are cookouts in summer and hot cider by the fire in winter. *Rte. 16B, Jackson; (800) 677-5737; (603) 383-8916.*

135

GOOD EATS

Brandli's ★/$-$$

Nestled in the Settlers' Green O.V.P. outlet mall, this is a nice, clean place to eat if you don't want sit-down service. Order pizza, hot heroes, baked ziti, and chef's salads at the counter, pick a table, and enjoy. The shopping center's playground is right outside the restaurant. *Rte. 16, Settlers' Green O.V.P., North Conway; (603) 356-7878.*

Common Man ★★★★/$$$

As much a gathering place as a restaurant, this eatery includes a pub with stone fireplace, where folks listen to live music and meet to play "snag." (Similar to ringtoss, the game involves hurling a ring attached to a rope toward a hook.) The food is as good as the atmosphere. Young diners can choose pasta and hot dogs from the kids' menu or order a half-portion of many adult entrées. *Exit 32 off I-93, Lincoln; (603) 745-DINE; www.thecman.com*

Fabyan's Station ★/$$

Just down the street from the grand Mount Washington Hotel, this restaurant capitalizes on the area's train theme by offering a Little Engineer's Menu. Kids can get a Caboose (hot dog platter), Brakeman (hamburger), and Choo-Choo Charlie (chicken fingers) at this former train station. Parents can dine on burgers and pub-style entrées. *Rte. 302, Bretton Woods; (603) 278-2222.*

Horsefeathers ★★/$$

Though their slogan, "the greatest eatery in the known universe," may be a slight exaggeration, there's no doubt that everyone in your family will find something to like here. The kids' menu features all the classics. For adults, there's pork tenderloin with spicy red beans, apple-smoked bacon-cheddar burgers, and white chocolate and Grand Marnier mousse. *Rte. 16/Main St., North Conway; (603) 356-6862.*

Italian Oasis ★★/$$

While exploring lovely Littleton, stop at this friendly restaurant, which has a deck overlooking the village. You can choose from the Mt. Washington ("the highest pizza in the northeast"), nachos, ribs, pasta dishes, burgers, seafood, and even a float made with homemade root beer. *Parker's Marketplace, 106 Main St., Littleton; (603) 444-6995.*

Mad River Tavern ★★/$$

Families who are visiting Waterville Valley will appreciate this laid-back restaurant, which dishes out delicious lunches and dinners at rea-

FUN FAMILY SKI RESORTS

For a complete list of the state's ski areas, call Ski New Hampshire at *800-88-SKI-NH;* www.skinh.com

Attitash Bear Peak
★★★/$$$$

This resort attracts families who want to ski and snowboard (check out the new 500-foot in-ground half-pipe) in one of the Mount Washington Valley's hot spots. Attitash has ski-in/ski-out accommodations in 143 rooms at the **Grand Summit Resort Hotel & Conference Center**, plus Snowcat grooming rides, cross-country skiing through Bear Notch Ski Touring Center, snowshoe tours, and Kids' Night Out pizza and movie parties for children 5 to 12. [280 skiable acres; 60 trails (20 percent beginner, 47 percent intermediate, 33 percent advanced); 12 lifts, including two high-speed quads; 97 percent snowmaking coverage. Family facilities: Child care for children 6 months to 6 years; Tiny Turns programs for skiers 3 to 5; Perfect Kids clinics for children 4 to 6; Adventure Kids programs for children 7 to 12; Learn-to-Ski and Learn-to-Ride programs; Family Fun Zone mini terrain park for those who want to improve their ski and snowboard techniques.] In the summer, the resort converts to a warm-weather playground with an Alpine slide and more. *Route 302, Bartlett; (603) 374-0946 (snow phone); (800) 223-SNOW; (888) 554-2900 (lodging);* www.attitash.com

Black Mountain
★★★/$$$$

Popular with families who want to ski and snowboard in a low-key atmosphere, Black Mountain features affordable lift tickets and a special Family Passport that allows two parents and two kids to ski for one low price. Lodging options include **Whitneys' Inn** *(800/677-5737),* a short walk from the base lodge. [132 skiable acres; 40 trails (33 percent beginner, 33 percent intermediate, 33 percent advanced); 4 lifts; 98 percent snowmaking coverage. Family facilities: Child care for children ages 6 months to 5 years; Tots clinics for children 3 to 6; Black Mountain Kids programs for children ages 6 to 12.]

continued on next page

5 Mile Circuit Rd., Rte. 16B, Jackson; (603) 383-4490 (general); (800) 475-4669 (snow phone); (800) 698-4490 (reservations); www.black mt.com

Bretton Woods Mountain Resort
★★★/$$$$

Long a haven for beginners, Bretton Woods now has West Mountain (25 new trails) to appeal to experienced skiers and snowboarders as well. All runs lead to one base lodge; shuttle service takes you to the Mount Washington Hotel & Resort for cross-country skiing, snowshoeing, and horse-drawn sleigh rides. [330 skiable acres; 62 trails (32 percent beginner, 44 percent intermediate, 24 percent advanced); 6 lifts, including a detachable quad; 95 percent snowmaking coverage. Family facilities: Child care for children ages 2 months to 5 years; Babes in the Woods programs for children 3 to 5; Hobbit Ski and Snowboard School for children 4 to 12.] Family weeks include entertainment and activities (such as après-ski parties with magicians, sing-alongs, and storytelling) for children 4 to 12. The resort runs through the summer, too, with programs for families. *Rte. 302, Bretton Woods; (603) 278-3300; (603) 278-3333 (snow phone); (800) 258-0330 (lodging);* www. brettonwoods.com

Cranmore Mountain Resort
★★★/$$$$

Cranmore offers affordable lift tickets and packages, and a friendly environment where you can ski, snowboard, ice-skate, and tube. [192 skiable acres; 34 trails (36 percent beginner, 44 percent intermediate, 19 percent advanced); 9 lifts, including an express quad; 100 percent snowmaking coverage. Child care for children from 6 months to 6 years and Snowsports School for children 4 and up;] The resort also has indoor tennis courts, a pool, and climbing wall. *Skimobile Rd., North Conway; (603) 356-5543; (800) SUN-N-SKI (lodging); (603) 356-7070 (snow phone);* www.cranmore.com

Gunstock Recreation Area
★★★/$$$

Whatever the season, there's lots to do at this 2,000-acre recreation area owned by Belkap County. In winter, you can ski, snowboard, and glide on an inner tube down the mountains. In warmer weather, you can camp (there are sites and cabins to rent on 420 acres), take a guided horseback trip, hike, fish, and stroll along the Wetlands Boardwalk. At the Skate Park and Mountain Board Center, you can try out a mountain board (a snowboard with all-terrain tires) or in-line skates. Rental prices are reasonable. Given the many special events throughout the year, you may want to call ahead to see what's scheduled during your vacation. *Rte. 11A, Gilford* (about 20 miles southeast of Compton); *(800) GUNSTOCK; (603) 293-4341.*

Jackson Ski Touring Foundation
★★★★/$$

With about 55 miles of beautifully groomed trails for cross-country skiing, this trail network is rated number one in the East by top ski magazines, and is considered among the world's best. Situated in picturesque Jackson, the village is a haven for Nordic skiers who consider the sport a way of life. Folks travel to the market on skis. They also ski between the 18 inns and lodges by and near the trail system, stopping for hearty bowls of soup along the way. You need to join the non-profit foundation to use the trail system, but the fee is reasonable (especially compared to Alpine ski rates). The benefits include free clinics, trail maps, and special programs. Lessons are also available. Avid skiers may want to build a trip around the trail network. *Main St., Rte. 16A, Jackson Village; (800) XC-SNOWS; (603) 383-9355;* www.jacksonxc.org

King Pine Ski Area
★★★/$$$$

This small, affordable ski area (which has summer programs as well) offers downhill and cross-country skiing, snowboarding, tubing, ice-skating, and snowshoeing. The Hoyts run the nearby Purity Spring Resort, featuring an indoor pool, slope-side rooms, and midweek packages. [35 skiable acres; 17 trails (50 percent beginner, 30 percent intermediate, 20 percent expert); 6 lifts, including two triples; 100 percent snowmaking coverage. Family facilities: Child care; sports clinics for children 4 to 7; junior programs for kids 7 to 12; overnight youth ski camps for children 8 to 16, including lodging, meals, and instruction.] Two ski for the price of one on nonholiday Tuesdays. *Rte. 153, East Madison; (800) FREE-SKI (lodging); (603) 367-8896 (snow phone);* www.king pine.com

Mount Sunapee Resort
★★★/$$-$$$$

Operated by Vermont's Okemo Mountain Resort, this family-oriented ski area (kids 6 and under ski free) offers a variety of summer activities. Take a superquad chairlift to Mt. Sunapee's 2,700-foot-high summit, then walk a half mile to beautiful Lake Solitude. *Rte. 103, Newbury* (about 35 miles southwest of Plymouth); *(603) 763-2356;* www.mtsunapee.com

Loon Mountain
★★★★/$$$$

New Hampshire's most visited ski area combines a convenient location (directly off the interstate, 2 hours from Boston), a beautiful setting in the western White Mountains, and

continued on next page

a variety of activities. In winter, you can ski, snowboard, snowshoe, cross-country ski, ice skate, or tube. In summer, there's horseback riding, mountain biking, and tennis. The Octagon and Governor Adams base lodges are connected by a steam train. The Mountain Club offers slopeside condominium-style units, indoor and outdoor pools, and a kid-friendly restaurant. 275 skiable acres; 44 trails (20 percent beginner, 62 percent intermediate, 16 percent advanced); 8 lifts; 99 percent snowmaking coverage. There's childcare for ages 6 weeks to 6 years and lessons for kids age 3 and up. *Exit 32, off I-93, Lincoln. (800) 229-LOON general; (800) 227-4191 (lodging); (603) 745-8100 (snow phone);* www.loonmtn.com

Waterville Valley
★★★★/$$$$

Set on 500 acres of private land, this secluded family-friendly playland offers downhill and cross-country skiing, snowboarding, skating, tubing, horse-drawn sleigh rides, snow cats, and ski bikes. Accommodations include 2,500 beds in a variety of settings including inns, condominiums, and lodges. There are activities in the Town Square and several kid-friendly restaurants. [255 skiable acres; 52 trails (20 percent beginner, 60 percent intermediate, 20 percent advanced); 11 lifts, including 2 detachable high-speed quads; 100 percent snowmaking coverage. Family facilities: Child care for kids 6 months to 4 years; sports clinics for kids 3 and up; Winter Unlimited Family Fun weeks include storytelling, snowman contests, fireworks, and special rental prices.] In the summer, all-inclusive summer packages are also available. *Ski Area Rd., Waterville Valley; (603) 236-8311; (603) 236-4144 (snow phone); (800) 468-2553 (reservations);* www.waterville.com

For cross-country ski fans:
Ski Inn

Based in Intervale, the Mount Washington Valley Ski Touring Association—a nonprofit group of eight businesses and 49 landowners—invites the public to cross-country ski on more than 40 miles of trails that connect to several family-friendly inns, including the Buttonwood Inn, the New England Inn, and the Old Field House. Special events include the Annual Chocolate Festival, where families ski from inn to inn, indulging in rich chocolate creations. *For more information, call (603) 356-9920;* www.crosscountryskinh.com

sonable prices. Kids can feast on pita pizza and mini chopped sirloin, while parents dine on pasta, chicken, and fish. *Rte. 49, Campton; (603) 726-4290.*

Polly's Pancake Parlor
FamilyFun ★★★★/$-$$

MUST-SEE

Food critics have declared that Polly's serves "the best pancakes in America," and few would deny the claim. In this former 1830s carriage shed, decorated with antique tools and family photos, you can feast on light, fluffy buckwheat, cornmeal, oatmeal buttermilk, and whole-wheat pancakes. All are made from scratch and can be dressed up with such items as blueberries, walnuts, or coconut. A family business since 1899, Polly's is adamant about using the best ingredients, including maple syrup they make themselves. You can even order a Maple Hurricane Sundae here. *Hildex Farm, Rte. 117, Sugar Hill; (603) 823-5575;* www.pollyspancakeparlor.com

Red Fox Pub & Restaurant
★★/$$

Located across from the Jackson Ski Touring Center, this restaurant has a reasonably priced Sunday morning breakfast buffet that includes jazz music, along with country-baked ham, Belgian waffles, fresh fruit, muffins, and custom-made omelettes. Weekday meals, ranging from Reubens to chicken potpie, are terrific, too. Kids will find hot dogs, spaghetti, and kiddie kocktails here, plus a children's playroom they can visit when the mood strikes. *Rte. 16A, Jackson Village; (603) 383 6659;* www.redfoxpub.com

Red Parka Pub
★★/$$

Decorated with antique skis, this restaurant is as cozy as a red parka. The friendly staff dishes up burgers and pizza for kids, provides pictures to color, and will even remove the skin from chicken dishes. *Rtes. 16 and 302, Glen; (603) 383-4344.*

FamilyFun READER'S TIP

Time in a Bottle

Our kids (Kiersten, 12, Nicolai, 10, Jarin, 4, and Micah, 1) love to collect rocks, so whenever we go someplace special, we choose one to mark the trip. We write on them—where we went, the date, the initials of those who were there, —and save them in glass jars. We love looking at the rocks and remembering the places we've been and the people who were with us. For instance, one rock says "Horseback Riding, September 27, 1997" and includes the names of family members and the horses we rode. Memories of Sunday drives, camping trips, fairs, and family vacations are all recorded and "bottled."

Ron and Marci Clawson, Sandy, Utah

141

Scarecrow Pub ★★★/$$

Crows don't stand a chance in this friendly pub. It's decorated with hundreds of scarecrows, many given to the owners by faithful customers. The atmosphere is relaxed, the staff is very friendly, and the fare is reasonably priced. You'll find everything from baked ziti and succulent burgers to potato skins and spaghetti. **NOTE:** No credit cards accepted. *Rte. 16, Intervale; (603) 356-2287.*

Sunny Day Diner
★★★/$$

It's always sunny in this diner, where toy monkeys hang from the ceiling, the big jukebox plays favorite tunes, and the chef will gladly make Mickey Mouse–shaped pancakes. The owners are culinary-school graduates, so baked goods are made from scratch, and since specials are based on "whims and availabilities," you never know what you'll get. Chances are, you can count on fancy scrambled eggs, hot meatball sandwiches, sweet pecan rolls, and homemade ice cream. *Rte. 3, Lincoln; (603) 745-4833.*

Whitney's ★★/$$-$$$

This terrific, family-oriented inn is a great place to eat, even if you don't stay overnight. The menu includes kids' classics, plus New England crab cakes, roast turkey, and stuffed veal. Every Friday night, there's a pasta and salad bar. *Rte. 16B, Jackson; (603) 383-8916.*

Woodstock Station
★★★/$$

One of the best family restaurants in the White Mountains features more than 40 items that are all under $10. Housed in a former train station (big families can even eat in the ticket booth), Woodstock Station doesn't leave anyone—or anything—out. The 148 items include generous portions of Mexican, Italian, American, and Chinese fare, which you can enjoy on the outdoor patio. The kids' train-themed activity menu offers Better-Than-Mom's Meat Loaf, Hot Dog Wellington (a wiener baked with cheese in a puff pastry), and kid-size pizzas. *Rte. 3, N. Woodstock; (603) 745-3951.*

SOUVENIR HUNTING

Christie's Maple Farm

Leif the Elf welcomes families to this scenic outpost, east of Santa's Village. Maple lovers can taste test homemade syrups and creams and tour the maple museum. You can also visit the sugarhouse, where the sap of 10,000 taps is turned into savory syrups. These, of course, are for sale in the gift shop. *Rte. 2, Lancaster; (800) 788-2118.*

Chutter General Store

The sweetest place to shop in the White Mountains has made it into the *Guinness Book of World Records.* Here, more than 600 jars of candy line a 111-foot-long counter, creating the World's Longest Continuous Candy Counter. Treats include cow tails (25 cents), pucker suckers (25 cents), reindeer corn (35 cents), and root beer jelly beans. *43 Main St., Littleton; (603) 444-5787.* In North Conway, **Zeb's General Store** has a 67-foot-long candy counter; *Rte. 16; (603) 356-9294.*

Village Bookstore

This bookstore is the second-best reason (after Chutter's) to visit the lovely hamlet of Littleton. The bottom floor of the 9,000-square-foot emporium is completely devoted to kids; you'll find everything from marionettes to squeaking rocks here. Upstairs, the extensive books section stocks all the Appalachian Mountain Club guides, children's picture books about New Hampshire, and specialized travel books, including *Best Hikes with Children in Vermont, New Hampshire and Maine* (The Mountaineers, $13). *81 Main St., Littleton; (800) 640-WORD.*

Spend a week on Squam Lake with no TV, just swimming, fishing, and kicking back. You can rent *On Golden Pond* (it was filmed here) when you get home.

The Lakes and Seacoast Region

LAKE WINNIPESAUKEE, often translated from the Native American as "Smile of the Great Spirit," is big in every way imaginable. New Hampshire's largest lake measures 28 by 13 miles and contains 274 islands. The anchor of the Lakes Region, "Winnie" offers a ton of fun, from boat rides and water slides to arcades, miniature-golf courses, and go-cart tracks.

Nature-loving families will also enjoy the superb Squam Lakes Natural Science Center and its wildlife tours. Also popular is Lake Ossipee, where families can rent a cottage and fish, swim, and canoe for the week. Though widely regarded as a summer destination, the Lakes Region is also an excellent winter getaway. It boasts great family skiing at the county-owned Gunstock recreation area (see "Fun Family Ski Resorts," page 137), as well as ice-skating, tubing, and snowshoeing.

Weirs Beach may seem a bit frayed, but kids can't get enough of its two water slide parks, gargantuan arcade, go-cart track, popular sandy beach, boardwalk, and one of the state's only drive-in movie theaters.

THE FamilyFun LIST

MUST-SEE · MUST-SEE

Squam Lakes Natural Science Center (page 148)

Strawbery Banke Museum (page 155)

Water Country (page 155)

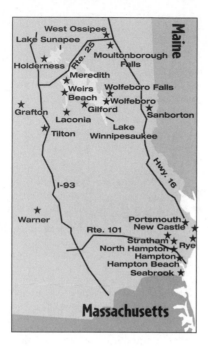

Families who are looking for a bit more polish will find it just a few miles north in Meredith. In this lakeside resort town, you can munch on fried clams by the waterfront and stay in some of the region's swankier hotels, such as the lovely Inn at Mill Falls, just across the street from the lake.

In the bygone hamlet of Moultonborough, you'll find the Old Country Store with its scent of dill pickles soaking in a barrel. You can also travel to a hilltop mansion known as Castle in the Clouds. Wolfeboro, the "oldest summer resort in America" has welcomed travelers since 1763. Here you can tour the lake on *Millie B*, a Gatsby-

style mahogany and chrome speedboat (see page 153) and visit Bailey's, a landmark restaurant for a sundae topped with homemade hot fudge sauce (see page 152).

The Lakes Region teems with special events, particularly in summer. For a list of family-oriented theatrical productions and town concerts, as well as the names of outfitters who rent boats, pick up a copy of *The Laker* (*800/339-5257;* www.thelaker.com), a free publication that's widely available at area attractions.

As if the beautiful lakes weren't enough, New Hampshire has 18 miles of seashore as well, packed with family-oriented beaches and parks; it's also home to New Hampshire's liveliest city, Portsmouth.

Though hard to believe now, parts of this 380-year-old port town were once so run-down that they were slated for demolition. Today, the city is one of the state's top tourist destinations, thanks to its museums (including an excellent children's museum), picturesque harbor, and bustling Market Square, the city's commercial center since the 1700s, when Portsmouth was a major shipbuilding port. For a living history adventure, wander along the Black Heritage Trail. Lined with 24 churches, living quarters, workplaces, and even auction sites, this route offers a look at the life of African Americans during Portsmouth's era of slavery. And you won't want to miss Strawbery Bank (Portsmouth's original name), where you can visit homes that date back to 1690 and chat with costumed role players.

Though it's a treat to visit Portsmouth any time of year, it's particularly fun in summer. The city's recreational jewel is Prescott Park, host to the Prescott Park Arts Festival. This summerlong celebration features children's theater, toe-tapping concerts, and family entertainers. (For more information, log on to www.artfest.org) During a summer vacation, you might also take in a children's show at the Seacoast Repertory Theatre (125 Bow St.; 603/433-4472; www. seacoastrep.org), or sail out to the Isles of Shoals. These nine rocky islands—five of which are in Maine, four in New Hampshire—are havens for seabirds.

Portsmouth is also an excellent base from which to visit the Seacoast's other key attractions, including Water Country and Rye's Seacoast Science Center at Odiorne State Park. For a memorable road trip along the shore, drive along Route 1B to the one-square-mile island of New Castle. This lovely community is home to Fort Constitution, Fort Stark, New Castle Lighthouse, and the Great Island Common, a seaside park with a very pretty beach. (*For information, contact the New Castle Town Hall, 49 Main St.; 603/431-6710.*) After encir-

Vacation Rewards

Set up a Souvenir Budget

FamilyFun readers, the Howells of Morgan Hill, California, aren't the only ones who swear by giving their two kids a set amount of money for vacation souvenirs and letting the kids choose how to spend it. Putting them in charge has not only eliminated those grating requests to Mom and Dad, but has also put the kids in touch with how much things cost. "They're more inclined to pinch pennies," mom Cindy says, "when it's their pennies."

Institute a Good Deed Bank

A trip to see Mickey Mouse inspired the Mohan family of Eden Prairie, Minnesota, to start a Good Deed Bank. "We knew that after paying for the trip we would have little money left for extras at the park," recalls Marci Mohan. So she had her kids decorate a coffee-can bank to look like Mickey Mouse. In the weeks leading up to the trip, whenever Hannah, age 9, or Dylan, 6, got caught doing something helpful, their parents dropped a coin in the bank. The kids' good deeds earned them a chunk of change to spend on vacation. And, says Marci, "We had a more considerate household."

cling the island, cross the bridge into Rye and take a break at the Ice House (*112 Wentworth Rd.; 603/431-3086*), a casual, seasonal spot where you can feast on fried clams. Up ahead, Route 1B intersects with Route 1A, which you'll follow through Rye and North Hampton, past majestic mansions that overlook the crashing surf. You'll know immediately when you arrive at Hampton Beach, on the southern end of New Hampshire's seacoast. It seems as if everyone from Massachusetts has come to cruise along Ocean Boulevard, munch on fried dough (there are 20 flavors at Blink's, including chocolate with jimmies), drop some change at one of the world's biggest arcades, and soak up the sun at the four-and-a-half-mile-long sandy beach.

The Lakes

CULTURAL ADVENTURES

Mount Kearsage Indian Museum ★★★/$

Delve into Native American history and culture at this surprise of a museum. The exhibit hall is filled with hundreds of beautiful handmade items, from moose hair and porcupine embroidery to baskets to canoes. Outside, you can roam through Medicine Woods, which contains 100 plants that Native Americans used for medicine, food, and building materials. Bring a picnic to enjoy at the 100-acre site, located in a pretty village with views of Mount Kearsage. Have fun crawling into the pit house, sweat lodge, and birch-bark wigwam. *Kearsage Mountain Rd., Warner; (603) 456-2600;* www.indianmuseum.org

Sandy Point Discovery Center ★★/Free

New Hampshire's Great Bay Estuary is one of only 25 National Estuarine Research Reserves in the country, and the discovery center is the place to explore this treasure. Learn about the natural history of estuaries, handle crabs in the touch tank, climb into a dry-docked lobster boat, and walk on a boardwalk through freshwater wetlands and salt marsh. *89 Depot Rd., Stratham; (603) 778-0015.*

MUST-SEE FamilyFun MUST-SEE Squam Lakes Natural Science Center ★★★★/$

Your appreciation of New Hampshire's natural wonders will increase exponentially after a visit to this top-notch center, which offers many special programs for families. For starters, walk along the Gephart Exhibit Trail, a three-quarter-mile boardwalk that leads you into the woods to meet bears, hawks, otters, foxes, and more. The roomy enclosures look so real that you'll almost think you happened upon these animals in the woods. Kids will love the Gordon Children's Center, where they can climb on a giant spiderweb, burrow inside a two-story tree, and play pollination tic-tac-toe. In summer, naturalists present trailside talks. You also can stroll around beautiful Kirkwood Gardens (designed to attract butterflies and hummingbirds). *Rte. 113, Holderness; (603) 968-7194; www.nhnature.org*

JUST FOR FUN

Fun Family Ski Resorts

For all-season information on Gunstock, see pages 138–139.

Funspot ★★★/$-$$$$

This aptly named, indoor entertainment complex features more than 500 token-operated games (from virtual motorcycle races to air hockey), plus a 20-lane bowling center, kiddie bumper cars, a miniature-golf course dotted with New Hampshire landmarks, and a driving range. This is more than a place for kids; you'll see plenty of parents perfecting their Skee-Ball skills. *Rte. 3, Weirs Beach; (603) 366-4377;* www.funspotnh.com

Klickety-Klack Model Railroad ★/$

The tiny resort town of Wolfeboro is filled with 150 locomotives, 400 freight cars, and 20 bridges—all within this museum. Kids can ring a trolley bell and church bells, make smoke waft from a factory chimney, blast a ship's horn, make figure skaters glide on ice, and operate two Thomas the Tank Engine trains. This model railroad empire also contains a miniature circus, zoo, granite quarry, and beaches. *8 Elm St., Wolfeboro Falls; (603) 569-5384.*

Ruggles Mine ★★★★/$$

Kids will have a field day at this mine, where they can walk through

Mail Sail

Travel aboard the **M/V** *Sophie C* **mail boat** as it delivers letters to residents on Lake Winnipesaukee's many islands. The route takes about two hours, but time flies because of all the stops. The same company also offers a two-and-a-half-hour trip aboard the 230-foot-long M/S *Mount Washington*, but that journey is too long for many kids. If you have your heart set on a trip on this famous three-decked boat, consider a one-way ticket, which could cut the length of your journey in half; the catch to this is that you need someone to pick you up. Home port for both boats is *Weirs Beach; (888) THE-MOUNT; (603) 366-5531.*

caves and tunnels with a pick and chip off pieces of mica, feldspar, and beryl. Visitors have discovered more than 150 minerals here (finders keepers), so bring a collection sack, or rent one along with tools and flashlights. The 200-year-old mine sits atop Isinglass Mountain. *To get there, take the auto road to the summit. Off Rte. 4, Grafton; (603) 523-4275; www.rugglesmine.com*

Male and female **loons** share the duty of incubating eggs.

Surf Coaster ★★/$$$

One of the family draws of Weirs Beach, this water park has a big wave pool, Crazy River raft ride, kiddie slides, and the totally tubular Twin Boomerangs (whoosh through a Plexiglas tube). There's a sundeck and snack bar, too. *Rte. 11B, Weirs Beach; (603) 366-5600.* (At the entrance to Weirs Beach, you'll find the **Weirs Beach Waterslide**, where slides run through and around a smoldering volcano. Kids have several choices, some more daring than others. *Rte. 3, Weirs Beach; 603/366-5161.*)

Winnipesaukee Scenic Railroad ★★★/$

Rail fans can choose between one-hour (departing from Weirs Beach) and two-hour (departing from Meredith) journeys along Lake Winnipesaukee. Either way, you'll travel in restored 1920s or 1930s railcars equipped with the all-important Ice Cream Parlor Car. For extra fun, get a Hobo Picnic lunch: a sandwich, chips, drink, and a cookie, in a sack that's tied to a stick. Dinner trains feature scrumptious roast turkey from Hart's Turkey Farm Restaurant (see page 152). *For information, call (603) 745-2135; www.hoborr.com*

BUNKING DOWN

B. Mae's Resort Inn & Suites ★★★/$$

This terrific family spot features appealing suites and standard rooms for families who want a relaxing getaway near Lake Winnipesaukee. It's a short walk on a nature trail to a lakefront beach. You can swim in indoor or outdoor pools, or check out the action at Weirs Beach, just a few miles away. The modern, air-conditioned rooms have cable TV and private decks or patios; the suites have contemporary kitchens and dining areas. *Rte. 11 at 11B, Gilford; (800) 458-3977; (603) 293-7526.*

Best Western Seabrook Inn ★★/$-$$

It's not the Ritz, but who cares when there are so many activities for kids? There's an on-site petting zoo, pony rides, a Moon Bounce, heated outdoor pools with a frog slide (slither down the tongue) and water slide, and even a mini Ferris wheel. All of these attractions—plus continental breakfast—are included in the low rate. You can get standard motel rooms, or suites with full-size kitchens. A free trolley takes you to Hampton Beach. *Corner of Stard Rd. and Rte. 107, Seabrook; (603) 474-3078;* www.bestwestern.com

Inn at Mill Falls ★★★/$$$

One of a trio of nearby inns collectively called the Inns at Mill Falls, this property is a special, slightly extravagant place for families to stay. Located directly across the street from Lake Winnipesaukee, the inn has spacious rooms with a queen-size bed and pullout sofa, a small indoor pool, and a beautiful lobby area with a welcoming fireplace. If you want to splurge even more, cross the street to the Inn at Bay Point for big suites and a location directly on the lake. Winter is an especially fun time to visit, as guests can borrow ice skates, try ice fishing, take a horse and wagon ride, and enjoy hot chocolate by the bonfire. *Rtes. 3 and 25, Meredith; (800) 622-MILL; (603) 279-7006;* www.millfalls.com

The Margate ★★★/$$-$$$

Though it's one of the fancier places in the Lakes Region, you'll feel perfectly comfortable bringing the kids here. The on-site restaurant has a kids' menu, plus there are lovely indoor and outdoor pools, and a private, 400-foot-long white-sand beach. You can opt for standard rooms or two-room units, with or without lake views. *76 Lake St., Laconia; (800) 396-3769; (603) 524-5210.*

Steele Hill Resorts ★★/$$

This family-oriented resort has one- and two-bedroom suites, two indoor pools, two outdoor pools, a game room, a kid-friendly restaurant, and an activities director who schedules ice-cream parties and scavenger hunts to make sure kids have a blast during their stay. Though it's near Lakes Region attractions, the facility has so much on-site recreation (including golf, ice-skating, cross-country skiing, nature walks, and snowshoeing), you may want to stay put. *516 Steele Rd., Sanbornton; (800) 284-6985; (603) 524-0500.*

- - - - - - - - - - - - - - - - - - - -

Belle of the Lake

You'll think you've wandered into a Huck Finn adventure when you board the old-time paddle-wheel *Winnipesaukee Belle*, which tools across Lake Winnipesaukee on a 90-minute trip. Depending on who the captain is, you might sail past serpent-shaped Rattlesnake Island or search for wildlife in Alton Bay. The captain welcomes visitors at his station in the center of the boat. You can get snacks and drinks aboard, too. *Town Docks, Wolfeboro; (603) 569-3016.*

GOOD EATS

Bailey's ★★/$-$$

Slide into an old wooden booth and get set for home-grown family fare at this landmark, operated by the Bailey family for more than 60 years. You'll find everything from burgers and clubs to fresh fish and prime rib, plus an extensive kids' menu. The real claim to fame, however, is the home-made hot fudge sauce that tops delectable sundaes. Maybe you should eat dessert first? *286 S. Main St. (Rte. 28), Wolfeboro; (603) 569-3662.*

CAMP ★★★★/$$

Everyone's a happy camper at this fun-loving restaurant, where the inspired menu features s'mores, complete with flaming marshmallows. A rustic lodge, CAMP's decor includes a mounted moose head, camp gear hanging from the rafters, and black-and-white photos of fishermen and kids lazing on the dock. CAMP "counselors" enthusiastical-

ly deliver fried green tomatoes, camp crackers (cheese-topped flatbread on a long narrow wood tray), and "fun guy" camper sandwiches. Kids can order pizza and "bsghetti" off their menu or half-size portions of adult entrées. *Chase House Inn, Meredith; (603) 279-3003.*

Hart's Turkey Farm Restaurant and Gift Shop ★★★★/$$

Head over to this family-owned restaurant for a home-cooked meal featuring all of your Thanksgiving favorites. (On a busy day, the Hart family dishes up a ton of turkey, 40 gallons of gravy, and 1,000 pounds of potatoes.) The extensive menu includes turkey pie, turkey nuggets, turkey livers, and turkey tempura, plus dozens of seafood, beef, and stir-fry dishes. Along with their own menu, kids get crayons, coloring sheets, and a friendly greeting from a staff that specializes in catering to young diners. *Rtes. 3 and 104, Meredith; (603) 279-6212.*

Meredith Bay Bakery & Café ★/$

Pleasant and affordable, this restaurant offers kid-size breakfasts and a lunch menu including American chop suey, PB&J, and grilled cheese. We bet you won't be able to resist the eye-popping bakery goodies, including big cinnamon rolls, cookies, and homemade pie. *7 Main St., Meredith; (603) 279-2279.*

Tilt'n Diner ★★★/$$

This stainless steel diner is an excellent place to fuel up before that shopping expedition at the nearby Lakes Region Factory Stores. Play your cards right, and the waitresses may even stop by for a game of tic-tac-toe. As the jukebox plays, kids can munch on fish-and-chips, macaroni and cheese, hot dogs, and chicken tenders. You can try the White Mountain meat loaf, served in a mountain of mashed potatoes. For your drink, there's Cherry Coke; for dessert, warm slices of Toll House Pie. You can buy vintage comic books here, too. *61 Laconia Rd., Tilton; (603) 286-2204.*

Town Docks ★★★★/$

Don't squander those splendid summer nights by eating indoors. You can order takeout hot dogs and ice cream from the small snack shack or step into the main restaurant for an expanded menu of chowder, fried clams, burgers, and sandwiches. If you stake out a table by Lake Winnipesaukee, you'll see sailboats and darling ducks—you may even catch the sunset. Part of the Common Man family of restaurants, the establishment's food is excellent. *Next to the public docks, Meredith Bay; (603) 279-3445.*

Yankee Smokehouse ★★/$-$$

Here's a place that's sure to tickle your ribs. Even the motto—"We will sell no swine before its time"—is

---

Built for Speed

An outing on the *Millie B* is great for kids for two reasons. The trip is just a half hour, and kids love the **Gatsby-style speedboat**, which tools around Lake Winnipesaukee at speeds of up to 50 mph. Modeled after a 1928 craft, the handsome mahogany-and-chrome boat has a triple cockpit and an informed captain who'll show you the wonders of the southern end of the lake. *Town docks, Wolfeboro; (603) 569-1080.*

---

good for a chuckle. Kids can pig out on sliced-pork sandwiches, chili dogs, barbecued chicken, and smokehouse ribs. Piggy banks, pig figurines, and pig cookie jars will please any pig fans. *Junctions of Rtes. 16 and 25, West Ossipee; (603) 539-RIBS.*

SOUVENIR HUNTING

Annalee Doll Museum & Gift Shop

In 1934, New Hampshire native Annalee Thorndike began making soft-bodied dolls and animals with impish grins. Today, her cottage industry has bloomed into a world-renowned business. You can see the dolls being made, learn the history of the company in the on-site museum, and of course, pick a souvenir from thousands of dolls in the gift shop. There's a playground and picnic area, too. *Off Rte. 104 onto Hemlock Dr., Meredith; (603) 279-6542.*

Innisfree Book Shop

This exceptional bookstore stocks a fantastic selection of kids' toys (you'll even find Spyrograph key chains here), plus an awesome display of books for Mom and Dad. *Mill Falls Marketplace, Meredith (603/279-3905), and Millfront Marketplace, Lincoln (about 25 miles north of Holderness); (603) 745-6107.*

Kellerhaus

It's a gigantic gift shop, an ice-cream emporium, and a candy store rolled into one delicious outing. An institution since 1906, this sweet spot features a sundae bar where kids can douse their scoop of homemade ice cream with 12 toppings. Breakfast, including hot Belgian waffles, is served, too. *Rte. 3, Weirs Beach; (888) KLR-HAUS; (603) 366-4466.*

The Old Country Store

Choose from chubby dills in pickle barrels, penny candy, locally made cheeses, bags filled with polished rocks, and much more at this old-fashioned general store. The atmosphere is classic, too: creaking, sloping floors, a vintage cash register, and a player piano. *Rtes. 25 and 109, Moultonborough; (603) 476-5750.*

Portsmouth & the Coast

CULTURAL ADVENTURES

The Children's Museum of Portsmouth ★★★/$

The trolley parked out front makes it easy to spot this museum, which is located in a former town meeting house. Inside, you'll find 19 hands-on exhibits that invite you to explore a submarine equipped with tunnels and slides, floss gigantic teeth, steer a lobster boat, try on ornamental masks, command a space shuttle, and even unearth bones at a dinosaur dig. There's a special section just for toddlers, where they can play with trains on a large track. *280 Marcy St., Portsmouth; (603) 436-3853;* www.childrens-museum.org

Seacoast Science Center ★★/$

Managed by the Audubon Society of New Hampshire, this center features aquarium exhibits of the varied habitats—from salt marshes to freshwater ponds—that you'll discover at nearby Odiorne Point. Kids will have fun at the touch tank and, depending on what's scheduled during your visit, you can hear talks about lobsters, lighthouses, and other marine topics. The science center is in 380-acre Odiorne State Park, an ideal place to have a picnic, go bird-watching, try your hand at tide-pooling for starfish, or sign up for a guided nature walk. *570 Ocean Blvd., Rye; (603) 436-8043.*

Strawbery Banke Museum ★★★★/$$

MUST-SEE FamilyFun MUST-SEE Centuries of history are preserved at this friendly village, where the structures range from those built in the 1690s to 1950s. Role players in period costumes help keep things fun. The hot spot for children is the Family Activity Center, where kids can play period games (such as "hoops" from the Victorian era), piece together tavern puzzles, and create crafts. If your children are fans of the American Girl dolls, ask about programs inspired by Molly McIntire, a doll based on a 9-year-old girl circa 1944. Program participants practice an air-raid drill, shop with ration coupons, and feast on popular foods of the day. *Marcy St., Portsmouth; (603) 433-1100.* For the Molly program, call *(603) 433-1106;* www.strawberybanke.org

USS *Albacore* ★/$

Hungry for a 205-foot-long sub? Head to Albacore Park to have your fill of fun facts about this locally built submarine. The teardrop-shaped vessel served with the U.S. Navy for 19 years and never went to war. As you tour the vessel, your kids won't believe that 55 men worked and lived together on this 27-foot-wide floating laboratory. *600 Market St., Portsmouth; (603) 436-3680.*

JUST FOR FUN

Water Country ★★★★/$$$

MUST-SEE FamilyFun MUST-SEE Sure, New England's largest water park is big, but its size doesn't refer just to the 20 acres of rides. Water Country is also big on friendliness, cleanliness, and safety, making a daylong outing extra enjoyable for kids and parents. From the lightning-fast Double Geronimo water slide to the white-water thrills of Thunder Falls—plus a giant wave pool and the pitch-black Warp-8— the park turns every visit into a prune-skinned party. You're welcome to bring a picnic, too. *Rte. 1, Portsmouth; (603) 427-1111.*

STARFISH are capable of regenerating arms that have been severed. A new starfish can also grow from one loose arm as long as a piece of the main sea star's body remains.

155

PATRIOT GAMES

Visit **Fort Constitution**, where Revolutionary War patriots committed the first overt act of aggression against the crown by raiding weapons at the British stronghold (the former Fort William and Mary). There's no picnicking, but you can feast on views of the Fort Point Lighthouse. *Rte. 1B, New Castle; (603) 436-1552.*

BUNKING DOWN

Hampton Inn
★★/$$

Owned by the Hilton, the Hampton Inn is a cut above the average chain. There's a big indoor/outdoor pool, and the clean rooms come equipped with HBO and Nintendo. At the dining area overlooking the pool, you can enjoy a complimentary, deluxe continental breakfast. A free shuttle whisks you to attractions in downtown Portsmouth. *99 Durgin La., Portsmouth; (603) 431-6111;* www.hampton-inn-nh.com

Marriott Residence Inn
★★/$$

Superclean and well run, this property is a great pick for vacationing families. You can get a studio, one-bedroom, or two-bedroom suite with a full kitchen and dining area, and the staff will even do the grocery shopping for you. There's an indoor pool, and the lobby is stocked with Candy Land and Colorforms.

1 International Dr., Portsmouth; (800) 331-3131; (603) 436-8880; www.marriott.com

Sheraton Harborside Portsmouth ★★/$$-$$$

If you want to be within walking distance of Portsmouth's downtown activities, this is a nice place that has the added benefit of letting you avoid the hassle of looking for downtown parking. On weekdays, the elegant retreat caters primarily to a business crowd, but families pack the house on weekends. Choose from guest rooms or condominium suites. There's also a large, heated indoor pool. *250 Market St., Portsmouth; (800) 325-3535; (603) 431-2300;* www.sheraton.com

Wallis Sands Place
★★/$$

Located on scenic Route 1A, this property offers ten well-kept efficiency cottages just across the street from Wallis Sands Beach. Some of the cottages are traditional; some are modern. All include cable TV;

kitchens with stoves, microwaves, and refrigerators; and use of shady picnic areas. For many families, the clean, sandy beach is the main draw. *1035 Ocean Blvd., Rye; (603) 436-5882.*

GOOD EATS

Cataqua Public House at the Redhook Ale Brewery
★★/$$$
This contemporary restaurant has the feeling of a big ski lodge. It's loud, so any noise your kids make blends right in. The kids' menu is small but serviceable. In winter, you can gather in the lounge by the crackling fire and play games or read books. *35 Corporate Dr., Portsmouth; (603) 430-8600.*

Muddy River Smokehouse
★★★/$$
From the street, this restaurant looks like a bar, but in back you'll discover a large, inviting dining room. The staff is great with kids. They get baskets of celery sticks and peanut butter, Wikki Stix to bend, and crayons and a coloring book/menu. Kids' choices include a pulled-pork sandwich, chicken fingers, and grilled cheese. Parents can order mouthwatering ribs, barbecued chicken, and more. Lunch or early dinner is your best bet, as the place becomes a swinging music hall at night. *21 Congress St., Portsmouth; (603) 430-9582.*

Newick's Fisherman's Landing
★★★/$$
One of a group of four popular seafood restaurants in New Hampshire and Maine, this large eatery extends a warm welcome to kids. They get to color, snack on Teddy Grahams, and munch on favorites from hot dogs to fish-and-chips. As for the rest of the menu, if it comes from the sea, you'll probably find it here—you can get everything from a basic scallop roll to a full-blown baked seafood platter. *845 Lafayette Rd., Hampton; (603) 926-7646; www.newicks.com*

Mornings at The Inn at East Hill Farm, the henhouse is filled with kids clutching baskets and waiting for hens to shake, wiggle, cluck, and lay. (Kids get to take home the eggs they collect.)

South/Southwest New Hampshire

START YOUR VACATION IN Concord? What a capital idea. Located on Interstate 93, just 35 miles from the Massachusetts border, New Hampshire's thriving capital is an ideal place to introduce children to the Granite State. With fewer than 40,000 residents, Concord feels more like a friendly town than a big city. Its South Main Street and North Main Street are lined with historic buildings, happening restaurants (you can even eat in a jail cell; see page 164), and toy and candy shops where proprietors will give you a warm welcome. No skyscrapers here, though kids will look up to the gold-domed capital building, where the legislature has convened since 1819. Open to the public, it's worth a walk-through to view portraits of the state's movers and shakers.

Across the street at the Museum of New Hampshire History, kids can join a treasure hunt that will challenge them to learn about the state's Native American heritage, its history as a maritime center, and early modes of transportation. Another must: the interactive celestial show at the Christa McAuliffe Planetarium, dedicated to the local social studies

THE FamilyFun LIST

MUST-SEE
MUST-SEE

Christa McAuliffe Planetarium
(page 162)

Fort at No. 4/Living History Museum (page 167)

Museum of New Hampshire History (page 162)

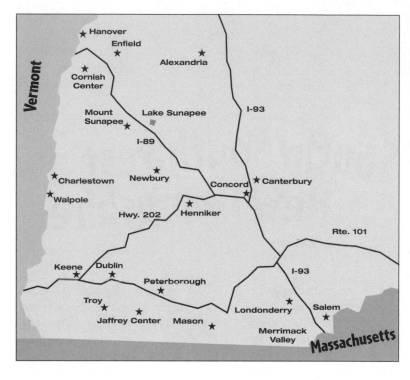

teacher who was killed in 1986 aboard the space shuttle *Challenger*.

Concord is one of dozens of communities that are part of **the Merrimack Valley**, the most populated part of the state. Its location along the scenic Merrimack River makes the capital city an outdoor destination as well. You can hike along the river at the headquarters of the Society for the Protection of New Hampshire Forests, take a canoe trip (see page 163), and ski at nearby Pat's Peak.

The **Merrimack Valley**, like the other regions profiled in this section, is home to less flashy, and therefore

less well known, vacation gems that are worth visiting—especially if you're looking for places to go that will take you off the beaten path.

The **Monadnock Region**, known as the Currier & Ives corner, contains about 40 historic communities that seem virtually untouched by time. At Silver Ranch in Jaffrey, you can take a horse-drawn sleigh ride through a peaceful, wooded landscape. At the Inn at East Hill Farm in Troy, kids can gather eggs in the morning, learn to milk a goat, and drink pitchers full of chocolate milk in the communal dining room. For more information on this area, call the **Monadnock**

Travel Council at *(800) 432-7864*.

The **Upper Connecticut River Valley** region refers to the ribbon of 25 or so Vermont and New Hampshire towns that flank the Connecticut River. The anchor attraction on the Vermont side is the Montshire Museum of Science in Norwich (see page 194). In New Hampshire, Hanover's Dartmouth College hosts everything from the Big Apple Circus to monster movies.

(For a schedule, call *603/646-2422* or log on to www.hop.dartmouth.edu) Nearby, West Lebanon's main artery (Rte. 10) is packed with family restaurants and inns and chain hotels.

For more information about the Dartmouth area, call the **Hanover Chamber of Commerce** at *(603) 643-3115;* www.hanoverchamber. org *or* www.hop.dartmouth.edu

Merrimack Valley

CULTURAL ADVENTURES

Canterbury Shaker Village
★★/$$

Set on 694 acres of open fields, woods, and ponds, this nonprofit historic site will introduce your kids to the crafts, traditions, and beliefs of the Shaker community. Members lived here from 1792 until 1990, putting their "hands to work and hearts to God." A 90-minute tour will take you through the picturesque village of 25 original buildings, including stops at the schoolhouse and immense laundry room; then you can sample homemade ice cream, and hike on the extensive

REWARD GOOD BACKSEAT BEHAVIOR

Backseat squabbles were a big problem for the Niehues family of Red Wing, Minnesota, on long car trips. "Four kids can find a lot to fight about!" says mom Mary. Now, though, Mom and Dad give each of the kids a roll of quarters at the beginning of the trip. Every time they have to correct a child's behavior, the culprit forfeits a quarter. But any quarters still remaining at the trip's end are the child's to keep.

trail system. *288 Shaker Rd., Canterbury; (800) 982-9511; (603) 783-9511;* www.shakers.org

Children's Metamorphosis
★★/$

On rainy days, there's no better place than this museum geared to children ages 1 to 9. Its many themed areas give kids the chance to play doctor in the emergency room, put on a puppet show for Mom and Dad, play with trucks in a sandbox, and assemble sculptures in the "sticky room." *217 Rockingham Rd., Londonderry; (603) 425-2560.*

 ### Christa McAuliffe Planetarium
★★★★/$

Dedicated to the local schoolteacher who perished aboard the space shuttle *Challenger* in 1986, this place gives kids the chance to become space explorers through a variety of interactive shows. Using the control boxes at their seats, they can make choices about what to discover. Depending on the schedule, you might take a three-dimensional mission to Mars, see the universe

through the eyes of the Hubble telescope, or (especially for preschoolers) learn about rainbows and stars with the help of friends from *Sesame Street. 3 Institute Dr., Concord; (603) 271-7827;* www.starhop.com

 ### Museum of New Hampshire History
★★★★/$

A terrific starting point for a visit to New Hampshire, this museum introduces families to the key personalities, inventions, and dramatic terrain that shape the Granite State. Take the kids on a self-guided family tour (sheets are available at the front desk), during which they can hear Abenaki Indian tales inside a wigwam and smell spices that were imported from the West Indies two centuries ago. You also can check out the Concord Coach, the most elegant and practical transportation of its day. Kids will enjoy climbing up a re-created fire tower to the second floor of exhibits. The gift shop sells activity books, crafts kits, and historical games. *Eagle Sq., Concord; (603) 226-3189.*

JUST FOR FUN

Canobie Lake Park ★★★★/$$$

At 80 or so acres, this well-maintained park is the perfect size for families. Its 45 rides—including four coasters—are within an easy walk of each other, and you'll find plenty of shady spots where you can take a break. You'll find lots of laid-back pleasures, including an antique carousel, a riverboat and pontoon boat, and a 24-gauge steam train. For thrill seekers, there's the Yankee Cannonball Coaster, the log flume, and the Boston Tea Party Shoot-the-Chute Ride, which douses anyone within a few feet of the splashdown area. Between the amusements, games of chance, live entertainment (Bozo the clown is a regular), boat rides, and fireworks, you could easily spend all day into evening here. *Exit 2 off I-93, Salem; (603) 893-3506.*

Society for the Protection of New Hampshire Forests
★★★/Free
With 100 acres of trails along the Merrimack River, this is a beautiful place no matter what the season. Bring a picnic lunch (no place to buy food here) and eat it on the outdoor deck at the conservation center in sight of the river. Young environmentalists may enjoy the self-guided tour of the passive-solar center, ingeniously designed for optimum energy efficiency. A non-profit conservation organization, the society owns more than 100 forests statewide, where families can have fun hiking, picnicking, boating, and cross-country skiing. At its Bethlehem's Rocks Christmas Tree Farm, you can even pick out a Christmas tree. Ask the SPNHF for

Have Canoe, Will Paddle

For a fun, inexpensive outing, try canoeing on the Merrimack River, which has a nice sandy bottom and plenty of beaches where you can stop for a break. **Hannah's Paddles** can shuttle families to a five-mile stretch of shallow river for a self-guided paddling adventure, during which you may see herons, osprey, ducks, and turtles. Visitors watch a short safety video before each trip. The company rents kayaks as well as canoes. *15 Hannah Dustin Rd., Concord; (603) 753-6695.*

a map that highlights the properties. *54 Portsmouth St., Concord; (603) 224-9945;* www.spnhf.org

BUNKING DOWN

Fairfield Inn ★★★/$$
Part of a national chain run by the Marriott, this property is convenient to all Concord attractions. There's an indoor heated pool, free HBO, complimentary breakfast in a pleasant dining area, and coin-operated guest laundry. Choose a room with two double beds or opt for an executive king room with a refrigerator, microwave, and pullout sofa bed. *4 Gulf St., Concord; (800) 228-2800; (603) 224-4011.*

GOOD EATS

Beefside ★★/$

This unpretentious local haunt serves delicious roast beef sandwiches topped with special BBQ sauce, horseradish, and/or bacon and cheese. If you prefer, you can order fried seafood, chicken nuggets, and grilled cheese sandwiches—for takeout or eating in. The atmosphere is basic, but the food is anything but. *106 Manchester St., Concord; (603) 228-0208.*

Intervale Farms Pancake House ★★★/$

If you flip over flapjacks, stop here to sample apple, blueberry, or chocolate-chip stacks drenched in homemade maple syrup. Kids can order a single pancake or split an order with a sibling. *Rte. 114 and Flanders Rd., Henniker; (603) 428-7196.*

Margaritas ★★★★/$$

It'd be a crime to skip this joint, where you and the kids can dine in the cells of the former Concord Jail. Supposedly, the restaurant is haunted by a former inmate—a rumor that only enhances the atmosphere. The fare is Mexican (enchiladas, burritos, fajitas) and leagues above prison grub. Little jailbirds will find all their cheesy favorites on the kids' menu/coloring sheet, plus they can do time playing with waxy Wikki Stix. We guarantee you'll be repeat offenders. *Bicentennial Sq., Concord; (603) 224-2821.* (There's another Margaritas *at 775 Lafayette Rd., in Portsmouth, 603/431-5828,* but, alas, it's not in a jail.)

Monadnock Region

JUST FOR FUN

Friendly Farm ★★/$

Talk about a warm welcome. The animals at this five-acre farm are so congenial that they'll cuddle up with your kids. Get the camera ready: some of your favorite vacation shots will be the pictures of your kids cradling chicks, feeding goats, hugging sheep, and trading oinks with pigs. There's also a working beehive, proud peacocks, and a maternity ward for barnyard babies. *Rte. 101, Dublin; (603) 563-8444.*

Miller State Park ★★/$

Kids can easily tackle Pack Monadnock, a smaller version of Mount Monadnock, at this park. To get to the 2,290-foot peak, drive along a one-and-a-third-mile auto road to the parking area. There's a half-mile-

Pumpkin City

During its annual Pumpkin Festival in 2000, the city of Keene set a record for the largest number of jack-o'-lanterns in one place. That night, 23,727 pumpkins were tallied, but Keene doesn't rest on its laurels. The past couple of years, the city has tried, albeit unsuccessfully, to beat its own record.

long trail around the summit. *Rte. 101, Peterborough; (603) 924-3672.*

Mount Monadnock ★★★/$
The second-most frequently hiked mountain in the world (the first is Japan's Mount Fuji) ends in a bald, rocky peak, from which you can see Mount Washington and even Boston. Stop at the visitors' center for a map. The ranger will probably suggest climbing the White Dot Trail, the quickest route to the 3,165-foot-high summit. With children, the hike will take about four hours round-trip, allowing time for stops at a pretty spring and rests at scenic overlooks. There are no facilities on the mountain, so you'll need to carry your water and snacks. *Dublin Rd. from Rte. 124, Jaffrey Center; (603) 532-8862.*

Silver Ranch ★★/$$$
Hi, ho, Silver! Whenever you travel to the scenic Monadnock region, you're in for a fun ride here. Depending on the season, you can take a pony ride, horse-drawn sleigh ride, or hayride. Riding lessons are also available. Snacks match the season; in autumn, for example, you can feast on homemade doughnuts and sip sweet cider. *Rte. 124, Jaffrey; (603) 532-7363.*

BUNKING DOWN

Days Inn ★★★/$$
If your family wants to enjoy contemporary comforts while exploring the "Currier and Ives" corner, this is a good bet. There's an indoor pool and complimentary breakfast, and the motel is near many family-oriented chain restaurants. *175 Key Rd., Keene; (800) DAYS-INN; (603) 352-7616; www.daysinn.com*

Inn at East Hill Farm ★★★★/$$$
When it comes to farm vacations, this resort is a special breed. In fact, it's one of the best lodges for families in all of New England—any place that advertises it's a place "Where Kids are Kings" is tops with us. In this picturesque, 15-acre farm at the foot of

Mount Monadnock, you can stay in a historic inn, cottage, or bunkhouse; enjoy three home-cooked meals a day; and join a dizzying list of kid-pleasing activities, from goat-milking to hikes up the mountain. If you'd rather do your own thing, you can swim in two outdoor pools, take a boat out on the lake, play tennis, sign up for a horseback ride, or just loaf. In the barnyard, kids can collect eggs from the chicken coop, feed the pigs, and milk the cows. Open year-round, the farm features cross-country skiing, sledding, ice-skating, visits to newborn baby lambs, and swimming in a heated indoor pool in winter. Rates include all meals and most activities. *Jaffrey Rd., Troy; (800) 242-6495; (603) 242-6495.*

GOOD EATS

Monadnock Mountain View Restaurant
★★★/$-$$

Feast on a view of the region's primo peak at this family restaurant, which dishes out burgers, tuna rolls, honey-glazed fried chicken, and PB&J. Come for the sunset or visit in fall, when the mountains wear a spectacular, colored coat. *Rte. 12, Troy; (603) 242-3300.*

Parker's Maple Barn and Sugar House ★★★/$

Hungry for pancakes drenched in homemade syrup? Come here any time of day to satisfy your craving. With nine varieties of flapjacks, there's no doubt about the house specialty in this old bar. Breakfast is served all day, but you can also get lunch (how about a peanut-butter-and-maple-cream sandwich?) and dinner (try maple-glazed ribs). In sugaring season, families can tour the maple sugar house and sample sugar-on-snow, a dish of snow topped with caramelized maple syrup. Lines can get long on weekends, but you can walk along a nature trail while you wait. *1316 Brookline Rd., Mason; (800) 832-2308; (603) 878-2308.*

SOUVENIR HUNTING

Steeplegate Mall

The Merrimack Valley's major mall has more than 65 stores, including toy shops, kids' clothing retailers, and plenty of fast food. *270 Loudon Rd., Concord; (603) 224-1523.*

Toadstool Bookshop

This popular bookstore has a terrific section of children's books and a kid-friendly café. Aesop's Table dishes out PB&J, hot chocolate, and giant homemade chocolate chip cookies. In summer, there's also an ice-cream window. *12 Depot Sq., Peterborough; (603) 924-3543.* (There's another location, sans the café, in the Colony Mill Marketplace.)

Upper Connecticut River Valley

CULTURAL ADVENTURES

Enfield Shaker Village ★★/$

Set in a lush valley between Mount Assurance and Lake Mascoma, "Chosen Vale" was home to Shaker families between 1793 and 1923. During that time, residents built the Great Stone Dwelling (see The Shaker Inn on page 168), farmed on more than 3,000 acres, and dedicated themselves to a life defined by equality, celibacy, pacifism, and industriousness. On a self-guided tour, you can see eight of the original buildings, walk to the beautiful Shaker Sacred Feast Ground (part of a state-owned 2,500-acre nature preserve), and watch artisans make Shaker crafts. For optimum fun, register in advance for a kids' craft workshop (perhaps basket-making or broom-making). *24 Caleb Dyer La., Enfield; (603) 632-4346; www. shakermuse um.org*

 **Fort at No. 4/ Living History Museum ★★★/$**

From the 1740s to the 1760s, Fort No. 4 was the northernmost British settlement, 30 miles north of its nearest neighbor. At this 20-acre site along the Connecticut River, you can explore a perfect re-creation of the original fort (which was actually located two miles away). You also can meet costumed interpreters who depict colonists and Native Americans of the French and Indian War era. You'll see them caring for animals, demonstrating hearth cooking, and tending the gardens. All told, there are about a dozen

River Journey

Pack a picnic lunch and sign on for **North Star Canoe Rentals'** two-hour self-guided journey on the Connecticut River. (You can turn your outing into a longer or shorter adventure, depending on your pace.) As you travel along the Vermont border, you'll paddle under the Windsor-Cornish Covered Bridge, the longest in America. Keep your eyes open for deer, eagles, beaver, and other wildlife. The company is accustomed to planning family outings and is happy to offer free instruction. It also provides shuttle service, and rents kayaks and six-person rafts. *Rte. 12A, Cornish Center; (603) 542-5802.*

structures within and outside the palisade wall. Kids will especially enjoy climbing the watchtower, petting the sheep, and visiting the blacksmith. Fun Shops allow children ages 7 to 12 to immerse themselves in the period for four hours and learn about Native American culture, butter-making, and militia skills. Held several times during the summer, these programs require preregistration. Longer summer camps are also offered. *Rte. 11, Charlestown; (888) 367-8284; (603) 826-5700;* www.fortat4.com

BUNKING DOWN

Inn at Valley Farms ★★★/$$
If you want to stay in the country and get away from it all—and forego television and water slides—consider this 105-acre working organic farm. Its two cottages are just right for families. (There's a main inn as well, but it's not particularly suited to children.) Kids can meet goats, a horse, and chickens in the barn. Breakfast is part of the deal, and includes a basket of fresh-baked goodies delivered to your door. *Wentworth Rd., Walpole; (877) 327-2855; (603) 756-2855.*

The Shaker Inn ★★★/$$
The movers and shakers in your family will enjoy staying at this inn, which turns a routine overnight into a learning adventure. Built from 1837

to 1841, this inn—aka the Great Stone Dwelling—is the largest main dwelling ever built by a Shaker community. (See "Enfield Shaker Village" on page 167.) Families who stay in one of the 24 authentically furnished guest rooms will get a feel for the Shakers' practical, yet beautiful style. Because the inn is on the grounds of the museum, you have a ready-made educational experience at the door. You can also hike, snowshoe, or ski on the nearby nature trails, or hang out at the beach on Lake Mascoma, which is a quick walk from the inn. Breakfast is included. During prime vacation weeks, there are family packages with lots of kids' activities (such as snow-cave making). *447 Rte. 4A, Enfield; (603) 632-7810; (888) 707-4257;* www.theshaker inn.com

GOOD EATS

Everything but Anchovies ★★★/$-$$
For Ivy League–caliber pizza, head to this friendly restaurant near the Dartmouth campus. The food is terrific, the staff is friendly, and kids will love the offerings—kid-size pizzas and spaghetti plates, homemade chocolate-chip cookies, and meatball subs. There are plenty of healthful options, too. Don't let the name fool you: you can get just about anything on your pizza, including anchovies. *5 Allen St., Hanover; (603) 643-6135.*

LAKE SUNAPEE AREA

THOUGH THE **Lake Sunapee area** is just 30 miles west of gargantuan Lake Winnipesaukee, Lake Sunapee and its neighbor lakes differ in both size and character. Crystal-clear Lake Sunapee is considerably smaller (ten miles long and three miles wide) than the commercial, fun-loving "Winnie." It's also a lot less crowded. You won't find wild water slides here or an abundance of lakeside lodging. What you will find are gorgeous views atop 2,743-foot-high Mount Sunapee, enjoyable boat rides, and a chance to soak up a natural paradise without the crowds. You'll also find great family skiing at the **Mount Sunapee Resort** (see "Fun Family Ski Resorts, page 139). For more information, call the **Lake Sunapee Business Association** at *(877) 526-6575;* www. sunapee.vacations.com Here are two of our favorite places to bunk down in the area:

Best Western Sunapee Lake Lodge ★★★/$$

This is a great base for families who've come to enjoy the region's many recreational pleasures. Just a four-minute walk to the beach at Mount Sunapee State Park, the lodge is also within easy striking distance of swimming, boating, mountain biking, and skiing. For fun, there's an indoor pool, game room, and, depending on the season, ice-skating in the rink out back or sand volleyball. The adjacent restaurant, Murphy's Grille, serves up kids' favorites and features Murphy's Underground, a playroom where kids can listen to music, watch videos on a wide-screen TV, and play games before, during, or after the meal. *1403 Rte. 103, Mt. Sunapee; (800) 606-5253; (603) 763-2010;* www.best western.com

Cardigan Lodge ★★★★/$$$

Families who like to hike will enjoy staying at this AMC-operated lodge, located at the base of 3,155-foot-tall Mount Cardigan. The lodge has 13 rooms, most with a mix of twin and bunk beds; guests share one of two large bathrooms. Ask about Family Fun Weeks and special programs geared to children. The rate includes breakfast, dinner, and food to pack for your own trail lunches. Unlike the AMC's high huts, which can be reached only on foot, you can reach Cardigan Lodge by car. *774 Shem Valley Rd., Alexandria; (603) 744-8011.*

Vermont

THE GREEN MOUNTAIN State is home to more than 360,000 acres of national forest, 602 major lakes and streams, 223 mountains more than 2,000 feet high, 7,099 miles of rivers, and the most ski areas on the East Coast. Only 588,000 people live in New England's second-largest state, so there's plenty of space to play without encountering crowds. Campers, especially, will have a field day.

Nature is Vermont's top attraction. Flanked by 435-square-mile Lake Champlain on the west and the Connecticut River on the east, the state

Northern Vermont

Central Vermont

Southern Vermont

is a paradise for fishermen (kids under age 15 fish free), canoers, and kayakers. The same holds true for hikers and cyclists, skiers and skaters, and, in autumn, leaf-peepers. No wonder Vermont's tag line is "The way life should be." Travelers may not be aware that Vermont has a fifth season: maple-sugaring season, when sugarmakers prepare a world-record half million gallons a year.

Nature notwithstanding, Vermont's top tourist attraction is the tour at Ben & Jerry's Ice Cream in Waterbury, where you can sample the sweet stuff and watch as it's made. Then there's the Vermont Teddy Bear Factory in Shelburne, where you can watch the bears being made, and design your own.

ATTRACTIONS	
$	under $10
$$	$10 - $20
$$$	$20 - $30
$$$$	$30 +

HOTELS/MOTELS/CAMPGROUNDS	
$	under $100
$$	$100 - $200
$$$	$200 - $300
$$$$	$300 +

RESTAURANTS	
$	under $10
$$	$10 - $20
$$$	$20 - $30
$$$$	$30 +

FAMILYFUN RATED	
★	Fine
★★	Good
★★★	Very Good
★★★★	*FamilyFun* Recommended

Après-ski activities at Mount Snow include sledding, tubing, dogsledding, and catching rides on the grooming machines.

Southern Vermont

A S IS TRUE IN OTHER AREAS of the state, southern Vermont's signature attractions are its natural wonders. Kids will have a blast tubing down the Battenkill River, splashing in Buttermilk Falls, hiking around Emerald Lake, and exploring the southern portion of the Green Mountain National Forest.

The bottom quarter of the state, southern Vermont has four family-friendly ski areas (Okemo, Bromley, Stratton, and Mount Snow; see "Fun Family Ski Resorts," page 179), numerous ski touring centers, and inns where you can shake off the chills with hot cocoa and cozy quilts.

In Arlington, where the artist Norman Rockwell lived for 14 years, you can tube down the Battenkill River, stay in an authentic log cabin (see Roaring Branch Log Cabin Resort on page 185), and see 500 of Rockwell's paintings in the Arlington Gallery. Take your time as you tool through town a much-photographed sign on the crimson-covered Chiselville covered bridge warns: "One dollar fine for driving faster than a walk on this bridge."

THE FamilyFun LIST

Adams Farm (page 176)

Extreme Tubing! (page 177)

Norman Rockwell Exhibition at the Arlington Gallery (page 175)

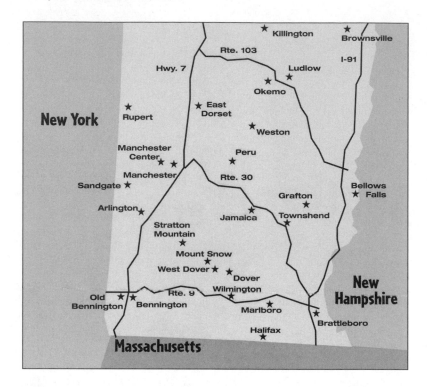

One of the region's most photo-genic towns is Grafton, where families can visit the village blacksmith, the local flock of sheep, the kid-friendly Nature Museum at Grafton, and the Grafton Cheese Company, where you can watch as award-winning cheddar is made. Manchester has been a resort town since the Civil War, and is now an upscale tourist enclave packed with tony shopping outlets and plenty of natural, cultural, and gastronomic wonders. Families can feast on a picnic lunch and amazing views at the top of Mount Equinox, and visit Hildene, the home of Abraham Lincoln's son, Robert Todd Lincoln. Manchester is a good base from which to visit nearby Bromley and Stratton Mountains, Rupert's Merck Forest, and North Dorset's Emerald Lake State Park.

The standout in Wilmington is Adams Farm, run by the sixth generation of the Adams family. Other kid-pleasing outings include swimming and boating in the Harriman Reservoir (aka Lake Whitingham), playing (in winter and summer) on the slopes of nearby Mount Snow, and exploring the general store and other shops in the historic downtown.

CULTURAL ADVENTURES

Bennington Monument
★★/$

You can learn a bit about the Revolutionary War—and get a great view of Southern Vermont—at this 306-foot-tall limestone monument. Ride the elevator to an observation point, where you can soak up the scenery and examine a diorama depicting the 1777 battle between Gen. John Stark and British and Hessian forces. *Rte. 9, Old Bennington; (802) 447 0550.*

Hildene ★★/$

Robert Todd Lincoln, Abe's son, summered in this 24-room Georgian Revival mansion, with its lush formal gardens. Visitors can take a one-hour guided tour, including a ten-minute introductory video and a walk through the home. Inside, you'll see one of Abe Lincoln's stovepipe hats, as well as tin soldiers, dolls, and other toys used by the Lincoln children. The tours are geared to adults, though guides will usually adapt talks when kids are in tow. You may want to visit during a special family-oriented event (check the Website below) or come in winter to cross-country ski on 11 miles of trails. Kids in grades five and up might get a bit more out of a visit by first reading *Thunder in October*, by local author (and former Hildene caretaker) Peter Campbell Copp *($10; call 802/362-0074 to order).* It's an adventure story about a boy whose father is, not coincidentally, caretaker of the famed estate. *Rte. 7A, Manchester; (802) 362-1788; www.hildene.org*

Norman Rockwell Exhibition at the Arlington Gallery
★★★/$

At this gallery, not only can you view Norman Rockwell's paintings, but you may get to meet someone who modeled for his pictures. An Arlington resident from 1939 to 1953, Rockwell was drawn to the

Canoe Under a Covered Bridge

If you and your kids enjoy canoeing, you'll be in heaven on the Battenkill River. This waterway flows for 45 miles, through Vermont's countryside and under four covered bridges, on its way to New York's Hudson River. **BattenKill Canoe Ltd.** can help plan a trip that's appropriate for your crew, whether you prefer a two-hour, daylong, or multiday adventure. The outfitter also provides safety tips, maps, and shuttle service. If you opt for a longer outing, plans include overnights at campsites and country inns. *Rte. 7A, Arlington; (800) 421-5268; (802) 362-2800;* www.battenkill.com

honest faces of his neighbors and friends, and he used them liberally in his illustrations. Marjorie and Larry Brush, for example, posed with their now grown-up daughter for *The Country Doctor* in 1947. If they're around, they'll be happy to share all the details. Housed in a historic 1875 church, the museum also offers a 15-minute film. *3772 Rte. 7A, Arlington; (802) 375-6423; www.normanrockwellexhibit.com*

Southern Vermont Natural History Museum ★★/$

Stop here and you're sure to see more than 500 species of native New England birds and mammals. This museum is filled with 150 dioramas of mounted specimens, from black bears to the extinct passenger pigeon. Kids will most enjoy meeting several live raptors (including a red-tailed hawk and a barred owl) and standing against a wall to compare their "wingspan" to that of several birds. *Rte. 9, Marlboro; (802) 464-0048.*

JUST FOR FUN

MUST-SEE FamilyFun **MUST-SEE** **Adams Farm** ★★★★/$

Run for six generations by the Adams family, this 210-acre farm is one of southern Vermont's most memorable spots for kids. For starters, young visitors can take a basket filled with carrots, apples, and grain to the indoor petting barn and feed potbellied pigs, angora rabbits, dairy goats, llamas, and dozens of other creatures.

Other activities include tractor rides on an old John Deere, goat-milking demonstrations, and cuddling sessions with kittens and bunnies. In sugaring season, you can watch as sap from 3,500 taps is boiled into 800 gallons of maple syrup. There are pony rides, barn dances, bonfire parties, and hayrides, including the standout 90-minute Haunted Hayride, complete with a live reenactment of a ghost story.

In winter, you can climb aboard a sleigh led by Belgian draft horses and ride through meadows and maple groves. *15 Higley Hill Rd., Wilmington; (802) 464-3762; www.adamsfamilyfarm .com*

Buttermilk Falls ★★/Free

A popular place to chill out, this wooded spot features a wide river with two separate falls where splash-happy kids can combat the summer's heat. The water's chilly, but you wouldn't know it from the sound of laughing children. *Near the junction of Rtes. 100 and 103, Ludlow.*

Emerald Lake State Park
★★★/$

Pack a picnic and head for the beach at this 430-acre park, where you can swim, rent a paddleboat, and fish, while soaking up views of Dorset Mountain. *Rte. 7, E. Dorset; (802) 362-1655; www.vtstateparks.com/htm/emerald/.cfm*

Equinox Skyline Drive
★★★/$

This journey to the highest peak in the Taconic Range is tops. The view from the toll road (it's about five miles long) is of lakes, rivers, valleys, and villages typical of Vermont. At the top of 3,816-foot Mount Equinox, you can behold the view from Lookout Point and search for wildflowers on a hiking trail. *Rte. 7A, Manchester; (802) 362-1114.*

Extreme Tubing!
FamilyFun ★★★/$$

For the ultimate winter blast, rent tubes for the kids and send them down the 700-foot hill (with a 400-foot runoff) by the White House Inn. Tubers can reach speeds of up to 40 miles per hour, so toddlers are better off on the kiddie hill. What goes down must come up on foot, but young tubers don't seem to mind. The White House Inn is also home to the Tubbs

Snowshoe Center, where folks ages 5 and up can rent equipment and wander on 20 miles of trails. If families want to stay at the inn, the best bet is the guesthouse, which has seven rooms (all with private bath), a common room with a TV, VCR, and fireplace, plus a large kitchenette. *White House Inn, Rte. 9, Wilmington; (800) 541-2135; (802) 464-2135.*

Fun Family Ski Resorts

For all-season information on Bromley, Mount Snow, Okemo, and Stratton ski resorts, see pages 179–182.

Grafton Ponds
★★/$$-$$$$

This year-round family recreation area is filled with fun for children. In winter, kids can slide through culverts (imbedded tubes) down a 20-foot-high tubing hill. They also can ice-skate, snowshoe, and cross-country ski on about 17 miles of groomed trails. In summer, there's hiking, cycling, and special five-day kids' camps, where activities may include swimming, panning for gold, and exploring a beaver pond. *Townshend Rd., Grafton; (802) 843-2400.*

Green Mountain Flyer ★★/$$

All aboard for a two-hour train ride between Bellows Falls and Chester Depot. You and your kids sit in restored 1930s passenger coaches and pass covered bridges, farmlands, and a cascading waterfall. The narration isn't generally geared to kids, but on many special trains it is. There's a Santa's Express in December, a Sugar-on-Snow Excursion (you can sample the sweet treat), and an Easter Bunny Express. For dates, log on to www.rails-vt.com **NOTE:** The Green Mountain Railroad, which operates the train, also offers trips on the Vermont Valley Flyer (between Manchester and North Bennington), the Champlain Valley Weekender (between Burlington and Middlebury), and the River Valley Rambler (White River Junction to Norwich). *The Green Mountain Flyer departs from 54 Depot S., Bellows Falls; (800) 707-3530; (802) 463-3069.*

FamilyFun GAME

I Could Eat an Alphabet

Let your half-starved brood describe how hungry they are in this game, best played about half an hour before you make a pit stop for food. This version of the I'm Packing for a Picnic game begins when you announce "I'm so hungry I could eat an aviator" ("alligator" or "apple"). The next player adds on with a B word. She might say, "I'm so hungry I could eat an aviator and a bunny rabbit" ("belly button" or "baseball"). See if you can keep it up until your family is eating zoos, zippers, or zigzags.

Hapgood Pond Recreational Area ★★/$

Part of the Green Mountain National Forest, this seven-acre pond is a popular spot to swim, hike, and camp. The Hapgood Pond Trail loops around the north edge of the pond and leads to a dam. *Hapgood Pond Rd., Peru. (For more information, contact the GMNF Manchester Ranger District, 2538 Depot St., Manchester Center; 802/362-2307.)*

Jamaica State Park ★★★/$-$$$

This 689-acre state park is a hit with families who want to camp (43 tent sites and 18 lean-tos are available), hike, or swim in Salmon Hole, the spot where three Frenchmen and some Indians ambushed British soldiers during the French and Indian War. An especially satisfying hike for families is the flat, Railroad Bed Trail, which meanders for two miles along the West River. **NOTE:** If you want to camp here in summer, make your reservations the previous January. *Depot St., Jamaica; (800) 299-3071 (winter); (802) 874-4600 (summer).*

Merck Forest & Farmland Center ★★/Free

Families can hike, camp, walk, cross-country ski, and snowshoe on 28 miles of trails at this 3,150-acre environmental education center. (In all cases, you need to bring your own equipment.) Children ages 3 to 5

FUN FAMILY SKI RESORTS

THE HEART OF New England's ski industry, Vermont is loaded with all-season ski and fun mountains. (For a list, contact Ski Vermont at *800/VERMONT, ext. 763; www.skivemont. com.* Here are our favorites for families.

Ascutney Mountain Resort
★★★/$$$$

At this four-season resort all trails lead to one base area, there's a 10-acre Learning Park for beginners, and all lodging is slope-side. You can go downhill skiing, snowboarding, tubing, ice-skating, and cross-country skiing. Other activities include swimming, treasure hunts, and bonfires. [130 skiable acres; 50 trails (26 percent beginner, 39 percent intermediate, 35 percent advanced); 6 lifts, including a milelong, high-speed detachable quad; 95 percent snowmaking coverage. Family facilities: Child care for children 6 and under; ski lessons for children 3 and up; snowboarding clinics for children 6 and up; on-site kid-friendly restaurants, a pizzeria, and a general store.] Ascutney offers a full array of summer packages and entertainment as well. *Rte. 44, Brownsville; (802) 484-7711; (800) 243-0011 (snow report and reservations);* www.ascutney.com

Bromley Mountain
★★★/$-$$$$

This low-key resort in southern Vermont is an affordable place to learn the sport or tackle more challenging trails. There's a base lodge, ski school, and après-ski activities. All trails lead to the lodge; ice-skating, sleigh rides, snowmobile tours, and cross-country skiing are just a short drive away. Lodging includes 300 condominium units, plus plenty of nearby family-friendly inns. [157 skiable acres; 43 trails (35 percent beginner, 34 percent intermediate, 31 percent advanced); 9 lifts, including a high-speed detachable quad; 84 percent snowmaking coverage. Family facilities: Child care for children 6 weeks to 6 years; ski clinics for children 3 and up; snowboard lessons for children 6 and up.] In the summer Bromley's got alpine and water slides and a zipline. *Rte. 11, Peru; (802) 824-5522; (802) 824-5522 (snow phone); (800) 865-4786 (reservations);* www.bromley.com

Killington/Pico
★★★/$$-$$$$

The east's largest ski resort is home to seven mountains, including the region's highest vertical drop (3,150 feet). The Rams Head Family Center

continued on next page

is serviced by four lifts, and offers ski and snowboard lessons, a food court, rentals, and family activities. Killington features more than 100 restaurants and clubs on its axis road, a staggering number of condominiums, inns, motels and lodges, and after-dark ice-skating, tubing, and snowboarding. Families Ski Wee Adventures include ice cream socials, horse-drawn sleigh rides, and family slalom races. [1,160 skiable acres; 200 trails (30 percent beginner, 39 percent intermediate, 31 percent advanced); 32 lifts, including the Rams Head Express Quad; 70 percent snowmaking coverage. Family facilities: Nursery and child care for children 6 weeks to 6 years; ski orientations for children 2 and up; snowboarding clinics for children 4 and up; Perfect Turn clinics using the Guaranteed Learning Method.] Summer highlights include mountain boarding (using a snowboard with nine-inch off-road tires). *Killington Rd., Killington; (802) 422-3333; (802) 422-3261 (snow phone); (800) 621-6867 (reservations);* www.killington.com

Mount Snow
★★★/$$$-$$$$

Vermont's southernmost family ski area wins raves from *FamilyFun* readers for its award-winning ski and snowboard programs and value-oriented packages. Night activities include tubing, sledding, grooming machine rides, family nights out, dog sledding, snowmobiling, and trips to the Galaxy Arcade. Accommodations include the Grand Summit Resort Hotel, condominiums, and Snow Lake Lodge. Several restaurants offer children's menus. [120 skiable acres; 130 trails (20 percent beginner, 60 percent intermediate, 20 percent advanced); 26 lifts, including 3 high-speed quads; 85 percent snowmaking coverage. Family facilities: Child care for children 6 weeks to 6 years, ski and snowboard clinics for children 3 to 12; and two-hour clinics for families with up to five participants (two adults, three children).] Check out their summer packages as well. *Rte. 100, West Dover; (802) 464-3333; (802) 464-2151 (snow phone); (800) 245-SNOW (reservations);* www.mountsnow.com

Okemo Mountain Resort
★★★★/$-$$$$

Okemo is known for its top-notch skiing and snowboarding terrain, kid-oriented instructors, and family-friendly policies. (Kids 6 and under ski free; kids 12 and under stay free with parents at Okemo Resort Properties.) Accommodations are available at Okemo Mountain Lodge or in one of 650 ski-in/ski-out and mountainside condominiums. Programs include Kids' Night Out, plus snowshoeing and cross-country skiing at nearby Okemo Valley Golf Club and Nordic Center. [520 skiable acres; 98 trails (25 percent beginner, 50 percent intermediate, 25 percent advanced); 14 lifts, including three super quads; 95 percent snowmaking coverage. Family facilities: Child care for children 6 weeks to 8 years; ski clinics for kids 4 to 18; snowboard clinics for children 5 to 18.] Open for summer pleasures, too. *77 Okemo Ridge Rd., Ludlow; (802) 228-4041; (802) 228-5222 (snow phone); (800) 78-OKEMO (reservations);* www.okemo.com

Smugglers' Notch
★★★★/$-$$$$

FamilyFun magazine readers laud this four-seasons resort in northern Vermont. Smugglers' Notch stretches for more than 1,000 acres over three mountains and offers top-notch amenities, award-winning ski and snowboard clinics, a staggering number of activities, and comprehensive packages. You'll find eight heated pools, three children's pools, three water slides, and six playgrounds, plus family snowshoe walks, magic shows, tubing, wacky science shows, cross-country skiing, and movie nights. Accommodations range from studios to five-bedroom town houses in the village, which has kid-pleasing restaurants, shops, 12 tennis courts, and a child-care center complete with a petting zoo. [260 skiable acres; 67 trails (22 percent beginner, 53 percent intermediate, 25 percent advanced); 9 lifts; 62 percent snowmaking coverage. Family facilities: Alice's Wonderland

Child Enrichment Center for children 6 months to 6 years; ski lessons for children 3 and up; snowboard clinics for children 6 and up.] For night fun, the Fun Zone interactive play area has a crawl-through whale, mini golf, basketball, and a 22-foot-long double slide. In the summer, Smugglers' has a full slate of family recreation, too. *Rte. 108, Smugglers' Notch; (802) 644-8851; (800) 644-1104 (snow phone); (800) 451-8752 (reservations);* www.smuggs.com

Stowe Mountain Resort
★★★/$$$-$$$$

Stowe combines great skiing with a picture-perfect setting and the amenities of a European-style resort. There's a New England village, a cozy lodge, numerous restaurants, and skiing and snowboarding on or near Vermont's highest peak (4,395-foot-high Mount Mansfield). Though Stowe has attracted advanced skiers for more than 60 years, the resort caters to young beginners at Spruce Peak; there's an exceptional cross-country trail network, too. [480 skiable acres; 47 trails (16 percent beginner, 59 percent intermediate, 25 percent advanced); 17 lifts, including an eight-person high-speed quad; 73 percent snowmaking coverage. Family facilities: Child care for children 6 weeks to 6 years; clinics for children 3 and up.] Area activities include sleigh rides, snowshoeing,

continued on next page

and ice-skating. In summer, check out the skate park, gondola rides, alpine slides, and hiking trails. *Rte. 108, Stowe; (802) 253-3000; (802) 253-3600 (snow phone); (888) 253-4849 (general information);* www. stowe.com

Stratton
★★★/$$-$$$$
Home to the U.S. Open Snowboarding Championships, Stratton is a good choice if you want to ski and snowboard in an upscale atmosphere offering deluxe accommodations; sophisticated, yet casual, restaurants; and top-notch instruction. There's a 45-acre Learning Park for beginners, plus snowshoe treks, ice-skating, sleigh rides, and cross-country skiing. Families can stay in condominiums, town homes, and lodges on or off the mountain. [583 skiable acres; 90 trails (35 percent beginner, 37 percent intermediate, 28 percent advanced); 14 lifts, including a 12-passenger, high-speed gondola and two six-passenger, high-speed detachable quads; 85 percent snowmaking coverage. Family facilities: Child care for children 6 weeks to 5 years; top-ranked ski and snowboard clinics for children 4 and up.] Summer highlights include tennis camp. *RR 1, Stratton Mountain; (802) 297-2200; (802) 297-4211 (snow phone); (800) 787-2886 (reservations);* www.stratton.com

will enjoy the short walk from the visitors' center to the farm to meet rare breeds of cows, pigs, sheep, and horses. Kids ages 6 and up favor the 30-minute walk along the Discovery Trail, which also leads to the farm. *Rte. 315, Rupert; (802) 394-7836;* www.merckforest.com

Retreat Petting Farm
★★/$
Wear your overalls, juice up your tractor, and come on down. Kids will love the chance to pet, cuddle, and feed the menagerie of farm animals at this working dairy farm. The please-touch environment includes 200 cows and 150 chickens, plus calves, heifers, emus, llamas, ponies, and pigs. This is the place to hold a baby chick, feed an ox, and milk a cow. *350 Linden St., Brattleboro; (802) 257-2240.*

Riley Rink at Hunter Park
★★/$
Take your kids for a spin at this beautiful, Olympic-size indoor ice-skating rink. You can rent skates, and there's a snack bar. *Rte. 7A, Manchester; (802) 362-0150.*

Sun Bowl Ranch
★★/$$$-$$$$
Set on Stratton Mountain, the ranch offers one- and two-hour trail rides for children ages 6 and up. On winter sleigh rides, families receive a goodie basket, pile into the sleigh pulled by two friendly Belgian

horses, Smoky and Bandit, and ride through the woods. Your destination: a bonfire where you can roast s'mores and sip hot chocolate (ingredients are in the goodie basket). The trip takes about an hour. *Stratton Mountain, Stratton; (802) 297-9210.*

Taylor Farm Sleigh Rides
★★/$$$

For the archetypal winter Vermont experience, bundle up, climb into a sleigh pulled by a Belgian horse, cuddle under a blanket, and enjoy a 45-minute ride through the woods. Along the way, you'll stop for hot cider and marshmallows by the fire. If you'd like something more substantial, you can preorder a picnic lunch, featuring bread, the farm's own cheese, and cookies. While visiting Taylor Farm, you'll also get the chance to meet 40 Holstein cows and, most likely, a newborn calf. *Rte. 11, Londonderry; (802) 824-5690.*

BUNKING DOWN

Colonial House Inn & Motel
★★★/$$

Located a mile and a half from the center of historic Weston, the motel has TVs in every room, but you'll probably be too busy skiing, sledding, hiking, and swimming nearby. The big draw at this homey inn/motel is the stupendous, complimentary breakfast. Depending on the day, your morning fare may include pumpkin muffins, hot Lumberjack Mush topped with pure maple syrup, buttermilk pancakes (more maple syrup), made-to-order omelettes, or bread that's baked on the premises. Pies, breads, scones, sticky buns, and cookies are also for sale here. Dinner (an extra fee) is a casual yet sophisticated affair with such entrées as pan-fried trout, London broil, and leg of lamb (again,

---

FamilyFun READER'S TIP

Travel Trivia

My husband and I wanted our family trip to be both educational and fun for our 9- and 11-year-old boys. To engage their interest, we devised a game to play while sight-seeing. Every morning I would give my sons three questions pertaining to the places we would visit that day. If they answered all three they could order the dessert of their choice at dinner. They could use any resource, including a plaque at the site, a tour guide, brochures, and the like. They thought it was great fun to win a dessert off Mom and Dad, and they were so successful that we bought a round every night. Websites and guidebooks were our sources for the questions. With that little bit of preparation, our kids ended up not only having a great time but learning a lot, too.

Kathy Davis, Charlotte, North Carolina

the menu varies). There are plenty of options for kids, too. *287 Rte. 100, Weston; (800) 639-5033; (802) 824-6286.*

Combes Family Inn
★★★/$$$

Built in 1891 as a dairy farm, this cozy, family-owned inn is a place to enjoy old-fashioned pursuits like spying on butterflies, taking a dip in Buttermilk Falls, visiting neighboring llamas, and swimming in Echo Lake. The country-style inn is set on 50 acres of rolling meadows. It accommodates families with rooms in the main farmhouse and in the attached motel-style unit. There's a closet full of games, a large common room with a TV, and a sledding hill (you can borrow sleds). Many guests consider the breakfasts to be the best part of the stay. *953 E. Lake View Rd., Ludlow; (800) 822-8799.*

Four Winds Country Motel
★★★/$

This clean, family-friendly motel is situated on spacious grounds where kids can play horseshoes, basketball, and go sledding. The motel features big, classically furnished rooms (some of them connect) with cable color TV and refrigerators. There's also an outdoor pool and an appealing breakfast room where guests enjoy complimentary breakfast. A popular spot for family reunions, this is probably Manchester's best bargain. *7379 Historic Rte. 7A, Manchester Center; (877) 456-7654; (802) 362-1105;* www.fourwinds motel.com

Green River Inn ★★/$$

Kids will love visiting the sheep, llama, and Scottish highland cattle at the inn's working farm. Set on 450 acres by the Green River, this pastoral retreat offers simple pleasures, such as fishing, hiking, sledding, stargazing, and snowman building. You can also go downhill skiing at nearby Bromley or Stratton. The historic inn has two family rooms (with a king-size bed and sleep sofa; no TVs), and a kids' playroom with a TV and VCR. Kid-friendly meals are served in the dining room (breakfast is included in the room rate). *2480 Sandgate Rd., Sandgate; (802) 375-2272.*

Hill Farm Inn
★★★/$$-$$$

Set on 50 acres of farmland on the Battenkill River, this is the perfect spot if you and your crew want to rise with the roosters, indulge in tasty home cooking, and soak up Vermont's country spirit. Young guests enjoy canoeing, making new friends around the fireplace, meet-

> Although Vermont was almost entirely deforested by the **timber industry** in the late 1800s, the state is now more than 75 percent wooded.

ing barnyard animals, and playing on the swing set in the spacious yard. Families can stay in the 1830 main inn, 1790 guesthouse (both contain two-room suites), or cabins (available from May to October) with porches and showers. *Hillfarm Rd., Arlington; (800) 882-2545; (802) 375-2269.*

Johnny Seesaw's
★★★/$$-$$$

Built as a rowdy roadhouse in the 1920s by Russian logger Ivan Sesow, Johnny Seesaw's is now a favorite place for families to stay and eat. The rooms (suites are best if you're traveling with kids) have a cozy, lived-in look, and a laid-back spirit pervades the place. There's an entertainment room with video games and two fireplaces, and the popular (yet rather pricey) restaurant serves kids' favorites. In summer and fall, you can use the tennis courts and Olympic-size outdoor pool. You can rent cottages, too. *Rte. 11, Peru; (800) 424-CSAW; (802) 824-5533.*

Londonderry Inn ★★★/$$

The 25 rooms at this rambling inn seem to go on forever, but every inch is geared to children. Chris and Maya Kearn, their three kids, and a menagerie of pets run this historic property, and they've made it more family-friendly than ever. In place of the former bar is a movie room where kids can watch videos. For dinner, homemade soup and bread are available as an alternative to pricey restaurant meals. There are teddy bears on every bed, and Maya's colorful paintings decorate the walls. Several rooms can accommodate families, and the Kearns are excellent at recommending activities for families. The spring-fed swimming pool is open in summer. *Rte. 100, Londonderry; (802) 824-5226;* www.londonderryinn.com

Manchester Highlands Inn
★★★/$$-$$$

This fancy Victorian inn blends scenery (the lodge overlooks Mount Equinox) and character. The carriage house, behind the main inn, has several rooms that accommodate families, plus there's a game room where you can play Ping-Pong and piece together puzzles. Best of all, you can walk to a cozy television lounge (rooms have no TVs) via an underground tunnel decorated with the graffiti of past guests. (Here, it's no crime to write on the walls.) You can relax in the sunroom in the main house, indulge in country breakfasts, and snack on homemade cookies. (Breakfast and cookies are included in the rate.) *Highland Ave., Manchester; (800) 743-4565; (802) 362-4565.*

Roaring Branch Log Cabin Resort ★★/$$

If you're pining for a hideaway in the woods, consider staying in a log

185

cabin nestled among 37 acres of white pine forest. Built between 1912 and 1917, each of the rough-hewn cabins has a stone fireplace, living area, fully stocked kitchen, and one to three bedrooms. Set along the Roaring Branch of the Battenkill River, the camps are a great place to swim and fish for trout. There's also a playground, two tennis courts, and a Ping-Pong pavilion. You need to bring your own linens and towels. *Sunderland Hill Rd., Arlington; (802) 375-6401.*

Shearer Hill Farm
★★★/$$

You and your kids can swing in a hammock, make new friends in the common room (which has a video library), and swim at nearby Harriman Reservoir. Animal lovers can meet a white-faced Hereford bull calf named Valentine, and other four-legged friends, in the grassy field. Stay in the main inn, or a free-standing house that offers more space and privacy. Breakfast in the inn's dining room is a treat, especially the prize-winning scones, featured in *Yankee* magazine. *Shearer Hill Rd., Halifax; (800) 437-3104; (802) 464-3253;* www.shearerhill farm.com

Wiley Inn
★★★/$$-$$$

This inn offers romantic getaways in "couples rooms," but also rolls out the red carpet for parents and kids.

Set on ten scenic acres, the ten-room inn has two-bedroom suites and family rooms, and the rates include a hearty breakfast in the dining room. You can play Chinese checkers by the fire, have fun on-line in the library (Internet use is free for guests), and watch family movies on comfy sofas in the lounge. In summer and fall, young guests love swimming in the outdoor pool, and dropping trout food into the pond and watching the fish jump. The Wiley Inn is near four downhill ski areas, six cross-country centers, and hiking, biking, and snowmobile trails. *Rte. 11, Peru; (802) 824-6600;* www.wileyinn.com

GOOD EATS

Alonzo's Pasta and Grille
★★/$$

Known for its selection of kids' meals for under $3, this casual restaurant offers a creative range of pasta dishes (ever tried straw and hay pasta?), burgers, ribs, and fajitas. If you have room, share the Chocolate Lava Pie à la mode—it has a hot

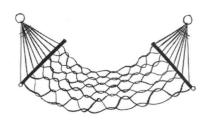

molten chocolate core. *At the Crafts Inn, West Main St., Wilmington; (802) 464-2355.*

Best Diner
★★★/$

True to its name, this is one of Manchester's top spots for families. Kids can get silver-dollar pancakes, hot dogs, and macaroni and cheese, plus strawberry milk shakes, plain cheese pizza, and Toll House cookie pie. Every night of the week, your crew can order family-style dinners, from meat loaf on Monday to fish-and chips on Friday. *Rtes. 11/30, Manchester Center; (802) 362-5657.*

D.J.'s Restaurant
★★/$$

After skiing or hiking at Okemo, families like chowing down at this local restaurant, which only serves dinner. No crayons or coloring books here—just good, consistent food, a friendly staff, and a comfortable atmosphere. Young diners can order chicken fingers and pasta, while parents dig into the signature steaks, seafood, and salad bar. *146 Main St., Ludlow; (802) 228-5374.*

Dot's ★★/$

This popular local spot is a hit with visiting families and anyone else who loves home cooking at reasonable prices. The berry pancakes are so good that you'll probably come back several times during your vacation. At breakfast, lunch, and dinner,

High Country Snowmobile Tours

One of Vermont's top winter sports is snowmobiling, and this family-owned outfitter can guide your crew on an hour-long tour through the **Green Mountain National Forest. Wendy and Mark Pederson have two kids, so they know how to make a trip safe and fun. High Country's instructors are well-versed in teaching beginners and will lead families on an exciting 12- to 15-mile journey along the state's extensive trail system.** You'll pass scenic vistas and wide-open fields, and may even spot moose and deer. Families of four typically rent two Ski Doo snowmobiles, with a child riding behind each parent. (Kids 18 and under ride free.)

High Country also rents wave runners and boats on Lake Whitingham (aka the Harriman Reservoir), the largest body of water completely within Vermont. The outfitter is located *at Mount Snow Ski Resort* (see page 180) and *on Rte. 9 in Searsburg.* For reservations, call *(800) 627-7533* or *(802) 464-2108;* www.high-country-tours.com

kids can color while they nosh on all of their favorites. If you like chili, get it while it's hot—really hot—here. Two locations: *Rte. 9 W., Wilmington (802/464-7284); and Rte. 100, W. Dover (802/464-6476).*

Laney's
★★★/$$

Kids of all ages will find lots to keep them entertained at this restaurant. The walls are festooned with autographed glossies of Hollywood stars, a player piano plunks "Roll Out the Barrel," and there's an old-time Mutoscope through which you can watch a Charlie Chaplin flick. The children's activity menu features themed meals (Muppets is cheese pizza) that come with a Shirley Temple, milk, soda, or juice, plus a scoop of Ben & Jerry's ice cream. Laney's bottles its own root beer, supplies kids with balloons, and invites young diners to draw on the paper tablecloths. Parents will find everything from ribs and chicken to seafood and pasta. *Rtes. 11/30, Manchester; (802) 362-4456.*

FamilyFun GAME

A Tougher Tic-tac-toe

Make the classic game of tic-tac-toe a little more lively and a bit tougher with this one basic change: with each turn, a player can fill in the empty space of his choice with either an X or an O.

Mother Myrick's ★★★/$

The tag line says it best: "Save $50. The next time you want a great dessert, skip dinner." Specialties at this famous dessert maker include Lemon Lulu Cake, hot fudge sundaes with fresh whipped cream, Creamsicle coolers, milk shake floats, and home-baked peanut-butter bars. *Rte. 7A, Manchester; (802) 362-1560.*

Mulligan's ★★★/$$

It may look like a Bennigan's, but the fare here is a cut above that at a big chain. Mulligan's is known for its expertly grilled steaks, as well as ribs and seafood. Food is cooked to order, and there's plenty of TLC for the kids, who get crayons, coloring books, and novelty cups. All of their favorites—from hot dogs to pasta— are served up with a smile. Open for lunch and dinner. *Rte. 7A, Manchester Center; (802) 362-3663.*

Sirloin Saloon ★★/$$

The name of the game here is succulent beef, seafood, and chicken dishes, plus an appealing salad bar that features fresh vegetables from local growers. Your kids' attention, however, will probably be focused on the art and artifacts that give the place so much character. Mounted animal heads survey you from the walls, and western landscapes, Native American beadwork, and arrowheads are on display. *Rtes. 11/30, Manchester Center; (802) 362-2600; www.sirloinsaloon.com*

SOUVENIR HUNTING

Apple Barn and Country Bake Shop

This purveyor of agritainment invites you to pick your own raspberries, taste 30 varieties of apples, and stock up on apple-cider doughnuts, but what kids like best are the special events. In fall, for example, young visitors can challenge Maize Quest, a two-acre cornfield maze where puzzles and games lead to the Magic Apple. Kids can also shoot a pumpkin slingshot, launching pumpkins 300 feet into the air in an attempt to hit the dragon target. At Halloween, you can wander through a haunted cornfield maze. Call for a schedule of year-round activities; you're sure to leave here with such yummy souvenirs as apples, chocolates, cheese, and jams. *Rte. 7, Bennington; (888) 8-APPLES; (802) 447-7780.*

Big Black Bear Shop

Since 1933, Vermont toy maker Mary Meyer has crafted some of the softest, cutest, and most huggable toys in the business. Chances are you won't be able to resist buying a turtle that shimmies out of her shell, a pudgy sawtooth beaver, or a brown-eyed black bear. *Rte. 30, Townshend; (888) 758-BEAR; (802) 365-4160.*

Northshire Bookstore

Housed in the historic Colburn House, this outstanding bookstore invites kids to pluck a book from its well-displayed collection, find a comfortable chair, and dig in. The selection is amazing. Be sure to check the schedule to see if your favorite author will be in town for a reading. *4869 Main St., Manchester Center; (800) 437-3700; (802) 362-2200.*

Tom and Sally's Handmade Chocolates

You can watch gourmet candies being made at this friendly factory, but it's even more fun to taste the goodies. Try the cow chips. (Don't worry, the tag line reads: Pure Chocolate, No Doo Doo.) *Rte. 30, Brattleboro; factory tour information: (802) 254-4200.*

Find out if you like Strawberry or Chocolate Chip Cookie Dough—or Karamel Sutra or One Sweet Whirled, for that matter—in the FlavoRoom during Ben & Jerry's Ice Cream Factory Tour.

Central Vermont

SOME OF VERMONT'S BEST
vacation spots are located
smack in the 88-mile stretch
between Waterbury and Springfield.
Here you can sun yourself by Lake
Champlain at the family-oriented
Basin Harbor Club, visit the Ben &
Jerry's factory in Waterbury, order a
Moxie soda at the general store where
President Calvin Coolidge hung out
as a boy, and hike on scenic trails at
the state's only national historical
park (Woodstock's Marsh-Billings
Historical Park). What's more, you
can peer into Quechee Gorge, enjoy
dozens of hands-on exhibits at
Montshire Museum in Norwich, and
attend a family-oriented performance at Rutland's restored theater,
the Paramount.

At Okemo, Ascutney, Killington,
and Pico (see "Fun Family Ski
Resorts" on page 179), you can ski

THE FamilyFun LIST

MUST-SEE
MUST-SEE

Ben & Jerry's Ice Cream
   Factory Tour (page 196)

Billings Farm & Museum (page 193)

Lake Champlain Maritime Museum
   (page 194)

Montshire Museum of Science
   (page 194)

President Calvin Coolidge
   State Historic Site (page 195)

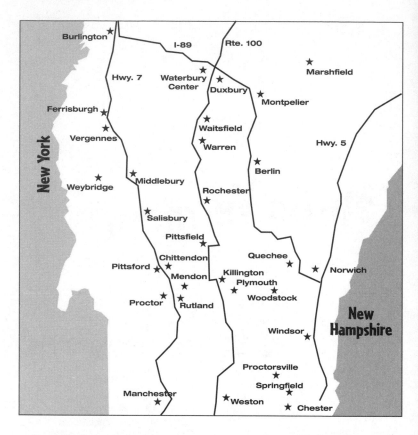

and snowboard on some of the best trails in the east. Plus, you can tube along the White River; ride a horse through the Green Mountain National Forest; boat, swim, and relax on lakes Champlain, Bomoseen, and St. Catherine; fish in the Ottauquechee River; and hike along Ripton's Robert Frost Trail.

Montpelier's downtown is filled with kid-friendly restaurants and awesome bookstores. Make time to tour the gold-domed state capital *(State St.; 802/828-2228)*, where you can challenge the kids to spot fossils in the marble floor of the lobby. Quechee is a good bet for summer. In June, you can float in for the annual Quechee Hot Air Balloon & Crafts Fair, one of the state's top tourist events. If you miss the event, there's still plenty to see, including Quechee Gorge, and glassblowing and pottery-making at Simon Pearce.

Stay around the Rutland/ Killington area if you long for the familiarity of chain hotels and restaurants. From here, venture on outings to Lake Bomoseen, Branbury State Park, the New England Maple Museum in Pittsford, and to Killington. The biggest ski resort in the east offers lots to do in summer, too, and you'll find leagues of family-friendly restaurants and outfitters along Route 4 and Killington Road.

The Upper Connecticut River Valley region includes 24 towns in New Hampshire and Vermont along a 20-mile stretch of the Connecticut River. The area's cultural center is Dartmouth College in Hanover, New Hampshire, but Vermont has its share of plum spots, too, notably Norwich's Montshire Museum of Science and Ascutney Mountain Resort in Brownsville. Thanks to Vital Communities, an education-oriented nonprofit organization, families can embark on more than 50 treasure hunts through forests and past waterfalls, historic cemeteries, and one-room schoolhouses. To get started, you'll need to purchase *The Valley Quest Map Book* ($7), available at two dozen retailers in the region and from Valley Quest *(104 Railroad Row, White River Junction, VT 05001; 802/291-9100)*. Along Woodstock's leafy streets, lined with Colonial and Federal-style homes, you'll find the state's only national historical park (Marsh-Billings-Rockefeller National Historical Park), a working farm that's open to families (Billings Farm & Museum), and a nature center where kids can meet eagles, vultures, and other raptors (the Vermont Raptor Center).

Cultural Adventures

Billings Farm & Museum
★★★★/$

Founded by Frederick Billings in 1871, this working dairy farm is part of the Marsh-Billings-Rockefeller National Historical Park (described on page 194). Here, kids can meet a herd of sweet-faced Jerseys, peek into the calf nursery, greet a flock of sheep, and tour an 1890s farmhouse. You also can try your hand at old-time farm activities, such as butter-making and milking the cows.

Set amid emerald-green hills, this is one of Vermont's prettiest farms, and the staff loves sharing it with families. Special events include Cow Appreciation Day, Children's Day, and holiday sleigh rides. Kids who are especially interested in farming will enjoy the indoor exhibits on plowing, seeding, and harvesting, and the 30-minute Oscar-nominated film, *A Place in the Land. Rte. 12, Woodstock; (802) 457-2355; www.billingsfarm.org*

Vermont's nickname, the **Green Mountain State**, comes from its French translation.

Lake Champlain Maritime Museum ★★★/$$

What a fun place to learn about the history of Lake Champlain. Set on three acres, this museum has ten exhibit buildings with plenty of hands-on activities for kids. In the children's activity center, known as the Roost, young guests can play with toys, do crafts, and participate in programs with nautical themes. Kids also enjoy roaming around the property and visiting the blacksmith, watching craftsmen make full-size and model boats, and climbing aboard the 54-foot gunboat *Philadelphia*. Special programs are routinely offered and include family canoe treks, kids' colonial crafts programs, and children's boating programs. *4472 Basin Harbor Rd., Vergennes; (802) 475-2022;* www.lcmm.org

Marsh-Billings-Rockefeller National Historical Park ★★★/$

You can combine fun with lessons on caring for the land at this, the only national park to focus on stewardship and conservation. In the Carriage Barn visitors' center, parents can read about America's great conservationists, while kids head for their own computer station where they can create their own virtual parks. Outside, you can hike to Mount Tom or enjoy a picnic by the scenic lake called the Pogue. The park is named in honor of four individuals: George Perkins Marsh, an environmentalist who grew up on the property; Fred Billings, who created the carriage roads and opened them to the public; and Billings's granddaughter, Mary French Rockefeller, and her husband, Laurance S. Rockefeller. The Rockefellers created the park and the Billings Farm & Museum. *Rte. 12, Woodstock; (802) 457-3368;* www.nps.gov/mabi

Montshire Museum of Science ★★★★/$

You'll find science lessons everywhere at this museum, located on 100 wooded acres alongside the Connecticut River. In the outdoor playground, for example, a simple seesaw is a momentum machine that illustrates the laws of physics.

MAPLE SYRUP producers create four types of syrup from the tree sap. Fancy Grade, Grade A Medium Amber, Grade A Dark Amber, and Grade B all differ in color and taste, so you'll have to try them all out to see which one you like best.

Inside, toddlers to teens will find lots of hands-on fun, including making giant bubbles, examining a leaf-cutting ant farm, pulling up to the counter for "soda-fountain science," viewing freshwater and saltwater aquariums, and playing at Andy's Place, an activity center for pre-schoolers. Visitors are welcome to walk along the outdoor trails, which also serve as the setting for many activities. *One Montshire Rd., Norwich; (802) 649-2200;* www. montshire.org

New England Maple Museum ★★/$

At this old-fashioned, low-tech museum you can learn how it takes 40 gallons of sap to produce one gallon of maple syrup. Through a wall mural, a film, and a collection of sugaring artifacts, Vermont's springtime ritual becomes a fun science lesson. Best of all, you can sample different grades of syrup, and, of course, purchase your favorites in the gift shop. *Rte. 7, Pittsford; (802) 483-9414.*

President Calvin Coolidge State Historic Site ★★★★/Free

Even those who know little about Calvin Coolidge will gain new respect for our 30th president after visiting his birthplace and boyhood home. The village looks much as it did when Coolidge was president (1923-1929), prompting visitors to marvel at his humble beginnings. You can visit the very buildings where Calvin was born, worshiped, and was sworn in by his father as Warren Harding's successor to the presidency. You can also tour the summer White House and buy Moxie soda (Calvin's favorite) at the general store where John Coolidge, Calvin's father, was storekeeper. Throughout your visit, pay attention to the details, such as the "Tumbling Blocks" quilt that Calvin hand-stitched as a boy. Also, part of the site is the Plymouth Cemetery, where six generations of Coolidges are buried. A simple, granite headstone marks the president's grave. *Rte. 100A, Plymouth; (802) 672-3773; (802) 672-3612.*

University of Vermont Morgan Horse Farm ★★/$

Located about two and a half miles from Middlebury, this scenic farm is the place to horse around with up to eight dashing Morgans, America's first breed of horse. You can take a guided tour of the main barn, view a 15-minute video, picnic on the spacious lawn, and watch Morgans trot in the Training Hall. In spring, you can visit the mares and foals. *74 Battell Dr., Weybridge; (802) 388-2011;* www.uvm.edu/cals/farms/mhfarm.htm

Vermont Marble Exhibit ★★/$

Your chips off the old block will enjoy meeting the resident sculptor at the world's largest marble exhibit. Kids can don goggles and chip away at a marble block, while parents watch in the observation area. The museum highlights the history of the Vermont Marble Co. and introduces you to marble from around the world and throughout the ages. Children will want to visit the new geology exhibit, Earth Alive, to check out fluorescent minerals, fossils of a 22-foot-long triceratops and ancient horse, and a 160-foot mural depicting the earth's composition. Junior geologists can even pose questions to the museum's kid-friendly geology expert, "Doc Rock," before your visit (send e-mail via www.vermont-marble.com), and get the answers on arrival. *52 Main St., Proctor; (800) 427-1390; (802) 459-2300;* www.vermont-marble. com

Vermont Raptor Center
★★★/$

At this educational center and clinic, you can get close looks at bald eagles, peregrine falcons, snowy owls, and more than 20 other high-flying hunters. Some of the raptors are permanent residents; others are recovering from injuries. Programs are held throughout the day, and you can wander along self-guided trails on the 78-acre nature preserve. Make time to visit the nature center to check out the snakes, turtles, spiders, and the gift shop. *Church Hill Rd., Woodstock; (802) 457-2779.*

(The Vermont Institute of Natural Science, which operates the facility, has two other sites with family-friendly hiking trails: *North Branch Nature Center, 713 Elm St./Rte. 12, Montpelier; 802/229-6206;* and *VINS-Manchester, 109 Union St., Manchester; 802/362-4374.*)

JUST FOR FUN

Ben & Jerry's Ice Cream Factory Tour
★★★★/$

Get the scoop on how Ben & Jerry's ice cream is made during a 30-minute guided tour that includes scrumptious samples. Although the ice-cream company is now owned by corporate giant Unilever, and Ben and Jerry are no longer at the helm, you wouldn't know it from the seven-minute introductory video that shows how childhood chums Ben Cohen and Jerry Greenfield

turned a $5 correspondence course into a global business. After the video, it's off to an observation deck where you can watch ice-cream makers in action. Then, get your licks in in the Flavoroom. Then you can order up to 40 flavors at the ice cream shop. **NOTE:** There's no ice cream production on Sundays, holidays, and special celebration days, but most likely you'll still be able to take an abbreviated tour. *Rte. 100, Waterbury; (802) 882-1260; www.benjerry.com/ tourinfo.tmpl*

Branbury State Park ★★★/$
Located on the eastern shore of Lake Dunmore, this 69-acre park has a 1,000-foot-long natural sandy beach, grassy picnic areas, and boat rentals. Hiking trails lead to scenic waterfalls, caves, and mountain lakes. *Hwy. 53, Salisbury; (802) 247-5925; www.vt stateparks.com/ htm.branbury/.cfm*

Button Bay State Park ★★★/$
Named for buttonlike, clay formations along its shoreline, this 253-acre park on a bluff on Lake Champlain has a swimming pool with lifeguards, boat rentals, and a nature center. *Button Bay State Park Rd., Vergennes; (802) 475-2377; www.vtstateparks. com/htm/button/bay.cfm*

Cavendish Trail Rides ★★/$$-$$$
Kids over age 8 can hit the trail on horseback at this riding center.

Choose from half-hour and hour-long rides through 500 acres of woods and meadows. Younger kids can take pony rides, plus there are seasonal wagon rides and hayrides. You can also hunt for treasures in the ongoing barn sale. *Twenty Mile Stream Rd., Proctorsville; (802) 226-7821.*

Fun Family Ski Resorts
For all-season information on Ascutney, Pico, and Killington ski resorts, see page 179.

Green Mountain National Forest ★★★/Free
The northern half of the forest offers many special hikes for families. Along the easy, milelong Robert Frost Interpretive Trail, for example, you'll find several of Frost's poems mounted in woods and fields. For information on this and other hikes, contact the **Middlebury Ranger District** (*1007 Rte. 7 S., Middlebury; 802/388-4362*), the **Rochester Ranger District** (*99 Ranger Rd., Rochester; 802/767-4261*), or the **Forest Supervisor's Office** (*231 N. Main St., Rutland; 802/747-6700*).

Green Mountain Rock Climbing Center ★★/$$
Kids as young as 3 have made it to the top of the 26-foot-high artificial rock walls at this popular climbing center. After you're fitted for protective gear and receive a safety lesson, you're ready to scale some of the 34

walls, which depict great American vistas. The grips are labeled, indicating levels of difficulty. *223 Woodstock Ave. (Rte. 4), Rutland; (802) 773-3343.* There's a second, seasonal location at Snowshed Ski Lodge at Killington Ski Resort.

Lots O' Balls ★★★/$

This 19-hole miniature-golf course was voted Number one by *Vermont Golf Magazine* in part because of the creative obstacles inspired by Vermont landmarks. Kids can hit balls through a famous round barn, gristmill, Congregational church, and covered bridge. There's a snack bar, too. *Rte. 100, Duxbury; (802) 244-5874.* **NOTE:** In Quechee, an older, 18-hole course, Quechee Gorge Minigolf *(Rte. 4, Quechee; 802-296-6669),* invites kids to putt under waterfalls and over a miniature recreation of Quechee Gorge.

MUST-SEE FamilyFun Quechee Gorge ★★★/Free

Carved by the Ottauquechee River, Vermont's "little Grand Canyon" is more than a mile long and 165 feet deep. You can view this natural wonder from the Quechee Bridge on Route 4, which spans the chasm. For a closer look, hike on a gorgeside trail that leads past a beaver pond, a waterfall, and a stand of sugar maples. The Quechee Chamber of Commerce information booth *(Rte. 4, Quechee; 802/295-7900)* can provide maps.

BUNKING DOWN

Basin Harbor Club
★★★★/$$$$

It doesn't get much better than this. For four generations, the Beach family has welcomed families to this 700-acre retreat on Lake Champlain. The 77 cottages were handcrafted generations ago by the Beaches, and they've been beautifully updated with phones, refrigerators, and classy yet comfortable furnishings (no TVs). The main lodge has a dining room overlooking the lake. There's an 18-hole golf course, tennis courts, a large swimming pool, boating, and an exceptional playground. You also can enjoy special events, such as hayrides, bonfires, family picnics, and (in summer) a complimentary children's program. Kids can play in the children's garden, take swimming lessons, go fishing, and more. Summer guests must sign on for the full American plan, which includes three meals a day. If your family chooses, kids can eat and play with their new friends and staff counselors, while parents savor sophisticated fare in the fancy dining room. *Off Panton Rd., Vergennes; (800) 622-4000; (802) 475-2311; www.basin harbor.com*

The Bridges Family Resort & Tennis Club ★★★/$$$

If your family likes to play tennis, you just scored. This resort features

12 tennis courts, with lessons for children and adults of every level, and tennis packages that let you volley all day long. Set in the Mad River Valley, the resort has one-, two,- and three-bedroom condos with full kitchens, fireplaces or woodstoves, and views of the Green Mountains from private decks. You also can enjoy three swimming pools, a playground, and game room. Just a third of a mile from Sugarbush ski area and seven miles from Mad River Glen, the Bridges also offers several family ski packages (prices vary widely, depending on the package you select and your length of stay). *202 Bridge Circle, Warren; (800) 453-2922; (802) 583-2922;* www.bridge resort.com

Cortina Inn
★★★/$$$

The family rooms at this inn have a master bedroom for Mom and Dad, and an adjoining, log-cabin-themed room with bunk beds for the kids. Another option is a mountain loft suite, with master bedroom and loft area with three twin beds. On-site activities include ice-skating, sleigh rides, swimming in the indoor pool, guided mountain bike trips, tennis, and a game room (plus massages for weary parents). There also are two on-site restaurants: one fancy, one casual. Laid-back Theodore's Tavern features a weekly all-you-can-eat pasta buffet with three savory sauces. An abundant break-fast buffet, complete with carving station, is included in the rate. *103 Rte. 4, Killlington; (800) 451-6108; (802) 773-3331;* www.cortinainn.com

Deer Brook Inn ★★/$$

Your hosts at this B&B are Brian and Rosemary McGinty and their sociable children, all excellent resources on what the area holds for kids. The inn has five rooms (the

Good Sports

Want to learn to canoe or kayak? Paddle on over to the Mad River Valley, where **Clearwater Sports** will take your family on a guided trip (or offer suggestions for a self-guided journey) on the Winooski River. The instructors build in time to swim with the kids and have lunch on the rocks overlooking a small set of rapids. One price includes equipment, transportation, and instruction. A Mad Yakkers day camp for paddlers ages 7 to 14 includes games, animal tracking, and flatwater paddling. For kids ages 11 to 16, there are three- or five-day kayak programs (the latter involves overnights in Maine and New Hampshire). Bike rentals are available, as are autumn nature programs. *Rte. 100, Waitsfield; (802) 496-2708;* www.clearwater sports.com best option for families is the two-room suite with TV), a spacious yard, and a rabbit and dog that enjoy attention. Rosemary's breakfasts are delicious. *535 Rte. 4, Woodstock; (802) 672-3713.*

Holiday Inn ★★★/$$

This property goes above and beyond the call for families. During school vacations, the hotel sets up a game room with foosball, Ping-Pong, television, and board games. In winter, you can take sleigh rides along wooded trails in a custom-made Austrian sleigh. In warm weather, you can hike on those same trails, have fun at the playground, and, any time of year, order pizza by the beautiful indoor pool. Young guests eat free at pleasant Paynter's Restaurant when an adult orders an entrée. *476 US Rt. 75, Rutland; (800) 462-4810; (802) 775-1911;* www.bass hotels.com/holiday-inn

Hollister Hill Farm ★★/$$

The inn has a family suite (a main bedroom for Mom and Dad, plus a small adjoining bedroom that can accommodate two kids), as well as a second bedroom that can accommodate three people (by employing a rollaway cot). There are no TVs in the rooms, but there's a common area with puzzles and games. Kids can meet the farm animals and learn about maple sugaring. *2193 Hollister Hill Rd., Marshfield; (802) 454-7725.*

Hugging Bear Inn & Shoppe ★★/$$

This six-bedroom Victorian inn is as warm and fuzzy as it gets. A crib contains a family of huggable bears that you can adopt during your stay. The Winnie the Pooh–themed room is suitable for two parents and a child; two other bear-themed rooms with two double beds are each suit-

Terrific Task Masters

When our family goes on vacation, we assign each of our seven children an important task for the duration of the trip, one that will make each child an active part of planning. On a trip to Orlando, Florida, these were their assignments. Sylvia, age 15, navigator and accountant, kept track of mileage, maps, and money; TamiSue, 13, photographer, had to use two rolls of film a day; Joshua, 10, auto mechanic, pumped gas and checked oil and tire pressure; Bryan, 7, mailman, got postcards and stamps and mailed the cards kids write to themselves each day; Libby, 7, dietitian, made sure the cooler was stocked; Andrew, 6, activities coordinator and music director, was solely in charge of the tape player; and Katie, 5, referee, settled all road disputes.

Wendy Lira, Alma, Kansas

able for four. The den contains toys, games, and a TV, and full breakfast is included. The shop stocks more than 10,000 bears costing $2 and up. *244 Main St., Chester; (800) 325-0519; (802) 875-2412;* www.hugging bear.com

Liberty Hill Farm
★★★★/$$$$

Readers of *FamilyFun* magazine rave about this place, which deserves its excellent reputation for hospitality and fun. The Kennett Family welcomes kids and parents to their dairy farm, home to 120 Holsteins, baby calves, and kittens. Families stay in seven guest rooms (with four shared baths) and enjoy delicious, home-cooked breakfasts and dinners (included in the rate). The activities are delightfully old-fashioned. You can swing on a tire, tube down the Green River (tubes provided), feed the farm babies, or piece together a puzzle on the front porch. Rates include breakfast and dinner. *511 Liberty Hill Rd., Rochester; (802) 767-3926;* www.libertyhillfarm.com

Mountain Meadows Lodge
★★★★/$$-$$$

Michelle Werle and her family have converted an 1850s farm into one of Vermont's best places for families. The 13-acre retreat, on Kent Lake and surrounded by national forest, is a veritable children's playland. Depending on what time of year you come, you can cook popcorn in

HEADS—AND CAPS—UP!

Middlebury College's midyear graduates celebrate the completion of their degrees with a unique tradition. Every February, the honored students—in full cap and gown—ride the Snow Bowl chairlift up into the Green Mountains. Every graduate hurtles down the mountain on skis, snowboard, sled, or snowshoes to the sounds of the cheering crowd waiting at the bottom.

----

the fireplace, pet the animals in the barn, go animal tracking, canoe or kayak, hike from the lodge to the Appalachian Trail, take a pony ride, swim in the pool, or join a marshmallow roast. The Mountain Meadows Cross-Country Ski Center can outfit your family for a snowshoeing or ski trip along 37 miles of groomed trails. An on-site kids' program features barnyard activities, arts and crafts, hikes, and themed lunches. Meals feature everything from veal to vegetarian options. Accommodations range from standard rooms to junior suites, and you can choose lodging plans that include breakfast or breakfast and dinner. *285 Thundering Brook Rd., Killington; (800) 370-4567.*

Mountain Top Inn
★★★/$$$$

Set on 1,330 acres high in the Green Mountain National Forest, this resort is a grand place for families who want to relax or enjoy an array of activities right on the premises. Any time of year, you'll find lots to do, from horseback riding, golf, and boating to cross-country skiing, snowshoeing, and horse-drawn sleigh rides. There's a sandy beach at the nearby lake, and the dining room dishes out children's favorites. (The Modified American Plan includes lunch and dinner.) You can stay in the inn or rent a cottage with a fireplace. *Mountain Top Rd., Chittenden; (802) 483-2311.*

FamilyFun SNACK

Cereal Solution

Before you leave on vacation, empty all your cereal boxes and create this snack mix.

In a large bowl, combine 3 cups of assorted cereals with ⅓ cup each of raisins, peanuts, and pretzels. Melt 4 ounces of white chocolate according to package directions and stir it into the cereal mixture until the bits are well coated. Chill for 20 to 30 minutes. Place in ziplock bags.

Vermont Inn
★★/$$$-$$$$

Country elegance meets comfort at this family-run inn, which caters to honeymooners and families with kids ages 6 and up. Several rooms accommodate four, with queen and trundle beds, for example. Although the dining room menu is sophisticated, it also offers traditional comfort foods for kids. They can even dig into a homemade brownie sundae. There's an outdoor pool, TV room, game room, and tennis court. The price reflects the MAP, which includes breakfast and dinner (breakfast-only plans are available, too). *Rte. 4, Killington; (800) 541-7795; (802) 775-0708;* www.vermont inn.com

Woodstock Inn
★★★/$$$$

Travel magazines hail this 200-year-old inn as one of North America's best, and most families would agree. Located on Woodstock's bucolic green, this classy but comfortable inn welcomes children with appealing menus in the dining rooms, spacious guest rooms, indoor and outdoor pools, and first-class recreational facilities. Enjoy downhill skiing on 22 trails at Suicide Six (don't let the name scare you), also home to a snowboard park. Cross-country ski on 37 miles of beautifully groomed trails at the Woodstock Ski Touring Center (which has kids' rentals). Other activities include golf, video games in the game room, cycling, tennis, and hiking to Mount Tom and Mount Peg. You also can choose from a variety of packages. Family Ski Weeks, for example, include lift tickets, breakfast, ski lessons, a sleigh ride, and family movies in the parlor. *14 The Green, Woodstock; (802) 457-1100;* www. woodstockinn.com

GOOD EATS

A&W Rootbeer Stand
★★★/$

Since 1952, the only A&W in Vermont has invited families to pull into a parking spot, wait for the carhop, and enjoy all-American meals in the comfort of the car. Kids love watching the action (sometimes, the carhops wear skates) and feasting on root beer floats, burgers, chicken fingers, milk shakes, and banana splits. Open seasonally. *1557 Rte. 7, Middlebury; (802) 388-2876.*

Casey's Caboose
★★★/$$

Chug on over to this choo-choo for pasta, potato skins, seafood, steak, and chicken dishes, and more than 20 kids' favorites. You can even eat in the observation cupola or watch a Lionel train make its way around the overhead tracks in the bar. *Killington Rd., Killington; (802) 422-3795.* (The same management company, Killington's Best Restaurants,

also owns Peppers Bar & Grill, where oranges travel across the room in Willy Wonka fashion to a machine that dispenses fresh-squeezed juice. *Killington Rd., Killington; 802/422-3177.*)

Fire & Ice
★★★★/$$

Not to be confused with the custom stir-fry restaurants of the same name (profiled on previous pages), this classy eatery boasts a unique innovation for families. Before, during, or after meals, kids (and parents) can escape to a small video theater off one of the dining rooms, shut the curtain, plunk down on pillows, and watch their favorite movies. The restaurant is filled with interesting artifacts and memorabilia, from a 1921 Hackercraft motorboat to more than 50 model boats and ships. Kids will find all of their favorites here, and parents can order everything from steaks and baked potatoes to cashew chicken stir-fry. The salad bar is tops. *26 Seymour St., Middlebury; (800) 367-7166; (802) 388-7166.*

A Travel Scrapbook

This suitcase-style scrapbook is just right for your child to pack with mementos of his vacation adventures — and it's a cinch to make.

Start with two cardboard report covers. Use one for the suitcase itself and one to cut out two U-shaped handles and two 1½- by 18-inch straps.

Attach one handle to the front of the suitcase by gluing the ends to the inside of the upper edge. Match up the second handle with the first one and glue it to the back side. Now close the suitcase and glue on the straps. Position the strap tops on the front of the suitcase one inch down from the upper edge, then wrap the straps around the back of the suitcase. Finally, fold down the strap ends so that they overlap the tops and attach stick-on Velcro-type fasteners.

For a handy photo pocket, glue a large open envelope to the inner cover. Then, fill the suitcase with manila folders for storing ticket stubs, brochures, and other souvenirs.

Grist Mill
★★/$$

Delicious chicken, ribs, burgers, and seafood dishes are just part of the reason to go to this restaurant. Set on the edge of Summit Pond, the Grist Mill invites families to sit on the front porch and soak up mountain views. In winter, you can rent ice skates and glide across the pond. *Killington Rd., Killington; (802) 422-3970.*

Hyde Away Restaurant
★★★/$$

Located near Sugarloaf ski resort, this 200-year-old farmstead welcomes families for dinner in a cozy, kid-friendly atmosphere. Classic children's meals are all here, plus there's a playroom with plenty of toys, a table and chairs for coloring, and a cable TV where kids can watch Nickelodeon. Grown-up dinners (try cheddar meat loaf) come with homemade bread and salad with maple-mustard house dressing. *Rte. 17, Waitsfield; (802) 496-2322.*

Main Street Grill & Bar
★★/$$

Here's your chance to sample cutting-edge dishes in a restaurant that's hip, yet comfortable for kids. A training facility for the New England Culinary Institute, this eatery features meals prepared by student chefs. Kids can dine on the classics (posted on the backs of working Etch A Sketches), while parents try creatively prepared salads, sandwiches, and main dishes. Because the menu changes constantly, we can't quote specifics. Suffice it to say, it's all very good. *118 Main St., Montpelier; (802) 223-3188.* (For a list of six other NECI dining facilities in Vermont, log on to www. neculinary.com)

Mountain Creamery Café ★★/$

Enjoy a hearty breakfast or lunch at this popular Woodstock restaurant. The country cooking will fill you up for all your adventures, and the treats are out of this world. Dip into pancakes, sandwiches, and burgers, but be sure to save room for the mile-high (not much of an exaggeration) pies, cookies, ice cream, and cakes—all of which are homemade. *33 Central St., Woodstock; (802) 457-1715.*

Rosie's Restaurant ★★★/$-$$

Families love the large, homey dining rooms and friendly spirit at this popular restaurant. The kids' menu offers 20 or so meal options, and children's dinners include a choice of two fruits or vegetables, not just the customary fries (though they're here, too). The main menu is a delightful, mixed bag. You'll find spaghetti, fried clams, roast turkey, and Reubens, and everything's delicious. *Rte. 7, Middlebury; (802) 388-7052.*

Sugar & Spice ★★/$

Before you eat, take a moment to watch maple syrup being made—and to draw off a sample to take to the upstairs dining room. There, you can pour the fresh syrup on French toast, waffles, and pancakes. (During lunch, sandwiches are on the menu, too.) The staff routinely makes maple candy and churns homemade ice cream in wooden buckets. (The maple ice cream is delicious.) You can even walk through a sugar bush adjacent to the restaurant. *Rte. 4, Mendon; (802) 773-7832.*

Wayside Restaurant & Bakery ★★★★/$

This restaurant is one in a million. It's inexpensive, the food is first rate, and the staff goes the extra mile to make kids feel welcome. Though not a fancy place, there are plenty of touches for families—shelves stacked with children's books, homebrewed cream soda, a *Peanuts*-themed menu for kids (Linus's Weakness is chicken nuggets), crayons and drawing paper, and more than 200 menu items, many priced under $2. Choose from old standbys, like chicken potpie and meat loaf, plus Yankee favorites, such as boiled dinners, salt pork and gravy, and stuffed perch. The fresh-made sugar doughnuts, praised by *The New York Times*, are extraordinary. *1873 Rte. 302, Berlin; (802) 223-6611.*

- -

It's in the Cards

My family loves to travel, and I have found a wonderful way to preserve our vacation memories. First, we buy postcards at all the different locations we visit. On the back, I jot down the highlights of the trip or funny things that happened while we were there. After we have returned home, I laminate all the postcards, punch holes in the top left corners, and put them all on a ring clip. It's exciting to see all of the places we have been, and the cards are inexpensive souvenirs of our travels.

Stefanie Wirths, Camdenton, Missouri

Windsor Station
★★/$-$$

Chug on over to this working train station in the Upper Connecticut River Valley for lunches and dinners with kid appeal. Dine in the casual lounge, where young guests can color trains on an activity sheet and see and hear Amtrak trains coming and going at the station. Kid fare includes fish-and-chips, burgers, and more; the main menu offers everything from fried scallops to chicken teriyaki. There's also a dimly lighted main dining room where Frank Sinatra recordings croon, and where kids are welcome but not always as happy as their parents. *Depot Ave., Windsor; (802) 674-2052.*

SOUVENIR HUNTING

All Things Bright and Beautiful

If you love stuffed animals, you'll be in heaven here. Housed in a two-story Victorian home, this store fea-

tures 12 rooms, each dedicated to specific soft species. In the cat and dog room, for example, you'll find 12 types of golden retrievers. Be sure to visit the teddy-bear den and the porch filled with swinging monkeys. *Bridge St., Waitsfield; (802) 496-3997.*

Cold Hollow Cider Mill

Just down the street from the Ben & Jerry's ice cream tour, this free attraction invites families to watch cider being made and dip into samples. The store stocks apple pies, fruit butters, pancake mixes, and cider doughnuts. *Rte. 100, Waterbury Center; (800) 3-APPLES; (802) 244-8771.*

Dakin Farm

Better wear stretch pants at this place, where the staff will ply you with free samples of cheese and other specialty foods. You also can tour the smokehouse and the maple syrup cannery. During sugaring season, the farm hosts popular pancake breakfasts and sugar-on-snow parties. *Rte. 7, Ferrisburgh; (800) 993-2546.*

Morse Farm

Dedicated to teaching families about maple sugaring, this farm is home to the Woodshed Theatre and an 18-minute video about the sugaring process. The real hit for kids, however, is the collection of animals and curmudgeons carved with a chain saw. To satisfy your sweet tooth, sample sugar-on-snow. In summer and fall, you can walk along the farm's Maple Trail, and, of course, watch the sap drip during sugaring season. *The County Road, Montpelier; (800) 242-2740; (802) 223-2740.*

Simon Pearce Glass

The fiery colors and bendable shapes make glassblowing fascinating for kids. Founded by famed Irish glass-maker Simon Pearce, this factory features a basement workshop where you can watch glassblowers and potters at work. Kids can even shape clay into their own take-home creations. *The Mill, Main St., Quechee; (802) 295-2711.*

Sugarbush Farm

Take a scenic, five-mile journey from Woodstock's village green to this 550-acre, family-owned farm, which produces exceptional cheese and maple syrup. Kids can taste test the fare and watch cheese packers hand-wrap and dip the blocks in wax to preserve freshness. The delicious products are all for sale in the store. You also can meander down the Maple and Nature Trail, used by draft horses to transport syrup from the sugarbush to the sugar-house. *591 Sugarbush Farm Rd., Woodstock; (800) 281-1757; (802) 457-1757*

Vermont Country Store

This 55-year-old, must-see attraction features thousands of items that practically beckon from the shelves, calling out, "You won't find me anywhere else." The goods include penny candy, manual typewriters, wall-mounted pencil sharpeners, British hot-water bottles, cobweb eliminators, and plenty of toys for the kids. *Rte. 100, Weston; (802) 824-3184. (There's also a store in Rockingham—Rte. 103; 802/463-2224.)*

Smugglers' Notch has been courting the family ski trade for decades. Just some of the evidence: 8 heated pools; 3 water slides; 6 playgrounds; indoor mini golf; and—get this—a child-care center with a petting zoo.

Northern Vermont

No MATTER WHAT YOUR taste in vacations, your family will find bliss in northern Vermont. This region is home to the state's largest city, Burlington (population: 40,000), and Vermont's most remote, hauntingly beautiful area, the Northeast Kingdom. The Lake Champlain Islands let visitors escape to an agricultural paradise filled with farm stands, lakeside getaways, and beautiful sandy beaches, while the village of Stowe combines the best of a New England burg with a first-class European resort.

If you really want to treat yourselves, stop at one of the region's top family resorts: The Tyler Place in Highgate Springs, the Wildflower Inn in Lyndonville, or Highland Lodge in Greensboro.

The different faces of northern Vermont are distinctive—and worth a visit. Situated on 120-mile-long Lake Champlain, the outdoor-oriented city of Burlington turns every day into a play day. A seven-mile-long recreational path runs along the waterfront, linking eight parks

THE FamilyFun LIST
MUST-SEE · MUST-SEE

Shelburne Farms (see page 214)

Shelburne Museum (see page 213)

Stowe Recreation Path
(see page 215)

**Vermont Teddy Bear Company
Factory Tours** (see page 215)

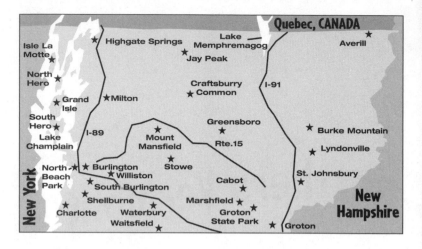

that have sandy beaches, playgrounds, camping facilities, and picnic shelters. Families can explore the lake by ferry or tour boat, or rent a vessel. In winter, you can snowshoe, cross-country and downhill ski, and snowboard. Any time of year you can wander through Church Street Marketplace, a four-block pedestrian mall teeming with kid-friendly restaurants, specialty shops, and street performers. For a cultural fix, take in a show at the Art Deco–style Flynn Theater *(call 802-863-5966 for a schedule)* or attend any of the arts, musical, and holiday festivals held throughout the year.

Just six miles south of the city in Shelburne is the Vermont Teddy Bear Company Factory and Museum. Shelburne is also home to two exceptional other attactions: the Shelburne Museum and Shelburne Farms.

The Lake Champlain Islands are made up of the Alburg Peninsula,

Isle la Motte, North Hero, and South Hero/Grand Isle. The small agricultural islands lure families with outdoor fun. You can loaf on the pretty beaches, or go fishing, apple picking, and cycling.

With its classic New England downtown and incredible views of 4,395-feet-tall Mount Mansfield, Vermont's highest peak, **Stowe** has lured skiers since the 1930s (see "Fun Family Ski Resorts" on page 179) but these days, the most popular month to visit is August, when families can skate, walk, or cycle along the town's recreational path, which is a bit more than five miles long. Seasoned hikers can ride the Stowe Mountain Resort gondola to Cliff House Station, then hike up a rocky trail to Mount Mansfield's summit for views of New Hampshire's Mount Washington. Smugglers' Notch State Park is a 4,000-acre gap, located between

Mount Mansfield and Sterling Peak and packed with rock formations.

The **Northeast Kingdom**, stretching for 2,053 miles from East Ryegate to Derby Line on the Canadian border, is home to two family downhill ski areas (Jay Peak and Burke Mountain), several cross-country centers, and a vast network of snowmobile trails. In summer, families hit the trails at Groton State Forest and Willoughby State Forest and swim in Harvey's Lake, Lake Willoughby, and Lake Memphremagog. If you don't mind venturing far afield for a camping adventure, head to Vermont's most remote park, Maidstone State Park, where you may spot a moose.

As isolated as this area can seem, you're never very far from a family-friendly lodge. Lyndonville's Wildflower Inn and Greensboro's Highland Lodge are two of the best resorts in the state. The town of St. Johnsbury ("St. J") is a wonderful base for families, as it's filled with

one-of-a-kind treasures, including the Fairbanks Museum & Planetarium, the St. Johnsbury Athenaeum & Gallery, and Maple Grove Farms of Vermont.

CULTURAL ADVENTURES

Ethan Allen Homestead
★★★/$

History buffs know Ethan Allen as head of the Green Mountain Boys and one of the Revolutionary War's most exciting personalities. A short drive from downtown Burlington, the homestead offers a hands-on history lesson, and since all objects are reproductions, kids can have a field day touching things. The staff may invite children to try on a yoke and bucket, sniff herbs in the garden, or even catch a frog on the banks of the Winooski River. For background, head to the Education Center to watch the *Tavern Tale*, a multimedia show that depicts life in 1791 through the eyes of a boy who has just arrived in Vermont. You can also take in History Under Foot, an archaeology show during which kids can dig for artifacts in a fake pit. Be sure to ask for a History Haversack, a backpack filled with activities, stories, and ideas for family scavenger hunts at the homestead. *1 Ethan Allen Homestead, Burlington; (802) 865-4556.*

Fairbanks Museum & Planetarium ★★★/$

Housed in an 1889 Victorian building with a barrel-vaulted ceiling, the museum is home to curiosities (including dinosaur artifacts) acquired by Franklin Fairbanks, a prominent businessman who wanted to share the wonders of the world with his community. Old-fashioned cases display more than 4,500 mounted animals (including a scary polar bear), a saber collection, fossils, rocks, crystals, Civil War artifacts, Zulu war shields, and even a letter to a local girl from Robert Louis

FamilyFun TIP

Car Trip Countdown

In hopes of avoiding the dreaded "When will we be there" question during a road trip from Detroit to Daytona Beach, *FamilyFun* reader Michelle Marek of Rochester, Michigan, came up with a way to make the drive pass more quickly for her kids. She wrote a series of mile measurements on clothespins, starting with "1,200 miles to go" and continuing with one pin for every 50 miles, right down to "50 miles to go," and finally "we made it." She hung a string in the van where all the kids could reach it and attached the pins in consecutive order. As she drove, her kids took turns taking the pins off the string, allowing them to keep track of the trip and see how close to their destination they were getting.

Stevenson. The museum houses the only public planetarium in Vermont. It's small, but the shows are fun. In summer, there's a hands-on nature corner for children. *Main and Prospect Sts., St. Johnsbury; (802) 748-2372;* www.fairbanksmuseum.com

Original Maple Grove Maple Museum and Factory ★★/$

America's largest packer of pure maple syrup is happy to share its secrets. On your tour, you'll see maple syrup packed on the filling line and watch maple-sugar candy being made. At the Sugar House Museum, you'll learn about the sugaring process. Best of all, you can shop for sweet treats in the gift shop. *1052 Portland St., St. Johnsbury; (802) 748-5141.*

St. Johnsbury Athenaeum & Gallery ★★/Free

This public library and National Historic Landmark is home to Alfred Bierstadt's painting *Domes of Yosemite,* which is nearly as wide as the wall on which it hangs. The light-filled landscape will make you want to hightail it to California to gaze upon the real thing. It's just one of several landscapes and portraits in this public library, which also has a terrific children's section, and towering shelves and spiral staircases that turn the clock back to 1871. *1171 Main St., St. Johnsbury; (802) 748-8291;* www.stjathenaeum.com

⭐ Shelburne Museum
FamilyFun ★★★★/$$

With 37 exhibit buildings and historic structures spread over 45 acres, this museum can seem overwhelming. Thanks to Owl Cottage, however, a family trip here is manageable. Depending on the day, kids can draw, paint, sculpt, and try on costumes. In summer, they can join the Surprise and Delight program, featuring projects such as papermaking, crafting birdhouses, and painting fish decoys. Many of the main exhibits have a Touch & Learn component for little visitors. Aboard the 1906 steamboat *Ticonderoga*, for example, kids can rifle through objects in one of the staterooms to determine passengers' identities. Other kid favorites: riding the 1920s carousel, visiting the blacksmith and weaver, and viewing the miniature circus parade. There's a café and refreshment stand, too. *Rte. 7, Shelburne; (802) 985-3346.*

JUST FOR FUN

Allenholm Farm ★★/$
Founded in 1870, Vermont's oldest commercial apple orchard sells some of the tastiest varieties around, including Vermont Gold, a sweet, thin-skinned fruit that's bursting with flavor. In the fall, you can ride the hay wagon to pick your own, and anytime you come, you can feed and pet the donkeys, horses, goats, sheep, and heifers in the petting paddock. The Allen family also rents out a suite on the first floor of the house. The unit has two bedrooms, a living room, and private bath, plus TV and toys for the kids. On the last morning of your stay, you'll be treated to a Vermont specialty: homemade pie and cheese at breakfast. *111 South St., South Hero; (802) 372-5566.*

Cabot Visitors' Center
★★/$
Say cheese. At this farmer-owned dairy, you'll see and taste plenty of it. Tour the plant to learn how a variety of cheeses are prepared, then taste samples in the cheese shop. Kids also get a Cabot coloring book. *Main St., Cabot; (800) 837-4261; (802) 563-3393.*

Craftsbury Outdoor Center
★★★/$$$
Sports-minded families will be in paradise at this 140-acre recreational center. The rate includes accommodations in simple rooms (many with shared bath) or cottages, all meals, and many activities. In winter, families can snowshoe, ski on a 62-mile trail network, and glide over a lighted skating pond. The staff enjoys teaching beginners (you can rent pull sleds for children too young to ski), and special activities are offered during family weeks. Summer activities include swimming at Hosmer Lake, lounging at

the beach, sculling, cycling, and hiking. *Craftsbury Common; (800) 729-7751; www.craftsbury.com*

Fun Family Ski Resorts

For all-season information on Smugglers' Notch and Stowe ski resorts, see page 181.

Groton State Park ★★★/$$$

The largest recreational facility operated by Vermont State Parks offers 25,000 wooded acres where families can camp, swim, hike, fly-fish, and go boating. Several state parks comprise this serene area, including **Boulder Beach** (a day-use park with swimming; *802/584-3823*), **Ricker Pond** (good for camping; 8*02/584-3821*), **Seyon Ranch** (a fly-fishing family's paradise; *802/584-3829*), **Stillwater** (camping and a swimming beach; *802/584-3822*), and **New Discovery** (camping; *802/426-3042*). All parks are located in Groton, except New Discovery, which is located in Marshfield. *For more information, call (800) VER-MONT; (802) 476-0170.*

Mount Philo State Park ★★★/Free

For a refreshing workout and amazing views, climb the Main Trail from the base of 968-foot-high Mount Philo to the summit. The moderately difficult trip takes about an hour and rewards you with vistas of the Lake Champlain Valley and Adirondack Mountains. You also can drive up a steep, narrow road to the mountaintop and unpack your basket in the picnic area. *5425 Mount Philo Rd., Charlotte; (802) 425-2390 (summer); (802) 483-2001 (winter).*

Sandbar State Park ★★★/$

This 15-acre park is packed with families all summer—and for good reason. The 2,000-foot-long beach fronts a sandy-bottomed lake that stays shallow well out from shore. There are picnic facilities, a bathhouse, and an adjacent wildlife refuge. *Rte. 2, Milton; (802) 893-2825 (summer); (802) 879-5674 (winter).*

Shelburne Farms

MUST-SEE FamilyFun MUST-SEE ★★★★/$

At this 1,400-acre estate-cum-environmental center alongside Lake Champlain, kids can collect eggs, milk cows, and brush horses in the Children's Farmyard. In the cheese-making facility, you can watch the staff make prizewinning cheddar using milk from the farm's Brown Swiss cows. For lakeside views, head for the walking trails. There's also a 90-minute tour (not geared to kids) on the history of this stunning estate, designed in 1886 by Dr. William Seward Webb and Lila Vanderbilt Webb. *1611 Harbor Rd., Shelburne; (802) 985-8686.*

Stowe Golf Park ★★★/$

Unlike traditional miniature-golf courses with spinning windmills and other novelties, this Stowe Golf

Park simulates real golf greens. The 18-hole course is located at the Sun & Ski Motor Inn, but you're welcome even if you're not staying there. *1613 Mountain Rd., Stowe; (802) 253-7159.*

Stowe Recreation Path
FamilyFun ★★★★/Free

One of the most beautiful routes of its kind, this five-and-a-half-mile path starts behind the Stowe Community Church on Main Street and meanders toward Mount Mansfield. Along the way, you'll pass wildflower fields, grazing cows, and the West Branch River. There are plenty of points to stop, rest, and swim, and several outfitters (including AJ's on Mountain Road; *800/226-6257; 802/253-4593*) can equip you with bicycles or in-line skates for the journey. For a full list of outfitters, contact the **Stowe Area Association** *(800/49-STOWE).*

Burlington offers a seven-mile recreational path that winds along Lake Champlain, through eight parks, some with sandy beaches and playgrounds. Campers can even pitch a tent at North Beach.

Vermont Teddy Bear
FamilyFun Company Factory
Tours ★★★★/$

The folks inside this massive, multicolored building produce 350,000 bears a year, making this the nation's largest producer of handcrafted teddies. On a 30-minute tour, you'll see employees cut the fur, stitch, stuff, and groom the bears. In the Make-A-Friend-For-Life Room, you can make your own bear for under $25. You'll choose your bear's fur and personality traits, cut the umbilical string, and fill out a birth certificate. From July to October, the factory also hosts a three-acre Giant Corn Maze, complete with three

KAYAKING FOR KIDS Kayak Stowe's scenic waterways with the help of **Umiak Outfitters**, which supplies equipment, lessons, and kid-friendly service on guided adventures. (You can also take self-guided trips.) In addition to family excursions, the outfitter offers Kids in Kayaks, a half- or full-day program featuring instructions and games for paddlers ages 8 to 13. Three-day Kids Adventure Camps include kayaking, canoeing, and orienteering. *Rte. 100 in the lower village, Stowe; (802) 253-2317.*

miles of walking paths, footbridges, and dead-end surprises. *6655 Shelburne Rd., Shelburne; (800) 829-BEAR; (802) 985-3001.*

BUNKING DOWN

Commodores Inn ★★★/$$

Being located on a small pond has its advantages. In winter, you can ice-skate; in warmer weather you can watch members of the Stowe Yacht Club race model yachts. The guest rooms have cable TV, plus there are indoor and outdoor pools, a living room with a fieldstone fireplace and wide-screen TV, and a family restaurant. *Rte. 100, Stowe; (800) 44-STOWE; (802) 253-7131.*

Golden Eagle Resort ★★★/$$

This value-priced lodge is one of Stowe's best places for families. Surrounded by 80 acres of land, the property is home to two stocked fishing ponds, two outdoor pools, a fitness center with a 50-foot-long indoor swimming pool, a playground, and casual and fancy restaurants. Nature trails on the adjacent Eagle Reserve offer the opportunity to spy whitetail deer, red fox, and snowshoe hares. The resort features 89 spacious rooms and suites with cable TV; some also have fireplaces and kitchenettes. A summer children's program invites kids to enjoy nature walks, crafts, and special events, such as a fishing derby and pizza night. *Mountain Rd., Stowe; (800) 626-1010; (802) 253-4811.*

Highland Lodge ★★★★/$$$$

For three generations, the Smith family has welcomed young travelers to one of Vermont's best family inns. Located in the Northeast Kingdom by spring-fed Caspian Lake, Highland Lodge is a year-round haven for those who appreciate the outdoors. Guests can stay in the historic 11-room lodge (an 1860s farmhouse) or one of 11 surrounding cottages (the best bet for families). In summer, kids ages 4 to 9 can join a supervised—and free—morning program that includes hikes, crafts, and art projects. They can even create pictures for the

ALL BEARS PURCHASED from Vermont Teddy Bear can get free, lifetime health care at the company's on-site Bear Hospital. You can even E-mail customer service to check on the health status of your injured bear while he or she is in Shelburne.

Forest of Art—a grove of trees where children's paintings are exhibited. It's a short walk across the country road to the sandy beach, where you can swim, fish, rent a boat, and search for crayfish. You also can play tennis or croquet, hike in the Barr Hill Nature Preserve, and join weekly family picnics on the beach. In winter, you can snowshoe or cross-country ski on 40 miles of scenic trails (the inn's ski shop offers clinics for beginners), go tobogganing, play Ping-Pong in the game room, or sip hot chocolate by the fire. Equally important, the dishes are delicious. The rate includes a full country breakfast and dinner. For lunch, you can dine on the porch or preorder a picnic. *Caspian Lake, Greensboro; (802) 533-2647.*

Howard Johnson Hotel & Suites
★★/$-$$

This is a good base camp for families who are exploring the sights in Burlington or Shelburne. The hotel offers an indoor pool, 121 rooms and suites, and complimentary breakfast. Next door, the Lake-View Bar & Grille, an American chophouse, has a kids' menu with meals that include dessert and beverage. *1720 Shelburne Rd., S. Burlington; (800) 874-1554; (802) 860-6000.* The same enclave of hotels includes a **Holiday Inn Express Hotel & Suites** *(800/HOLIDAY)*, which has an indoor pool and game room, and **Smart Suites** *(877/862-6800).*

Beware the Champ

Lake Champlain plays host to its own version of the Loch Ness Monster. Champ, as the creature is known, has mostly eluded photographers since he was first observed in the early 1600s. More than 300 sightings have been reported, including one by the lake's namesake Samuel de Champlain.

Quimby Country
★★★/$$$

Since 1894, Vermont's oldest fishing lodge has invited folks to the remote, northeast corner of the Northeast Kingdom to fish, relax, and commune with wildlife at nearby Great Averill Pond. Families can stay in one of 20 cottages on 65-acre Forest Lake, eat three homemade meals a day in the communal dining room, and enjoy a variety of kids' activities and natural wonders. To keep the intimate, summer-camp spirit, Quimby Country only accommodates 65 guests at a time. Young guests can fish, swim, watch wildlife, hang out at the playground, and join special events such as kids-only campouts. After all these years, the cottages are a little crooked, but they're clean, and families spend much of their time outdoors anyway. Located two miles down a dirt road, the resort is a safe haven, where parents feel comfortable letting their children roam. The rate includes three meals a day, and there's no minimum stay. *Forest Lake Rd., Averill; (802) 822-5533.*

Shore Acres Inn & Restaurant
★★★/$$

Set on 50 beautiful acres along Lake Champlain, this lodge has many units that face the lake and Green Mountains. There's a half-mile of private shore for swimming, tennis courts, a driving range, lawn games, and 100-foot dock for fishing. The 23 rooms have two doubles or queens, and TVs. Meals aren't included, but are available at the on-site restaurant. *Rte. 2, N. Hero; (802) 372-8722.*

Stowe Motel & Snowdrift
★★★/$-$$

It may not be as swanky as its neighbors, but this pleasant property is one of Stowe's biggest bargains. The rooms and efficiencies have cable TV and a refrigerator, plus there are two heated outdoor pools, a game room, picnic tables, barbecue grills, and a tennis court. The owners will even lend you mountain bikes to use on the town's recreational path. *2043 Mountain Rd., Stowe; (800) 829-7629; (802) 253-7629.*

Sun & Ski Motor Inn ★★★/$-$$

This is no ordinary motor inn. The staff delivers your breakfast in a basket (or, you can partake in the breakfast buffet in the morning room), the

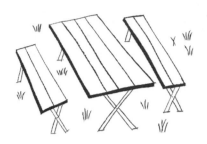

West Branch River trickles through the property, and there's a beautiful 18-hole miniature-golf course. The nine-acre grounds give kids plenty of space to run around, plus there's a beautiful, indoor heated pool (102 degrees in winter). The 25 spacious rooms and loft suites have refrigerators and cable TV. *1613 Mountain Rd., Stowe; (802) 253-7159.*

Terry Lodge ★★/$$$

At this lakeside lodge on the Lake Champlain Islands, you can fish off the dock, swim in Lake Champlain, enjoy spectacular sunsets and views of New York's Adirondacks, and pal around with other families. Guests can choose a meal plan that includes breakfast or breakfast and dinner, and can stay in a simply furnished, two-room suite in the 1800s farmhouse. One room has a full-size bed for parents; the adjoining room has twin beds for kids (no TV). If you prefer, rent a two-bedroom cottage with a TV, and cook in or choose a meal plan. Family-style dinner is served in the dining room each night. If the kids finish early, a staff member may supervise them outside while parents complete their meals. There's also a central living room with a VCR and lots of board games. *West Shore Rd., Isle La Motte; (802) 928-3264.*

Trapp Family Lodge ★★★/$$$

The hills are alive with the sound of families enjoying a vacation at this Alpine retreat. The lodge is owned by the von Trapp Family, whose story was depicted in *The Sound of Music.* Every week, Rosmarie von Trapp, the youngest daughter of Baron and Baroness von Trapp, leads a sing-along. There are plenty of other treats, too, including panoramic views of Stowe, one indoor and two outdoor pools, and tennis. Guests can hike and cross-country ski on 40 miles of trails. For kids ages 3 to 12, the Mountain Kids Club offers storytelling, nature walks, horseback riding, and special excursions. Families can stay in one of 116 guest rooms or 100 guesthouses. *Trapp Hill Rd., Stowe; (800) 826-7000; (802) 253-8511.*

The Tyler Place ★★★★/$$$$

Run for generations by the Tyler family, this 165-acre retreat just shy of the Canadian border proves that summer camp isn't just for kids. Located near woods, meadows, and a mile of undeveloped shoreline along Lake Champlain, this all-inclusive resort offers a multitude of activities for parents and children to enjoy separately and together.

Children's programs are designed for kids from birth to teens and include everything from visiting the petting farm and pontoon-boat rides to cycling adventures and making crafts. In the morning, kids play with their peers, and parents can try mountain biking, rock climbing, aqua aerobics, and yoga. After lunch (kids and parents tend to eat separately), families participate in joint activities, such as fishing trips. For dinner, adults dine together, and kids join their new friends for cookouts, pool parties, and campfires. After the young guests go to bed, parents can hire a sitter and join other adults for dancing and socializing. For most of the summer, the minimum stay is a week (guests check in and out on Saturday). Accommodations include 28 cottages, rooms in the country inn, and family suites; rates include all meals and activities. The resort also boasts heated indoor and outdoor pools, a climbing wall, sailboats, and tennis courts. This is not an inexpensive vacation, but many families consider it money well spent, especially since all activities are planned and provided for you. *Rte. 7, Highgate Springs; (802) 868-4000.*

Wildflower Inn
★★★★/$$-$$$

One of New England's best places for families, this inn offers an array of children's activities in a bucolic backdrop. Set on a 570-acre farm in the

Northeast Kingdom, Wildflower Inn is surrounded by mountains and wildflower fields, where you can watch Belted Galloways (also known as Oreo-cookie cows) graze. Innkeepers Jim and Mary O'Reilly have drawn on their experiences as the parents of eight children to make kids feel welcome. In the children's playroom, kids can try on dress-up clothes, hang out in the reading loft, play bumper pool, and watch movies. They can meet animals in the petting barn, swim in the outdoor heated pool, and scale a climbing tower in the outdoor play area. They also can take in a performance of the Vermont Children's Theater (in one of the barns), learn a new craft, skate in the outdoor

---

FamilyFun TIP

Hit the Trail

Just a 20-minute drive from Burlington, **Catamount Outdoor Center**, a family-owned outfit, offers the chance to mountain bike, walk, snowshoe, or cross-country ski on 20 miles of trails. In winter, you can iceskate, too. (Rental equipment is available for children and adults.) A mix of fields, forest, and various terrain, the trails are suitable for beginners and advanced athletes. The staff provides instruction for families who are just learning to cross-country ski. *592 Governor Chittenden Rd., Williston; (802) 879-6001.*

---

rink, and snowshoe, sled, and cross-country ski. Meals are served in the dining room and are superb. (Breakfast and afternoon snacks are included in the rate, but much of the year you can eat dinner here, too.) You can rent a room in the carriage house or a family suite, some of which have cooking facilities. *Darling Hill Rd., Lyndonville; (800) 627-8301; (802) 626-8310.*

GOOD EATS

Arvad's Grill & Pub ★★/$-$$

After the Ben & Jerry's ice cream tour, head to this casual restaurant for lunch or dinner. The creative menu includes salads, burgers, pita sandwiches, cheese fries, steak, and chicken entrées. Kids get crayons and an activity menu filled with fun favorites, including Waterbury's PB&J (served with raspberry jam on oatmeal bread), clam strips, and franks. You'll enjoy looking at the colorful wall mural of old-time Waterbury. *3 S. Main St., Waterbury; (802) 244-8973. (Arvad's is also located on Rte. 100 in Waitsfield; 802/496-9800.)*

Depot Street Malt Shop ★★★/$

Zip up your poodle skirts, slick back your hair, and hightail it to this 1950s-style diner, complete with soda fountain, doo-wop music, and fun memorabilia. From burgers to spaghetti, all the kids' favorites are here. You'll also find sandwiches, salads, hot turkey sandwiches, and loads of fountain treats, including egg creams, Cherry Coke, and old-fashioned ice-cream sodas. *Depot St., Stowe; (802) 253-4269.*

Dutch Pancake Cafe ★★★/$

If your kids crave pancakes, they'll love this unusual restaurant. The 12-inch, crepe-style pancakes include traditional, fruity (how about banana chocolate coconut?), hearty (ever heard of broccoli and cheese pancakes?), and sweet-tooth (one choice is apples, blueberries, and ice cream) varieties. Kids can get eight-inch versions of several pancakes, complete with a surprise and the chance to decorate their meals with sprinkles and whipped cream. *900 Mountain Rd., at the Grey Fox Inn, Stowe; (802) 253-5330.*

Miss Lyndonville Diner ★★/$

Kids eat free every Tuesday night at this friendly diner (the deal even includes a special dessert). The extensive children's menu features breakfast, lunch, and dinner offerings. You can get everything from one strawberry pancake to a hot turkey sandwich. For parents, comfort food abounds. *Rte. 5, Lyndonville; (802) 626-9890.*

Shanty on the Shore
★★★/$$

Located along Burlington's waterfront, this casual seafood restaurant

provides interesting views both inside and out. Kids can watch boats dock and depart on Lake Champlain, or turn their eyes indoors to crustaceans in a lobster tank. Decorated with nautical novelties, the Shanty dishes out kids' burger and hot dog baskets, spaghetti, and fish dinners, plus lots of fresh seafood dinners for parents. *181 Battery St., Burlington; (802) 864-0238.*

Sweetwaters
★★★/$-$$

You're in the center of the action at this terrific restaurant, located on the Church Street Marketplace. A popular spot at Happy Hour, it's also a great place to bring kids for lunch and dinner. Young diners get a fun activity menu, balloon, and special cup, plus pita pizza, burgers, spaghetti, and a special Sunday brunch menu. Fare runs from imaginative sandwiches and wraps to bison cheeseburgers and steak. *120 Church St., Burlington; (802) 864-9800.*

Whiskers ★★★/$$

If you're looking for a special night out, this is the place for dinner. Intriguing antiques (including a Flexible Flyer sled used in the movie *Ethan Frome*), Tiffany lamps, and a crackling fire make the atmosphere memorable. All the kids' classics are here, plus they can embellish their ice cream at the toppings bar. Parents can dig into lobster, prime rib, chicken entrées, and a 40-item salad bar. In summer, you can eat out on the porch and stroll through an acre of perennial gardens. *1652 Mountain Rd., Stowe; (800) 649-8996; (802) 253-8996.*

SOUVENIR HUNTING

Dog Mountain

If you're a dog lover with a sense of humor, visit this 150-acre canine shrine masterminded by Vermont artist Stephen Hunick. (You've probably seen his books *My Dog's Brain* and *Sally Goes to the Beach.*) Known for his whimsical, detailed art and furnishings (including begging dachshund table lamps), Hunick has reached new heights with Dog Mountain. The pet paradise includes a gallery (dogs allowed) and outdoor sculpture garden. There's even a dog chapel, where pets and their owners can meditate while gazing at stained-glass windows featuring—yes, you guessed it—canine companions. Books and postcards (canine-related, of course) are for sale here. *Spaulding Rd. (off Rte. 2), St. Johnsbury; (802) 748-2700.*

Farmer's Daughter Gift Barn, Country Store & Museum

One of New England's largest and oldest gift barns isn't just a fun spot to shop—it's a great place to step back in time. True to its name, the store is housed in an open-post-and-beam barn (built without nails). Its shelves are filled with candy, maple syrup, pancake mixes, deerskin moccasins, and enough stocking stuffers to take you through the next ten holidays. The "museum" refers to the collection of antiques on display, including a sleigh that was used to deliver groceries a century ago. When you get tired of shopping, you can feed the resident sheep and ducks. *Rte. 2, St. Johnsbury; (802) 748-3994.*

Lake Champlain Chocolates

If the smell of rich, custom-made chocolate doesn't get you, the taste will. In this factory store, you can watch through an observation window and see the chocolate-dipped pretzels, homemade fudge, and specialty figurines (we love the chocolate Labs) being made. You also can taste samples and buy factory seconds that are just as scrumptious as the firsts. *750 Pine St., Burlington; (800) 634-8105.*

Stowe Mercantile

With more than 50 kinds of penny candy, fresh homemade fudge, a menagerie of stuffed animals, and a piano to plunk, chances are you'll be making at least one trip to this fun general store. *Main St., Stowe ; (802) 253-4554.*

CONVERSATION STARTERS

IME ON THE ROAD offers families the perfect opportunity to reconnect by having conversations that don't revolve around car pools, chores, or eating all your vegetables. If you have trouble switching conversational gears, try asking your kids these questions or similar variations. You can give them the wheel sometimes, too, letting them ask you probing queries! Or you can turn this less-than-idle chat into a game by writing questions on slips of paper, placing them in a hat, and passing the hat—the question you pick out is the one you must answer, honestly. Make your queries silly or serious, but be sure they cannot be answered by just saying yes or no.

- If you could make up a holiday, what would it be and how would you celebrate it?
- What is the first thing you would do if you became president?
- Would you rather be a butterfly or a fish? Why?
- Do you think dogs are smarter than cats? Are dogs smarter than horses?
- What did settlers on the prairie have for breakfast 100 years ago? What will we be eating for breakfast in 100 years?
- If you had to lose one of your five senses, which would it be? Which one sense would you choose if you could only have one? Why?
- Would you like to have sonar like a bat, or be able to run as fast as a gazelle? Why?
- If you could choose five animal qualities for yourself from the animal kingdom, what would they be?
- What is the best book you've read recently, and why did you like it?
- What's the silliest thing you ever did?
- What will you do this summer?
- What's your earliest memory?
- What do you think the surface of the moon looks like?
- If you were going to write a book, what would it be about?
- What will you be doing in ten years?
- If you discovered a new island what do you imagine would be on it?
- What one thing would you change about school?
- Who is your hero and why?
- What should we surprise Mom with for her birthday this year?
- What is the best—and the worst—thing you have ever eaten?
- What is an item of international news that you have heard or read about in the past few months?

Massachu

O N ANY MAP of New England, it's easy to see that Massachusetts is the heart of the region. The 190-mile-long state borders each of the other New England states (except Maine), plus New York. From the top of 3,491-foot-high Mount Greylock to the tip of Cape Cod's sandy hook (one of the East Coast's distinguishing characteristics), it's clear that the Bay State loves the limelight—and it adores families who come to bask in it.

The hard part is choosing among the many wonderful and diverse attractions. In Western Massachusetts' Pioneer

Western Massachusetts
Central Massachusetts
Merrimack Valley
North Shore
Boston ★
South Shore
Cape Cod

setts

Valley, families can take a white-water-rafting trip. In Boston, city creatures can explore historic streets on the two-and-a-half-mile-long Freedom Trail. On the coast, beach lovers will find 80 sandy playgrounds upon which to build their castles.

The sixth state to join the union is blessed with not one, but two, fun-loving capes—famous 70-mile-long Cape Cod on the South Shore, and the smaller, but magical, rocky Cape Ann on the North Shore. Factor in the state's 2,800 lakes, ponds, and rivers, 107 state parks and forests, two popular offshore islands (Nantucket and Martha's Vineyard), and 170 museums, and you've got yourselves a vacation powerhouse.

ATTRACTIONS	
$	under $10
$$	$10 - $20
$$$	$20 - $30
$$$$	$30 +

HOTELS/MOTELS/CAMPGROUNDS	
$	under $100
$$	$100 - $200
$$$	$200 - $300
$$$$	$300 +

RESTAURANTS	
$	under $10
$$	$10 - $20
$$$	$20 - $30
$$$$	$30 +

FAMILYFUN RATED	
★	Fine
★★	Good
★★★	Very Good
★★★★	FamilyFun Recommended

Riding the swan boats in Boston's Public Garden has been a tourist tradition here since 1887.

Boston

WHEN IT COMES TO welcoming families, the historic city of Boston is revolutionary. Plain and simple, Beantown is an exceptionally fun city for children. At dozens of world-class attractions and museums, kids can indulge their dreams of becoming an astronaut, hanging out with Sesame Street characters, and riding an old-fashioned swan boat, a tradition since 1887. The city's thriving harbor invites families to take a whale watch or help collect sea specimens, and hotels roll out the red carpet for kids.

Perhaps the city's greatest plus, however, is its gift for making learning fun. What better way to teach kids about the Boston Tea Party—the notorious 1773 rebellion against British taxes on tea—than by inviting children to become Patriots, charge aboard a cargo ship, and toss crates of tea into Boston Harbor? The city's two-and-a-half-mile-long Freedom Trail makes it easy and enjoyable to view the sites. Just fol-

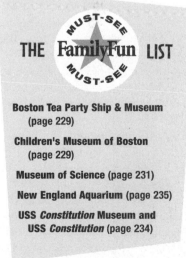

THE **FamilyFun** LIST

MUST-SEE MUST-SEE

Boston Tea Party Ship & Museum
(page 229)

Children's Museum of Boston
(page 229)

Museum of Science (page 231)

New England Aquarium (page 235)

USS *Constitution* Museum and USS *Constitution* (page 234)

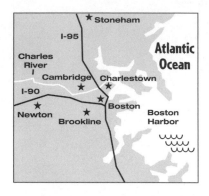

low the red line past 16 historic gems, including Paul Revere's house (1680), the gold-domed State House (1795), and the USS *Constitution*. From April to September, you're bound to run into the Freedom Trail Players, costumed colonists with a gift for gab who'll gladly answer kids' questions. The players also offer many family programs. Little kids will go for Mother Goose Storytelling, in which a player portraying Boston's beloved Elizabeth Vergoose, aka Mother Goose, reads her poems, and explains how she got her famous nickname. *(For information, call 617/227-8800.)*

Walking is the best way to explore Boston's distinctive neighborhoods, from the nation's third-largest Chinatown to the Italian North End.

In Beacon Hill, you can still see original panes of purple glass in classic brownstones. Bring your fun money to the boutique-lined Back Bay, home of the ultimate toy palace, FAO Schwarz. Throughout your travels, be sure to point out to the kids the intriguing juxtaposition of Boston's silver skyscrapers and its 18th-century brick landmarks.

Boston is currently in the midst of the more than $7 billion Big Dig (www.bigdig.com), the largest urban infrastructure project in American history, which makes driving in the city's famed tangle of streets extra difficult. Fortunately, the city has an excellent public transportation system known as "the T." You and your kids can use the water taxis, trolleys, subways, and buses to reach attractions in an efficient, affordable manner. Boston's Visitor Passports, good for one, three, or seven days, grant you unlimited rides for one low price; call the Massachusetts Bay Transportation Authority at *(617) 222-3200.*

Just across the Charles River is the city of Cambridge, which is well worth a visit. Cambridge offers fun shops and street musicians in hopping Harvard Square. You'll also

FORT EXPLORERS

Take a ferry to **Georges Island** and **Fort Warren,** a granite fort where Confederate prisoners were held during the Civil War. There are ranger programs and picnicking. *Boston Harbor Islands State Park, Boston; (617) 727-5290.* For ferry information, call *Boston Harbor Cruises, (617) 227-4321.*

want to make time to explore Harvard University and its Museums of Cultural and Natural History. Outside city limits, in what is known as Greater Boston, are several must-see attractions as well.

CULTURAL ADVENTURES

Boston Tea Party Ship & Museum
★★★★/$

It's 1773, the British have imposed a steep tax on tea, and you and the other Patriots aren't going to stand for it anymore. Here, your young rabble-rousers are encouraged to replay one of the key chapters in the city's history by dressing up like Indians, climbing aboard the Brig *Beaver II*, and throwing (plastic foam) tea chests overboard to express their dissatisfaction with the Crown. They can also explore the 110-foot-long ship and meet costumed interpreters. At press time, the museum was closed due to fire damage, so call to see if it has reopened. *Congress Street Bridge, Boston; (617) 338-1773;* www.bostonteaparty ship.com

Boston by Little Feet ★★★★/$
No stuffy speeches on this hour-long tour, where guides lead kids and their parents on an easy walk past ten historic sites. On any given day, guides might challenge kids to find the lion and unicorn atop the Old State House, play hopscotch on the City Carpet (a brass, glass, and ceramic sidewalk mosaic decorated with the names of two famous Boston Latin School alums, Benjamin Franklin and Sam Adams), and find the gravestone of Elizabeth Vergoose, better known as Mother Goose. *For reservations, call (617) 367-2345.*

Bunker Hill Monument
★★★/Free

A high point of any Boston vacation, this 221-foot-tall granite obelisk commemorates the 1775 Battle of Bunker Hill. Families can climb a spiral staircase to the top for dramatic views. Then check out the dioramas at the base of the monument that depict the battle. *Breed's Hill, Charlestown; (617) 242-5641;* www.charlestown.ma.us/monu ment.html

Children's Museum of Boston ★★★★/$
Look for the oversize milk bottle (a snack bar) outside New England's largest children's museum, and get ready for three levels of hands-on fun. Here, your kids can easily spend half a day blowing gigantic bubbles, climbing on a two-story maze, playing dress-up, attending children's theatrical shows, hanging out with their friends on *Sesame Street*, and polishing their drilling and loading skills at the

Construction Zone. Fuel up for your adventures at the adjacent McDonald's. *300 Congress St., Boston; (617) 426-8855;* www.bostonkids.org

Dreams of Freedom Museum
★★★/$

This museum honors immigrants past and present through a series of educational exhibits. You and the kids can tour exhibit halls filled with interactive displays and experience the trials of an immigrant voyage aboard a re-created ship; you can look into the trunks and suitcases of passengers, wander through a virtual customs gate, and even conduct your own genealogy search. *One Milk St., Boston; (617) 695-9990;* www. dreamsoffreedom.com

Harvard University Museums of Natural History and the Peabody Museum of Archaeology and Ethnology
★★★★/$

Every child should get the chance to go to Harvard, and here's your ticket. Through 26 old-fashioned galleries, these two museums on the university campus introduce youngsters to the wonders of the world. At the natural history museum (composed of three major galleries), you can peek at the world-famous glass flowers in the botanical galleries. This collection of 3,000 amazingly lifelike glass models was created over a period of 50 years by Leopold Blaschka and his son. In the

sparkling mineralogical galleries, you'll see a 1,600-pound amethyst geode; in the zoological galleries is the world's only mounted Kronosaurus, a 42-foot-long prehistoric marine reptile. At the Peabody, kids will enjoy the elaborate African masks, Maya monuments, and items from Lewis and Clark's expedition (1804–1806). *Harvard Museum of Natural History: 26 Oxford St., Cambridge; (617) 495-3045; Peabody Museum: 11 Divinity Ave., Cambridge; (617) 496-1027;* www. hmnh.harvard.edu

John F. Kennedy Library and Museum ★★★/$

You don't have to head to Washington to take a White House tour: at the nation's official memorial to hometown hero JFK, families can step back in time to the 1960s and wander through the halls of the Kennedy White House to learn more

about our 35th president. For an overview, see the 18-minute biographical film about Kennedy. Then wander through 25 multimedia exhibits that depict a 1960s Main Street (complete with vintage appliances and political posters in the shop windows), the Oval Office, and a tribute to the First Lady (featuring exotic gifts that Jacqueline Kennedy received from world leaders). Though your kids won't understand much about the Cold War and the Bay of Pigs, they can take a treasure hunt (get the forms from the staff) that makes the visit more meaningful. Come on Saturday morning, when the museum offers a free children's hour featuring music and storytelling. *Columbia Point, Boston; (617) 929-4523; www.cs.umb.edu/jfklibrary*

The Mapparium ★★★/$

This 30-foot stained-glass walk-through globe has entertained and informed children since 1935. Part of the new Mary Baker Eddy Library for the Betterment of Humanity, the Mapparium features a state-of-the-art light and sound system that projects 16 million colors onto the sparkling spheres. There are 605 glass panels, a glass pedestrian bridge, and unusual acoustics (a whisper from one end of the globe can be heard clear across the other side). Library visitors can also peek into the newsroom of the Pulitzer Prize–winning *Christian Science*

Name That Cat

Massachusetts children have played a role in choosing several of their state symbols. School children successfully lobbied Bay State legislators to name the chocolate-chip and the tabby as the state cookie and cat, respectively.

Monitor to see how the staff gathers and reports stories. *200 Massachusetts Ave., Boston; (617) 450-7000.*

Museum of Science
FamilyFun ★★★★/$-$$

There's no end to the fun here. Located on the banks of the Charles River, this vacation blockbuster features 600 hands-on exhibits, an amazing planetarium, and the five-story Mugar Omni Theater, which is home to the city's largest movie screen. Seats in the planetarium are equipped with armrests whose push buttons allow you to interact with celestial programs (for example, the narrator may ask you a question about a planet and request that you press the A, B, or C button; the votes are tallied and you can see how the group voted), and a rooftop observatory where you can stargaze on Friday night. Kids can learn about Newton's law of physics by playing on seesaws and

continued on page 234

EIGHT WAYS TO HAVE FUN WITH KIDS IN BOSTON

Sea Boston

If you've taken a tour by land, why not take two by sea. The city offers a bundle of boat trips, including whale watches (see page 234) and the **Boston by Sea tour**. This 90-minute, living history cruise uses film, theater, song, pirate legends, and face painting to add kid appeal to its tour of Boston Harbor. *(Boston Harbor Cruises, One Long Wharf, Boston; 617/227-4321.)* The company also offers Boston Harbor tours to the Boston Harbor Islands.

The **Charles Riverboat Company** does 55-minute trips along the Charles River. *100 Cambridgeside Pl., Suite 320, Cambridge; (617) 621-3001.*

The **New England Aquarium** features 90-minute Science at Sea tours, where young scientists can climb aboard the *Doc Edgarton* and haul in lobster traps and tow for plankton. *Central Wharf, Boston; (617) 973-5206.*

If you'd rather float your own boat, you can rent one from **Charles River Canoe & Kayak**. *2401 Commonwealth Ave., Newton; (617) 965-5510.*

Have an island adventure.

Thirty islands dot the waters off Boston Harbor, and your family can ferry to several of them. Twenty-eight-acre **George's Island** is the kid pleaser, where you can explore Fort Warren (1883), stock up at the snack bar, and picnic in open fields. From here, you can also take a free water taxi to the other islands. **Gallops**, another family favorite, has a sandy beach, hiking paths, and spectacular views of Boston. **Lovell** is a camper's paradise. Park rangers are stationed at the islands and give tours and family programs. *Call (617) 223-8666 or log on to www.Bostonislands.com For ferry information, call (617) 227-4321.*

Quack up.

Your little ducklings will love the city's webbed-footed wonders. **Boston Ducks** (amphibious landing vehicles) take families on a wacky street tour, then splash down into the Charles River. Fans of Robert McCloskey's *Make Way for Ducklings* will want to waddle over to the Public Garden to visit the bronze statues of Mrs. Mallard and her eight fuzzy charges (Jack, Kack, Lack, Mack, Nack, Ouack, Pack, and Quack), who, as you may remember from the book, settled in the pretty park. The **Historic Neighborhood Foundation** sponsors 90-minute tours that retrace the steps of Mrs.

Mallard and her brood, with guides introducing kids to Boston's architectural treasures along the way. Speaking of birds, don't forget to ride the historic **swan boats in the Public Garden**, a treat for families since 1877. *Call (617) 522-1966.*

Visit the Green Monster.
Fenway Park's ferocious, 37-foot-high cement wall in left field defies players to hit a ball out of the historic stadium. That's one reason Red Sox games are so much fun. Baseball buffs can also tour the 1912 ball field. The Sox frequently sponsor special family-discount games and kids' promotions. *4 Yawkey Way, Boston. Call (617) 267-1700 or log on to* www.redsox.com

Go for the show.
Many arts organizations offer special performances for kids. Some favorites include the world-famous **Boston Pops** *(Symphony Hall, Boston; 617/266-1492)*, the **Puppet Showplace Theater** *(32 Station St., Brookline Village; 617/731-6400)*,

The **Coolidge Corner Theatre** *(290 Harvard St., Brookline; 617/734-2501)*, and the **Boston Children's Theatre** *(Suffolk University, 55 Temple St., Boston; 617/424-6634)*.

Take the T.
Avoid traffic during the Big Dig (the city's $7+ billion construction project) by taking **public transportation**. Save for your feet, it's the least expensive, easiest way to get around town. *Call (617) 222-3200.*

Enjoy winter's wonders.
Boston wraps herself up in style for the holidays. Your kids will love the **tree-lighting ceremonies**, the dazzling store windows, the animated **Enchanted Village at City Hall Plaza**, and the **Teddy Bear Tea at the Four Seasons** *(617/338-4400)*.

Affect that local accent.
To get the hang of Boston-speak, repeat several times quickly: *Pahk your cah in Hahvahd yahd.* The trick is to drop r's where they belong and insert them where they don't.

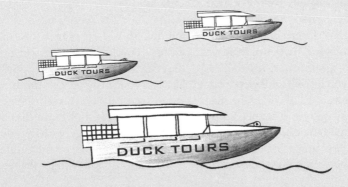

WHALE WATCHING AROUND BOSTON

Boston Harbor Cruises *(1 Long Wharf; 617/227-4321)* offers three-hour trips aboard high-speed catamarans.

swings at Science in the Park. They also can create their own computerized fish species in the Virtual Fish Tank, meet boa constrictors at live animal demonstrations, watch a dramatic lightning storm in the Theater of Electricity, and race solar cars at "Investigate!" There's a wonderful gift shop and several cafeteria-style food outlets. You can even have Skyline Sunday Brunch here, which includes a ticket to the Omni theater. *Science Park, Boston; (617) 723-2500;* www.mos.org

USS *Constitution* Museum and USS *Constitution* (Old Ironsides)
★★★★/Free

Built in 1797, the three-masted frigate known as Old Ironsides is so tough that cannonballs bounced off her two-foot oak hull. Yes, that's how she earned her nickname. It also means she can definitely withstand the pitter-patter of little feet. On a 30-minute tour *(call 617/242-5670)*, you'll see Paul Revere's contribution (a metalworker, he made the ship's bolts and copper sheathing), touch the cannons, and learn about the courageous powder monkeys (the young boys who carried

gunpowder to the ship's gunners during battle). Afterward, head for the adjacent USS *Constitution* Museum, where your youngsters can try their hands at shipbuilding, view models of Old Ironsides, and blast the British with cannons in a video game. The museum also, from time to time, holds children's programs and costumed reenactments. Call *(617) 426-1812*. Both attractions are in the Charlestown Navy Yard. **NOTE:** Instead of driving, *take the MBTA Water Shuttle from Long Wharf, near the New England Aquarium; for a schedule, call (617)227-4320;* www.ussconstitutionmuseum.org

JUST FOR FUN

Franklin Park Zoo
★★/$

More than 200 species make their home at this 72-acre site in Boston's historic Franklin Park. Kids will love monkeying around with the gorillas and mandrills in the humongous Tropical Forest, seeing more than 1,000 beautiful butterflies at Butterfly Landing, visiting the world's tallest animal on the Giraffe Savannah, and following wallabies, emus, and kangaroos on the Australian Outback Trail. From May to October, zookeepers share the tricks of their trade at special weekend programs. You can also sign up for one of many family classes, such as nature drawing. Save yourself the drive by hopping on the Zoo Mobile at Faneuil Hall or Copley Place (call for a schedule). *1 Franklin Park Rd., Boston; (617) 541-LION.* Zoo New England, the nonprofit agency that oversees the zoo, also operates the Stone Zoo. *149 Pond St., Stoneham; (781) 438-5100;* www.zoonewengland.com

 New England Aquarium
★★★★/$$

One of New England's best attractions, the aquarium wows kids the instant they walk through the door and see penguins making mischief in their ground-level colony. Peer into the giant ocean tank (it's 24 feet deep and holds 200,000 gallons) to view a tropical reef that's home to sharks, barracudas, and colorful fish usually seen only by deep-sea divers. You can watch veterinarians care for sick animals at the on-site medical center; visit Abra and Nellie, the popular sea otters; climb upon a fiberglass rocky shore and touch sea urchins and horseshoe crabs; and get splashed at a sea lion show. The aquarium also offers family-oriented boat trips. *Central Wharf, Boston; (617) 973-5200;* www.neaq.org

Prudential Skywalk
★★★★/$

Sadly, the city's tallest tower, the John Hancock Observatory, closed permanently after September 11, but you can still get a bird's-eye view of Boston from the 50th floor of the Pru. From these lofty heights, see if you and the kids can spot the city's "miniature" landmarks, such as the gold-domed State House and legendary Fenway Park. Fun facts are posted throughout the observation deck. Did you know the Red Sox go through about six dozen balls in a single baseball game? *800 Boylston St., Boston; (617) 859-0648.*

BUNKING DOWN

Bed & Breakfast Agency of Boston
★★★/$$-$$$

Boston folks are so accommodating, they'll let you move into their homes. If you're tired of hotels, call this agency and ask to be matched

---

FamilyFun TIP

Follow the Freedom Trail

It's easier to get a handle on history when someone memorable leads the way. Try the **Freedom Trail Players**, friendly costumed guides who portray patriots reliving dramatic events in their lives. For information on the 90-minute tour, call *(617) 227-0800.*

up with an apartment in a prime locale. Rentals are available for a night or more. With locations in Beacon Hill, the Back Bay, and other neighborhoods, these accommodations give a feel for how Bostonians really live. If it's your pleasure, you can have fun going to the market and cooking your own meals. The agency's office is at *47 Commercial Wharf, Boston; (800) 248-9262; (617) 720-3540;* www. boston-bnbagency. com

Boston Marriott Long Wharf
★★★/$$-$$$$

You can't beat the location of this 402-room hotel on Boston Harbor: it's next door to the New England Aquarium and boat tour operators, and across the street from Faneuil Hall. The guest rooms have super-large closets and bathrooms, and the hotel's cruise-ship-themed restaurant, Oceana, offers lots of kid pleasers. After sight-seeing, the indoor pool and sundeck overlooking the ocean is a perfect place to wind down. *296 State St., Boston (617) 227-0800;* www.marriott.com

The Colonnade
★★★/$$$

In Boston's historic Back Bay (home to FAO Schwarz), the 285-room hotel has the city's only rooftop swimming pool. Its on-site French restaurant, Brasserie Jo, has a Little Jo menu for kids. Some of the many family packages may include a kid-pleasing fanny pack stuffed with goodies, passes to area attractions, and complimentary parking (this last perk is for Mom and Dad). *120 Huntington Ave., Boston; (617) 424-7000;* www.colonnadehotel.com

Four Seasons Hotel
★★★★/$$$$

Nobody does it better. For the ultimate splurge, check into this deluxe hotel for an evening of pampering that you'll remember for years to come. The royal treatment includes an excellent concierge (who can help you plan family outings, choose restaurants, and provide food for ducks and squirrels), use of kid-size robes, a beautiful indoor pool, before-bed goodies, and a kid-friendly restaurant where children can pick their meals by clicking through a View-Master. The location, across the street from Boston's Public Garden and the famous swan boats, is also a plus. Over the holidays, treat yourselves to the dress-up Teddy Bear Tea: children bring a teddy bear to donate to Boston's needy kids and, in return, receive bear-shaped tea sandwiches and hugs from a costumed bear. *200 Boylston St., Boston; (800) 332-3442; (617) 338-4400;* www.fourseasons.com

Le Meridien ★★★/$$-$$$$

This 326-room Rennaissance Revival hotel may have a sophisticated, European flair, but it's also friendly to families. Through Meridien Magic packages, young guests get a gift on check-in and use of the gorgeous indoor pool, plus a plush, kid-size robe, and bedtime milk and cookies. Treat yourselves to the elegant Sunday brunch, a gastronomic feast featuring a kids-only station with hot dogs, minipizzas, and mac and-cheese. It's just a short walk to Faneuil Hall. *250 Franklin St., Boston; (617) 451-1900.*

Royal Sonesta Hotel ★★★★/$$$-$$$$

Plenty of TLC for families is only one of the advantages of staying at this 400-room Cambridge Hotel alongside the Charles River. Some of the others are: gorgeous views of Boston's skyline, a convenient location just down the street from Boston's Museum of Science, and a fabulous, atrium-style indoor swimming pool. Available at select times throughout the year, family weekends include passes to area attractions, bedtime milk and cookies, and a complimentary courtesy van that follows a daily route to such places as Harvard Square, Faneuil Hall Marketplace, and the Prudential Center. Summerfest packages give you complimentary bikes (bike paths along the city's esplanade are just outside the door), free boat rides, and free ice cream. Another bonus: the CambridgeSide Galleria, packed with kid-pleasing shops and restaurants, is just across the street. *5 Cambridge Pkwy., Cambridge; (800) SONESTA; (617) 806-4200;* www.sonesta.com

Seaport Hotel ★★★/$$$-$$$$

In the up-and-coming Seaport District (across the street from the World Trade Center), this sophisticated, 427-room hotel goes out of its way to make kids feel special. With 18 stories, it offers beautiful views of

Hi-Tech Hi Jinx

The Boston press regularly publicizes "hacks" (in this case, pranks) perpetrated by students at the **Massachusetts Institute of Technology**. The practical jokers responsible for the hack are rarely identified, but are credited with pulling off humorous stunts that do not damage school property. One of the most memorable hacks in MIT history involved placing a fake campus police cruiser (complete with a box of doughnuts) on top of the Great Dome, one of the campus's more prominent structures.

High-Flying Games

Games that use a pen or pencil are perfect to play on airplanes, since you can lean on the tray top. The following ideas are especially enjoyed by players who are sitting in a row. Unlike backseat car games, which can get fairly boisterous, these plane pastimes are a bit quieter, so you won't make enemies of your fellow fliers.

CRAZY CREATURES

Create strange-looking people, beasts, or any combination of both by folding a piece of paper into three equal sections. One person draws the face in the top section, then folds down the paper so the next person can't see it. That person then draws the midsection of the body, folds down the paper, and passes it to the third person, who sketches the legs in the bottom section. Finally, unfold the paper and name your creature.

TOUCHY TELEPHONE

This is a good game for people sitting in a row. Player 1, on one end, thinks of a word. Player 2, next to 1, closes his or her eyes and holds out an arm. Using a finger, Player 1 "writes" the word on Player 2's arm. The word gets passed down the row – and maybe across the aisle – until it reaches the last person in your party. That person says the word he thinks was written on his arm out loud, and Player 1 says the original word. Let Player 2 start the next round, and so on.

Boston Harbor or the city skyline. The indoor swimming pool is gorgeous; service is kid-friendly at the stylish Aura restaurant (splurge on the hotel's signature dessert, the incredible cookie-and-sorbet carousel); and special packages may include welcome gifts, milk and cookies, and passes to the Children's Museum, just down the street. A progressive, "all-inclusive" policy means you don't have to worry about tipping, except at the restaurant. *One Seaport La., World Trade Center, Boston; (877) SEAPORT; (617) 385-4000.*

GOOD EATS

Durgin-Park Restaurant
★★★/$$

For generations, this historic restaurant has been the place to try such Yankee specialties as old-fashioned baked beans prepared in stone crocks, pot roast, New England corned beef and cabbage, and even coffee Jell-O (there are burgers and brownie sundaes, too). Order your favorites, sit down at one of the long tables, and dig in. *Faneuil Hall Marketplace, Boston; (617) 227-2038.*

Faneuil Hall Marketplace
★★★/$

If you can't decide whether to have pizza or Mexican, seafood or Chinese, head to this crowded, hopping marketplace. Composed of

three restored 19th-century buildings, "the Market" is home to more than 40 food vendors. Give everyone $6, order at your favorite counters, and then eat together at a table in center court. *Faneuil Hall Marketplace, Merchants Row, Boston; (617) 242-5642.*

Fire & Ice
★★★★/$$

A classic example of "eatertainment," this creative restaurant invites kids to design their own stir-fry meals by picking their favorite meat, fish, and veggie mix-ins from food stations, then watching as chefs sizzle the food on a 30-foot-round grill. Even if your kids decide to mix beets with swordfish, the young chefs treat every dinner as if it's a masterpiece. *50 Church St., Cambridge; (617) 547-9007.*

Full Moon
★★★★/$$

More restaurants should take a cue from this leading-edge spot. Masterminded by two sisters with kids, this eatery combines delicious, eclectic food with a creative play area. The royal treatment starts with a bucket of toys set on the table for youngsters and extends to awesome menu choices and a kid-savvy attitude. Children's meals are whipped up quickly, and your toddlers will be served their beverage in sippy cups. In the wonderful play area adjacent to the tables, the kids can pass the time with trains, a minikitchen, and a big blackboard. Bonus: kids' cooking classes are periodically offered here, and Henry Bear's Park, one of the area's finest toy stores, is just a short walk down the street. *344 Huron Ave., Cambridge; (617) 354-6699.*

Hard Rock Café
★★/$-$$

No matter how loud your kids get, this place will be louder. Decorated with rock-and-roll memorabilia (such as Eddie Van Halen's guitar and Keith Richards's jacket), this is a great place for parents who pine for classic rock, and for kids who want to belt out a song while they're coloring in their groovy Lil' Rocker menu/activity book. Kids' meals include Jimi Tenderstix. *131 Clarendon St., Boston; (617) 424-7625;* www.hardrockcafe.com

Legal Seafoods
★★★/$$-$$$

Not only does this restaurant dish out some of the best seafood anywhere, but its kids' menu is outstanding. Many children's selections go beyond the standard burger and fries, although, they're here, too. Kids can get easy-to-eat lobster (that's been taken out of, then replaced in, the shell), fresh-cod fish sticks, and even fish-shaped ravioli— all served with fresh fruit and vegetables (something you seldom see on children's menus). The chowder is outstanding. *26 Park Square, Boston; (617) 426-4444* (with many other locations); www.legalseafoods.com

Marche Movenpick
★★★★/$

The Canadian-based restaurant is one of the best places for families to refuel in Boston. Eat your way around the globe at this colorful marketplace, where you can wander to different stations and watch chefs prepare delicious delicacies. Try homemade pizza or a "pasta mountain," then wander to the Fruit Tree for a hand-blended juice drink, or try Bami Bam Bam (noodles) in the Far East. Exploring this "food

theater" is as much fun as nibbling the offerings. Parents and kids both will like the kids' playroom with videos and toys and—above and beyond the call of duty—kid-size bathroom stalls. *Prudential Center, Boston; (617) 578-9700;* www.trend maker.com/food/marche/

Pizzeria Regina
★★★/$-$$

The place to go for thin-crust pizza in the city's North End, the restaurant is casual and comfortable, with a high tolerance for noisy kids. *11½ Thatcher St., Boston; (617) 227-0765.*

Sluggers Dugout
★★/$

This place hits a home run with kids. The baseball-themed eatery features lots of colorful memorabilia, plus beloved ball game fare: hot dogs, fries, and ice cream. *254 Faneuil Hall Marketplace, Boston; (617) 723-3635;* www.sluggersdugout.net

Union Oyster House
★★★/$$

Mix history with hot dogs at the nation's oldest, continuously operated restaurant. Famous for its semicircular oyster bar, the brick

BOSTON BAKED BEANS have been a favored food since Colonial times. The beans are slow-cooked in molasses for their unique flavor. The popular dish is the reason behind the city's nickname—Beantown.

landmark is also renowned for making families feel at home. Kids get a marvelous activity/coloring book that explains the building's history, and the excellent kids' menu features Ye Olde Peanut Butter and Jelly. *41 Union St., Boston; (617) 227-2750.*

SOUVENIR HUNTING

Curious George Goes to Wordsworth

Your little monkeys will love the Curious George–themed watches, posters, and backpacks in this fun shop, along with the cache of other educational toys, games, and books. *1 JFK St., Harvard Sq., Cambridge; (617) 498-0062.*

Faneuil Hall Marketplace

With more than 125 boutiques, shops, and pushcart vendors, as well as street entertainers, face painters, and special events, you can bet you'll be stopping here more than once during your trip. *Merchants Row, Boston; (617) 242-5642.*

FAO Schwarz

The 6,000-pound bronze teddy bear outside the store hints at what's inside this two-story toy shrine: a colossal selection of windup, computerized, push-button, collectible, and just plain cuddly playthings. Animated displays and a continuously playing theme song round out the experience. *440 Boylston St., Boston; (617) 262-5900;* www.fao.com

The **Boston Celtics** have won 16 NBA Championships, more than any other team in history.

Henry Bear's Park

Since 1976, this appealing, independently owned toy store has delighted families with fun, educational offerings sure to get a giggle from your kids. There's an excellent children's books department, along with Groovy Girls rag dolls, Radio Flyer wagons, hip backpacks, and much more. *361 Huron Ave., Cambridge; (617) 547-8424.*

See the town of Rockport with Footprints Walking Tours and your kids might learn to tie sailor's knots or make paper pirate ships.

North Shore and Merrimack Valley

Wᴴᴱɴ Mᴀꜱꜱᴀᴄʜᴜꜱᴇᴛᴛꜱ folks refer to the Cape, chances are they're talking about Cape Cod. There's a second Cape, however, also blessed with gorgeous family beaches, steeped in history, and packed with attractions. Cape Ann may be small in comparison to Cape Cod, but this North Shore promontory is big on fun.

Cape Ann's byways lead families past seaside villages, memorable vistas of the Atlantic, and working harbors where fishermen have cast their nets for generations. No wonder artists have long come to paint along its granite shores. Most families target the communities of Gloucester and Rockport.

Founded in 1623, the port of **Gloucester** has the oldest working harbor in the country. You can pay tribute to the 10,000 fishermen

who've perished at sea (including the *Andrea Gail* crew, depicted in the best-selling book and film *The Perfect Storm*) by visiting the

THE **FamilyFun** LIST

Hammond Castle Museum
(page 247)

The House of the Seven Gables
(page 247)

Lowell National Historical Park
(page 247)

Minute Man National Historical Park (page 248)

Wolf Hollow (page 253)

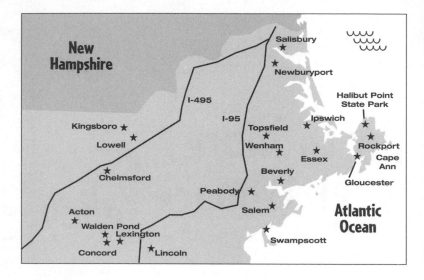

Fishermen's Memorial along the waterfront. Boat excursions, from whale watches to schooner cruises, are popular here. The kids will also like Good Harbor and Wingaersheek beaches *(call 800/649-6839 for either beach)*.

Gloucester's creative sister, **Rockport**, attracts legions of artists. For their part, kids love wandering past the tiny shops along Bearskin Neck and climbing on the rocks at Halibut Point Park to see if they can spot a seal.

Cape Ann is a fine launching point for exploring other communities (there are 34 in all) on the state's North Shore. The **North of Boston Convention and Visitors Bureau** (*17 Peabody Square, Peabody; 800/742-5306; 978/977-7760; www.northofboston.org*) is an excellent source of information; request the *North of Boston Visitor Guide.*

Here's some of our favorites:

In **Ipswich**, stake out a spot of white sand at four-and-a-half-mile-long Crane Beach, and take a boat trip through the magical Crane Wildlife Refuge.

Most people associate **Salem** with the Salem Witch Trials of 1692. Tourists come by the busloads to such sites as the Salem Witch Museum to learn the disturbing yet fascinating story. The town's Peabody-Essex Museum has more than a million objects brought home by sea captains from back when Salem was known as the "Venice of the New World."

For many families, summer isn't complete without visiting the carnival-style amusement area of **Salisbury Beach**, where your kids can munch cotton candy along the boardwalk, try their luck at a game of chance, and build castles on the five-mile-long beach. *Rte. 1A; (978) 465-3581.*

Just west of the North Shore lies the **Merrimack Valley**, encompassing 15 towns where families will find great adventures. Lowell National Historical Park, for example, brings the Industrial Revolution to life, with trolley rides and boat trips, and hands-on activities at the Boott Cotton Mills Museum.

Make sure to visit Minute Man National Historic Park and walk along the very road where Paul Revere—as legend has it—rode his horse and shouted, "The British are coming!"

Fans of Louisa May Alcott will have fun touring her modest yet marvelous Concord home. You can also swim in Walden Pond, near where Henry David Thoreau lived while writing his classic book, *Walden.* For more information on the Merrimack Valley, contact the **Greater Merrimack Valley Conven-** **tion and Visitors Bureau** (*9 Central St., Suite 201, Lowell; 800/443-3332; 978/459-6150;* www.merrimack valley.org).

CULTURAL ADVENTURES

American Textile History Museum ★★/$

You can still see and hear Lowell's legendary looms cranking out fabric at this renovated textile factory, now home to 100 exhibits that will weave a spell on your kids. The Textiles in America activity book invites children to color costumes, embark on a treasure hunt for inventions, and learn the process of turning raw wool into fabric. (Kids who complete the activities get a prize.) There's a play area in the gift shop and a delightful on-site café. *491 Dutton St., Lowell; (978) 441-0400;* www.athm.org

FamilyFun **READER'S TIP** -------------------------------

T Squares

My son, Jason, age 10¹/2, has a number of T-shirts from sports teams he's played on, camps he's gone to, and places we've visited. Jason's aunt, Linda, came up with a creative way to preserve those memories after he has outgrown the shirts. She cuts a section from the front and back of each shirt, sews them together, and lightly stuffs them to make mini-pillows. She then sews the pillows together to make a soft and comfortable quilt. It's a great keepsake, and as Jason gets older and taller, the quilt will keep on growing with him.

Debbie Emery, Northboro, Massachusetts

re-creates the pretrial of Salem's first accused witch. During the 50-minute program, your family becomes the jury, and most kids (best for the 5 and older set) love the chance to ponder the evidence, cross-examine witnesses, and question Bridget. The performance isn't scary; it's fun. *Old Town Hall, Derby Sq., Salem; (978) 927-2300, ext. 4747.*

The Crane Estate
★★★/$

The industrialist Richard T. Crane, Jr., made a fortune during America's Gilded Age, and families can share the spoils of his success by visiting this magnificent 2,000-acre reservation. Crane's 59-room, Stuart-style Great House has a half-mile-long lawn, known as the "grand allee," which rolls to the sea and is the perfect setting for summer concerts, Fourth of July celebrations, and children's holiday parties. In summer, kids bring their pails and shovels to four-and-a-half-mile-long Crane Beach to sculpt castles out of beautiful white sand (there's a big contest each year). Nature lovers can also tour the Crane Wildlife Refuge on a 90-minute land-sea trip. *Argilla Rd., off Rte. 1A, Ipswich; (978) 356-4351.*

"Cry Innocent: The People vs. Bridget Bishop"
★★/$

Even young children will enjoy this interactive stage production, which

Discovery Museums
★★★/$

Double your pleasure at this superb pair of museums, great for parents who are traveling with toddlers and older children. The Children's Discovery Museum is a brightly painted Victorian home where each room holds a surprise for babies and toddlers. As young ones wander around the colorful themed rooms, they can piece together a dinosaur skeleton, dress up like jungle animals, climb in a tree house, and play with bubbles in the water-discovery space. Next door, in the modern, light-filled Science Discovery Museum, kids ages 6 and up can visit three levels of hands-on math and science stations. Here, you can walk through a giant Tornado, experiment with sound waves, create gadgets in the inventor's workshop, and make circuits in the electricity room. Call for the schedule of special events, from Halloween parties to magic shows. *177 Main St., Acton; (978) 264-4200.* www.discoverymuseums.org

Hammond Castle
FamilyFun Museum ★★★★/$

Like a moonlit vision in a Dracula movie, this 16-room granite castle sits on the edge of the Atlantic, enticing families to explore its hallowed halls. The former home of the inventor Dr. John Hays Hammond, Jr., the castle once housed a hundred cats, seven dogs, and 20 birds (alas, no children). Today, kids will love inspecting the humongous 8,200-pipe organ, climbing 67 steps up a narrow staircase to the tower, walking through the Medieval Great Hall, and checking out Hammond's inventions (from a push-button radio to a guided torpedo system). If it isn't too crowded, the staff will even hand your child a helmet and sword and conduct a knighting ceremony, complete with certificate. In October, the castle operates one of the scariest haunted mansions ever. *80 Hesperus Ave., Gloucester; (978) 283-7673.*

The House of the
FamilyFun Seven Gables
★★★★/$

School-age children will enjoy the 25-minute tour of this mystical house, immortalized in Nathaniel Hawthorne's novel of the same name. The best part: climbing 20 steep steps up the secret staircase into the attic. Hawthorne was born in the adjacent house, where families can enjoy lace-making, bread-baking, and wool-spinning demonstrations.

You may want to get a combination ticket that includes admission to the **Salem 1630: Pioneer Village**; you can buy tickets at either place. *54 Turner St., Salem; (978) 744-0991; www.7gables.org*

Le Grand David
Spectacular Magic Company
★★★/$$

Add some magic to your vacation at the gorgeously restored Cabot Street Cinema Theatre, where, for 26 years, turban-topped Le Grand David and his sparkling cast have treated families to some of the best magic shows anywhere. Complete with dazzling costumes, levitations, sleight-of-hand tricks, and disappearing rabbits, the show captures the glory of vaudeville. Though the two-and-a-half-hour performance is fast-paced, it's still a bit long for younger kids. Nearby, at the **Larcom Theatre** *(13 Wallis St., Beverly)*, the company produces "An Anthology of State Magic." *The Cabot Street Cinema is at 286 Cabot St., Beverly. For either performance, call (978) 927-3677.*

Lowell National
FamilyFun Historical Park
★★★★/$

Once you've visited this park, you'll never look at a cotton shirt the same way again. Here, the Industrial Revolution comes alive through hands-on activities and programs. In the 1820s, Lowell became an industrial powerhouse, importing farm girls from New England's rural villages (and later, poorly paid immigrants) to live and work in the city's mills. You can get a taste for that time period at the orientation film in the visitors' center. In its play area, kids can weave, play with gears and pulleys, and read children's books about the era. The nearby **Boott Cotton Mills Museum** has a kids' Discovery Trail, where kids punch time clocks, don aprons, and try hands-on activities—such as spinning and carding wool—as they wander through the historic mill. (The weaving machines are so loud; you can even opt to wear earplugs.) In summer, families can tour the park by vintage trolley or cruise through the canals via boat. You'll also see an 1840s boarding house where the mill girls lived. The park sponsors a Junior Ranger Program and many special family-oriented events, including the Lowell Folk Festival and Canal Heritage Day. *67 Kirk St., Lowell; (978) 970-5000; www.nps.gov/lowe*

Minute Man National Historical Park
★★★★/Free

Start a revolution of your own by heading to this wonderful park for a lively lesson on the War of Independence. Exhibits center around the events of April 19, 1775, when Redcoats and Patriots fought along a 20-mile stretch of road between Boston and Concord, kicking off the Revolutionary War. Today, you and your kids can walk along the five-and-a-half-mile Battle Road and visit the site where Paul Revere was captured. Revere's fellow couriers, William Dawes (who turned back) and Samuel Prescott (after Revere's capture, he escaped, and carried the warning to Concord) and other Revolutionary War warriors—American and British—are profiled at the park. You can also cross the North Bridge, where embattled farmers, commonly known as Minutemen, marched in protest for their freedom. (It's fun to pose for a picture by the famous

---

FamilyFun READER'S TIP

Fledgling Photographers

Last summer, I put an extra flash in our vacation. Instead of having grown-ups be the only photographers, I bought each of our five children, whose ages range from 7 to 19, a 24-exposure disposable camera and let them snap their own pictures. The kids loved it, and we were able to see our vacation through their eyes. Plus, since they were inexpensive cameras, I didn't worry about them being dropped or lost. For very little money, these simple cameras brought our family a lot of smiles.

Kathi Kanuk, Chardon, Ohio

Minute Man statue, sculpted by Daniel Chester French.) At the Ephraim Hartwell Tavern, interpreters portray Ephraim and Elizabeth Hartwell and their children and invite your kids to play with colonial toys and try period crafts. Sign up for the Junior Ranger Program and don't miss the excellent, 30-minute multimedia show in the Minute Man Visitor Center. The park runs through Lexington, Concord, and Lincoln. **The Minute Man visitors' center** is on *Rte. 2A, Lexington; (781) 862-7753.* The **North Bridge visitors' center** is at *174 Liberty St., Concord; (978) 369-6993.* You may also want to stroll along Lexington's Battle Green, site of the war's first skirmish. *1875 Massachusetts Ave.; (781) 862-1450; www.nps.gov/mima*

During the **Salem Witch Trials** of 1692, more than 150 men and women were charged with practicing witchcraft; 19 of them were hanged.

New England Pirate Museum ★★/$

Here's your chance to rub salty elbows with Blackbeard, Kidd, and the rest of their bearded mates. On your search for buried treasure, you'll explore an 80-foot pirate cave. *274 Derby St., Salem; (978) 741-2800; www.piratemuseum.com*

Orchard House ★★★/$

Fans of *Little Women* (published in 1868) won't want to miss touring the house where Louisa May Alcott penned the beloved book. The Alcotts lived here from 1857 to 1877, and the tour provides a fascinating glimpse into the lives of the four sisters—Anna, Louisa, Elizabeth, and May— who inspired the novel. Families can see the very desk upon which Alcott wrote *Little Women*, and can take a look at the sisters' bedrooms. In May's room, for example, the walls are adorned with flowers and mythological figures, sketches that hint at the accomplished artist she would become. *399 Lexington Rd., Concord; (978) 369-4118.*

Peabody Essex Museum ★★★/$$

Founded in 1799 by seafaring entrepreneurs who collected art on their voyages, this museum contains more than a million art objects. The collection ranges from colorful figureheads that adorned New England ships to a sperm-whale jaw with 48 intimidating teeth. For hands-on fun, families gravitate to the Nature Culture Room, where kids can play games and join activities that change periodically. In the past, kids have donned silk costumes to explore the Silk Trade and sawed through a log to understand the gnawing power of beavers. *East India Sq., Salem; (978) 745-9500; www.pem.org*

Salem Maritime National Historic Site
★★★/$

Relive Salem's heyday as an international trading port at this collection of nine historic sites along the wharf. You can also stroll down **Derby Wharf** (the last of 50 original wharfs) to Salem's **1871 lighthouse**, tour the **1819 Custom House** where Nathaniel Hawthorne worked, and spend a few shillings at the **West India Goods Store** (1800). *174 Derby St., Salem; (978) 740-1660;* www.nps.gov/sama

Salem 1630: Pioneer Village
★★★/$

Meet some of Salem's early settlers at this re-created 17th-century village, where your kids can pet sheep and goats, crawl into a wigwam, and chat with costumed interpreters. You'll get the chance to try such hands-on activities as churning butter and spinning wool. Adjacent Forest River Park has a sandy beach with calm waters and lifeguards. *Forest River Park, Salem; (978) 745-0525.*

Salem Wax Museum of Witches & Seafarers
★★/$

Though the museum's 13 historical wax tableaux are supposed to be the draw, kids will gravitate to the hands-on area beneath the gallery. Here, you can make a gravestone rubbing, wait for someone to bail you out of a 17th-century jail cell, and learn how to make sailor's knots. *288 Derby St., Salem; (800) 298-2929.*

Salem Witch Museum
★★★/$

If you have time for just one witch

SEA ESCAPES

WITH ITS SCENIC COVES, schooner-filled harbors, and working fishing docks, the North Shore is a terrific place to cruise the waters. Whatever floats your boat, chances are, there's a tour for you. (You can even save yourself the drive to Boston by taking the 75-minute trip aboard the Salem ferry; *call Boston Harbor Cruises, 617/227-4321.*) Here are two family favorites:

Agawam Boat Charters
★★★/$$

Forget the canned narration and opt instead for a customized tour that's geared to your family's interests and budget. Captain Ted Marshall is full of colorful stories, which he'll gladly share with you aboard a pontoon or motorboat. He'll steer you past scenic islands, lighthouses, and barrier beaches and will even organize a family fishing attraction, hop on your broomstick and head to this popular site, where the hysteria of 1692 is played out on 13 stage sets. More like a multimedia show than a museum, the attraction features a deep-voiced narrator who grimly describes the course of events. It's probably too scary for kids under age 8. *Washington Sq., Salem; (978) 744-1692.*

Wenham Museum
★★/$

This little museum is big on wonder. Among its displays are more than a thousand dolls from all corners of the world (some dolls dating back to 1500 B.C.), six operating model train layouts, a three-foot-tall Addams Family dollhouse, and more. In the interactive room, kids can play with trains, building blocks, and puppets. *Rte. 1A, Wenham; (978) 468-2377.*

Just for Fun

Drumlin Farm Education Center & Wildlife Sanctuary ★★★/$

Run by the Massachusetts Audubon Society, this 232-acre farm gives kids the chance to poke into barns and sheds filled with cows, chickens, pigs, and goats and learn about the workings of a farm. After meeting the animals, hike up the dome-shape drumlin (for which the farm is named) to watch birds and butterflies. *208 S. Great Rd., Lincoln; (781) 259-9500.*

Foote Brothers Canoe Rentals ★★★/$

The slow-moving Ipswich River flows through a wildlife sanctuary and two state parks, making it ideal for family canoe trips. This afford-

trip or clambake. Bring along a picnic and bathing suits so you can take a swimming break. The captain's hourly rate is very reasonable (there's a 90-minute minimum), and he frequently offers specials. *21 Pickering St., Essex; (978) 768-1114.*

Moby Duck Tours
★★★/$$

Learn about the region's witches, pirates, and sea captains on this 55-minute amphibious tour, which starts on land and eventually

splashes into the harbor. *Harbor Loop, Rogers St., Gloucester; (978) 281-3825.*

able, family-owned outfitter can set you up in a 17-foot-long Grumman canoe that fits two adults and two small children. With nearly 50 years of experience catering to families, Foote Brothers can recommend a self-guided nature journey that suits your clan's expertise; there are no guided tours. *230 Topsfield Rd., Ipswich; (978) 356-9771; www.ipswichma.com/footbrothers/*

Footprints Walking Tours
★★★/$
On these kids' walking tours, you don't just learn about pirates, you become one. Your adventure begins at the company's base—a former fishing shack—where you don themed hats and then follow Charles and Vicki Hogan down the streets of Rockport. Along the way, you learn about the sea creatures, salty pirates, and captains that once inhabited this rocky wonderland. The Hogans draw on their experience as grandparents to charm your children. They'll even teach your family how to tie sailor's knots. Tours are customized to your children's interests and ages. *15 North Rd., Bearskin Neck, Rockport; (978) 546-7730; www.footprints ofRockport.com*

Goodale Orchards ★★★/Free
Open May to December, the orchard goes all out in fall with pick-your-own apples, lip-smacking cider doughnuts, hayrides, and the chance to see the busy cider mill at work.

Kids can also pet farm animals and shop for old-fashioned candy in the store. *143 Argilla Rd., Ipswich; (978) 356-5366.*

Ipswich River Wildlife Sanctuary
★★★/$
Massachusetts Audubon's largest sanctuary invites families to explore 2,800 acres of meadows, woods, and wetlands on ten miles of trails. The sanctuary has special events scheduled throughout the year, which range from guided nature walks and owl prowls to maple sugaring tours and nature festivals. *87 Perkins Row, Topsfield; (978) 887-9264.*

Parker River National Wildlife Refuge ★★★/$
For nature lovers, a visit to this 4,662-acre paradise on pretty Plum Island is a must. The refuge is home to more than 300 bird species, so bring your binoculars, walk along boardwalk trails, and train your eyes on piping plovers, blue herons, and other feathered friends. The sandy beach is great for strolling, but it's too rough to swim here. Plum Island is also a favorite cycling spot. *Plum Island, Newburyport; (978) 465-5753.*

Salem Willows ★★/Free-$$
There's a first time for everything, including the chop suey sandwiches that are a local (and tasty) favorite. This unusual repast isn't the only reason to visit this pay-by-the-ride amusement park. Families

can also enjoy the arcade, a livery where you can rent motorboats or kayaks, and legendary taffy and ice cream made from a recipe that dates back to 1883. *173 Fort Ave., Salem; (978) 745-0251;* www.salemwil lows.com

Volcano Park ★★/$

If your kids are getting antsy, don't erupt. Bring them to this 25,000-square-foot indoor theme park, with an 18-hole Polynesian-themed miniature-golf course (featuring a simmering volcano), bank-shot basketball, a Moon Bounce, arcade games, and a soft play area for younger kids. Pizza and hot dogs are plentiful. *164 Newbury St. (Rte. 1 South), Peabody; (978) 536-5123.*

Walden Pond ★★★/$

Henry David Thoreau immortalized this 64-acre pond in his 1854 book, *Walden,* and families can experience the beauty of the setting firsthand by swimming, hiking, and fishing here. You can also see a model of the writer's cabin at one end of the parking lot. *Rte. 126, Concord; (978) 369-3254.*

Wolf Hollow (North American Wolf Foundation) ★★★★/$

You stand a better chance of being hit by a meteorite than being killed by a wolf, but that doesn't stop some folks from fearing (and harming) them. This place will take the fear away through a remarkable presentations featuring the resident wolf pack. In fact, chances are you'll never look at the "big bad wolf" the same way again. During the presentations, you and your kids (best for ages 5 and older) sit in bleachers alongside the wolves' expansive, fenced habitat. You're introduced, one by one, to each member of the pack. You also get to witness the power of the pecking order, practice your howling skills, and watch the wolves heed the call for "cheese." *114 Essex Rd., Ipswich; (978) 356-0216.*

WE RECOMMEND two whale watching tours in Gloucester; **Cape Ann Whale Watch** *(Rose's Wharf; 800/877-5110; 978/283-5110)* has four-hour trips led by staff members from the Whale Conservation Institute, on which you can listen to whale songs with headsets. With **Seven Seas Whale Watch** *(Seven Seas Wharf, Rogers St.; 800/238-1776; 978/283-1776),* you can take four-and-a-half-hour trips aboard the *Privateer.*

BUNKING DOWN

Atlantis Motor Inn
★★/$$

Every one of the inn's 40 rooms has an ocean view, and the views get better (and the rates pricier) the higher up you stay. There's an outdoor seaside pool, an on-site coffee shop, and Good Harbor Beach is a short walk away. *125 Atlantic Rd., Gloucester; (800) 732-6313; (978) 281-8994; (978) 283-0014.*

Best Western Chelmsford Inn
★★/$$

A convenient base for exploring attractions in Lowell, this 120-room hotel has an outdoor pool, an adjoining Ground Round Restaurant, and a big backyard where kids can run off excess energy. *187 Chelmsford St., Chelmsford; (978) 256-7511;* www.bestwestern.com

---

I SPIED

Here's a variation on the classic game in which someone says, "I spy with my little eye something green," and whoever guesses the item correctly goes next. Get tricky and play I Spied, selecting items that you've already passed.

Capt'n Jack's Waterfront Inn
★★★/$$$

Just eight miles north of Boston, this inn rents rooms, suites, and even apartments. There's an oceanside pool, and it's a quick walk to the beach and ice-cream shops. *253 Humphery St., Swampscott; (800) 628-4671; (781) 595-7910.*

Homewood Suites
★★★/$$

Stay in one of these suites, and your family will be spoiled for life. Kids can sleep on the foldout sofa in the living room, while parents enjoy privacy in their own bedroom. Each room has cable TV, and the attractive kitchen is furnished with plates, utensils, and all appliances. You can also enjoy the indoor pool and the generous, complimentary continental breakfast that's served in the lobby. *57 Newbury St., Rte. 1, Peabody; (800) CALL-HOME; (978) 536-5050.*

Rocky Shores Inn & Cottages ★★/$$

This is a nice place to stay if you want to rent a cottage in Cape Ann for the week (in peak season, nightly rentals aren't available). The two- and three-bedroom Cape-style cottages have knotty-pine walls, eat-in kitchens, full bath, cable TV, and either ocean or garden views. Although there are no on-site activities for children, the beach is just a short walk away. *65 Eden Rd., Rockport; (800) 348-4003; (978) 546-2823;* www.rockportusa.com/rocky shores/

GOOD EATS

Athenian Corner
★★/$$

In the heart of Lowell National Historical Park, this restaurant serves exceptional Greek food in a family-oriented setting. You'll find moussaka, grape leaves, and shish kebab, along with cheeseburgers and spaghetti. *207 Market St., Lowell; (978) 458-7052.*

Bonkers Fun House Pizza
★★★/$

Rain or shine, this place is a haven for families. The colossal indoor play zone has a maze, merry-go-round, Ferris wheel, arcade games, and a special toddler activity area. Although pizza is the mainstay, you can also get subs, salads, and chicken fingers. *535 Lowell St., Peabody; (978) 535-8355.*

Brackett's Ocean View Restaurant ★★/$$

As its name suggests, diners get beautiful views of Sandy Bay along with their tasty meals. Though the restaurant may look a bit formal, it's child-friendly, with a classic kids' menu and accommodating waitresses. Parents will find everything from lobster and other seafood fare to London broil and chicken dishes. *27 Main St., Rockport; (978) 546-2797.*

Caffe Graziani ★★/$$

Feast on homemade linguini, ziti, and chicken parmigiana at this authentic Italian café, where you'll hear the beautiful language spoken behind the grill. The friendly waitresses will tempt your kids with spaghetti and meatballs, chicken nuggets, and pizza. *133 Washington St., Salem; (978) 741-4282;* www.salemweb.com/biz/graziani

David's Restaurant
★★★/$$-$$$

Kids won't be the least bit impressed with the grilled sea bass, but they'll love munching on hot dogs, watching videos on a big-screen TV, and playing games with their peers in their special room at this restaurant that's far ahead of others in its family-oriented arrangements. David's makes it possible for parents to eat a nice meal (there are two restaurants on the premises: casual David's and the fancier Rim), while kids have some fun of their own. Although children are welcome at either restaurant, once they get a peek at their special space, there's little hope you'll lasso them for a sit-down meal. The Kids' Room accepts children 18 months and over, and parents pay an hourly rate, just as you would for a sitter. *11 Brown Sq., Newburyport; (978) 462-8077.*

The Firehouse
★★/$$

Kids get all fired up about this restaurant, which is decorated with alarm bells, rescue ladders—and even a dummy sliding down a pole. The fare includes burgers, steaks, and seafood, along with typical kids' staples. *130 Middlesex Rd., Kingsboro; (978) 649-4118.*

Gloucester House Restaurant
★★★/$$

These folks turn Sunday into Funday. On summer Sundays, the staff hosts seed-spitting contests, musical chairs, and other goofy games out on the lawn. Winners of the afternoon events are rewarded with silly prizes. Of course, any time of the week you can get great seafood here, along with classic American dishes. Kids will find all of their favorites, too. *Seven Seas Wharf, Gloucester; (800) 238-1776; (978) 283-1812.*

Periwinkles ★★/$$

Kids can sip Playground Punch and munch on Kookie Monsters at this accommodating waterfront restaurant alongside the Essex River. Children can enjoy the usual favorites, while parents dine on fare with an unusual twist: depending on when you come (the menu changes periodically), you might find succulent Cuban sandwiches, jerk chicken, and grilled lobster pizza. *74 Main St., Essex; (978) 768-6320.*

The Rockmore Floating Restaurant
★★★/$$

Motor over to your supper on a 26-foot-launch (the restaurant ferries you for free), which drops families off at a converted barge anchored in Salem Harbor. Decked out with palms and bright Caribbean colors, the floating eatery is fun incarnate. Kids love watching oodles of fish swim under the docks and ordering their favorite dinners off a menu attached to an Etch A Sketch. The boat leaves from Pickering Wharf and from Marblehead's Village Street Pier. In the off-season, families can still enjoy the friendly service and festive food at the Rockmore's sister restaurant, the **Rockmore Dry Dock**, *Pickering Wharf, Salem; (978) 740-1001 (for both).*

Skip's ★★/$-$$

This local favorite dishes out big, tasty portions of spaghetti, meat loaf, and chicken dishes at reasonable prices. The waitresses are attuned to kids, providing crayons, a welcoming attitude, and scrumptious kids' meals. *116 Chelmsford St., Chelmsford; (978) 256-2631.*

Sylvan Street Grilles
★★★/$$

Peanut butter and marshmallow fluff is nowhere to be found on most menus, but it's here, along with your favorite characters (Barney, Arthur and D.W., and the Rugrats), who join families at special breakfasts the first and third Sunday of every month. No matter when you visit, kids get balloons and coloring sheets. Parents get to dine on scallop pie, sirloin steak, and shrimp linguine. This family-run restaurant has two locations: *195 Elm St., Salisbury (978/462-7919); and 12 Sylvan St., Peabody (978/774-1724).*

Woodman's
★★★★/$-$$

Coming to Essex and skipping Woodman's fried clams is like going to New York and passing on the bagels. In 1914, potato chip purveyor Lawrence "Chubby" Woodman dropped a clam in the fryer and started a culinary revolution. Ever since, families have flocked to this restaurant—now run by Chubby's descendants—for incredibly generous portions of plump, sweet Ipswich clams; colossal onion rings; chowder; lobster; and hot dogs. Dinner here is worth every clam. *Rte. 133, Essex; (978) 768-6451.*

SOUVENIR HUNTING

Tuck's Candies

For the ultimate summer pleasure, buy a bag of homemade peanut butter, cinnamon, and butter-rum taffy at this local institution (since 1929), and stroll along bear-claw-shaped Bearskin Neck, a shopping enclave packed with old fishing shacks that have been converted into galleries and specialty shops. *15 Main St., Rockport; (800) 569-2767; (978) 546-6352.*

Ye Olde Pepper Candy Companie

This candy is so good, Salem's sea captains packed it into their ships' hulls in the 1800s and traded it overseas. To this day, America's oldest candy company still makes Gibralters and Blackjacks, the very treats a sweet-toothed sailor would find irresistible. *122 Derby St., Salem; (978) 745-2744.*

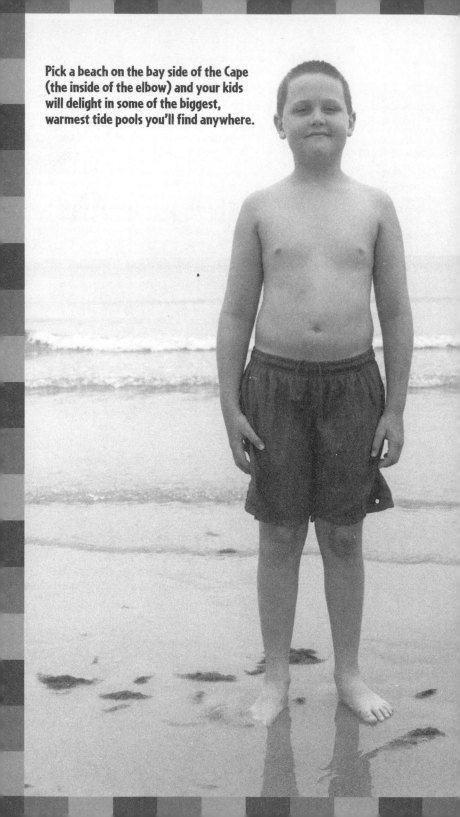

Pick a beach on the bay side of the Cape (the inside of the elbow) and your kids will delight in some of the biggest, warmest tide pools you'll find anywhere.

South Shore and Cape Cod

FOR MANY FAMILIES, Massachusetts' South Shore is the summer fun capital of New England, packed with beaches, family amusements, natural wonders, and historic attractions that lure millions of travelers to the area every year. In just one day, you can visit the spot where the Pilgrims set up shop, don a bandanna and face paint and set off on a pirate adventure, and relax on a stretch of beach that's so beautiful it's been declared a National Seashore.

The center of the action is 70-mile-long Cape Cod, the largest glacial peninsula in the world. Connected by the Sagamore and Bourne bridges to the Massachusetts mainland, the Cape consists of 15 towns whose population more than doubles during the summer. The Cape's beaches have won top honors in *FamilyFun*

THE FamilyFun LIST

MUST-SEE
MUST-SEE

Battleship Cove (page 262)

Cape Cod National Seashore (page 268)

Pilgrim Monument & Provincetown Museum (page 265)

Plimoth Plantation (page 266)

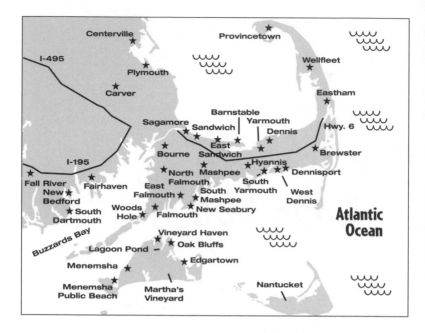

magazine's national travel survey, and it's easy to see why. With 300 miles of beach along four distinct bodies of water, families can easily find one that suits their tastes.

Formed by two-mile-thick ice sheets thousands of years ago, the Cape's shape is constantly changing due to wind and water, and families can learn about this process at the Cape Cod National Seashore visitors' center (see page 268). In addition to the sparkling ocean, families will find kettle ponds (round pockets of water formed by slow-melting ice chunks), streams, and lakes, which you can explore by canoe or kayak.

Where to vacation on the Cape is a matter of personal taste. Here are brief descriptions of some popular family destinations:

Dennis, located mid-Cape, has 18 beaches (including the kid-pleasing Mayflower Beach along the gentle shore of Cape Cod Bay). The town is also the starting point of the 20-mile-long Cape Cod Rail Trail and home to Sundae School *(381 Lower County Rd., Dennisport; 508/394-9122)*, a popular ice-cream parlor where kids can listen to a Victorian player piano as they dig into sundaes made with real whipped cream.

Falmouth, home to the renowned Woods Hole Oceanographic Institution in the village of Woods Hole, is the place for junior oceanographers to visit seals and other sea life at the local aquarium. You also can board a marine research vessel for a hands-on adventure at sea. Ask the **Falmouth Chamber of Commerce** *(800/526-8532; 508/548-8500)* for the entertaining children's activity book *Kids Catch Memories in Falmouth By-the-Sea.*

Hyannis, a section of the town of Barnstable, is the commercial hub of the Cape. It's also the place to learn more about John F. Kennedy and his family at the John F. Kennedy Hyannis Museum. Hyannis also offers a fun-filled pirate cruise and a tour of a potato-chip factory (see page 269). You can even hop on a carousel at the Courtyard Marketplace in the center of the main shopping district *(541 Main St.).*

Provincetown, or P-town, is out there in every way imaginable. Located at the lower tip of the Cape, this fun-loving town was the Pilgrims' first landing site before they moved to Plymouth. Here, you'll find artists, fishermen, purple-haired rebels, and families of every

sort jamming the sidewalks along festive Commercial Street. Those who want to escape the crowds can climb the 116 steps to the top of the Pilgrim Monument (the highest stone tower in the United States), take a dune tour (see page 267), or sign on for a whale watch.

In **Yarmouth,** kids can bounce on a trampoline, play pirate miniature golf, go bowling, and join a game of paintball along busy Route 28, which is jammed with family attractions.

The Cape is a perfect launching point for a couple of essential South Shore side trips, each of which is less than an hour from the Cape Cod Canal. Plan on a pilgrimage to **Plymouth,** to learn the story of the 102 men, women, and children who established the first permanent English settlement in the New World. Top-rated Plimoth Plantation, the *Mayflower II,* and the Plymouth National Wax Museum will help your kids understand the hardships and resourcefulness of this remarkable community.

To the west of Cape Cod in **Bristol County,** families can experience the golden age of whaling at New Bedford Whaling National Historic Park, a beautifully preserved 13-block waterfront area. As you amble past the historic mansions, wander into Seamen's Bethel, where mariners, including Herman Melville, have worshiped before going to sea.

CULTURAL ADVENTURES

⭐MUST-SEE FamilyFun ⭐MUST-SEE Battleship Cove
★★★/$

Make sure you and the kids are shipshape before you visit this park: There are six boats to tour, including the USS *Massachusetts* battleship (Big Mamie), which is longer than two football fields and as tall as a nine-story building. After walking her decks, you can climb aboard the destroyer USS *Joseph P. Kennedy*, named for JFK's brother, an aviator killed in World War II. The remaining vessels include a World War II submarine, the USS *Lionfish*; the Russian missile corvette *Hidden Sea*; and two rare patrol torpedo boats. If you're not up for all six, pick the *Massachusetts*, and then head for the nearby Fall River Carousel (see "Merry Carousels" on page 352) for a fun break. *Battleship Cove, Fall River; (800) 533-3194; (508) 678-1100; www.battleshipcove.com*

Cape Cod Museum of Natural History
★★★/$

Rain or shine, this 80-acre retreat is a great place to bring the kids. In the two-story main hall, you can meet indigenous plants and animals and learn how the Cape was formed by glaciers 20,000 years ago. Afterward, meander onto nature trails that wind past woodlands, marsh, and freshwater habitats. The center hosts a number of guided family programs, including family field walks (a mile-and-a-quarter walk to a scenic beach) and Mudflat Mania (find fiddler crabs and worms at low tide). You can also consider seal cruises and guided canoe and kayak trips. *869 Rte. 6A, Brewster; (508) 896-3867.*

Around Town

If you're driving through one of New England's many wonderful small towns, encourage your kids to do a little scavenger hunting from the car. Be on the lookout for these:

♦ A building more than 100 years old
♦ A humorous or out-of-date billboard
♦ A place where an important event occurred
♦ A dirt road

♦ A statue or outdoor sculpture
♦ A street with a great view
♦ A house painted in three colors
♦ A graveyard
♦ A lake or pond
♦ A factory where an everyday item is made
♦ A street named after someone famous
♦ A shop you've never visited
♦ A bear- or moose-crossing sign

Children's Museum in Dartmouth—and more
★★/$

Housed in a renovated dairy barn, this museum focuses on farming in New England—a great eye-opener to city kids. Throughout the year, you can join special events (such as maple sugaring programs) and group walks on 60 acres of agricultural fields, woodlands, and salt marsh. Inside, the exhibits (which will eventually change to better suit the farm theme) include a pirate ship, ambulance, grocery store, and puppet theater. *276 Gulf Rd., S. Dartmouth; (508) 993-3361.*

In comparison, the **Cape Cod Children's Museum** (★★/$) is a shrimp—just one large room of interactive exhibits geared to kids up to age 3. Here, kids can climb aboard a train, pirate ship, and fishing boat. *577 Great Neck Rd., S. Mashpee; (508) 539-8788.*

Colonial Lantern Tours
★★/$-$$

Some families mistake Plimouth Plantation for the site of the Pilgrims' original settlement. In fact, however, they established their first community in downtown Plymouth, and you can tour the area on a leisurely, lantern-lit walk geared to families with kids ages 6 and up. Throughout the 90-minute walk, you each hold a punched-tin colonial lantern, while educators share fascinating facts and points of interest

you'd easily miss without a guide. It's a good trip to take the evening before touring Plimoth Plantation. Ghost tours are offered, too. *Call for reservations and directions. (800) 698-5636; (508) 747-4161.*

Expedition *Whydah*
★★/$

Though there aren't a lot of hands-on exhibits at this small museum, the story is often enough to captivate kids. In 1984, Cape Codder Barry Clifford salvaged the only pirate ship ever recovered: the *Whydah*, which sank on April 26, 1717, and contained a boatload of treasures. Here, you'll watch footage of Clifford's expedition off the coast of Wellfleet. You'll also see pieces of eight, pirate pistols, and leather goods worn by pirates, and learn about the world's most feared pirates. *16 MacMillan Wharf, Provincetown; (508) 487-8899;* www.whydah.com

Heritage Plantation of Sandwich ★★/$

Set on 76 beautifully landscaped acres, this complex of American museums and gardens is making an effort to attract more families—and succeeding. At the front desk, you can pick up a fun pack filled with suggestions for activities to try inside the various exhibit halls. There also are several Touch and Teach kiosks (hands-on learning stations) on the premises. Kids will enjoy climbing on an antique car in the automobile

263

museum, checking out the miniature soldiers at the military museum, and riding on the 1912 carousel made by master craftsman Charles Looff. In summer, kids can also join activities in the children's garden (advance registration required), see family movies in the outdoor theater, sign up for crafts classes, and visit a historic windmill. *67 Grove St., Sandwich; (508) 888-3300.*

John F. Kennedy Hyannis Museum ★★/$

If you've made a pilgrimage to Hyannis to learn more about the Kennedys, this is the place to start. The small museum isn't as elaborate as Boston's Kennedy museum, but it tells the story of JFK's love affair with the Cape. Through family photographs and a video narrated by Walter Cronkite, you'll learn how the Kennedy Compound became JFK's summer White House. You'll also see plenty of pictures of a tanned Jackie, Caroline, John, Jr., and the young president enjoying happy times. *397 Main St., Hyannis; (508) 790-3077.*

FamilyFun TIP

Whale Watching on Cape Cod

Hyannis Whale Watcher *(Barnstable Harbor; 800/827-0374; 508/362-6088)* offers three- to four-hour trips aboard the M/V *Whale Watcher*, a jet-powered boat.

Lloyd Center for Environmental Studies ★★/$

If you're in the mood for a quiet activity off the beaten path, check out this 55-acre retreat along the Slocums River Estuary. A scenic ride past woods and wetlands will lead you to a laid-back center with six walking trails, one of which you can complete in ten minutes. The trails lead to a salt marsh, peaceful forest, and freshwater wetlands. In the center, you can handle creatures in a touch tank; meet Jitter, the green iguana; and, from the observation deck, take in a panoramic view of Buzzards Bay. Throughout the year, the center holds seasonally appropriate family programs that may include canoe trips and scavenger hunts; call for schedule. *430 Potomska Rd., S. Dartmouth; (508) 990-0505;* www.umassd.edu/spe cialprograms/lloyd/lloydcenter.html

Marine Museum at Fall River ★/$

Packed with intricately designed ship models, this museum will appeal to kids who are fascinated by the *Titanic*. Here, you can see videotapes of the wreckage discovered by Dr. Robert Ballard. Deck chairs, buttons, hair combs, and chocolate tins from the wreck are on display, plus there's an amazing 28-foot model of the ship designed by 20th Century Fox Studios for the 1953 *Titanic* movie. You can even hear a recorded account of the 1912 tragedy from a *Titanic* survivor. *70 Water St., Battleship Cove, Fall River; (508) 674-3533;* www.marine museum.org

Mayflower II ★★★/$

The first question kids will ask when you step onto this re-creation of the *Mayflower*: "How did 126 people fit on this boat?" Probably not very comfortably. As you roam the decks of the English merchant vessel (it was never meant to carry passengers), your grade-schoolers will gain a new understanding of the tenacity required to make the 66-day journey from England to the New World. From the traditional buff-brown hull to the hand-sewn linen canvas, the creators of the *Mayflower II* spared no effort in getting the details right. Interpreters are frequently on hand to answer the inevitable questions, such as, "Where did the Pilgrims sleep?" *State Pier, Plymouth; (508) 746-1622;* www.plimoth.org/ museum/mayflower/mayflowe.htm

New Bedford Whaling Museum ★★★/$

This is a whale of a way to learn about the industry that supported the region for so long. Here, kids can climb on the world's largest ship model, a half-scale replica of the New Bedford bark, *Lagoda*. They also can get a taste of life as a whaler by lying down in a cramped bunk. Suspended from the ceiling are skeletons of a 33-foot humpback and a rare, 65-foot blue whale. The largest animal ever to live on earth, the creature is so big you could park a Volkswagen on its tongue and have room to walk along the edge. Make sure to take in a view of New Bedford's historic harbor from the observation deck. If you're lucky, the 1894 schooner *Ernestina* will be in port. *18 Johnny Cake Hill, New Bedford; (508) 997-0046;* www.whal ingmuseum.org

Pilgrim Hall Museum ★★★/$

At this museum devoted to preserving the Pilgrims' possessions, kids can undertake a treasure hunt in search of a baby's cradle, William Bradford's chair, and dinnerware. *75 Court St., Rte. 3A, Plymouth; (508) 746-1620.*

☀MUST-SEE Pilgrim Monument & FamilyFun Provincetown ☀MUST-SEE Museum ★★★★/$

Some families will go to great heights to learn about the Pilgrims, who first came ashore November 11, 1620, in Provincetown. They remained here for five weeks before heading on to Plymouth—and this 252-foot-tall granite monument acknowledges their brief stay. The 116-step tower is modeled after the Torre Del Mangia in Siena, Italy. If your family makes it to the top, you're rewarded with a panoramic view of Cape Cod Bay and Provincetown Harbor. (Kids often finish the

CRANBERRY QUALITY is ensured by a bouncing test. Good cranberries bounce, but bad ones have soft spots that take away their Tigger-like qualities.

journey well before their parents.) It's also worth it to stop in the Provincetown Museum to see Pilgrim artifacts and view a 12-minute, kid-oriented video about the Pilgrims' journey. *High Pole Hill Rd., Provincetown; (800) 247-1620; (508) 487-1310;* www.pilgrim-mon ument.org

Plimoth Plantation
FamilyFun ★★★★/$$

How did the Pilgrims enjoy the ride on the *Mayflower*? What the heck is pottage? For answers to these and other Pilgrim-related questions, you can go right to the source at this living history museum. To get a handle on this extensive attraction, see the 15-minute orientation film in the visitors' center, check out the crafts center, then make your way to Pilgrim Village. Everyone in the village acts and speaks as if it's 1627. (Ask about Pokémon and you'll get a baffled stare.) The folks who portray the Pilgrims are amazingly immersed in their roles, and will gladly invite you to watch them cook a tansy (omelette) or weed the garden. After chatting with William Bradford, governor of the colony, and Captain Myles Standish, the

colony's military commander, mosey on over to Hobbamock's Homesite. Here, you'll learn about the Pokanoket Indian who served as the Pilgrim's interpreter. You'll also want to visit the Crafts Center to watch artisans use 17th-century techniques to make pottery, furniture, and shoes like those the Pilgrims would have brought with them or imported from Europe. In the Nye Barn, kids will love seeing Milking Devon cows, San Clemente Island goats, and Tamworth hogs, rare breeds that are similar to those that would have inhabited the 1620s settlement. You can get fast food here or sample 17th-century cuisine at Out of the Ordinarie. The Children's Shop has a wonderful selection of old-time toys and books. *Rte. 3A, Warren Ave., Plymouth; (508) 746-1622;* www. plimoth.org/museum/museum.htm

Plymouth National Wax Museum ★★/$

As you'll discover at this entertaining, educational museum, the Pilgrims were cut from a special mold. In 24 detailed scenes, you'll learn about these brave souls who crossed the Atlantic in search of religious freedom. You'll bear witness to the Pilgrims' pretrip persecution in

England, passage on the *Mayflower*, and the courtship of John Alden and Priscilla Mullins, both among the first settlers in New Plymouth. Open April to November. *16 Carver St., Plymouth; (508) 746-1622.*

Plymouth Rock ★/Free

It may not have the "aah" factor of, say, the Grand Canyon, but this famous chunk of bedrock is part of the Plymouth pilgrimage. After all, it's the rock the Pilgrims stepped on when they arrived on December 21, 1620. You'll find this surprisingly small chunk—along with hordes of tourists who've come to pay homage to it—at the portico on Plymouth's waterfront. www.state. ma.us/dem/parks/plgm.htm

Thornton W. Burgess Museum & Green Briar Nature Center and Jam Kitchen ★★★/$

These spots are gems for families who want to turn a love of reading into a special adventure. Born in 1874 in Sandwich (the Cape's oldest town), Thornton Burgess was a conservationist and beloved children's author. He began his 170-book career in 1910 with *Old Mother West Wind*, a tale that introduced children to the antics of Peter Rabbit (not to be confused with Beatrix Potter's Peter), Jimmy Skunk, Sammy Jay, and a cast of other animals. You can learn about this author, and his love of children and nature, in two nearby locations.

Throughout the year, the Thornton Burgess Society sponsors children's activities at the museum *(4 Water St., Sandwich; 508/888-6870)* and at the nature center *(6 Discovery Hill Rd., E. Sandwich; 508/888-6870)*, which is located on a 57-acre conservation area. Depending on the season, programs may include canoe trips, Peter Rabbit Day, full-moon walks, and Cape Cod safaris. During jam-making workshops, you can make plum jam and blueberry peach jam using turn-of-the-century methods. The adjacent gift shop stocks an inexpensive collection of Burgess's books.

JUST FOR FUN

Art's Dune Tours ★★★/$$

For 54 years, this outfit has given families a chance to explore the windswept dunes of Cape Cod National Seashore on narrated motor tours. These days, a Chevy Suburban shuttles passengers to the beach for hour-long adventures. On the journey, you'll explore sandy mounds covered with beach grass, tour areas where no one else goes,

BEACH BUTTERFLIES

Turn your family's beach finds into colorful keepsakes.

For each butterfly, you'll need a matching pair of small or medium-size clean, dry mussel, clam, or oyster shells. Arrange the pair side by side with the inner surfaces facedown and the hinged edges flush. Hot-glue the hinged edges together (a parent's job), creating a strong bond. Then bend a 6-inch pipe cleaner length into a V and curl the tips to create antennae. Hot-glue the base of the V to the top of the glued joint. Flip over the butterfly, and your child can use acrylic or puffy paint to adorn the inner shells with a distinctive wing pattern.

and even stop for a break so kids can slide down a sandy hill. Seasonal. *Commercial and Standish Sts., Provincetown; (800) 894-1951; (508) 487-1950.*

Cape Cod Central Railroad
★★/$$

Dining out can be a moving experience on this railroad, which offers a Family Supper Train during the summer. The two-hour dinner excursion features chicken fingers and pasta for the kids, pan-seared salmon and chicken merlot for the adults, and lots of on-board entertainment—including magicians, jugglers, and clowns. You'll chug past the scenic Cape Cod Canal and salt marshes, but the kids probably won't notice. They'll be too busy getting their faces painted. *252 Main St., Hyannis; (888) 797-RAIL; (508) 771-3800.*

Cape Cod National Seashore
★★★★/Free

Stretching 40 miles from Chatham to the tip of Provincetown, this beautiful natural wonder is one of the primary reasons people venture to the Cape. Here, you can loaf on the beach or bone up on your natural history. To get acclimated, stop by the **Salt Pond visitors' center** *(Nauset Rd., off Rte. 6, Eastham; 508/255-3421)* and watch the introductory movie, which explains how the glaciers formed the Cape millions of years ago. In the exhibit gallery, kids can also learn about the Cape's early settlers, the whaling industry, native wildlife, and the origins of the Cape Cod–style house. Special ranger-led programs include canoe lessons, lighthouse tours, shellfishing demonstrations, guided walks, and campfire talks on the beach. From the seashore's **Province Lands visitors' center** *(Race Point Rd., off Rte. 6, Provincetown; 508/ 487-1256)*, you get a dramatic view of the dunes from its upper deck.

On the upper Cape, rangers at the Cape Cod Canal in Buzzards Bay offer Junior Ranger Programs and other family activities that culminate with a campfire and marshmallows. *(508) 759-4431.*

Cape Cod Potato Chip Company Tour ★/Free

Take your chips off the old block to watch potatoes turn into crunchy snacks on a self-guided tour. Peer through the factory windows and see workers hand-cook batches of spuds; best of all, you'll get to taste free samples at the end of the line. *100 Breed's Hill Rd., Hyannis; (508) 775-7253.*

Cape Cod Storyland Golf ★★★/$

This contoured 18-hole course is filled with reproductions of Cape Cod landmarks. As you putt from Bourne to Barnstable, you'll see the salvage site of the pirate ship

Whydah and the spot where the Pilgrims signed the Mayflower Compact. *70 Center St., Hyannis; (508) 778-4339.*

Edaville Railroad ★★/$$

In an era of themed attractions, this railroad seems dated and old-fashioned, but it's still fun, particularly for children under 8. Here, you can take a five-and-a-half-mile trip on a steam train past cranberry bogs, enjoy a picnic, and play on six amusement rides, including a carousel and flying elephants. In November and December, riding the evening holiday train is a local tradition. *Rte. 58, S. Carver; (877) EDAVILLE; www.edaville.org*

Nickerson State Park ★★★/Free-$$

One of the most popular and least expensive camping places in these parts (there's a modest fee), the park is filled with about 2,000 acres of kettle ponds, hiking trails, and bike paths. No wonder it's one of the Cape's top recreational spots. You'll roll right through it if you're cycling along the Cape Cod Rail Trail, and it's the perfect place to stop for a picnic under a picturesque stand of pines. *3488 Rte. 6A, Brewster; (508) 896-3491.*

Pirate's Cove Adventure Golf ★★★/$

This pirate-themed golf course is a treasure. Choose from two 18-hole courses where pirate songs blare, and Blackbeard and his cohorts cackle in creepy dioramas. You'll wander through cool caves, spy sharks in the water, and negotiate challenging holes flanked by waterfalls and drawbridges. If you have some extra coins in your treasure chest, you can splurge on pirate gear in the gift shop. *728 Main St., S. Yarmouth; (508) 394-6200;* www.piratescove.net

SuperSports Family Fun Park
★★/$-$$

After your history lesson in Plymouth, reward your kids with a trip to this park (about a 15-minute ride from Plymoth Rock). Here, you can play miniature golf on a three-acre course, ride go-carts, play video games, and hop into a bumper boat in a 10,000-square-foot pool. You can even practice your golf swing at a 35-bay driving range. *Junction of Rtes. 44 and 58, Carver; (508) 866-8000;* www.pilgrims.net/super sports/attractions

Wellfleet Bay Wildlife Sanctuary ★★★/$

This 1,000-acre area encompasses salt marshes, beaches, and tidal flats, making it an awesome spot for nature-loving families. Summer activities include Family Frolics through the sanctuary to play bird bingo, behind-the-scenes aquarium tours, and kids-only sanctuary safaris. During Creature Features, kids can get the scoop on spiders and sharks. At crafts classes, you can make fish prints and wind socks; make reservations in advance. The center also offers cruises along Nauset Marsh and marine life trips. *Rte. 6, S. Wellfleet; (508) 349-2615.*

Zooquarium ★/$

This is a good place to escape from some of the Cape's more contrived attractions. Here, you can spy on fish found in local waters, catch a sea lion show, visit a bobcat, and feed creatures in a petting zoo. At interactive exhibits, you can even use a zookeeper's cookbook to prepare an animal's lunch, and study animal

---

Foil Boredom

This one is so simple you won't believe it. Just buy a roll of aluminum foil (make sure to remove the saw on the box), and toss it into the backseat. Although foil is hardly a traditional sculpture material, it works. In the hands of your kids, aluminum foil can be turned into snakes, crowns, masks, and more. (You might need to switch activities when it turns into a bat and balls.)

Angela de la Rocha, Sterling, Virginia

SETTING SAIL

With so much competition among tour operators in Southeast Massachusetts, companies have come up with a number of fun twists for boat trips. Since these tours are very popular, reservations are advised.

Duckmobile Tours

These tours are always a splash with families. You can board amphibious vehicles in Cape Cod (*Cape Cod Duckmobiles, 437 Main St., Hyannis; 800/225-DUCK; 508/362-1117*) and Plymouth (*Harbor Pl.; 800/225-4000; 508/747-7658*). Of course, the best part for kids is when the ducks drive straight into the harbor to begin the waterborne part of the tour.

Nauset Marsh Family Cruise

On the two-hour trip along a beautiful marsh, families take a pontoon-boat ride, search for shells along a barrier beach, dig for clams and sea worms, and seek out snails and crabs. Excursions are led by kid-friendly instructors from the Wellfleet Bay Audubon Society, which also offers marine life cruises. *Rte. 6, S. Wellfleet; (508) 349-2615.*

Oceanquest

Junior oceanographers can collect and examine sea creatures, learn about the wonders of the ocean, and soak up the beauty of Woods Hole during this 90-minute cruise aboard the *Sea Star*. Kid-friendly educators lead the way. *Waterfront Park, Water St., Woods Hole; (800) 376-2326.*

Plymouth Pirate Adventures

Wearing pirate hats, bandannas, and face paint, kids (and fun-loving parents) can embark on an hour-long adventure at sea to capture a wooden treasure chest. Alas, the bandits aboard the enemy ship *The Buccaneer* have the booty, and they'll do anything (including shooting off a smoky black cannon) to save it. Held from May to October, the trips are best suited to kids ages 4 to 12. Lobster Tales, which runs the trips, also offers hands-on lobster boat excursions where families can bait and haul traps. *Town Wharf, Plymouth; (508) 746-5342.*

Seal Watches

Passengers on the Monomoy Refuge Seal Expedition have seen as many as 1,000 gray seals at a time. During the two-hour trip, you'll observe the seals as they frolic in the water, collect data for the Cape Cod Stranding Network, and study seal ecology on a barrier beach. Year-round tours are offered by the Cape Cod Museum of Natural History. *(508) 896-3867.*

scat—better known as poop to parents and their small children—to garner clues about an animal's behavior. *674 Rte. 28, W. Yarmouth; (508) 775-8883.*

If you're in New Bedford, you can visit animals at the newly expanded **Buttonwood Park Zoo**, featuring Asian elephants, New England wildlife, and underwater exhibits focusing on the rivers and estuaries of Southern New England. *Buttonwood Park, Brownell Ave., New Bedford; (508) 979-1410.*

BUNKING DOWN

All Seasons Motor Inn
★★/$$
This clean, mid-Cape motel on busy Route 28 is convenient to miniature golf, area beaches, and Hyannis attractions. There are indoor and outdoor pools, a game room, and rooms with private patios or balconies. Families can enjoy a complimentary continental breakfast in the glass-enclosed greenhouse restaurant. *1199 Main St., Rte. 28, S. Yarmouth; (800) 527-0359; (508) 394-7600;* www.allseasons.com

Cape Codder Resort & Spa
★★★/$$-$$$
Though families flock to Cape Cod for the beaches, kids go wild over this 261-room mid-Cape hotel's pool. The 8,200-square-foot indoor wave pool has two-foot waves, an eight-

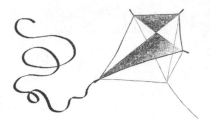

foot water slide, waterfalls, and dancing water fountains. In addition there's an on-site Hearth 'n' Kettle family restaurant, a playground, in-room Nintendo, and free trolley service to area beaches and the nearby Cape Cod Mall. *1225 Iyanough Rd. and Bearses Way, Hyannis; (888) 297-2200; (508) 771-3000.*

Cape Wind ★★/$$
This is a nice place for families who want to stay in a secluded spot that's easily accessible to Cape attractions. Located on a private road off Route 28, the horseshoe-shape, single-story motel overlooks a bay where you can visit ducks and swans and borrow a boat. Kids can romp on Cape Wind's gargantuan lawn and play on the swings, and there's an outdoor pool, too. Rooms range from standard units with two double beds to suites with kitchens. Though some units are a bit dated (while others have been newly renovated), the place is clean, affordable, and an all-around great pick for families. *34 Maravista Ave. Ext., Teaticket (part of E. Falmouth); (800) 267-3401; (508) 548-3400.*

Even' tide Motel and Cottages
★★★/$$

A popular family-operated retreat, it offers clean motel rooms with cable TV and several cottages for families who want to hang out in a low-key part of the Cape. The Cape Cod Rail Trail is right out the back door, and Marconi Beach is less than a mile away. Kids will enjoy the on-site playground and 60-foot indoor pool. Some rooms have a separate area with a pullout sofa bed. For extra privacy, seal off the area by closing the sliding door. *Rte. 6, S. Wellfleet; (800) 368-0007 (in Massachusetts); (508) 349-3410; www.eventidemotel.com*

Green Harbor Resort
★★/$$

Billed as an affordable place to enjoy a Cape Cod vacation, this mom-and-pop-style motel alongside Green Pond isn't polished, but it's friendly, well-kept, and fun for kids. You can borrow a paddleboat or rowboat, swim in the outdoor adult pool or kiddie pool, go crabbing and fishing, and cook up burgers on the outdoor grills. There are basic units with a microwave and refrigerator, as well as studios with a kitchenette and a three-bedroom cottage. Guests with boats can dock them here for free. Menauhant Beach is a short drive away. *134 Acapesket Rd., E. Falmouth; (800) 548-5556; (508) 548-4747; www.greenharborresort.com*

John Carver Inn
★★★/$$-$$$

Hold on to your Pilgrim hats. There's not another hotel pool like this in all New England. In an attempt to attract more families to Plymouth year-round, the Catania family spared no expense in fashioning the Pilgrim Cove Indoor

T's by the Sea

Here's a beach craft that will leave a lasting impression on your kids—or on their T-shirts, at least. Working right on the beach, you can use seashells and fabric paint (available at most art-supply stores) to print summery designs on a cotton shirt, hat, or beach towel.

First, clean each shell you plan to use and then press a ball of modeling clay onto its inner surface (this will serve as a convenient handle). Place newspaper between the front and back of the shirt to keep the paint from leaking through.

Next, pour some fabric paint onto a sponge. Press the outside of the shell into the paint and then onto the shirt. Repeat, experimenting with different colors (use a new shell and a clean portion of the sponge for each hue). At home, heat-set the dry paint according to the manufacturer's directions.

VISITING THE VINEYARD

LOCATED SEVEN MILES OFF the coast of Massachusetts, Martha's Vineyard boasts beautiful beaches lined with roses, awesome natural wonders (don't miss the colorful Aquinnah Cliffs), and miles of biking and hiking trails.

In lively Oak Bluffs, you'll find colorful gingerbread-style cottages, an oceanside gazebo that hosts summer band concerts, and a landmark carousel. The stately community of **Edgartown** (the setting for the 1976 movie *Jaws*) is home to well-preserved 18th-century streets, a scenic harbor, and a pretty town beach. **Vineyard Haven**, the island's commercial center, features a miniature-golf course (*Island Cove, State Rd.; 508/693-2611*), a harborside playground at Owen Park, and gift shops and restaurants galore. And the fishing village of **Menemsha** offers the chance to see lobstermen hauling in their catches. Many families enjoy sight-seeing by bicycle; bring your own or rent from one of the many outfitters.

The ferry to Martha's Vinyeard departs from several points, including **Falmouth** (a 35-minute trip; call the *Island Queen* at *508/548-4800*), **Woods Hole** (45 minutes; call the *Steamship Authority at 508/477-8600*), and **Hyannis** (one hour and 45 minutes; call *Hy-Line Cruises at 508/778-2600*).

When it's time to stop for a bite, kids feel welcome at **Papa's Pizza** (*199 Upper Main, Edgartown; 508/627-7784*), the **Black Dog Tavern** (*Beach St., Vineyard Haven; 508/693-9223*), and the **Wharf Pub** (*Lower Main St., Edgartown; 508/627-9966*).

Family-friendly lodges include the **Winnetu Inn & Resort** (*Katama Rd., Edgartown; 978/443-1733*), which has family suites and a children's program; the **Island Inn** (*Beach Rd., Oak Bluffs; 800/462-0269; 508/693-2002*), which has an outdoor pool and tennis courts; and the **Tisbury Inn** (*Main St., Vineyard Haven; 800/332-4112; 508/693-2200*), which has an indoor pool. For help planning a visit, contact the **Martha's Vineyard Chamber of Commerce** (*Beach Rd., Vineyard Haven; 508/693-0085*; www.mvy.com).

Here are some fun things to do:

1. Get sand in your shoes. With its gentle surf and shallow water, **Joseph Sylvia State Beach** (on Beach Road between Oak Bluffs and Edgartown) is popular with parents of young children. Kids who want a bit of wave action enjoy **Menemsha Public Beach**, next to Menemsha Harbor.

2. Bike with tykes. The six-mile-long **oceanside route** from Oak Bluffs to Edgartown is especially popular with families. For added convenience, take the ferry directly to Oak Bluffs (not Vineyard Haven) and rent bikes there, too. The Chamber can provide a list of family-oriented outfitters.

3. Get back to nature. With its well-marked trails and scenic habitats, the 300-acre **Felix Neck Wildlife Sanctuary**, run by the Massachusetts Audubon Society, is the perfect place to hike with kids. Stop by the nature center for an overview of this special peninsula, then walk along color-coded paths where you might spot otters, ospreys, deer, and painted turtles.

4. Get crabby. If you're not up for a charter fishing expedition, tie a piece of raw chicken to a string and catch crabs with a dime-store net instead. Crabbing hot spots include the waters across the street from Edgartown's **Bend-in-the-Road Beach** and around Maciel Marine on Vineyard Haven's **Lagoon Pond**. Remember: you need to release egg-bearing females, recognized by the dark, orange-brown mass under their belly flap.

5. Hoof it to Oak Bluffs. A trip to Martha's Vineyard isn't complete without a ride on the historic **Flying Horses Carousel** (*Circuit Ave., Oak Bluffs*), where you can even try to catch the brass ring.

Theme Pool. Here, you can soak in a hot tub that's imbedded in a re-creation of Plymouth Rock. You can also zoom down a water slide that slithers through a 40-foot scale replica of the *Mayflower*, complete with wooden masts. Periodically, water bombs shoot off the side of the boat to the delight of kids, who no doubt prefer this place to the real *Mayflower*. The inn is classy and comfortable, with early American decor. The on-site family restaurant, the Hearth 'n Kettle (which has many locations throughout the region), dishes out all the kids' classics. The John Carver Inn is an easy walk to attractions. *25 Summer St., Plymouth; (800) 274-1620; (508) 746-7100.* (The Catania family also owns the **Daniel Webster Inn** on the Cape; *149 Main St., Sandwich; 508/888-3622,* but, alas, it doesn't have a Pilgrim pool.) www.john-carverinn.com

Lighthouse Inn
★★★/$$$

Though the West Dennis Lighthouse is privately owned by the Stone Family, they're more than happy to share it. In fact, the 1855 light is the focal point of the Lighthouse Inn, a resort on Nantucket Sound for families who don't mind paying a bit more to vacation at a secluded, nine-acre retreat with a gorgeous view and on-site amenities. You can choose to stay in rooms at the main inn (the lighthouse is the center section), or in Cape Cod-style cottages with one-, two-, or three-bedroom suites especially suited to families. The many amenities include a 700-foot-long private beach, an outdoor heated pool, tennis, and a game room. In summer, there are supervised kids' programs (extra fee), including crafts, storytelling, and meals. The rate includes breakfast in the waterfront dining rooms; you can get dinner here, too. *Lighthouse Inn Rd., West Dennis; (508) 398-2244.*

New Seabury
★★★/$$$-$$$$

Looking for a congenial country club atmosphere on the Cape? This self-contained village on 2,300 acres is great for families who want to stay in modern condos within easy walking distance of many on-site activities. Located along a three-mile stretch of beach on Nantucket Sound, the upscale resort offers a variety of lodging options in different settings, plus 16 tennis courts, two golf courses,

FamilyFun TIP

Eco Etiquette

When snacking on the beach, make sure you throw away plastic bags and garbage, which can easily drift into the water. Eating garbage is one of the leading causes of death in aquatic animals. Turtles, ocean sunfish, and other animals often mistake plastic bags for jellyfish.

two outdoor pools, bike rentals, trails, and a slew of kids' activities. *Great Oak Rd., New Seabury; (800) 999-9033; (508) 477-9400.*

Ocean Vista on the Beach
★★/$$$

One of many waterfront lodges in Dennis, this spot is good for families interested in weekly rentals of one-, two-, three-, or four-bedroom condos equipped with kitchens. Though the units are about 50 years old, the owners take good care of them, and you can't beat the location: on an 800-foot-long sandy beach along the town's calm bay side. *Mandigo Rd., Dennis; (508) 385-3029.*

Pilgrim Sands Motel ★★/$$

The closest motel to Plimoth Plantation also has the advantage of being right on the beach. The rooms are basic, but the motel offers everything to make your family feel at home in Pilgrimland: indoor and outdoor pools, free HBO, and a coffee shop where you can get a continental breakfast (for a fee). *150 Warren Ave., Rte. 3A, Plymouth; (800) 729-SANDS; (508) 747-0900;* www.pilgrimsands.com

Red Jacket Beach Resort, Yarmouth ★★★★/$$$

This place has it all: an awesome location on both the Atlantic Ocean and Parkers River, dozens of activities, an ocean-side restaurant with

Shadow Giants

Here's a fun way for kids to pass the time when it's sunny but too chilly to go in for a dip. All you need is a stretch of hard-packed sand.

To start, one child strikes a pose. Depending on the angle of the sun, his shadow may be very long and distorted, at least two or three times his height. His partner traces around the shadow with a stick. Then both kids can decorate the figure with a shell face, pebble buttons, or seaweed hair. You can't take this beach giant home with you, but the mosaic makes a great photograph—especially if you put the picture in a frame decorated with glued-on shells.

kids' meals, on-site laundry, and accommodations that suit families big and small. Why leave the grounds when it's all here? You can enjoy miniature golf, indoor and outdoor pools, a private beach, a playground, and free movies. There also are kayak, canoe, and jet-boat rentals, and, in the summer, a friendly penguin mascot who roams the premises dispensing free ice pops. Other summer treats include weekday kids' activities (free to guests), such as crafts, lawn games, and beach kickball. On Wednesdays, there are special family programs. The best value for families is a "family room"—for an extra $30, you get a small connector room with bunk beds for the kids. Town houses are also available. *1 S. Shore Dr., S. Yarmouth; (508) 398-6941.*

SeaCrest Oceanfront Resort
★★★/$$$

Located on Old Silver Beach, one of the Cape's best family beaches, this full-service resort isn't for those on a tight budget, but you do get a lot for your money. In addition to a 684-foot stretch of private beach, there are indoor and outdoor pools, an oceanfront dining room with a kids' menu, a game room, and tennis courts. In summer, there's a children's day camp that's (unbelievably) free to young guests ages 3 to 12. Campers can do crafts, play water games, fly kites, and more. Special family events are offered, and babysitting can be arranged. *350 Quaker Rd., N. Falmouth; (508) 540-9401; (508) 540-9400.*

Sheraton Four Points Hotel
★★★/$$$

This member of the national chain has a beautiful indoor pool in a tropical atrium that's home to live parrots. The rooms have small refrigerators, the Cape Cod Rail Trail is just out the back door, and the on-site restaurant, Arturo's, dishes out pizza and pasta. During school vacation weeks in February and April, family programs (included in the

room rate) are in full swing, with magic shows, poolside pizza parties, and more. *Rte. 6, Eastham; (800) 533-3986; (508) 255-5000.* There's another Sheraton with an indoor pool in downtown Plymouth *(180 Water St.; 508/747-4900)* within walking distance of the *Mayflower II*; www.sheraton.com

Shoreway Acres Resort ★★/$$

Just a short walk to Falmouth Village and Surf Drive Beach, this hotel has contemporary and colonial rooms, indoor and outdoor pools, and games like badminton and volleyball on the expansive lawn. The location—on a lovely historic street— is a plus, as is the on-site restaurant that offers a free breakfast buffet. You can get packages that include other meals, too. Open all year, the hotel offers many school vacation packages. *Shore St., Falmouth; (800) 352-7100; (508) 540-3000.* www. shorewayacresinn.com

Viking Shores ★★/$$

Located on the Cape Cod Rail Trail, this family-run spot is perfect if you and your kids enjoy cycling and want easy access to the Cape Cod National Seashore. The rooms are basic but clean, and you can get adjoining ones. There's an outdoor pool, tennis courts, a big yard where kids can run around, and the property abuts a miniature-golf course and seafood restaurant. Continental breakfast is included. A fine—and very reasonably priced—pick for families who want a comfortable, affordable Cape getaway. *Rte. 6, N. Eastham; (800) 242-2131; (508) 255-3200.*

GOOD EATS

Barbyann's ★★/$$

A great family find, this restaurant dishes out all your kids' favorites in a comfortable atmosphere complete with crayons and activity menus. Mom and Dad can indulge in prime rib or shrimp scampi, or they can join the kids with tuna melts or burgers. *120 Airport Rd., Hyannis; (508) 775-9795.*

Betsy's Diner ★★★/$

Here's the place to get delicious, home-cooked meals at reasonable prices. Decorated with antique signs, appealingly mismatched furniture, and a corner jukebox, this gleaming silver diner has a children's menu (with cheeseburgers, pasta, and more) and such classic favorites as roast turkey dinner, franks and beans, meat loaf, and big slices of chocolate cream pie. *457 Main St., Falmouth; (508) 540-0060 or (508) 540-4446.*

Box Lunch ★★★/$

On a sunny day at the Cape, who wants to eat in? This outfit offers more than 50 selections of takeout lunches that you can tote to the beach or bike path. You'll find a lip-smacking list of rollwiches (sand-wiches rolled in soft pita bread), including inexpensive kids' favorites such as Boring (plain old melted cheese) and PB&J. Other selections include Gilded Lobster (lobster, avo-cado, and Swiss), Jaws I (roast beef and horseradish), and John Alden (turkey and cranberry sauce). *Locations include Falmouth (781 Main St.; 508/457-ROLS), Yarmouth (Union Sq.; 508/862-2186), and Wellfleet (50 Briar La.; 508/349-2178).*

Cooke's ★★★/$$

As seafood connoisseurs know, the success of fried clams rests in the batter—in this case, an old family recipe. Cooke's dishes out heaping plates of expertly fried clams, shrimp, scrod, and sole, along with broiled and baked delicacies. The kids' menu includes hamburgers, cheeseburgers, and fish-and-chips. Slide into a big comfy booth and enjoy hanging out. *Locations in Hyannis (1120 Rte. 132; 508/775-*

0450) and Mashpee (7 Ryan's Way, Mashpee; 508/477-9595).

Four Seas ★★★/$

Sure, you can get sandwiches here, but that would mean less room for the old-fashioned ice-cream sodas, sundaes, and banana splits that make this place famous. Depending on when you come, you might get to try creamy scoops of penuche pecan, rum and butter, and pistachio nut pineapple. Open May to through Labor Day. *360 S. Main St., Centerville; (508) 775-1394.*

Lobster Hut ★★★/$$

For a casual lunch on pretty Ply-mouth Harbor, order fresh, reason-ably priced seafood at the counter or find a table on the deck, and soak up the view. There are hot dogs, burg-ers, and fried chicken for those who want to skip the fish. *Town Wharf, Plymouth; (508) 746-2270.*

Baskets on Board

In 1856, Nantucket commissioned lightships to anchor off the island shores and warn other boats about the dangerous shoals. Since time passed slowly during their duties, sailors brought basket-making materials with them. Today, Nantucket lightship baskets are synonymous with the island.

Lobster Trap
★★★/$$

Hungry for lobster the minute you cross the Bourne Bridge? Head for this casual restaurant overlooking Buzzards Bay. The breezy, screened porch is filled with colorful buoys, lanterns, and easy-wipe resin furniture and is a pleasant place to eat fried clams, lobster rolls, and (from the kids' menu) hamburgers and hot dogs. *290 Shore Rd., Bourne;* *(508) 759-3992. Other locations in Centerville (Bell Tower Mall, Rte. 28; 508/778-5010) and S. Yarmouth (Union Station; 508/394-8360).*

Moby Dick's
★★★/$$

Families with a whale of an appetite love this friendly, relaxed restaurant, where making a mess comes with the territory. Here, you can feast on clambakes, Nantucket buckets

SET SAIL FOR NANTUCKET

FAMILYFUN magazine readers consistently praise Nantucket for its beautiful beaches, which stretch for more than 50 miles around the island. Once home to whaling captains, the 14-mile-wide island is now known for its cobblestone streets, historic homes (many of which have been converted into fancy inns), and upscale bistros. Nantucket encourages families to bring their bikes to explore the six paved paths that lead to its beaches and scenic vistas.

If there's a downside to staying here, it's the cost. Families can find plenty of affordable activities to enjoy during day trips (*see the list below*), but overnight stays can break the bank. With its outdoor pool and location near Jetties Beach, the **Beachside** (*30 North Beach St.; 800/322-4433*) is one of the more affordable (by Nantucket standards) choices for families. If you're staying for a week, your most economical option is to rent a cottage (the Nantucket Island Chamber of Commerce, listed below, can supply names of rental agencies).

Kid-friendly restaurants include **Cap'n Tobey's Chowder House** (*20 Straight Wharf; 508/228-0836*), **Henry's Sandwich Shop** (*2 Broad St.; 508/228-0123*), and **Nantucket Pharmacy** (*45 Main St.; 508/228-0180*), which dishes out frappés, hot dogs, and tasty cones.

Nantucket is 30 miles south of Cape Cod. Ferry options include the two-and-a-half-hour trip from Hyannis (call the **Steamship Authority**; *508/477-8600*) and the one-hour, and thus pricier, **Fast Ferry from Hyannis** (*508/495-3278*). **The Nantucket Island Chamber of (buckets with steamers, mussels, and corn), fried seafood, and chowder. Kids can play with crayons and Trivial Pursuit cards; their menu features hot dogs, burgers, and smaller-sized seafood baskets. *Rte. 6, Wellfleet; (508) 349-9795.*

Morgan's ★/$-$$

Run by the Bettencourt family, this small, cozy eatery is the place to get a bountiful breakfast (try the pump-kin walnut pancakes or specialty omelettes) or lunch. Nearby, at **Fort Phoenix State Beach** *(Green St., Fairhaven; 508/992-4524)*, kids can climb on cannons overlooking the Achushnet River breakwater. *58 Washington St., Fairhaven; (508) 997-4443.*

Sam Diego's ★★★/$$

You know a restaurant is hot when it's housed in a former fire station.

Commerce *(48 Main St.; 508/228-1700; www.nantucketchamber.org)* can provide more options, along with maps and suggestions.

For starters, try these affordable activities with children.

1. Hit the beach. With its playground, snack bar, water activities, skateboarding park, rest rooms, and lifeguards (in season), **Jetties Beach** on calm Nantucket Sound is tops with families. On the south side of the island, Surfside Beach has more waves, plus a snack bar, rest rooms, and lifeguards (in season).

2. Reach for the sky. Bring a kite to fly at the beach, or buy a cool one at Sky's the Limit *(5 The Courtyard, Lower Main St.; 508/228-4633).*

3. Use your pedal power. Nantucket is famous for its paved bike paths. Outfitters (such as **Young's Bicycle Shop**, *6 Broad St.;* *508/228-1151)* can provide helmets, cycles, and maps. The three-mile-long, flat Surfside Bike Path has benches and water fountains and leads directly to Surfside Beach. If you want a slightly hillier, longer ride, take the eight-mile-long Polpis Bike Path past cranberry bogs, wetlands, and a lighthouse.

4. Have a whale of a good time. At the **Nantucket Whaling Museum** *(13 Broad St.; 508/228-1736)*, kids can see a 43-foot-long skeleton of a finback whale, a fully rigged whaleboat, and the lens from the Sankaty Lighthouse. In July and August, children's programs focus on whaling lore and colonial days.

5. See the sea. Try a pirate cruise aboard the 31-foot Friendship sloop *Endeavor (Slip 15, Straight Wharf; 508/228-5585)* and the ice-cream cruise with **Harbor Cruises** *(Slip 11, Straight Wharf; 508/228-1444).*

Teaching Your Kids How to Pack

Encourage your kids to think of mix and match outfits for various activities, just as they do when dressing paper dolls. (You even can have them practice by packing a doll wardrobe — trying out the different outfits — while they pack for themselves.) For example, ask a preschooler, "We're going hiking. Which of your comfortable pants do you want to wear?" After he lays these out, ask him to match them with two T-shirts (for two outfits), a sweatshirt in case it is cold, and a pair of comfortable walking shoes. Then, consider another vacation activity. Ask him to find two bathing suits, with a sun cover-up and a hat. Next, ask him to think about nighttime, laying out toothbrush and toothpaste, pajamas, a beloved but small stuffed animal, a bathrobe, and slippers.

Here you'll find a Young Juan's menu featuring mini-burritos, tacos, and kid coladas, plus crayons, activity sheets, and friendly service. The decor—bright lights, ornamental suns, and colorful blankets—would make even the most stone-faced Pilgrim crack a smile. *51 Main St., Plymouth; (508) 747-0048. There's also a location in Hyannis (950 Iyanough Rd.; 508/771-8816).*

Seafood Sam's
★★★/$$

You may not get an ocean view, but you'll get great seafood at this group of restaurants that wins rave reviews from local families. For kids who don't want to feast on fried clams, broiled scallops, or crabmeat salad, there are hot dogs, hamburgers, and fried chicken. The place is clean and casual, the prices are reasonable, and the portions are generous. Eat in, or bring your order out to a picnic table. *Located in S. Yarmouth (1006 Rte. 28; 508/394-3504), Harwichport (Rte. 28; 508/432-1422), Sandwich (Coast Guard Rd.; 508/888-4629), and Falmouth (Rte. 28, Palmer Ave.; 508/540-7877).*

SOUVENIR HUNTING

Cuffy's/Cuffy's Kids Factory Store

Your hosts at this factory store are a pack of animatronic characters, including Lenny the Lizard, a chatty fisherman, and a band of six sea creatures in Hawaiian shirts. They'll entertain you with rock-and-roll hits while you shop for comfy Cape Cod sweatshirts and T-shirts. Clothes are made on the premises, and you can watch the embroidery and screenprinting machines at work. The designs are terrific, and you'll love the prices: ten T-shirts, on special, cost $35. *1 Reardon Circle, Yarmouth; (508) 394-1371.*

Eight Cousins

Named for one of Louisa May Alcott's less famous books, this all-children's bookstore has shelves full of wonderful titles, a helpful staff—and it hosts story hours. Once you start browsing, it's a sure bet that you'll forget the beach is right down the street. *189 Main St., Falmouth; (508) 548-5548.*

Elaine's T-Shirts & Costumes

Folks in Martha's Vineyard bark about their ubiquitous Black Dog (see page 274), but in New Bedford, Herman Melville's old haunt, they're spouting off about their blubbery mascot, the black whale. As official purveyor of all things emblazoned with the black whale logo, Elaine's can outfit you with T-shirts, mugs, and hats. *772 Purchase St., New Bedford; (508) 999-2166.*

Wellfleet Bookstore & Restaurant

Digest a tasty meal and a great book at this kid-friendly hangout overlooking Wellfleet Harbor. Turn your kids loose in the bookstore to search for a comic book, then enjoy a literary and culinary feast in the restaurant (great views on the second floor). The menu includes creatively prepared breakfasts, lunches, and dinners, with plenty of kids' options. *50 Kendrick Ave., Wellfleet; (508) 349-3154.*

FOOTPRINTS IN THE SAND

On beach vacations, sand seems to end up everywhere, especially between the toes. The simple plaster-casting project lets your child capture that sandy barefoot feeling—and a record of his feet.

MATERIALS
- Plaster of paris
- Small bucket
- Freshwater
- 4-inch lengths of string or wire (for hangers, if desired)

Choose a site to cast your molds—the moist, hard-packed sand near (but not too near!) the water's edge works best. Have your child firmly press both feet into the sand. The prints should be about 1½ to 2 inches deep. If your child can't press down that hard, he can use his finger to dig down into the print, following its shape. Mix up the plaster, according to the directions on the package, so that it has a thick, creamy consistency. Pour the wet plaster gently into the footprints.

If you want to make hangers, tie a knot about a half inch from each end of your pieces of string or wire. As the plaster begins to harden, push the knotted ends into the plaster and let dry. After 20 to 25 minutes, gently dig the footprints out of the molds and brush away any excess sand. Set sole-side up in the sun (away from the rising tide) for about an hour to let harden.

From the inside it's an enormous domed basketball court; from the outside the new Basketball Hall of Fame looks like—you guessed it—a basketball. Other rooms contain interactive displays that let kids measure their jump shots, trivia prowess, and shoe size (against Bob Lanier's).

Western Massachusetts

THE MOUNTAIN LOVER'S answer to Cape Cod's shining sea, western Massachusetts is a four-season playland for families who like to camp, fish, hike, cycle, canoe, and picnic by waterfalls. You can venture to small, friendly towns right off a Norman Rockwell canvas. In fact, the artist made his home in Stockbridge, in the Berkshires, for 25 years and set many of his paintings at area luncheonettes and fishing holes.

This chapter covers two distinct areas of Western Massachusetts: the Berkshires and Pioneer Valley. Known for generations as the summer retreat for wealthy, culturally minded families, the Berkshires comprises 30 mountain communities near the New York border. In summer, leagues of New Yorkers and Bostonians gather on the lush lawns at Tanglewood in Lenox for outdoor concerts by the Boston Symphony Orchestra. As is true with many of the area's arts organizations, the famous symphony offers special children's performances *(888/266-1200; 413/637-5240)* You can also enjoy family offerings at the Jacob's Pillow Dance

THE **FamilyFun** LIST

Basketball Hall of Fame (page 287)

Eric Carle Museum of Picture Book Art (page 288)

Glacial potholes (page 291)

Hancock Shaker Village (page 289)

Six Flags New England (page 294)

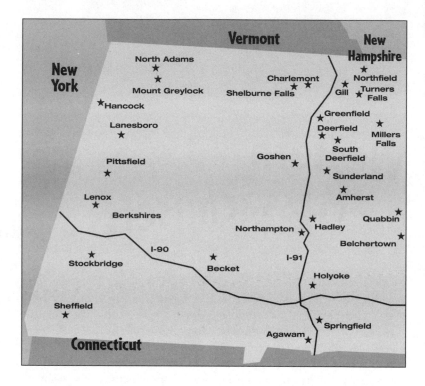

Festival in Becket *(413/243-0745)*, Berkshire Theater Festival in Stockbridge *(413/298-5536)*, and Shakespeare & Company in Lenox *(413/637-1199 or 413/637-3353)*, among others. In this hilly region, families can also take 19th-century penmanship lessons at Pittsfield's Hancock Shaker Village; sleep in the old stone lodge atop Mount Grey lock, the state's highest peak; and ride the Alpine slide (in summer) or ski (in winter) at Hancock's Jiminy Peak.

Just east of the Berkshires, the Pioneer Valley (named for the area's early fur traders) is a 50-mile-wide ribbon of towns along the Con-

necticut River. Here, you'll find rivers to raft, paths to cycle, canoes to paddle, and historic towns to explore. Home to the "five colleges"—Smith, Mount Holyoke, Amherst, Hampshire, and the University of Massachusetts—the region also hosts a never-ending lineup of events families will enjoy, from balloon festivals to country fairs. Although the area's best-known man-made attraction is the Six Flags New England amusement/water park in Agawam, there are plenty of other pleasures, too.

The **Mohawk Trail**, a 63-mile-long old trading road (Route 2), stretches across the northern border of the state from the New York line to Millers Falls. There are plenty of trinket shops where kids can buy Indian-themed souvenirs and maple-sugar candy. (For more information, log on to www.mohawktrail.com)

Northampton is an artsy college town with leagues of inexpensive restaurants where families can sample Middle Eastern, Indian, Thai, Mexican, and other ethnic cuisine. (Yes, you can get pizza and hamburgers here, too.) Look Park's waterspray area provides relief on a hot day.

Known worldwide for its arts events and fancy inns, **Lenox** has a kid-pleasing surprise: the public can use the town's sandy beach, free of charge. In summer, lifeguards are on duty, and visiting kids can borrow from the basket of beach toys. *Rte. 20, Lenox; (413) 637-5530.*

Chill out in the summer by heading for **Shelburne Falls**. Don your bathing suits and splash among 50 glacial potholes at the base of scenic Salmon Falls. Home to world-renowned glassblowers, the town also invites families to watch artists practice their craft at studios, including North River Glass on Deerfield Avenue *(413/625-6422).*

Springfield (population: 157,000) gets the credit for inventing the game of basketball. Families can practice their hook shots at the Basketball Hall of Fame. The hometown of Dr. Seuss, Springfield recently created a sculpture park in the author's honor.

CULTURAL ADVENTURES

 **Basketball Hall of Fame**
★★★★/$

This attraction—in an impressive new, $103 million facility—is devoted to all levels of basketball, from amateur to professional. Packed with hands-on (and feet-on) exhibits, the museum invites kids to see if they can jump as high as Michael Jordan, play Shaq Attaq pinball, and measure their feet against Bob Lanier's size 22 shoe. Kids can also play touch-screen basketball trivia, check out the contents of Rebecca Lobo's locker, and even inspect a piece of the actual floor where Michael Jordan made his final career basket—against the Utah Jazz in 1998. By far the biggest draw is the Spaulding Shootout, where kids can practice their throws in 15 baskets of varying difficulty. **HINT:** If you want kids to learn some

FamilyFun TIP

Essentials

The Magellan's catalog (800-962-4943) has inflatable pillows (saving graces on long trips) and a variety of light, durable travel essentials, such as hair dryers, luggage straps, alarms, adapter plugs, and clothing organizers.

BAG O' BUGS

Place a few graham crackers in a plastic bag, seal it shut, and crush the crackers into a fine sand using a large spoon. Add a few raisins and let your kids dig for bugs in the sand. Experiment with other tasty critters: dried cranberry ladybugs, chocolate- or carob-chip ants, even gummy worms, snakes, or spiders.

----

of the history of the game, which originated in Springfield, start on the upper floors and work your way down to the shootout. *1100 W. Columbus Ave., Springfield; (413) 781-6500;* www.hoophall.com

Berkshire Museum ★★★/$

The nation's oldest museum combines art, natural science, and history under one roof. Kids will enjoy meeting Wally the stegosaurus on the front lawn. Once inside, children can visit an Egyptian mummy, a 143-pound meteorite, a tankful of piranhas in the 26-tank aquarium, and an art gallery that contains 13 refrigerator doors decorated with kids' masterpieces. Even getting a snack is an adventure, as kids can

drop coins into a wacky Vend-o-Mat, complete with pressure gauges and pulleys. Though the mounted animal exhibits have an old-time feel, the staff has made the galleries feel more contemporary with kiosks that help a young audience interpret the collection through fun activities. (You can study mammal scat, for example.) *39 South St., Rte. 7, Pittsfield; (413) 443-7171;* www.berk shiremuseum.org

Children's Museum at Holyoke ★★/$

At this regional museum kids can cut loose and learn something in the process. Youngsters can tunnel through the human body on an indoor climber. In the village, they can shop for pretend vegetables at La Bodega, and then dish them out in the diner. There's also a Lego play area, a giant bubblemaker, and a construction site. *Heritage State Park, Holyoke; (413) 536-KIDS.* Just across the street, families can ride on a restored 1929 carousel (see "Merry Carousels" on page 352), featuring 48 hand-carved steeds.

Eric Carle Museum of Picture Book Art ★★★★/$$

This sprawling new museum is a monument to the talents of founder Eric Carle (of *The Very Hungry Caterpillar* fame). Set in an apple orchard next to Hampshire College, its mission is to open up the hearts and minds of kids and adults alike to the beauty of children's book art. Carle's work is exhibited, as well as legends such as Maurice Sendak and Leo Lionni. Call ahead to find out about readings, performances, and art activities for kids, and then make an afternoon of it — there's even a café so your family can refuel. *125 West Bay Road, Amherst; (413) 586-8934;* www.picturebookart.org

Hancock FamilyFun Shaker Village
★★★/$$

From 1790 to 1960, this village was an active Shaker community, which sought to create heaven on earth in the peaceful setting of the Berkshires. Committed to celibacy, equality, and the separation of the sexes, the Shakers held all property in common and established a progressive farm complete with an intriguing round stone barn. Families can have plenty of hands-on fun while touring 20 original Shaker buildings set on 1,200 acres. In the Discovery Room, kids can try spinning wool, basket-weaving, and milking Mary Jane. This life-size model of a Holstein cow comes complete with a squishy udder. Kids also can practice their penmanship using a quill pen in the one-room schoolhouse (1820), and can watch black-smithing, cheese-making, and woodworking demonstrations. Stop by the visitors' center first and watch the brief orientation film for a helpful overview. *Junction of Rtes. 20 and 41, Pittsfield; (800) 817-1137; (413) 443-0188;* www. hancockshaker village.org

Historic Deerfield
★★★/$$

At this pleasant neighborhood, you'll find 14 historic buildings filled with 20,000 objects that were made or used in America between 1630 and 1840. Families can pick up a *Family Activity Guide* that turns an ordinary walk into a trip back in time. Visit the **Wapping Schoolhouse** and the **Wells-Thorn House**, where you'll learn about the young slave, Lucy Terry, who became the nation's first black female poet. In **Memorial Hall** *(413/774-7476)*, kids can see Native-American artifacts, view one of the nation's oldest dolls, and join activities in the nearby Indian House (in summer—for example, the staff offers a free series of themed weeks, where young visitors might grind and sift corn, bundle and hang herbs, or marbleize paper). The **Channing Blake Meadow Walk** leads families through a working dairy farm to the Deerfield River. *The Hall Tavern visitors' center is on "The Street," in Deerfield; (413) 774-5581;* www.his toric-deerfield.org/

Northampton is home to **Smith College**, the largest women's college in the country, with just under 3,000 students.

Lyman Conservatory
★★/Free

This leafy paradise lets you visit the tropics without leaving the country. Located on the Smith College campus, the conservatory features 2,500 plant species from all over the world. Kids love to play hide-and-seek behind the banana trees. *Smith College, Northampton; (413) 585-2740.*

MASS MoCA
★★/$

The Massachusetts Museum of Contemporary Art is the nation's largest center for modern visual and performing arts. Its 13-acre campus of renovated factories offers ample space for artists at work and for exhibitions. The campus also is home to Kidspace, a 2,300-square-foot art gallery/studio that gives young artists the chance to make creations of their own. Kidspace is only open to the public on certain days of the week, so call ahead. *87 Marshall St., N. Adams; (413) 664-4481;* www.massmoca.org

Norman Rockwell Museum
★★/$

Norman Rockwell's lifelike, idealistic works made him one of the most popular artists of the 20th century. This museum is located on 36 country acres in Rockwell's adopted home of Stockbridge, where he lived for the last 25 years of his life. Kids can view the artist's *Saturday Evening Post* covers, visit his studio, crawl on outdoor sculptures created by Rockwell's son, Peter, and create their own drawings in a small workshop. *Rte. 183, Stockbridge; (413) 298-4100;* www.nrm.org

Old Greenfield Village
★★/$

Talk about Yankee ingenuity—and enterprise. Retired schoolteacher Waine Morse admires his hometown of Greenfield so much, he spent 30 years collecting antique artifacts and assembling a historic replica of the village for families to view on a self-guided tour. (There's a taped recording in each building to orient you.) You'll find a dry-goods shop, toy shop, apothecary, print shop, ice-cream parlor with a marble soda fountain, and more. *Rte. 2 W., Greenfield; (413) 774-7138.*

Pratt Museum of Natural History ★★/$

In the Pioneer Valley, rainy days can still be dino-mite. This college muse-

um gives kids the chance to inspect locally discovered dinosaur tracks, the skeletal legs of an 87-foot-long diplodocus, and the skeleton of a wooly mammoth. *Amherst College, Amherst; (413) 542-2165.*

The Quadrangle/ The Springfield Museums ★★★/$

One of the area's great bargains, this museum complex invites families to tour four facilities at one low price. In the **Springfield Science Museum**, kids can view a 20-foot-tall replica of Tyrannosaurus rex, watch a show in the nation's oldest American-built planetarium (1937), and peer at frolicking fish in the Solutia Eco-Center. The **George Walter Vincent Smith Art Museum** has an intriguing collection of samurai armor and swords, while the **Connecticut Valley Historical Museum** contains information on Springfield's famous resident, Dr. Seuss, born Theodor Geisel in 1904. Outside, the Dr. Seuss National Memorial Sculpture Garden features bronze statues of familiar characters like the Cat in the Hat, the Lorax, and Horton the Elephant. Another sculpture shows the author working at his drawing table. The funky **Cafe on the Quad**, dishes out peanut-butter-and-jelly sandwiches. The Quadrangle hosts free, toe-tapping summer jazz concerts. *220 State St., Springfield; (413) 263-6800;* www.quadrangle.org

JUST FOR FUN

Berkshire Scenic Railway Museum ★★/$

For kids with short attention spans, this attraction is just the right length: 15 minutes. During your ride on the short shuttle, you can enjoy views of October Mountain and Woods Pond. Like Newport, Rhode Island, the Berkshires attracted wealthy families who built 30 room "cottages" in the area during the Gilded Age (1870–1920). Many of the travelers arrived at this very train station. Inside, you can see some period photos and two model railroads. *Housatonic St. and Willow Creek Rd., Lenox; (413) 637-2210.* You can also take a 15-minute ride aboard an 1896 trolley at the **Shelburne Falls Trolley Museum**. *14 Depot St., Shelburne Falls; (413) 625-9443.*

DAR State Forest ★★/Free-$

A favorite camping spot for families, the wooded retreat has hiking trails leading to 1,697-foot-high Moore's Hill. Although it's a shrimp compared to its mountain neighbors, the peak still affords big views. *Off Route 116 in Goshen; (413) 268-7098.*

Glacial potholes
FamilyFun ★★★★/Free
One of the state's best roadside wonders, this geological gem in Shelburne Falls is the place

291

Ski, Slide, or Bike

The largest ski and snowboard resort in the Berkshires, **Jiminy Peak** offers plenty of summer activities as well. First for skiers: Jiminy features snowboard and ski trails that all lead to the base lodge. Accommodations include 1,400 beds on the mountain; another lodging option is the all-suites **Country Inn** (800/882-8859), with an on-site restaurant, heated outdoor pool, hot tub, and game room. Jiminy has 40 trails (35 percent beginner, 40 percent intermediate, 25 percent advanced); 9 lifts, including a six-passenger high-speed lift; and 93 percent snowmaking coverage. Family facilities include Ski Wee programs for children 4 to 8; Explorer programs for kids 8 to 12; private lessons; mountaintop meals at Hendricks Summit Lodge; family favorites at Christianson's Tavern at the base and snow tubing at nearby Brodie Mountain.

In summertime, families can ride on the six-passenger chairlift to take in views of Jericho Valley and Mount Greylock, ride the alpine slide down a 3,000-foot-long bobsled run, play miniature golf, fish in the stocked trout pond, and test the mountain bike trails (the trail system includes two lifts). For winter information: *37 Corey Rd., Hancock; (800) 882-8859; (413) 738-5500.* For summer information: *Rte. 43, Hancock; (413) 738-5500;* www.jiminypeak.com

to chill out on a hot day. The 50 potholes—the country's largest collection—were formed from granite during the Glacial age. These days, they're lounge chairs of sorts, providing kids and parents a place to stretch out and dangle their feet at the base of Salmon Falls. *You'll find the walkway to the potholes behind Mole Hollow Candles on Deerfield Avenue. Shelburne Falls.*

Ioka Valley Farm ★★★/$

No matter when you visit this 600-acre family farm, you'll have a blast. In summer, kids can play in Uncle Don's Barnyard and pet the friendly animals, crawl through a hay tunnel, push dump trucks in a giant sandbox, and ride swings in a farm-themed playground. In fall, they can pick a pumpkin and take a Halloween hayride. In winter you can all cut your own holiday tree, and in spring you can visit the maple barn and taste fresh syrup on homemade pancakes. *3475 Rte. 43, Hancock; (413) 738-5915.*

Look Park
★★/$

It's hard not to envy the kids of Northampton. Their 150-acre local park is the ultimate kiddieland, with miniature golf, a water-spray park, bumper boats and pedal boats on Willow Lake, pretty picnic grounds, and a train that encircles a small zoo. *300 N. Main St., Northampton; (413) 584-5457;* www.lookpark.org

Magic Wings Butterfly Conservatory and Gardens ★★★/$

Butterflies only live for about two weeks, but you can spend some quality time with them at this facility, the largest butterfly conservatory in the northeast. Magic Wings was created by a Dad who enjoys sharing his love of butterflies with kids of all ages. After you learn the difference between Royal Fritillaries and Mourning Cloaks, stroll past fountains and play areas in the abundant gardens. For a treat, sample Painted Lady Pistachio Italian ice in the Magic Wings café. *281 Greenfield Rd., S. Deerfield; (800) 556-4117 or (413) 665-2805.*

Mount Greylock State Reservation ★★★/Free

At 3,491 feet, Mount Greylock is the state's highest peak. Here, families can climb the 92-foot-high Summit Veteran Memorial Tower for a view of five states. You can even stay overnight on the summit at **Bascom** Lodge (see Bunking Down), a 1930s fieldstone lodge run by the Appalachian Mountain Club. *Rockwell Rd. (between Rtes. 7 and 8), Lanesboro; (413) 499-4262 or (413) 499-4263;* www.berkshire web.com/mohawktrail/mtgrey lock.html

Mount Sugarloaf State Reservation ★★★/Free

Drive up a winding road to the 652-foot-high summit, climb the observation tower, and soak up great views of the valley. The reservation also is an excellent spot for picnics and kid-pleasing hikes. *Off Rte. 116, S. Deerfield;* www.state.ma.us/dem/ parks/msug.htm

Mount Tom State Reservation ★★/$

Take your family for a hike through 1,800 mountaintop acres. Then, for a change of pace, view the nature exhibits in the Robert Cole Museum. *Rte. 5, Holyoke; (413) 534-1186.*

GUIDES AT THE BARTON COVE campground can set families up on a two-hour (or longer) canoe or kayak adventure, where you might spot bald eagles and other cool creatures along the banks of the Connecticut River. The river's slow-moving current makes it ideal for kids. Beginners will enjoy the popular Riverview Trip, which leads families on a five-and-a-half-mile journey through French King Gorge. *Rte. 2, Gill; (413) 863-9300.*

IN THE 1930s AND 40s the Quabbin Reservoir was created to provide water to Boston residents. The towns of Dana, Enfield, Greenwich, and Prescott were shut down and residents were required to move so the Quabbin could be built. Parts of the flooded towns can still be found underwater.

Norwottuck Rail Trail
★★★/Free

One of the state's most popular rail trails, this ten-mile-long paved path leads cyclists (and in-line skaters, cross-country skiers, and walkers) past farmland, mountain scenery, and across an iron bridge over the Connecticut River. You can rent bikes, trailers, and tandems at **Valley Bicycles** (*8 Railroad St., Hadley; 413/584-4466*). The bike path traverses the towns of Northampton, Hadley, and Amherst, and you can reach it from such spots as Mountain Farms Mall (*Rte. 9, Hadley*) and Elwell State Park (*Damon Rd., Northampton*). *For information on the trail, call the Connecticut River Greenway State Park at (413) 586-8706.*

Northfield Mountain Recreation and Environmental Center
★★★/Free-$

One of the area's premiere family spots for four-season recreation, this 2,000-acre retreat offers 25 miles of hiking trails (fees), mountain biking (fees), 20 miles of cross-country ski trails (where families can take lessons), plus camping, shady waterside picnic areas, and canoeing in nearby Barton Cove. In summer, you can also cruise 12 miles along the Connecticut River on the *Quinnetukut II Riverboat*, and learn about the area's natural and cultural history. *Rte. 63, Northfield; (800) 859-2960; (413) 659-3714.*

Quabbin Reservoir
★★★/Free

Claimed by both western and central Massachusetts as a premiere hiking spot, this 18-mile-long reservoir (which supplies drinking water to two and a half million residents) is surrounded by 81,000 acres of woods and meadows that families love to explore. Start your adventure at the southern end of the reservoir at Quabbin Park, a 3,200-acre reserve that contains 20 miles of hiking trails and a visitors' center. *485 Ware Rd. (off Rte. 9), Belchertown; (413) 323-7221.*

Six Flags New England
FamilyFun ★★★★/$$$

In 1840, families gravitated to Gallup's Grove in Agawam

for clambakes along the Connecticut River. Today, that grove is the region's largest amusement park. The 235-acre Six Flags features dozens of rides, including six roller coasters; the giant water park, Island Kingdom; and plenty of chances to meet the park's mascots: Looney Tunes characters and comic-book superheroes. One of the biggest thrills is the 22-story (that's taller than the Statue of Liberty) hyper coaster, Superman Ride of Steel. At speeds of up to 70 miles per hour, it catapults riders 13 feet below the earth. The free-fall ride Scream lives up to its name with a stomach-churning, 20-story drop. Other highlights include the pint-size rides at Looney Tunes Movie Town, the 500,000-gallon Commotion Ocean wave pool, and Batman Thrill Spectacular, where fans of the Caped Crusader can cheer him on during a special-effects show complete with fireworks. When it's time for a break, families can relax at a grassy park on the riverbanks. *1623 Main St., Agawam; (877) 4-SIX-FLAGS; (413) 786-9300;* www.sixflags.com

Skinner State Park
★★★/Free

Drive to the peak of Mount Holyoke (the westernmost mountain in the nine-mile-long Holyoke Range) and enjoy a summer concert at the mountaintop inn, the Summit House. No doubt you'll appreciate the view as much as the music. It's the very vista that inspired artist Thomas Cole to paint the landscape "The Oxbow" in 1836. *Rte. 47, Hadley; (413) 586-0350;* www.state. ma.us/dem/parks/skin.htm

The Zoo in Forest Park
★★★/$

Pack up a picnic and spend a few hours at this appealing zoo surrounded by a 735-acre park. The zoo is home to more than 200 animals, from black bears to muntjac deer. It has a petting area and discovery room, and offers special family programs, a playground, train ride, lush lawns, ponds, and a mausoleum that kids love to explore. If you're traveling in the area over the holidays, don't miss Bright Nights, a two-mile-long drive-through light show featuring illuminated Dr. Seuss characters. *Sumner Ave., Springfield; Zoo: (413) 733-2251; park: (413) 787-6440.*

FamilyFun TIP

Something Fishy

From May through July, **Turners Falls Fish Ladder** is one of several places in the state where kids can park themselves in front of viewing windows and watch as shad, salmon, and striped bass migrate back to the streams of their birth. After the show, your little ones can stretch their own fins at the nearby playground. *Off Rte. 2, Turners Falls; (413) 659-3713.*

BUNKING DOWN

Bascom Lodge ★★/$-$$

If you don't mind communal quarters (families share bathrooms and bunk rooms here), get set for a peak experience at this stone lodge on the 3,491-foot-high summit of Mount Greylock. Run by the Appalachian Mountain Club, this lodge offers many family programs (llama trekking, backpacking); hearty, family-style meals; incredible views of the Berkshires and surrounding ranges; and access to 50 miles of trails. Four private rooms that sleep two are also available. *For information, call the Mount Greylock visitors' center at (413) 528-6333 or (413) 743-1591.*

Blue Heron Farm ★★/$$

Stay in one of three freestanding housekeeping cottages and pitch in with farm chores, or simply relax and soak up the views of the Berkshires. Kids will love trying to milk the Nubian and French Alpine dairy goats, grooming the personable Norwegian fjord horses, and harvesting high-bush blueberries. Since the farm is at 1,500-feet elevation, views of the nighttime sky are incredible. *Warner Hill Rd., Charlemont; (413) 339-4045; www.blueheronfarm.com*

Clarion Hotel and Conference Center ★★/$$

With clean, modern rooms, indoor and outdoor pools, a game room, lighted tennis courts, and convenient access to the highway, this is a great choice for families who are vacationing in the Pioneer Valley. *1 Atwood Dr., Northampton; (413) 586-1211.*

Holiday Inn ★★/$$

This hotel makes an effort to provide families with personalized service, from reduced-price tickets (for both guests and nonguests) to nearby Six

Pet Savvy

It's easier than ever to **bring your pet along on vacation.** A number of hotels now accept pets, and some even offer exercise areas and pet room service. (A few go so far as to bring dog biscuits and bottled water to your room on a silver tray!)

Ready Buddy for travel by making sure his ID tags are complete and by taking him on short trips close to home (so he doesn't think getting in the car means going to the vet). Try calling these hotel and motel chains to find out their pet policies: Best Western (800-528-1234); Four Seasons (800-332-3442); Holiday Inn (800-465-4329); Loews (800-235-6397); and Motel 6 (800-466-8356).

Flags New England to the Friendly's takeout stand in the lobby, where you can buy ice cream and baked goodies. There's a big, heated indoor pool, a video game room, and laundry room. The 12th-floor restaurant, Zaffinos, has terrific views of the valley, and kids eat free here when accompanied by an adult who orders an entrée. *711 Dwight St., Springfield; (800) 465-4329; (413) 781-0900;* www.basshotels.com/holiday-inn/

Race Brook Lodge
★★★/$$

Amidst the proper Inns of neighboring Stockbridge, this relaxed retreat is a surprise. Steeped in the spirit of Taos, New Mexico, the lodge has wild gardens, Native American rugs on the walls, and funky artwork. There's even an outdoor café by a babbling brook. Families will enjoy walking on the inn's one-and-a-half-mile Race Brook Trail, running around in the big yard, and swinging in the hammocks. Your best bet is to rent a room with two double beds in one of the cottages, or you can spring for the marvelous guesthouse with exposed beams and a full kitchen. The home-cooked breakfasts offer an abundance of choices—there's a buffet, or you can order from the menu; in any event, portions are huge. *864 S. Under-mountain Rd., Sheffield; (413) 229-2916;* www.rblodge.com

Yankee Inn ★★/$$

Situated on seven and a half acres, this 96-room, roadside lodge is a good base camp for a trip to the Berkshires. You'll find a variety of room sizes, an outdoor pool with flowing waterfalls, and an indoor pool and spa. *461 Pittsfield Rd., Lenox; (800) 835-2364; (413) 499-3700.*

GOOD EATS

Bub's Barbecue
★★/$$$

The motto at this ultracasual restaurant is "pig out in style." Families can chow down on award-winning pulled pork, baby back ribs, and Cajun specialties that make for finger-licking fun. Spice up your meal even more by playing tunes on the free jukebox. *Rte. 116/Amherst Rd., Sunderland; (413) 548-9630.*

Who Lives There?

Travel exposes your family to new places and different styles of living. As you pass a lime-green house with a yard full of plastic pink flamingos and a working waterwheel, it's hard not to wonder what type of family lives there. Why not run with that? Suggest that your kids speculate on who lives inside the houses you pass and what they might be doing at that moment. Perhaps the people in the green house invented mint chocolate-chip ice cream. Perhaps they have seven children and three pets— a Lhasa apso, an iguana, and a Persian cat wearing a pink leather collar. If it's dinnertime, perhaps they're gathered around the kitchen table enjoying tuna casserole topped with potato chips that will be followed by a dessert of cherries flambé. They'll be playing a game of Pictionary after dinner and, well, you get the idea.

Cha Cha Cha
★★/$

One of many places in Northampton to get an ethnic feast, this restaurant is quick and affordable, the atmosphere is cool and casual, and the Mexican food is mighty tasty. Order burritos, tacos, and cilantro chicken salad at the main counter, choose your favorite salsa, and snack on chips while you wait for the busy chefs to call your number. *134 Main St., Northampton; (413) 586-7311.*

Pastas Wood Fired Pizza
★★/$-$$

These folks have their antennae up for cool ideas. Each booth is equipped with its own small TV, so you can channel-surf while you chomp on pizza. Kids can get "puppy pizza" shaped like a dog bone, or try the pasta or grilled cheese sandwiches. *Rte. 8, Lanesboro; (413) 499-5562.*

Pizzeria Paradiso
★★/$-$$

Create your own pie, crowned with toppings ranging from goat cheese and caramelized onions to fresh tomatoes and spinach. Kids can play with pizza dough while they wait (you need to ask for it). They also can color on activity menus, and order kids' selections including Shirley Temples, chicken tenders, and linguine. *12 Crafts Ave., Northampton; (413) 586-1468.*

The Pub
★★/$-$$
Mark your calendar for Wednesday night, when kids eat free, and a magician entertains your crew at this neighborhood pub. Burgers, fries, and homemade soup are on tap here. *15 E. Pleasant St., Amherst; (413) 549-1200.*

Red Rose Pizzeria
★★/$-$$
Springfield's favorite spot for hand-tossed pizza, this restaurant also dishes up meatball grinders, pasta, and eggplant parmigiana in a friendly setting. No kids' menu, but splitting plates is fine. *1060 Main St., Springfield; (413) 739-8510.*

Sophia's
★★/$-$$
From rotisserie chicken and seafood plates to baby back ribs and triple-decker clubs, this family-run restaurant will satisfy everyone's cravings. Kids can color while they wait for clam strips, chicken tenders, and grilled cheese. *Rtes. 7 and 20, Lenox; (413) 499-1101.*

SOUVENIR HUNTING

Thorne's Marketplace
In the center of downtown Northampton, this funky mall is a fun place to find fresh-picked daisies, educational toys, exotic beads, rubber ducks, and fresh-baked chocolate-chip cookies. *150 Main St., Northampton; (413) 584-5582.*

Yankee Candle Company
It's much more than a great place to buy scented candles. You can also dip your own candles, watch costumed craftsmen make antique-style tapers in the Candle Museum, and view Ferraris and Porsche Speedsters in the Yankee Candle Car Museum. Kids will love wandering through the Bavarian Christmas Village, complete with a miniature train, snow-covered dioramas, and a drawbridge leading to Nutcracker Castle (where you can pose in oak thrones). Shopping at Kringle Village and Santa's Toy Shop is fun, too. *Rtes. 5 and 10, S. Deerfield; (877) 636-7707; (413) 665-2929;* www.yankeecandle.com

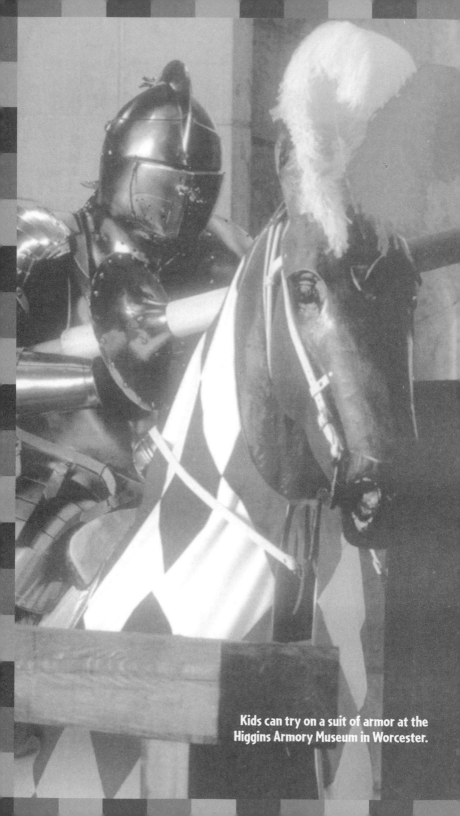

Kids can try on a suit of armor at the
Higgins Armory Museum in Worcester.

Central Massachusetts

SANDWICHED BETWEEN THE flashier metro Boston to the east and the peaks of the Berkshires and Pioneer Valley to the west, central Massachusetts consists of four distinct districts filled with natural and cultural gems.

Families can leave 21st-century trappings behind at Old Sturbridge Village, where ladies in bonnets and bespectacled peddlers demonstrate the crafts and trades practiced more than 170 years ago. Many families combine a trip to Plimoth Plantation (depicting Pilgrim life in the 1600s; see page 266) with a trip here (life in the 1830s). Given the range of kids' activities at both attractions, it makes sense to spend a day at each.

Families who like their history blended with outdoor pursuits will enjoy the **Blackstone River Valley**, composed of 11 historic towns along the Rhode Island border. In 1986, Congress established the bistate Blackstone River Valley National Historic Corridor, a 44-mile-long region that extends south of Worcester to Pawtucket, Rhode Island.

THE FamilyFun LIST

MUST-SEE · MUST-SEE

Davis' Farmland (page 305)

Davis' Mega Maze (page 306)

Higgins Armory Museum (page 304)

Old Sturbridge Village (page 305)

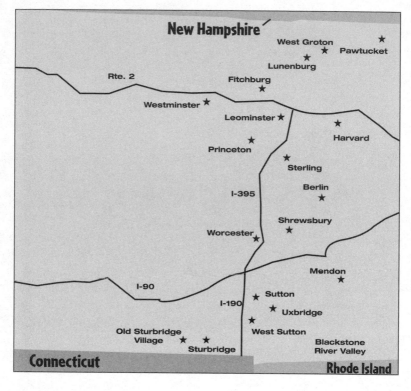

Here you will find scenic hiking and biking trails, swimming spots (check out West Hill Dam in Uxbridge), canoe programs for beginners, and family-oriented events. Stop by River Bend Farm (287 Oak St., Uxbridge; 508/278-7604) at Blackstone River & Canal Heritage State Park for a schedule of events, from riverboat rides aboard the Blackstone Valley Explorer to sleigh rides at West Sutton's Waters Farm.

The state's second-largest city, **Worcester,** provides a day—and a "knight"—to remember. It's home to the world's most important col-

lection of shining armor, the Higgins Armory Museum (see page 304). Just a short drive away, families can visit polar bears at the Ecotarium (see page 303), a 60-acre urban oasis that specializes in making science fun for kids. Trivia fans take note: Shredded Wheat, the ubiquitous smiley face, and drugstore valentines were all invented in Worcester.

The Johnny Appleseed Trail is the catchall name for 25 communities along Route 2 in north-central Massachusetts; this is a great place for families to go apple-picking at one of the area's abundant orchards.

Family favorites include Berlin Orchards *(200 Central St., Berlin; 978/838-2400)* and Hamilton Orchards *(Rte. 202 and West St., New Salem; 978/544-6867)*. To make your trip more meaningful, read a book about Johnny Appleseed (born John Chapman in 1774 in Leominster; you can visit the town's Main Street statue in his honor). The **Johnny Appleseed Trail visitors' center** *(Rte. 2, W. Lancaster; 978/534-2302)* can refer you to the area's chief attractions. These include Wachusett Mountain, a popular family ski and recreational area in Princeton, and Davis' Farmland and Mega Maze in Sterling. To make your visit extra sweet, pick up a bag of locally made apple chips (they look like potato chips but taste like apples) at the visitors' center.

CULTURAL ADVENTURES

Ecotarium
★★★/$

The high point of a visit here is the tree canopy walkway, where kids literally explore the treetops. During this seasonal program (there's an extra charge), kids don harnesses and helmets and walk across 40-foot-high platforms and swinging bridges. The walkway is indicative of the new energy at this 60-acre "center for environmental exploration,"

which is home to 200 animals. At outdoor habitats, kids can visit bald eagles and the polar bears, Ursa Minor and Kenda. Inside, you can take in a planetarium show, enjoy three floors of interactive exhibits, and even ride on a narrow-gauge railroad. Special programs, from jazz concerts to Halloween events, are held throughout the year. *22 Harrington Way, Worcester; (508) 929-2700;* www.ecotarium.org

Fruitlands ★★/$

Set in the lush, rolling hills of the Nashoba Valley, this "museum of

Old Sturbridge Village

Sturbridge offers special events during the various seasons. Here are some that may happen during particular months. Ask, too, about Kids Club events, some of which are open to nonmembers. (For more information, see page 305.)

- ♦ In December and January A Winter Wonderland, 1830s Style
- ♦ In March Maple Sugaring Camp
- ♦ In April Barnyard Babies
- ♦ In May All About Wool: From Lamb to Loom
- ♦ In June The Village Garden Blooms
- ♦ In July Independence Day with a Bang
- ♦ In August Village Craftsmen Display Wares
- ♦ In September 1830s Agriculture

Vacation Display

To beat the winter blues, our elementary school held a Family Travel Night in February, inviting families to bring souvenirs, pictures, and other items from places they had visited or lived. Each family set up a display in the cafeteria. The school even handed out homemade passports for the kids to get stamped at each stop. My family was so inspired after talking with another family that had lived in Nova Scotia that we have since taken a camping trip there.

Elise Anton, Dorset, Vermont

the American landscape" is actually four museums. The focal point is the farmhouse where Louisa May Alcott lived while her father, Bronson, conducted a short-lived utopian experiment. (**The other museums include the Shaker Museum, Indian Museum, and Picture Gallery.**) If you plan a bit ahead, you can register for a special family program, where you might look for animal tracks on the Fruitlands' three-mile trail system, listen to one of Louisa May Alcott's short stories, or even become an apprentice archaeologist. Treat yourselves to lunch in the tearoom, or bring a picnic so you can sit outside and enjoy views of Mount Wachusett and Mount Monadnock. Open seasonally. *102 Prospect Hill Rd., Harvard; (978) 456-3924.*

Higgins Armory
FamilyFun **Museum ★★★★/$**
It's worth jousting for a spot at this special museum, home to

the western hemisphere's largest collection of arms, armor, and art. Kids love wandering through this castle-like building into the low-lit Great Hall, complete with soaring arches, colorful flags, and faux stone walls. Here they can inspect armor made for knights, kids, and even dogs. In the Quest Gallery, children can try on a suit of armor, play chess, and make brass rubbings. The museum also offers a variety of special programs, from medieval fairs to knighting ceremonies. *100 Barber Ave., Worcester; (508) 853-6015;* www.higgins.com

National Plastics Center and Museum ★★/$

Leominster, aka the Pioneer Plastics City, pays tribute to polymers at this surprisingly kid-friendly museum. But then, what else would you expect from the town that invented the pink lawn flamingo? (Millions have been manufactured at Union Products, just across the street.) During your visit to this museum, kids can learn interesting facts, such as what makes car bumpers absorb power. You also can make plastic products using molding machines, create sculptures with plastic blocks, and learn about landmark plastic products, from Bakelite to Band-Aids. *210 Lancaster St., Leominster; (978) 537-9529; www.npcm.plastics.com*

Old Sturbridge Village
FamilyFun ★★★★/$$

You may have the most fun in history at this remarkable, 200-acre community that re-creates life in New England from 1790 to 1840. Forty original buildings were moved from different parts of the region to create this living history museum. As you explore the blacksmith shop, town parsonage, and working gristmill, you'll meet friendly, costumed interpreters who'll gladly show you how to make cheese and master a 19th-century dance. They'll even share the latest village gossip. Although these guides don't stay in character all the time (except during scheduled events), you can count on them to be animated when it comes to answering kids' questions. Sturbridge Village goes all out for families, with dozens of daily activities, such as parlor games and storytelling, and special events that include family days, where you can play games from the 1830s. At the Samson's Children's Museum, kids can don period costumes and play school in an old-time schoolhouse.

In summer, you can take a boat ride along the Quinebaug River and sign up for the Village at Twilight, an after-hours event during which you can ride in a horse-drawn carriage around the town green, eat a filling tavern meal, and enjoy period entertainment. Open all year, the village also features Halloween programs, Thanksgiving and Christmas feasts, and kids' camps, where children can make period crafts. *1 Old Sturbridge Village Rd., Sturbridge; (800) SEE-1830; www.osv.org*

JUST FOR FUN

Davis' Farmland
FamilyFun ★★★★/$

Cow-abunga! Bring your party animals to this 250-acre family farm for four-legged fun. Though the friendly animals are the focal point here (you'll meet rare livestock, along with goats, pigs, and more), there's much more. Kids can try their luck in the fishing pond, take a hayride, hop on a pony, wander through a kids' maze, have fun in the themed play areas, and join special daily activities. The Herd Rock Cafe will keep you fortified with pizza, hot dogs, and ice cream. You can even sign up for an animal slumber party, where you pitch your tent in the field, join a campfire cookout, and snooze by the creatures. *Redstone Hill, Sterling; (978) 422-MOOO.*

FamilyFun TIP

Calling all Paddlers

Blessed with scenic lakes, rivers, and streams, Central Massachusetts is a canoe lover's delight. Before you embark on a family trip, stop by the **River Bend Farm visitors' center** at the Blackstone River & Canal Heritage State Park *(287 Oak St., Uxbridge; 508/278-7604)* to pick up a free, 40-page guide that outlines canoe routes for beginners and experienced paddlers. The center periodically hosts canoe clinics for families (check with the front desk), but does not rent canoes. You can get them at the **Great Canadian Canoe Company** *(Rte. 146, Sutton; 508/865-0010; 800/98-CANOE)*.

For canoeing along the Johnny Appleseed Trail, stop by **Nashoba Paddler Rentals** *(Rte. 225, W. Groton; 978/448-8699)*. The outfitter rents supersize canoes that fit two adults and up to five kids, and can help you plan a pleasant trip down the slow-moving Nashua River. Watch out for those turtles!

Davis' Mega Maze
FamilyFun ★★★★/$

Go ahead and get lost at this maize maze, cut from the cornfields at the Davis family farm. Designed by world-renowned maze maker, Adrian Fisher, the maze's theme changes every year (pirates,

dragons, etc.), but the challenge remains the same. Holding a flag (so the staff can keep tabs on you), your family negotiates endless cornhusk pathways, dead ends, and bridges to find your way out. If you really get desperate, wave your flag and surrender—the staff will come get you. As part of your adventure, you can complete a themed scavenger hunt and be rewarded with a prize. Call ahead for hours of operation. *Redstone Hill, Sterling; (978) 422-8888;* www.davisfarmland.com/megamaze

Hyland Orchards and Brewery
★★/Free

Kids appreciate the chance to run around at this 150-acre farm, located at the end of a country road. There are animals to pet and feed, a playground, an ice-cream bar, picnic areas, and seasonal special events. *199 Arnold Rd., Sturbridge; (508) 347-7500.*

Southwick's Zoo ★★★/$$

One of the highlights of a visit to the Blackstone Valley, this family-run zoo invites kids to meet 500 animals, from African elephants and rhinos, to lions, tigers, and bears. You'll have fun feeding deer in the 35-acre deer forest, watching live animal shows, hanging out at the playground, and riding atop elephants, camels, and ponies. *2 Southwick St., Mendon; 800-258-9182; (508) 883-9182.*

Wachusett Mountain State Reservation ★★★/Free

The state's second-tallest peak, Wachusett Mountain is a monadnock. That means it weathered erosion better than the surrounding land and, as a result, stands above the nearby, lower hills. In this case, it also means sweeping views of Boston, the Berkshires, and New Hampshire's Mount Monadnock, plus the chance to see hawks and other birds during migration season. You can drive to the top of the 2,006-foot peak and hike on 17 miles of trails. For a map, stop at the **John Hitchcock visitors' center** *(Mountain Road, Princeton; 978/464-2987).*

BUNKING DOWN

Old Sturbridge Village Lodges ★★/$

Run by the folks who operate Old Sturbridge Village, which is right next door, this lodge offers 47 first-floor rooms (with phones and cable TV), an outdoor pool, and small playground. Ask about family packages that include admission to the village. *Rte. 20, Sturbridge; (508) 347-3327; www.osv.org/pages/lodges.htm*

Publick House Country Motor Lodge ★★/$$

This casual, clean lodge overlooks the famous Publick House, which was established in 1771. Guest rooms and suites have phones, cable TV, and private balconies. If your family prefers a suite, ask about accommodations in the Chamberlain House. Special winter weekend packages are available. *On the common, Sturbridge; (800) PUBLICK; (508) 347-3313; www.publick house.com*

Quaker Motor Lodge ★/$

A nice base for exploring the Blackstone River Valley, this 38-room motel has a heated outdoor pool and complimentary continental breakfast. Refrigerators and cable TV are standard in each room. *442 Quaker Hwy., Uxbridge; (508) 278-2445.*

Sheraton Four Points ★★/$$

Located in Johnny Appleseed's hometown of Leominster, this seven-story hotel has attractive rooms, a heated indoor pool, and an on-site restaurant with a kids' menu. *99 Erdman Way, Leominster; (978) 534-9000; www.fourpoints.com*

Sturbridge Host Hotel & Conference Center ★★★/$$

Turn a trip to Sturbridge Village into an all-out getaway at this lakeside resort. Here you'll find more than 250 rooms; a beach for swimming, boating, and fishing; an indoor pool; miniature golf; and on-site restaurants. *366 Main St., Sturbridge; (800) 582-3232; (508) 347-7393; www.fine-hotels.com*

Wachusett Inn
★★/$$

Just four miles away from Wachusett Mountain, this country-style inn is a terrific place to bunk in any season. Families can stay in guest rooms or suites, swim in the outdoor or heated indoor pool, enjoy sleigh rides and hayrides (in season), and venture out on cross-country skiing and hiking trails. *9 Village Inn Rd., Westminster; (800) 342-1905; (978) 874-2000;* www.wachusettvillage inn.com

GOOD EATS

Lowell's
★★/$$$

For a century, this family-owned restaurant has been filling hungry tummies with home-cooked, reasonably priced meals. Kids will find all of their favorites here and, while

they wait to be served, can color the animal-themed menus. Seafood is a specialty, and families crowd in on weekends for the fish-and-chips. For dessert, pull up a swivel stool at the ice-cream counter and dig into an ice-cream sundae. *Rte. 16, Mendon; (508) 473-1073.*

Old Mill Restaurant
★★/$$

Set alongside an old mill stream, this family-owned restaurant will satisfy your appetite with tasty sandwiches, chicken and beef dishes, and seafood. Kids will find the classics on their menu. The staff will gladly give you food to throw to the resident ducks. *Rte. 2A, Westminster; (978) 874-5941.*

Publick House
★★★/$$-$$$

Built in 1771 by Ebenezer Crafts, this historic inn dishes out hearty, New England meals in period dining rooms that warm the soul. Turkey dinners, hearth-roasted chicken, and kettle-chip crusted scrod are just a few of the specialties for big appetites. Kids can choose from petit filet mignon, smaller turkey dinners, hamburgers, and banana splits. The friendly staff will provide crayons and scrumptious pecan rolls, which you can also buy in the bakeshop. To save money, come for breakfast. *On the common; (800) PUBLICK; (508) 347-3313;* www.publickhouse.com

SOUVENIR HUNTING

Eaton Farm Confectioners

In the Blackstone River Valley, you can take a factory tour at this sweet place where candymakers use recipes dating back to *1892. Burbank Rd., Sutton; (800) 434-9300 or (508) 865-5235.*

Ewen's Sleepy Hollow Sugar House

Come in any time of year for maple syrup and maple creams and candies. In March, you can also watch as sugarmakers boil maple syrup. *66 Elmwood Rd., Lunenberg; (877) 320-3958; (978) 582 6655.*

Hebert Candy Mansion

Family-owned since 1917, "America's First Roadside Candy Store" dishes up chocolates, cream filled confections, and lots of fun. The mansion hosts everything from 50-themed car shows to haunted candy mansions. It also offers mouthwatering factory tours. *575 Hartford Pike, Rte. 20, Shrewsbury; (800) 642-7702, ext. 333 (events hotline); (508) 845-8051; www.hebert-candies.com*

FamilyFun GAME

One Minute of Words

Everybody gets a pencil and paper. Someone has to be the timekeeper (a good job for a grown-up). The timekeeper picks a letter, tells it to everyone else, and shouts "Go!" Players write as many words as possible that start with that letter. When a minute is up, the timekeeper says "Stop!" and all the players put down their pencils. Whoever has the most legitimate words wins. Decide in advance whether you can finish writing a word you've already started when the game ends. Now, give yourself one more minute to write a sentence with as many of the words as you can.

Marshall Farm

This hilltop farm is a favorite place to search for a souvenir (how about a bag of apple chips?) or to pick your own apples. When you're ready to eat, have a country lunch in the on-site restaurant, or enjoy a picnic and savor views of Wachusett Mountain. *340 Marshall Rd., Fitchburg; (978) 343-6255.*

Rhode Island

ONLY 37 MILES WIDE and 48 miles long, Rhode Island is so small it could fit into Texas 227 times.

However, when it comes to packing a vacation punch, Little Rhody, as it's fondly called, is no pipsqueak. True to its name, the Ocean State boasts 400 miles of sandy coastline beaches, from the frisky, amusement-packed town of Misquamicut to the gentle waves of Roger Wheeler State Beach. Bike paths, walking trails, and canoe routes that meander past old mill villages make Rhode Island a paradise for nature lovers (see "Rhode Island Greenways" on page 317).

Greater
Providence

Newport

South
County

Block Island

Like its founder, Roger Williams, a cleric who fled the Massachusetts Bay Colony to escape the oppression of Puritanism, Rhode Island has a quirky, independent streak. You can see this in the state's fun food traditions. Here, many children grow up drinking coffee milk (made with a sweet coffee syrup), slurping coffee "cabinets" (milk shakes), and drinking Del's Lemonade (available at outlets throughout the state).

Whether you take a ferry to Block Island, head to the Providence River to watch WaterFire, or take the Cliff Walk in Newport, you'll see that Rhode Island may be small in size, but it's big on fun.

ATTRACTIONS	
$	under $10
$$	$10 - $20
$$$	$20 - $30
$$$$	$30 +

HOTELS/MOTELS/CAMPGROUNDS	
$	under $100
$$	$100 - $200
$$$	$200 - $300
$$$$	$300 +

RESTAURANTS	
$	under $10
$$	$10 - $20
$$$	$20 - $30
$$$$	$30 +

FAMILYFUN RATED	
★	Fine
★★	Good
★★★	Very Good
★★★★	*FamilyFun* Recommended

If catching sight of a sailboat or twenty in Newport Harbor whets your nautical appetite, your family can take a 90-minute tour on the 78-foot schooner *Adirondack*.

Newport

From a distance on a sunny, summer day, Newport Harbor looks like a gigantic bathtub jammed with toy boats. Schooners, motorboats, tour boats, J-boats, and mega-yachts glisten in the golden rays, waves happily splashing against their hulls.

Newport is filled with boat aficionados who have made playing—and competing—in world-class watercraft their consuming passion. Luckily, your family can join the fun, too, since megayachts aside, there is a fleet of vessels happy to escort you and your kids on a rollicking tour past lighthouses, historic Fort Adams, and the city's famous mansions.

Newport's golden age lasted a dizzying 40 years, from 1890 to 1930, when dozens of the nation's wealthiest families built gargantuan summer "cottages" along the shore for all to see and admire. Newport remains a vacation mecca for the privileged but, today, any visitor can tour the opulent mansions run by the Preservation Society of Newport. For

THE FamilyFun LIST

MUST-SEE · MUST-SEE

Astors' Beechwood (page 315)

The Breakers (page 315)

Cliff Walk (page 317)

Fort Adams State Park (page 317)

The Green Animals (page 317)

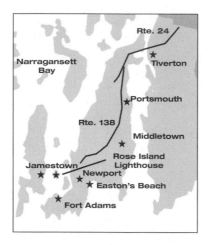

Preservation Society hosts special family events, such as a spring tea party at the kid-pleasing Green Animals site and an Easter egg hunt at Rosecliff. The visitors' center features a kiddie concierge (basically, buckets filled with kid-oriented brochures), and some hotels offer family packages. Though Newport is pricey, just beyond its borders is Middletown, where families will find many more affordable and kid-friendly hotels and restaurants. You may want to stay there at night and explore Newport by day.

many children, seeing the marble ballrooms and gold coaches is like wandering into a scene from *Cinderella*.

Speaking of fairy tales, kids are sure to enjoy *Cornelius Vandermouse, the Pride of Newport,* by Peter W. Barnes and Cheryl Shaw Barnes. The story concerns a fortunate mouse (he's a gifted sailor and lives in the colossal Breakers mansion) that searches Newport's famed estates for a good-luck token that will help him win the Commodore's Cup. You can buy the book at the mansion's museum shops.

Though Newport is still a magnet for tony yacht owners and honeymooners, it also warmly welcomes families. The town goes all out for Halloween, there are lavish, family-oriented celebrations during the holidays, and the city hosts a wonderful winter festival during February school vacation. The

CULTURAL ADVENTURES

The Artillery Company of Newport Armory and Museum ★★/$

This museum doesn't need interactive exhibits to make its point: this amazing collection of uniforms from 1741 to the present represents more than 100 countries; walking through with your kids (best for the school-age crew) will surely generate a lively discussion ("Wow, those guys in the Revolutionary War sure were tiny!"). Several celebrity uniforms are on hand, including those donated by King Hussein of Jordan, U.S. General Colin Powell, and HRH Prince Philip, the Duke of Edinburgh. *23 Clarke St., Newport; (401) 846-8488;* www. newportartillery.org

Astors' Beechwood
FamilyFun ★★★★/$

Come here for a mansion tour with a twist: when you walk through the grand doors of the Astors' 40-room "cottage," you have the definite feeling you've really gone back in time to 1891. Costumed actors portraying members of the esteemed family welcome you in. Kids will love the costumes, meeting the domestic staff and being addressed as "prince" or "princess." On the 45-minute tour, you might even be invited to join a game of croquet or badminton or to try out your dance steps in the ballroom. Although the home isn't as palatial as others in the neighborhood, the tour is especially fun for families. *580 Bellevue Ave., Newport; (401) 846-3772; www.astors beechwood.com*

The Breakers ★★★/$$
FamilyFun
The summer home of Cornelius Vanderbilt II, this is the grandest of the grand Newport cottages. Two of the 70 rooms were made in Paris and shipped to Newport for reassembly. While you'll gush over the ornate marble and gold dining room, and ooh and aah at the ocean views from the Renaissance-style upper loggia, the high point for kids is the children's cottage. An exact miniature of the original Breakers mansion, it was the playhouse for little Gladys Vanderbilt. No plastic sippy cups at her teddy-bear tea parties; Gladys's play china was pure Limoge. *Ochre Point Ave. at Ruggles Ave., Newport; (401) 847-1000.* For an extra fee, you can tour the **Breakers Stables** *(Coggeshall and Bateman Aves.; 401/847-1000)* and see a historic model train, coaches, and carriages.

The Elms ★★★/$
Edward J. Berwind modeled his mansion after French palaces, complete with a grand ballroom and marble staircase, but kids will be drawn to the subbasement area: Berwind, a coal magnate, engineered a progressive heating system that was remarkable for the time. Kids love climbing down to the lowest level of the house to see the underground railroad, which transported coal to the boiler room. The house and gardens are filled with adorable

WHY DO LOBSTERS TURN RED WHEN COOKED?

Lobsters have many colors in the shells, but red is the most stable one. The green and brown pigments, which dominate a live lobster's coloring, are destroyed by cooking.

marble cherubs. Start a game and see how many you can count. *Bellevue Ave., Newport; (401) 847-1000.*

International Tennis Hall of Fame and Museum ★★/$

If you and your kids love tennis, swing over to this museum, once a private club for the elite during the town's heyday. You can watch replays of the world's best matches, but it's even more fun to play tennis on one of the 13 grass courts, which are open to the public (reservations necessary; racquet rentals available; fee). Inside the museum, you'll find exhibits that trace the sport from its medieval roots to Andre Agassi and beyond; with a lot of items behind display cases, this spot is really geared to older kids or die-hard fans. *194 Bellevue Ave., Newport; (401) 849-3990;* www.tennisfame.org

Old Colony & Newport Railroad ★★/$

Landlubbers can still enjoy touring Newport Harbor by taking a very

entertaining 70-minute narrated ride on this train—composed of a 1904 Boston and Maine railroad coach and an 1884 Inter Colonial Ry Office car. The nine-mile ride chugs past rocky beaches and decommissioned U.S. naval ships (including the USS *Iowa* and the USS *Saratoga*). Picnic baskets and food are allowed. *The depot is at 19 America's Cup Ave., across from the Newport County Convention & Visitor's Bureau; (401) 624-6951.*

Rhode Island Fisherman and Whale Museum ★/$

This tiny museum, inside the Seamen's Church Institute, is a good option on a rainy day. Kids can don fishermen's gear, pilot a ship while listening to taped conversations of real fishermen, and even try quahogging. *18 Market Sq., Newport; (401) 847-4260.*

Thames Science Center ★★/$

Any place in Newport where kids can have hands-on fun is welcome.

Sight Sailing

Who wouldn't fall in love with **a sailboat called Valentine?** This Pearson Ensign sailboat takes up to six passengers on an exciting, 75-minute cruise through the harbor toward Narragansett Bay. You'll get close-up views of racing vessels and mega-yachts—and the captain may even let your child take the tiller and steer. Though the company also offers tours on *Starlight* (two-hour sails, up to six passengers) and *Sightsailer* (70-minute sails, up to 16 passengers), it recommends the *Valentine* for parents with young children because of the short sailing time and the one-on-one interaction with the captain. *Bowen's Wharf; (401) 849-3333.*

Depending on when you visit this small museum (the interactive stations are subject to change), you might experiment with waves and sound in a high-tech arcade, decode secret messages, play a giant music box, or use a thermal-imaging camera to map body heat. The museum offers special Saturday science workshops for children ages 7 to 10, plus a variety of themed programs (such as a yo-yo clinic) and speakers. The science store is exceptional. *77 Long Wharf, Newport; (800) 587-2872; (401) 849-6966;* www.thames science.org

JUST FOR FUN

Cliff Walk
FamilyFun ★★★★/Free

For magnificent views of the splendid mansions and the Atlantic Ocean pounding against the rocky shoreline, stroll this three-and-a-half-mile coastline walk and soak up the grandeur of bygone days without getting soaked by high prices (it's free). **NOTE:** Parents might want to stick to the north end of the path (Narragansett to Ruggles Avenue), which is fairly level; the southern end of the walk involves quite a bit of climbing, and it's not particularly suited to young kids. *Pick up the Cliff Walk at Memorial Boulevard, near the western end of Easton's Beach (parking is available at Easton's Beach).*

Rhode Island Greenways

Nature lovers take note: before you leave for Rhode Island, be sure to call and ask for a Greenways map. Greenways are extensive networks of trails, bike paths, and water routes that are perfect for those who prefer to experience the state's natural beauty at minimum expense—and away from the crowds. From oceanside bike paths and wooded hiking spots to scenic canoe routes and walking trails, the map highlights dozens of refreshing, low-cost outings. The Greenways system keeps expanding; for the latest information, call each site before you go. *To request your free map, call (800) 556-2484.*

Fort Adams State Park
FamilyFun ★★★★/Free

An active military fort from 1799 to 1945, the site features three tiers of guns and cannons, plus a picnic area, bathing beach, and boat launch on 21 acres along Narragansett Bay. *Ocean Dr., Newport; (401) 847-2400.*

The Green Animals
FamilyFun ★★★★/$

A colossal giraffe, elephant, dinosaur, and lion greet families who visit this historic topiary garden. It's a must for kids to pose for a picture by the two bears. The waterside setting makes this a gorgeous place to picnic, and you can also see some Victorian toys in the 1880 Brayton House. *Cory's La., Portsmouth; (401) 847-1000.*

New England Aquarium Exploration Center at Newport
★★/$

This small branch of Boston's New England Aquarium offers summer fun. Kids can pick up and meet sea stars and hermit crabs, take knot-tying lessons, and make prints at craft sessions. For a nominal charge, the center even offers family field trips that focus on sea life in Narragansett Bay. *175 Memorial Blvd., Easton's Beach; (401) 849-8430.*

Newport Butterfly Farm ★★/$
Enter this 30-by-100-foot greenhouse and see up to 1,000 butterflies of varying species (because butterflies only live between seven and ten days, the specimens are constantly changing). The keepers here are protective of their winged residents (you can't touch, chase, or bother the butterflies). Kids will have fun trying to identify the exquisite insects using a field guide, and meeting Nellie, a trained turtle who comes when called and begs for food. *1038 Aquidneck Ave., Middletown; (401) 849-9519.*

Newport Equestrian Academy
★★/$$$

Adjacent to the Norman Bird Sanctuary, this riding center offers two-hour horseback rides along the beach. Best suited to kids ages 6 and up, the price ($30 at press time) includes a half-hour lesson, followed by a 90-minute ride. Smaller kids can hop on a pony for a half-hour ride around this pretty, five-acre facility. If you really want to hoof it in style, consider a 90-minute horse-drawn carriage ride; as you trot by breathtaking vistas, you'll get a sense of what it might have been like to be an Astor or Vanderbilt. *287 Third Beach Rd., Middletown; (401) 848-5440.*

Norman Bird Sanctuary
★★★/$

Take a walk and sign up for family-oriented nature programs at this beautiful, 450-acre wooded retreat, which has seven miles of hiking trails. Depending on the season, the lineup might include a Halloween campout with s'mores and stories around the campfire; an owl prowl; or a Native American Thanksgiving. You'll also enjoy wandering through the nature center and attending spe-

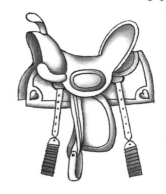

cial events, such as the Harvest Fair. *583 Third Beach Rd., Middletown; (401) 846-2577;* www.normanbird sanctuary.org

Roseland Acres
★★/$$-$$$
There's nothing snooty about this riding center, which is family-run and family-oriented. Depending on the season, families can enjoy hayrides, sleigh rides, or trail rides along miles of wooded bridle paths. There's a petting zoo, too. *594 East Rd., Tiverton; (401) 624-8866.*

Watson Farm
★★/$
This seaside, working farm has a two-mile scenic trail with expansive views of the bay. The best time to visit is in the spring, on Lamb Day. You'll see new lambs in the pastures and watch sheep-shearing demonstrations. To avoid disappointment, call first to see if the farm is open; hours vary. *455 North Rd., Jamestown; (401) 423-0005.*

BUNKING DOWN

Howard Johnson Lodge
★★/$$
This is a fine place if you're not looking for a destination resort—just a place to sleep and relax between excursions. The inn, on busy Route 138, has spacious rooms, tennis courts, and an indoor pool. *351 W.*

TALL SHIP

The 78-foot classic schooner *Adirondack* offers 90-minute and two-hour tours that welcome kids (the shorter tour is sufficient for most youngsters). On your journey, you'll sail by Fort Adams, the Rose Island Lighthouse, and even the playhouse that belonged to the young Jacqueline Bouvier (Kennedy Onassis). *Newport Yachting Center, America's Cup Ave., Newport; (401) 846-1600.*

Main Rd. (Rte. 138), Newport; (800) 1-GO-HOJO; (401) 849-2000.

Newport Marriott ★★★/$$$
Located on the harbor next to the visitors' center, this hotel is smack in the thick of everything. A game room, indoor pool, and kids' menu at the on-site restaurant have definite kid appeal. The Thames Science Center, a good place to visit on a rainy day, is on the ground floor of the hotel. The concierge desk is very helpful in assisting you with activity planning. *25 America's Cup Ave., Newport; (401) 831-4004;* www.marriott.com

Rose Island Lighthouse
★★★★/$$

If your family wants an illuminating experience, stay overnight in this 1870 lighthouse on Rose Island, a mile offshore from Newport Bridge. The first-floor quarters of the former lighthouse keepers have been turned into a cozy museum/apartment with a record player (and a collection of older records you can spin), a Mutoscope through which to view penny postcards, and old-fashioned board games. **NOTE:** Though the apartment has two bedrooms, this is not a typical inn—there is no on-site manager to deliver breakfast, and, in case of emergency, you'll need to contact the folks in the second-floor quarters upstairs who have paid for the privilege of being lighthouse keepers for the week (that's another program entirely; call for information).

The apartment for overnight guests is equipped with pots, pans, dishes, and utensils, and a single-burner gas hot plate. There's no running water (bottled drinking water is provided) or refrigeration (bring your food in a cooler) and wind-powered electricity must be used sparingly. In exchange for roughing it, you'll enjoy wraparound views of Narragansett Bay. On a sunny day don't forget to climb the steps that lead to the beacon, for more memorable views. A volunteer from the nonprofit Rose Island Lighthouse Foundation will transport you via boat to and from the lighthouse and explain all the rules. In warm weather families can swim or fish below the high-tide line, and in winter, you might spot harbor seals. *For information, call (401) 847-4242.*

SeaView Inn
★★★/$

This is one of the best places for families in the Newport area. The inn doesn't merely accept kids, it caters to them. Located two miles from downtown Newport on a hill with ocean views, the inn provides free breakfast, free use of bikes and kites, plus an indoor pool and a spacious lawn with lots of room to play. *240 Aquidneck Ave., Middletown; (800) 495-2046; (401) 846-5000.*

GOOD EATS

Brick Alley Pub ★★★/$$

This is one pub where kids seem to come first: trains chug along tiny tracks at the edge of the ceiling, colorful road signs adorn the walls,

---

FamilyFun TIP

A Boatload of Lobsters

The **Aquidneck Lobster Co.** *(31 Bowens Wharf, Newport)* takes in about a million pounds of lobster a year (plus fish). You can see the latest catch and even pick out a lobster — the staff will cook it for you to go.

there's a big shiny car by the salad bar, and crayons and an activity sheet/menu round out the experience. *140 Thames St., Newport; (401) 849-6334.*

Flo's Drive-In
★★/$-$$

Flo's has been serving tender, sweet, deep-fried clams and clam chowder, along with hot dogs and burgers, since 1936. While they're waiting for their order, kids love climbing on the model boat and playing in the sandy area in front of the restaurant. *Aquidneck Ave., Middletown; (401) 847-8141.*

Newport Creamery
★★/$

This famous restaurant chain is a godsend for families looking for good, affordable fare. The kids' menu is a bargain. And everyone must try an Awful Awful. *Bellevue Avenue in The Bellevue Gardens, Newport (401/846-6332); and 208 W. Main Rd., Middletown (401/846-2767).*

Rocco's Family Pizza
★★/$

Mama mia—do they make good pizza here! Choose thin- or thick-crust and pick your favorite toppings, sit back, and enjoy. This family-owned restaurant also dishes out calzones. *124 Broadway, Newport; (401) 848-4556.*

Sea Fare's American Café
★★/$$

If you crave gourmet fare but have pint-size appetites to satisfy, this place offers haute cuisine in a casually sophisticated atmosphere that welcomes children. While kids dine on their old standbys, parents can try sweet potato polenta, rack of lamb with mint risotto, or goat-cheese quesadillas. *Brick Market Pl., Newport; (401) 849-9188.*

Tito's Cantina ★★/$

Little amigos love this place, and so will you when you see the prices. The casual Mexican restaurant dishes up Batman burritos and Tito's (chicken) tenders for kids. *651 W. Main St., Middletown; (401) 849-4222.*

SOUVENIR HUNTING

Animal House

In this specialty toy store your kids can spend their fun money on stuffed animals, books, puzzles, stickers, and their favorite licensed characters. *395 Thames St., Newport; (401) 847-5209.*

High Flyers Flight Co.

Besides selling a jazzy array of kites, the store frequently sponsors public kite-flying contests at Brenton Park. The event is a colorful afternoon of free family fun. *492 Thames St., Newport; (401) 846-3262.*

Only 7 by 3 miles, the Block is a perfect island to bike around. Once you hit the beach, though, you'll never leave.

South County and Block Island

With 100 miles of coastline and dozens of sandy white playgrounds, South County offers you the opportunity to hang out at a different beach each day for a week and still have some to explore on your next visit. Are you in the mood to be entertained? Head to Misquamicut, with its jamming strip of amusements, water slides, and seaside snack bars. Want a safe haven for the little ones? Meet Blue Shutters, a small beach that caresses children with gentle waves. If you want a big state beach with major wave action, join the throngs at Scarborough. And if you want to watch die-hard surfers challenge some rambunctious waves, Narragansett Beach is the place.

With a selection like this, it's no wonder so many families migrate to South County each year (many rent cottages; see page 330). The area is a microcosm of New England's best in the hot season—in coastal communities such as Charlestown, Westerly, Narragansett, and the fishing village of Galilee, where you can eat seafood by the sea,

THE FamilyFun LIST

MUST-SEE MUST-SEE

Block Island (page 326)

The Fantastic Umbrella Factory (page 333)

Gilbert Stuart Museum (page 325)

Narrow River (page 327)

Watch Hill (page 330)

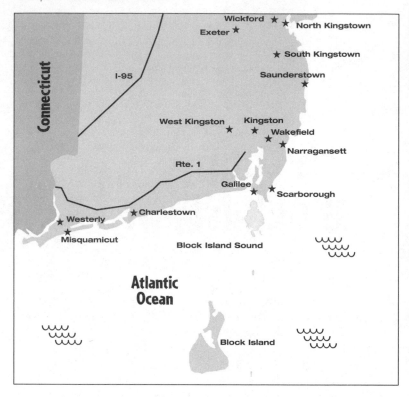

play miniature golf, indulge in creamy scoops of homemade ice cream, take a ferry to Block Island (12 miles off the coast), and ride a historic carousel. Families with children who aren't yet in school often wait until after the summer rush, when cool breezes, autumn colors, and fewer crowds make a visit even more enjoyable.

Beaches aren't the only reason to visit South County: farther inland, you'll find salt marshes, remote woodlands, farm stands, tiny villages—and history with a capital "H": there's the Gilbert Stuart Museum,

where you can learn about the talented little boy who grew up to paint George Washington's portrait, and the South County Museum, where your kids can play with the animals at the 18th-century Canonchet Farm.

South County has fun food traditions, too. The specialty here is johnnycakes, cornmeal pancakes of sorts that can be prepared thick (the South County way) or thin and crispy (Newport style). The "correct" formula is a subject of great debate among some locals. You can sample these breakfast treats at local restaurants (see Good Eats) and, if you like them enough, you can even drive out to the Kenyon Corn Meal Company, which has been grinding cornmeal using granite millstones since 1711.

As is true in Rhode Island's other regions, South County holds many fairs, festivals, and special events—from the Big Apple Circus to historic Wickford's holiday celebration—that are widely promoted in local free papers, such as *This Week in South County*.

CULTURAL ADVENTURES

Gilbert Stuart Museum
FamilyFun ★★★★/$

Sure, you know George Washington, but here's a chance to meet the man who painted his famous portraits (and created the classic image on the dollar bill). Gilbert Stuart was just 3 years old when he started picking up charcoal sticks from the fire and sketching portraits (at age 12, he was commissioned by a Newport doctor to create a portrait of the family canine). You can learn his fascinating story here, and kids can wander through Stuart's birthplace (1755) and see his cradle, visit the gristmill, and watch the waterwheel churn. On select weekends, well-informed kid docents, ages 5 to 12, lead the tours dressed in colonial garb. The best time to come is mid-April through July, during the herring run. More than 300,000 fish swim upstream, scaling the fish ladder on the property, to reach their spawning grounds—kids love to watch. *815 Gilbert Stuart Rd., N. Kingstown; (401) 294-3001.*

South County Museum and Farm ★★/$

In this pastoral setting, devoted to life in the region from the 1800s to the 1950s, visitors can wander through Canonchet Farm and see sheep, goats, ponies, and the state bird, the Rhode Island Red (a chicken). If you can lure the kids away from the animals, you'll want to tour the general store, working print shop, schoolroom, and country kitchen. There's also an activity room where kids can dress up in clothes of the time (slip into a mariner's oilskin outfit, for example). The gift shop sells penny candy, arrowheads, kaleidoscopes, and more. *Cononchet Farm, Strathmore St., Narragansett; (401) 783-5400.*

FamilyFun TIP

Look! Up in the Sky...

Stop by the **Frosty Drew Observatory** *(Ninigret Park, Rte. 1A, Charlestown)* at dusk on summer Fridays to view constellations through a high-powered telescope. Astronomers explain the magic of the night.

University of Rhode Island Coastal Institute Visitors Center
★/Free

A beach is much more than sun and sand. Learn about its hidden wonders at Living on the Edge, a small interactive science exhibit on URI's coastal campus. You can find out about lobsters and fish through interactive computer exhibits and play with a dune machine. The institute also occasionally offers family programs in summer. *South Ferry Rd., Narragansett; (401) 874-6211; www.crc.uri.edu*

JUST FOR FUN

Adventureland of Narragansett
★★/$-$$

At this playland on Narragansett's main shopping strip, families can spend the afternoon playing 18-hole miniature golf, testing their skills in the batting cage, and riding go-carts and bumper boats. *Point Judith Rd., Narragansett; (401) 789-0030;* www. visitri.com/waterwizz

Block Island
FamilyFun ★★★★/$-$$$$

Spend a day or a week. See "All Aboard for Block Island" page 328.

Casey Farm ★★/$

A thriving plantation in the mid-1700s, the farm now produces organically grown herbs, vegetables, and flowers, and you can learn about the process on guided tours. There's no hands-on component to the tour, so if you're looking for a place to pet the animals, head to the South County Museum. In summer, however, Casey Farm offers weeklong camps for kids ages 5 to 9, where they can pitch in with farm chores, make butter, and go for a hayride. *Rte. 1A, Saunderstown; (401) 295-1030.*

Fiddlesticks Driving Range
★★/$-$$

This outdoor entertainment center is an ideal place for families to try their skills in batting cages and a driving range and play miniature golf. One of the 18-hole courses meanders around a hot-air balloon, the other winds through caves. *Exit 5 off Rte. 4, N. Kingstown; (401) 295-1519.*

Misquamicut
★★/Free-$$$

Not a romantic getaway, this South County town is tailormade for kids, with a carousel, 2-mile-long state beach, giant water slides (**Water Wizz**; *401/322-0526*), and go-carts, bumper boats, mini-golf, and more

(Bayview Fun Park; *401/322-0800*). You get the idea.

Narragansett Ocean Club
★★/$

Spinning to the music of the 1950s around the gleaming wood roller rink, Mom and Dad can indulge in some nostalgia while their kids enjoy an afternoon of wholesome fun. The rink offers public skating sessions through the week, and there are special sessions just for kids that include lessons (parents get free coffee while they watch). The snack bar offers hot dogs and pizza. *360 S. Pier Rd., Narragansett; (401) 783 6120.*

Narrow River
FamilyFun ★★/$-$$

Rent kayaks or canoes from Narrow River Kayaks and take a self-guided tour down this scenic waterway that consists of a tidal inlet, salt marsh, estuary, and fjord-like pond. Its calm waters make it ideal for a family paddling adventure. On your journey, you'll likely spot herons and egrets and maybe even a coyote or a bear. *94 Middlebridge Rd., Narragansett; (401) 789-0334.*

Ninigret Pond and Park
★★/Free

For a low-cost outing, head to this park to play tennis, ride along an almost-milelong paved bike course, have fun at the playground, and (here's a secret) hang out at the fam-

Best Bets for Boats

THE KAYAK CENTER
With three locations in Rhode Island, this outfitter offers an exceptional schedule of programs and tours, with several geared to families. Two favorites are the **Wickford Harbor Tour**, where you explore the cove by scenic Wickford Village; and the **Newport Harbor Tour**, where paddlers get a close look at the city's America's Cup boats and mega-yachts. These tours last three hours and include equipment, snacks, and instruction. If you'd rather rent kayaks and head off on your own, consider paddling to Charlestown's Ninigret Pond, a calm, saltwater oasis packed with wildlife *(the Charlestown outlet is on Charlestown Beach Road; call 401/364-8000).* The outfitter also offers daylong kayak camps, where kids ages 9 to 13 learn about safe paddling techniques and skills. *9 Phillips St., Wickford; (888) SEA-KAYAK; (401) 295-4400.*

SOUTHLAND RIVERBOAT
Riding on this riverboat can be so much fun, it makes you feel like dancing—and that's exactly what happens on these one-and-three-quarter-hour tours. As Beach Boys tunes and other rock hits play, the kid-friendly captain may start **dancing on the deck,** inspiring you to shake, rattle, and roll. On the voyage, you'll cruise by 11 islands (and assorted windsurfers), see fishermen and lobstermen at work, and view snowy egrets, swans, and blue herons. *State Pier, Galilee; (401) 783-2954.*

ily-oriented beach at the three-acre spring-fed swimming pond. This beach is much less crowded than the ocean beaches, and lifeguards are on hand all summer. *Rte. 1A, Charlestown; (401) 334-1222.*

Smith's Castle
★★/$

First off, it's not a castle. It's a big white house that's believed to be the oldest surviving plantation house in the country. The site of trading centers established by Roger Williams and Richard Smith in 1638, the homestead gives families a chance to wander through 18th-century gardens, picnic in a cove by Narragansett Bay, and learn about Rhode Island's earliest residents, the Indians. Kids who tour the house can help docents hunt for the "castle mouse." The castle closes for the winter, but tours can be arranged by appointment. *Mill Cove, N. Kingstown; (401) 294-3521.*

ALL ABOARD FOR BLOCK ISLAND

ONCE YOU'VE explored the beaches along Rhode Island's southern coast, ferry 12 miles south to Block Island, which the Nature Conservancy rates as one of the top 12 "last great places in the Western Hemisphere." Just seven miles long and three miles wide, the island is packed with walking/hiking trails, 17 miles of sandy beaches, more than 40 rare and endangered species, and many miles of picturesque stone walls. Though the island doesn't seem touristy or commercial, you'll nevertheless find dozens of restaurants, kayak/ boat/ cycling rental shops, gift shops, and fishing charters.

To get to Block Island, take a ferry from Point Judith, Rhode Island, or New London, Connecticut (401/ 783-4613), or Montauk, Long Island (call the **Montauk Express** at *631/668-5709*). Wear sturdy hiking shoes and bring beach gear.

Family-friendly restaurants include **Finn's Seafood Restaurant** *(Water St., Old Harbor; 401/466-2473)*, **The Beachhead** *(Beach Ave., Old Harbor; 401/466-2249)*, **Sharky's** *(Corn Neck Rd., Old Harbor; 401/466-9900)*, and **Ballard's** *(42 Water St., Old Harbor; 401/466-2231)*, where kids can play on the half-mile-long beach while parents finish their meals.

If you decide to stay overnight, kid-friendly accommodations include the **Atlantic Inn**, with its lifesize dollhouse *(High St.; 401/466-5678)*, the **Barrington Inn** *(Beach Ave.; 401/466-5880)*; the **1661 Inn** *(Spring St., Old Harbor; 401/466-2421)*, and the **Hygeia House** *(Beach Ave.; 401/466-9616)*. For information on

South County Bike Path
★★/Free
On this scenic bike path, bicycle-toting families (there aren't any local rental shops) can travel four miles from the Kingston train station to the hamlet of Peacedale, passing farmland and diverse wildlife (the path's expansion to 11 miles, ending in Narragansett, was underway as we went to press). *You can park your car at the train station, off Rte. 138 in W. Kingstown; (800) 548-4662.*

Tower Hill Equestrian Center
★★/$$-$$$
The entire family should trot over to this horsey haven (which has a huge stable with about 50 horses) for some riding fun. Short pony rides on friendly, shaggy Shetlands are best for kids up to about age 12; older children and parents can opt for trail rides through the woods. *Tower Hill Rd., N. Kingstown; (401) 294-8190.*

cottage rentals and more, contact the Block Island Chamber of Commerce (*800/383-BIRI; 401/466-2474; blockislandinfo.com*).

Here are some fun things to do:

1. Meet the animals.
The Hotel Manisses (*1 Spring St., Old Harbor; 800/MANISSE; 401/466-2421*) is home to a Scottish Highland steer, a bevy of llamas, black swans, Egyptian geese, emus, and fainting goats (they faint when excited).

2. Hit the trail.
Head to the Nature Conservancy (*High St., Old Harbor; 401/466-2129*) for a map of scenic trails and a schedule of kid-oriented programs.

3. Opt for the ocean.
Families love Frederick J. Benson Town Beach (named for an Islander who used lottery winnings to fund a scholarship for local students),

with soft sand, beautiful ocean views, and free parking, plus showers, a snack bar, and umbrella rentals.

4. Lighten up.
Families can tour the Southeast Lighthouse, high on Mohegan Bluffs, and North Light, a beautiful spot to watch the sunset. For information, call the Block Island Historical Society (*401/466-2481*).

5. Play around.
In July and August, kids ages 7 to 14 can star in a performance of the Fairy Tale Theater. For 45 minutes on summer mornings, young thespians rehearse a fairy tale with their peers, then don costumes and perform at the Empire Theatre (*Water and High Sts., Old Harbor; 401/466-2555*). After the show, children of all ages are invited on stage to re-create the fairy tale. Your Cinderella and Prince Charming will love this.

Watch Hill
★★★/Free-$$

Picturesque, Victorian Watch Hill is a town to stroll about. Make stops at the **Watch Hill Lighthouse** and museum (on a clear day you can see Fishers Island, New York) and, of course, at the famous **Flying Horse Carousel**, one of the nation's oldest merry-go-rounds— its wooden horses were carved in 1867 *(Bay St.)*.

BUNKING DOWN

A terrific option for families planning to vacation here for at least a week is renting a beach cottage. Go to "realty/rentals" under "accomodations" at www.southcountyri.com

Breezeway Resort Motel
★★★/$$-$$$

This pleasant, family-owned resort provides a break from the bustle of Misquamicut Beach, just a short walk away. Kids like splashing in the on-site fountains; there also are colorful gardens, swings, a shuffleboad court, and a large outdoor heated pool. *70 Winnepaug Rd., Misquamicut; (800) 462-8872; (401) 348-8953.*

Cottrell Homestead ★/$-$$

If you long for the slower pace of farm life, consider staying at one of Rhode Island's last remaining dairy farms. Though rooms are modest, you'll feel like part of the farm family as you eat Mrs. Cottrell's home-cooked breakfasts, examine the blue ribbons the family has won at state fairs, and meander to the barn to see the Ayrshire cattle. *500 Waites Corner Rd., S. Kingstown; (401) 783-8665.*

Hamilton Village Inn
★★/$

If ratings were based exclusively on cleanliness, this roadside motel would earn four stars. This is one of the rare places that doesn't jack up its rates in the high season. Guests have access to an off-site swimming pool at Wickford Shipyard, and the Station House restaurant is next door. *642 Boston Neck Rd., N. Kingstown; (401) 295-0700.*

Sandy Shore Motel & Apartments ★★/$$

The beach is your backyard at this family-owned lodge at Misquamicut Beach. Families can choose one- or two-bedroom apartments with kitchenettes or standard motel rooms (there are minimum-stay requirements in summer). *149 Atlantic Ave., Misquamicut; (401) 596-5616.*

Village Inn
★★★/$

This gray-shingled inn, across the street from Narragansett Beach, offers many rooms with water views and balconies, an indoor pool, and an on-site restaurant with a deck. It abuts Pier Marketplace, a shopping area with a movie theater, ice-cream parlor (Nana's), and more. The only downside: heavy tourist traffic makes this a noisy place to rest your heads. *One Beach St., Narragansett; (800) THE-PIER; (401) 783-6767.*

GOOD EATS

Aunt Carrie's ★★/$$

Don't even think of coming to town without stopping here. For genera-tions, this restaurant (once a small lemonade stand run by a Mom of six, Carrie Cooper) has lured fam-ilies to Narragansett with its scrump tious clam cakes and chowder. So set up your chairs on the grassy lawn by the bay, and watch the boats sail by as you eat. *1240 Ocean Rd., Narragansett; (401) 783-7930.*

Champlin's ★★★/$-$$

This waterfront eatery in the fishing village of Galilee lures you with its generous portions of fried seafood (plus hot dogs and hamburgers), the ultracasual atmosphere (you can wear your bathing suit), and the views. Pick a table on the deck and watch the lobstermen, ferries, and tour boats in action. *Great Island Rd., Galilee; (401) 783-3152.*

Gregg's ★★★/$

Treat your family to home-cooked meals and mile-high desserts at this local favorite. *4120 Quaker La. (Rte. 2), N. Kingstown; (401) 294-5700.*

Lenny & Joe's Fish Tale ★★★/$$

This seafood lovers outpost dishes out tasty clams, lobster, scallops, shrimp, and more. If the kids don't want seafood, they can dig into franks or burger platters from their own menu. *138 Granite St., Westerly; (401) 348-9941.*

Picnic Basket ★/$

If you feel like having a picnic, stop here for supplies. For the kids, the dozens of to-go (or eat in) offerings include pizza slices and PB&J; Mom and Dad can choose from an equally large adult selection, includ-ing hummus-tabbouleh roll-ups and turkey and cranberry sandwiches. *20 Kingston Rd., Narragansett; (401) 782-2284.*

Tinsel Town

Any time of year, climb aboard a Belgian-style sleigh for a ride through the woods in the rural town of Essex. Since the sleds have wheels, you don't need snow to enjoy the journey. Afterward, you (Mom or Dad) may want to wander through the **Christmas House,** which bills itself as New England's largest year-round "holiday" gift shop, but you may want to leave the kids outside, due to the number of breakables. *1557 Ten Rod Rd. (Rte. 165), Exeter; (401) 397-4255.*

Pizza Place ★★★/$

Say cheese! This pizza spot is one of the most appealing in the area. While you're waiting for your thin-crust pies, kids can roam comfortably in the spacious dining room. All the familiar toppings are here, along with some more exotic ones, such as clams, pineapple, and barbecue chicken. *43 Broad St., Westerly; (401) 348-1803.*

Shell Painting

With rounded frames and smooth, chalklike surfaces that soak up paint, seashells make good palm-size canvases for your children's seascapes.

MATERIALS

♦ Seashells (chalkier, white shells work best)

♦ Jar of freshwater (for rinsing shells and mixing paint)

♦ Watercolor or acrylic paints and brushes

To start, rinse a few shells with freshwater and let them dry in the sun. Your child can paint pictures on the inside of each shell, being careful to let each color dry before adding the next for a crisp picture, or letting the colors blend for an abstract splash of color. Set out in the sun until dry.

Sea View Station ★★/$

Enjoy home cooking while you're on vacation at this immaculate family restaurant next to the old Sea View Railroad trolley tracks. Your kids will love their menu: "huge half-pound monster dogs unleashed from the grill," "swamp Yankee meat loaf," and other under-12 faves (kids' meals come with ice cream). Mom and Dad can feast on fresh-baked loaves of aromatic bread, railroad-themed breakfasts (the Motorman's special is a breakfast bonanza), johnnycakes, beef stew, and decadent desserts. *640 Boston Neck Rd. (Rte. 1A), N. Kingstown; (401) 295-8666.*

Station House Restaurant ★★/$

This pleasant, reasonably priced restaurant, near the South County bike path, is a great place to try johnnycakes (made with carpenter's grist white flint cornmeal), savory omelettes, burgers, and sandwiches. *3711 Kingstown Rd., S. Kingstown; (401) 783-0800.*

Term's ★★/$-$$

Better come early. Lines at this pub, a short walk from Narragansett Beach, snake out the door. Catering to a mix of locals and visitors, this place tempts young guests with hamburgers, grilled cheese, and ravioli, while their folks can choose from a selection of home-cooked pasta dinners, seafood platters, and meat entrées. *135 Boon St., Narragansett; (401) 782-4242.*

TOY TIDBIT

In 1952, Rhode Island–based Hasbro invented Mr. Potato Head.
The original toy kits only included pieces (ears, noses, eyes)—
children used real potatoes for the body.

SOUVENIR HUNTING

MUST-SEE FamilyFun The Fantastic Umbrella Factory

MUST-SEE Built in 1968, this unusual shopping enclave bills itself as a "19th Century Farmyard Paradise." During your visit you can wander through fragrant gardens and meet emus, sheep, and ornamental pheasants (for a quarter, you can buy a bag of feed), and shop for everything from penny candy and silly string to feather boas and cats'-eye marbles in the main store. *4820 Old Post Rd., Charlestown; (401) 364-6616.*

Juggles

This place features fun, educational gifts you can't find at big malls. The helpful staff knows the products and can help you select the toy that's right for your child. Summer months are highlighted by hour-long craft programs (you can make a volcano, for example); there's a nominal charge. *5600 Post Rd., E. Greenwich; (401) 885-4578; 560 Kingstown Rd., Wakefield; (401) 783-5778.*

Kenyon Cornmeal Company

If you've become addicted to johnnycakes during your visit, you can make them at home with a sack of Johnny Cake Corn Meal, manufactured using granite millstones since 1711 by this historic company. The folks at the company store, right across from the red clapboard gristmill, will be happy to supply recipes. *Glenrock Rd., South Kingstown; (800) 7-KENYON.*

World Store

If you like toys and activities that focus on nature, try this shop, also in Wickford Village. It sells hanging toy monkeys with Velcro feet you can attach around your waist, plus old-fashioned ant farms, and fossils. *16 W. Main St., Wickford; (401) 295-0081.*

On WaterFire nights, Providence's waterfront looks a bit like a festival in Venice.

Greater Providence

ON A SUMMER SATURDAY night, spectators jam Providence's waterfront for a firey display. As dreamy, rhythmic music pulses, more than 100 bonfires mounted in braziers atop the Providence River exude the heady scent of burning cedar logs. As gondolas float under the moon, children dance by waterways, mesmerized by the magical reflections on the water. For many families, this popular celebration, known as WaterFire, is one of the reasons for planning a family visit to Providence.

Thanks to a multimillion-dollar effort to rejuvenate this historic city, several other new attractions beckon as well. Besides WaterFire (which runs from April to October; log on to www.waterfire.org for dates and times), this so-called Renaissance City, home to Brown University and the Rhode Island School of Design has a new family-oriented all-season skating rink, an interactive children's museum, a massive new mall, and a series of Venetian-style footbridges that make a downtown walk seem like a brief trip to Italy.

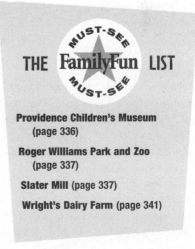

THE FamilyFun LIST

MUST-SEE
MUST-SEE

Providence Children's Museum (page 336)

Roger Williams Park and Zoo (page 337)

Slater Mill (page 337)

Wright's Dairy Farm (page 341)

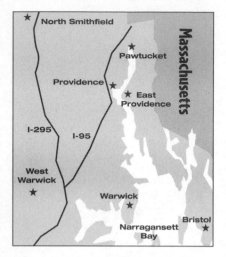

As always, one of the best reasons to bring kids to Providence remains Roger Williams Park, named for the city's independent-minded founder (see page 337). Staying in Providence comes at a cost, however. Room rates in the city are typically higher than those in surrounding areas, so you may want to visit the city for the day and perhaps stay in nearby hotel- and chain-restaurant-rich Warwick.

North of Providence, in Pawtucket, you'll want to make a stop at Slater Mill and Slater Memorial Park for an afternoon that nicely mixes history and relaxation.

CULTURAL ADVENTURES

Providence Children's Museum
★★★★/$

Head to Providence's jewelry district (the city was once the world's costume jewelry capital) for a day of fun at this 7,000-square-foot playground, packed with hands-on activities for even the youngest children. In seven themed areas, kids can climb down a manhole and explore the underworld at City Streets, build fountains and float boats in Water Ways, and meet immigrants from four different countries in Coming to Rhode

BAY PLAY

One of the reasons folks journey to Rhode Island is to play on Narragansett Bay, a watery playground filled with coves, islands, and beaches, which accounts for a quarter of the state's total area. Your family can explore the bay on an adventure sponsored by Save the Bay, a Providence-based environmental organization: hop in a kayak for a guided tour, try snorkeling around Point Judith (ages 6 and up), board a schooner and belt out sea chanteys, sign on for a seal-watch cruise aboard the *Brandaris,* or spend the day fishing. The organization frequently partners with area institutions, such as Connecticut's Mystic Aquarium, for special programs. *For price information and a schedule, call (401) 272-3540.*

Island. At Littlewoods, kids ages 4 and under can crawl through a cave, climb a tree, and try on animal costumes. There's a children's garden outside, and the museum hosts dragon hunts, crafts classes, a circus school, and themed teas throughout the year. *100 South St., Providence; (401) 273-KIDS.*

Slater Mill
FamilyFun ★★★/$

A visit to this national treasure shows how a visionary inventor named Samuel Slater built America's first water-powered cotton spinning mill in Pawtucket in 1793. So successful was his experiment, it spawned mills throughout Connecticut, Massachusetts, and Rhode Island, launching the Industrial Revolution. Here, kids can watch a 200-year-old machine spin cotton thread, see how a cotton gin processes fibers, and watch the waterwheel harness power from the Blackstone River. In the Sylvanus Brown House, kids glimpse the rather dreary lifestyles of families of the period, by stepping into their spare living quarters and learning about daily tasks. Youngsters particularly like watching guides turn strawlike flax into thread. The old-time gift shop features tin whistles, bracelets made by the woven braider machine, and souvenir bookmarks made on the narrow fabric loom. *67 Roosevelt Ave., Pawtucket; (401) 725-8638.*

JUST FOR FUN

Colt State Park ★★★/Free
This 464-acre paradise, on the shore of Narragansett Bay, offers four miles of hiking trails, six picnic groves, gardens, scenic kite-flying spots, and a three-mile bike loop that winds by pastoral coves and marshes. Swimming, however, is off-limits. *Rte. 114, Bristol; (401) 253-7482; www.riparks.com/colt.htm*

Fleet Skating Center ★★/$-$$
Twice the size of the skating rink in New York City's Rockefeller Center, Providence's 14,000-square-foot beauty invites families to take a spin "around town." Skaters glide across the downtown rink to the rhythm of loud, energizing music, taking in views of the historic Providence Biltmore and other downtown landmarks. Night skating is particularly fun, with the illuminated Art Deco office tower locally known as the Superman Building glowing in the dark. Ice-skating season is from October to March, in-line skating from April to September. Skate rentals are available. *2 Kennedy Plaza, Providence; (401) 331-5544; www.fleetskating.com*

Roger Williams
FamilyFun Park ★★★/Free-$

The hub of family activity in warm weather, this 430-acre Victorian park dotted with small scenic lakes is a city treasure. Besides the zoo (*see below*), the park features a Museum of Natural History with a planetarium, paddleboat rentals, a bandstand with summer concerts, and trolley rides. Carousel Village, a minipark for young children, offers a carousel, bumper boats, a miniature-golf course with model-size Rhode Island landmarks, a playground, and pony rides. Many families make a day of it, spending the morning at the zoo, and relaxing the rest of the day at the park. Admission to the park is free, but you need to buy tokens for individual attractions. To save money, buy a park pass, which includes zoo admission and several park activities for one price. *Elmwood Ave., Providence; (401) 467-0150.*

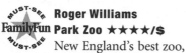 **Roger Williams Park Zoo ★★★★/$**
New England's best zoo, nationally recognized for its expan-

sive, naturalistic exhibits, lets kids come nose to nose with 160 species of rare animals. Youngsters love watching the elephants and ostriches in the Plains of Africa exhibit, seeing the polar bears swim in the underwater viewing area, and spotting snow leopards, moon bears, and other exotic creatures along the Marco Polo Trail. If you're going to other attractions in Roger Williams Park besides the zoo, consider buying a money-saving park pass. *1000 Elmwood Ave., Providence; (401) 785-3510;* www.rogerwilliamsparkzoo.org

Slater Memorial Park
★★/$

For families, this city park offers just the right blend of history and recreation. On a sunny afternoon, you can play tennis, rent paddleboats, ride the historic Looff carousel (see page 352), go horseback riding, or tour the historic Daggett House, the Revolutionary War–era home of General Nathaniel Green. Admission to the park is free, with nominal fees for activities. *Newport Ave., Rte. 1A, Pawtucket; (401) 728-0500.*

BUNKING DOWN

Providence Biltmore
★★★/$$$

Built in 1922, this historic landmark features 130 junior suites. The location—just across the street from the Fleet Skating Center—can't be beat,

---

FamilyFun TIP

Last Picture Show

Load your car with a cooler, lawn chairs, and sleeping bags, and join dozens of local families for an evening at **Rustic Drive-In** *(Rte. 146, North Smithfield; 410/769-7601),* Rhode Island's last operative drive-in theater. Hear the soundtrack by tuning the dial on your car radio or sit outside with a portable radio set up on the hood.

though be aware that if you're staying in a room overlooking the rink, the music can be loud. There's no pool here, but for recreation, it's an easy walk to the Providence Place Mall. *Kennedy Plaza, Providence; (800) 294-7799;* www.providence biltmore.com

Providence Marriott ★★/$$$
This hotel has a large indoor/outdoor pool that's popular with families, and you can bring your pet; another plus: the on-site Bluefin Grill offers a kids' menu at every meal. *1 Orms St., Providence; (800) 228-9290;* www.marriott.com

Sheraton Providence Airport ★★/$$
Though it caters primarily to a business clientele, this is a fine place for families who want a break from Providence's high hotel prices. New sleigh beds adorn every room, there's an indoor pool, complimentary breakfast is served daily, and there's a free shuttle to T. F. Green Airport, which is next door. *1850 Post Rd., Warwick; (401) 738-4000;* www. sheraton.com

Spring Hill Suites ★★/$$
Located just off the highway in an industrial park, this spot isn't going to win any prizes for ambience. But it's a fine base camp for families, and the rates are reasonable. The two-room suites have a bedroom and lounge area with a kitchenette

Row Your Boat

Providence isn't just a walking city—it's a rowing city. **Paddle Providence,** on the Providence Riverwalk, rents canoes and kayaks and can provide instruction as well. Beginners may want to paddle around for an hour along the Providence River, while advanced paddlers might take a trip out to Narragansett Bay or the Weekonk River. The company also offers canoe and kayak tours in Providence and throughout the state, tailoring custom trips to your family's interests. The organization even rents ten-person "war canoes," perfect for family reunions. *(401) 453-1622.*

(including a refrigerator and microwave), and each room has a TV. Operated by the Marriott Corporation, the property offers laundry facilities, a heated indoor pool, and a complimentary shuttle bus to the nearby airport. Kids will enjoy the afternoon snack of milk and cookies. *14 James P. Murphy Hwy., W. Warwick; (401) 732-6667;* www.marriott.com

GOOD EATS

Angelo's ★★/$
Mangia! At this family-oriented restaurant in the heart of Providence's Little Italy, you order home-cooked delicacies at prices so

low you'll feel as if you're in a time warp. Most kids are happy with the spaghetti and meatballs, plus there are meatball sandwiches, ravioli, fried peppers, and daily specials. Don't forget a colorful spumoni ice cream for dessert; there's also chocolate pudding and vanilla ice cream. *141 Atwells Ave., Providence; (401) 621-8171.*

Cheesecake Factory
★★/$-$$

With more than 200 items on the menu, everyone will find something they like at this casually elegant eatery that dishes up a whole lot more than cheesecake. You'll find barbecue chicken-topped pizza, California omelette, Baja fish tacos, and bodacious burgers. Of course, save room for the signature dessert; kids might prefer a hot fudge sundae, mud pie, or the giant brownie ice cream sandwich. *94 Providence Pl., Providence; (401) 270-4010.*

Fire + Ice: An Improvisational Grill
★★★★/$$

Let your kids make their own meals at this snazzy hot spot at the Providence Place Mall. Encouraged by signs inviting diners to create, savor and design, you wander through a food bar, filling your bowl with a custom combo of fresh vegetables and noodles, and chunks of beef, chicken, and seafood. After selecting one of 14 marinades from the sauce counter, bring your din-

ner to the 25-foot circular grill, where the chefs cook it as you watch. That's the "fire" part; the "ice" part comes from the salad bar, where you can create your own leafy masterpieces. *42 Providence Pl., Providence (with locations in Boston and Cambridge); (401) 270-4040.*

Gregg's ★★★/$

Everything a family could want in a restaurant, this place offers a casual, kid-loving atmosphere, home-cooked favorites at reasonable prices, friendly staff, activities for the kids, and humongous desserts. Kids' fare ranges from Red Riding Hood (spaghetti and meatballs) to Humpty Dumpty (a hamburger plate), while adults can feast on mile-high meat loaf, California roll-ups, and portobello focaccia. Save room for the chocolate layer cake. In the Providence area, the locations are at *1303 N. Main St., Providence (401/831-5700); 1940 Pawtucket Ave., E. Providence (401/438-5700); and 1359 Post Rd., Warwick (401/467-5700).*

Modern Diner ★★★/$

Since you're in the state that pioneered the American diner, this place is a must. A sterling streamliner from the 1930s, it's the first diner in the nation to be listed on the National Register of Historic Places. Seating is a bit cramped, but go anyway: this is the place to try a "coffee cabinet" (local lingo for a milk shake), plus homemade beef stew, burgers, meat loaf, or breakfast, which is served all day. *364 East Ave., Pawtucket; (401) 726-8390.*

Spike's Junkyard Dogs ★/$

If you're a fan of franks, head to this casual spot for lip-smacking, 100-percent all-beef dogs served on fresh-baked buns. Purists will want to order the Mutt (a plain dog), while more adventurous eaters might try the Samurai Dog (teriyaki sauce and sautéed onions) or the Buffalo Dog (buffalo wing sauce, blue cheese, and scallions). *273 Thayer St., Providence; (401) 454-1459.*

Wright's Farm Restaurant ★★★★/$

For a true family dining experience, try a Blackstone Valley tradition known as "chicken, family style." The meal consists of communal bowls of chicken so tender that it falls off the bone, served with fried potatoes or French fries, macaroni with rich tomato sauce, and dinner rolls. Of the dozens of Valley restaurants that dish out chicken family style, Wright's is one of the better known. This dining landmark can accommodate up to 2,000 diners, many of whom come from miles around to feast on the succulent, all-you-can-eat dinners. *84 Inman Rd., Nasonville, about 10 miles northeast of North Smithfield; (401) 769-2856.*

SOUVENIR HUNTING

Brown & Hopkins Country Store

The nation's oldest continuously operating general store (1809) features penny candy—as well as some that costs more. Clerks will happily fill your kids' brown bags with black licorice, root beer barrels, and gumballs, which cost a penny to a quarter each. Youngsters also will gravitate to the jump ropes, wooden yo-yos, and jewelry-making kits. *1179 Putnam Pike (Rte. 44), Chepachet, 8 miles northeast of North Smithfield; (401) 568-4830.*

MUST-SEE FamilyFun MUST-SEE Wright's Dairy Farm

For generations, this working dairy farm has produced quality milk and whipped-cream pastries, which you can buy in the bakery by the barn. Try to visit around 3:30 P.M. so you can watch the farmhands milk the cows. *200 Woonsocket Hill Rd., N. Smithfield; (800) 222-9734; (401) 767-3014.*

Connecticut

FAMILIES WHO ARE short on time but who long to share some vacation fun together find Connecticut to be the ideal retreat. The third-smallest state in the union, the Constitution State is just 60 miles long north to south and 100 miles east to west. Within three hours, you can drive between its two farthest points.

Small it may be, but Connecticut offers more than its share of four-star family attractions: dinosaurs (at Dinosaur State Park in Rocky Hill) dolphins, sharks, and sea lions (at two major aquariums), beaches (two miles of sandy shoreline at

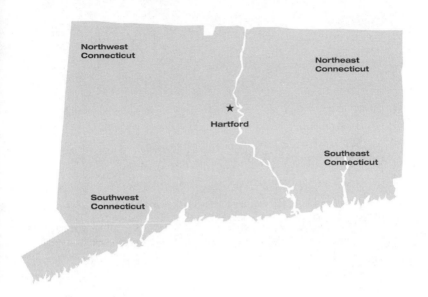

Northwest Connecticut

Northeast Connecticut

★ Hartford

Southeast Connecticut

Southwest Connecticut

Hammonassett State Beach in Madison, for instance), camping (in the Litchfield Hills), and amusement parks (two family theme parks). Connecticut is also packed with cultural offerings: visit an awesome children's museum, ramble around America's first town green, explore Mark Twain's home, and join a scavenger hunt at the nation's oldest public art museum.

In the countryside, families can ride a vintage steam train and then explore the Connecticut River by riverboat or milk a cow at one of the state's 4,100 farms. And Connecticut's 91 state parks and 30 state forests mean you're never far from a place where your family can have the landscape all to yourselves.

ATTRACTIONS

$	under $10
$$	$10 - $20
$$$	$20 - $30
$$$$	$30 +

HOTELS/MOTELS/CAMPGROUNDS

$	under $100
$$	$100 - $200
$$$	$200 - $300
$$$$	$300 +

RESTAURANTS

$	under $10
$$	$10 - $20
$$$	$20 - $30
$$$$	$30 +

FAMILYFUN RATED

★	Fine
★★	Good
★★★	Very Good
★★★★	FamilyFun Recommended

Depending on the season, your family can watch maple sugaring, sheep shearing, and cider making, or pick your own apples, peaches, and pumpkins here.

Southwest Connecticut

ONNECTICUT'S southern-most communities—Greenwich, Stamford, Darien—feel much more like an extension of New York City than a piece of New England. (They're closer to the Big Apple, too, with Greenwich just 30 miles from Times Square.) Heading north on I-95, your first stop is Fairfield County, home to Fortune 500 companies, New York City commuters, trophy homes, gleaming skyscrapers, and elite downtowns packed with pricey boutiques and chichi restaurants.

Despite the quick pace, southwest Connecticut remains a great family destination. In South Norwalk (also known as SoNo, Connecticut's version of New York's arty SoHo) you can visit Stepping Stones, Connecticut's best children's museum, a palace of hands-on wizardry and creative design, while at the city's Maritime Aquarium, you can meet sharks and seals and take in a film in the IMAX theater. In Bridgeport, stop in at the Barnum Museum, shrine to the city's flamboyant, one-time mayor, P. T. Barnum.

THE **FamilyFun** LIST

MUST-SEE
MUST-SEE

The Maritime Aquarium at Norwalk, South Norwalk (page 351)

Peabody Museum of Natural History at Yale (page 348)

Stepping Stones Museum for Children, South Norwalk (page 349)

345

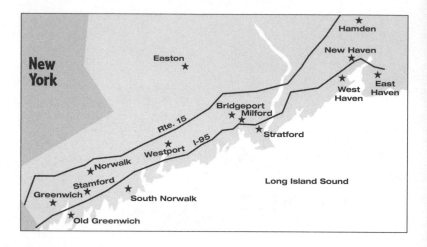

Just east of Fairfield County is New Haven, cultural mecca and site of Yale University. Just walking on the town's 16-acre green—the nation's first planned town green, expertly laid out with nine perfect squares—and roaming around Yale's Gothic campus will stimulate your brain cells. You'll also want to stop by Yale's Peabody Museum, which lures 35,000 kids a year to gaze in awe at gargantuan dinosaur skeletons.

The New Haven area is home to many a marvelous invention, including Eli Whitney's cotton gin (visit his namesake museum in Hamden), the lollipop (made in 1892 when George C. Smith of the Bradley Smith Candy Company plugged sticks into candy balls), and American football (invented in 1879 by Yale football captain, Walter Camp). And what kid wouldn't adore a town that invented pizza and the hamburger?

You can taste these kid-pleasing creations at the very places where they were conceived. At Louis' Lunch (see page 356), birthplace of the hamburger sandwich in 1900, you can still get a broiled beef patty served between two slices of toast. The first American pizza can also be traced back to 1900 and New Haven. Frank Pepe created the popular pie using a recipe he brought from Italy. Families still line up and wait for hours at Pepe's Pizzeria (see page 356).

Educational opportunities abound on Long Island Sound as well. From Stamford, you can sail out to Sheffield Lighthouse and climb up its old tower for spectacular views. You can also take an ecology cruise and examine crabs and jellyfish. New Haven is home port to *Amistad*, a reproduction of the Spanish cargo vessel *Amistad*. Here, families can learn the powerful, true story that inspired Steven Spielberg's movie of the same name made in Southern New England. The tale dates back to 1839, when the Spanish kidnapped 50 Africans, intending to sell them into slavery in Cuba. While aboard the slave vessel, the Africans seized the ship and ultimately sailed it to New Haven Harbor. Instead of finding freedom, they were jailed pending a U.S. Supreme Court ruling that allowed them to return home. Your family can witness this struggle during a visit to *Amistad (call Amistad America for details, 203/495-1839).* To complete the experience, make the pilgrimage to the 14-foot-tall *Amistad* Memorial *(165 Church St.),* the exact site where the Africans were jailed prior to the Supreme Court ruling.

Despite Southwest Connecticut's pricey reputation, you can still find rooms for reasonable rates. Most hotels cater to business crowds during the week and have excellent rates for families on weekends. New Haven also offers a VIP pass, good for discounts on several attractions and performances. *Call (800) 332-STAY; (203) 777-8550; or log on to* www.newhaven cvb.org

CULTURAL ADVENTURES

Barnum Museum ★★/$

The Barnum Museum chronicles the life and times of Bridgeport native Phineas Taylor Barnum (1810–1891), the showman who created America's first great circus. Though the museum could use some refreshing and more interactive exhibits, kids will still find plenty to entertain them. Say hello to Baby Bridgeport, a replica of the 700-pound pachyderm that set the record for smallest performing circus elephant. Discover Tom Thumb, another Bridgeport native who became one of Barnum's most successful performers. (His miniature carriages and costumes are on display.) Periodically, the museum hosts special family programs. *820 Main St., Bridgeport; (203) 331-1104.*

P.T. BARNUM was able to read his obituary in the newspaper before he died. After Barnum stated that the press only said good things about people after they had died, the *New York Sun* ran the circus man's obituary on the front page. The headline stated "Great and Only Barnum—He Wanted to Read His Obituary—Here it Is."

Discovery Museum
★★★/$

A combination fine arts gallery, science center, and children's museum, this attraction has more than 100 hands-on exhibits. Witness the power of a lightning bolt, gaze at stars at the on-site planetarium, and learn key science concepts while shooting basketball. The gem here is the Challenger Learning Center, created in memory of the astronauts who perished in 1986 on the space shuttle *Challenger*. Here, on a journey to Mars, kids can team up in a mission control and space station to perform experiments, collect data, and monitor their trip. The missions are available to families (with children ages 10 and up) on Saturdays; advance reservations are necessary; there's an additional fee. *4450 Park Ave., Bridgeport; (203) 372-3521;* www.discoverymuseum.org

Eli Whitney Museum
★★★/$-$$

Inspired by the New Haven genius who invented the cotton gin, this unusual museum (at this site of Whitney's first factory) will bring out your kids' entrepreneurial spirit. At weekend workshops, you can make pinball machines, galimotos (West African car toys), and rubber-band-powered cars. All inventing is done under the guidance of creative instructors who encourage clanging, banging, and out-of-the-box thinking. Geared to kids ages 7 to 12,

the museum includes an outdoor water-learning lab and a covered bridge leading to hiking trails. *915 Whitney Ave., Hamden; (203) 777-1833;* www.eliwhitney.org

Garbage Museum
★★/$

Every second, Americans throw away six tons of trash. That grim statistic takes on a playful, educational edge at this trashy treasure, where hands-on exhibits teach kids how to preserve our natural resources. You'll meet Trash-o-saurus, a 24-foot-long dino made entirely of refuse, and get to test your knowledge of environmental issues by playing the Trash Bash. Ever wonder how recyclables are processed? Just take a walk, over the 125-foot-long, glass-enclosed skywalk, to the local recycling center. *1410 Honeyspot Rd. Ext., Stratford; (203) 381-9571.*

Peabody Museum of Natural History at Yale
MUST-SEE FamilyFun MUST-SEE ★★★★/$

Though a bit dusty, this site houses one of the region's best collections of dinosaur skeletons. Thousands of schoolchildren travel here annually to roam through the Great Hall of Dinosaurs, where you can see the skeletons of a brontosaurus, stegosaurus, and the largest known fossil turtle, archelon ischyros. The humongous dinosaur mural, painted from 1940 to 1942 by Rudolph Zallinger, is almost reason enough to visit. Though many of the museum's 2,000 objects are solely for viewing, there is a bustling hands-on discovery lab where kids can touch fossils, tree bark, and the tooth of a Tyrannosaurus rex. Kids also go for the exhibit on ancient Egypt, fascinated by its two mummies. Stop by the gift shop for chocolate fossils, amber candy imbedded with real insects, and edible crickets. *Yale University. 170 Whitney Ave., New Haven; (203) 432-5050;* www.peabody.yale.edu

Shoreline Trolley Museum
★★★/$

A favorite of grandparents and grandkids, this National Historic Landmark offers the chance to take a three-mile round trip ride along the tracks of the oldest suburban trolley line in the United States. Though the ride is the fun part, you might also want to take time to explore the nearly 100 classic trolleys and poke around in the gift shop. Open Memorial Day to Labor Day. *17 River St., E. Haven; (203) 467-6927.* The **Connecticut Trolley Museum** *(58 North Rd., E. Windsor; 860/627-6540)* also offers three-mile rides on antique streetcars, but the overall facility isn't as polished.

Stamford Museum and Nature Center
★★★/$

Any time of year, you'll find family events on tap at this nature lover's retreat, where you can meet sheep, pigs, and peacocks at Heckscher Farm; stroll by a stream on a 300-foot-long boardwalk; study Native American culture at the People of the Dawn exhibit; take in a planetarium show; and even wander through a colorful art gallery. Depending on the season, special events may include horse-drawn wagon rides, sled-dog demonstrations, maple-sugaring, and sheepshearing. *39 Scofieldtown Rd., Stamford; (203) 322-1646;* www.stamfordmuseum.org

MUST-SEE FamilyFun Stepping Stones Museum for Children
★★★★/$

As soon as you set foot in the door, you know you've found a place that will keep children stimulated for hours. Your first view is of kids spinning the gears of a colorful, 27-foot-tall kinetic sculpture—and enjoying every second. This place has rein-

FamilyFun TIP

Wind Bags

Getting a homemade kite off the ground doesn't get much easier than this quick trick. First, tie together the handles of a plastic shopping bag with an end of a ball of string. Staple a few 2-foot lengths of ribbon to the bottom of the bag for kite tails. As you run, and the bag fills with air, slowly let out the string and the kite should begin to soar and dive.

vented the concept of children's museums by offering fresh, imaginative exhibits in space designed to pack fun into every square inch. Highlights include Waterscape, where kids don rain gear and conduct aqueous experiments; In the Works, where you can construct race cars and perform time tests; and I Spy Connecticut, where you can fly a helicopter, submerge in a submarine, and ride a train past the state's landmarks. *303 West Ave., Norwalk; (203) 899-0606.*

JUST FOR FUN

Beardsley Zoo
★★★/$

Connecticut's biggest zoo, this 33-acre property is easy to get around, well maintained, and has plenty to see, including wolves, ocelots, toucans, and Siberian tigers. Snakes and exotic monkeys make their home in the Rainforest Building, and goats and bunnies occupy the New England farmyard. Peacocks strut

their stuff and, when the wildflowers are in bloom, this is a lovely place for a picnic. There's a carousel in an enclosed pavilion, plus children's performances and other special events. *1875 Noble Ave., Bridgeport; (203) 394-6565;* www.beardsley zoo.org

Captain's Cove Seaport
★★★★/Free-$$

Since 1982, Captain's Cove has morphed from a vacant lot into a premier tourist attraction complete with boardwalk, Victorian and colonial shops, a kid-friendly dockside restaurant, and intriguing historical vessels. A fun, casual place to spend the afternoon, Captain's Cove blends maritime history with entertainment, routinely hosting concerts and festivals. In the 400-seat restaurant, kids can order cheeseburgers and clams and see a 40-foot model of the RMS *Titanic* suspended over the upstairs dance floor. For an adventure in Black Rock Harbor, board the *Chief* (a 40-foot Navy launch) and travel to Black Rock Lighthouse and Penfield Lighthouse. You can also climb aboard the lightship *Nantucket,* a floating lighthouse referred to as the Statue of Liberty of the Sea. Captain's Cove is the home port of the tall ship *Rose,* a reconstruction of a 1757 British frigate. If she's in port, stop by for a visit. *One Bostwick Ave., Bridgeport; (203) 335-1433;* www.captainscove seaport.com

Draw That Tune

Music has inspired many great artists. See how it moves your young Picassos. Sing standards, or turn the radio on, and let your kids draw whatever they hear. Oldies and country stations seem to work best: kids won't automatically know all the words, so they'll have to listen quietly, and you won't worry about lyrics you wouldn't want to see illustrated by anyone — particularly by your own children.

Some of these old lyrics are the silliest to draw — did you ever wonder what Benny and the Jets, Lucy in the Sky, or Superfly looks like? Others can be misinterpreted in a way that's more hysterical than motivational. You might find your kids have drawn a bathroom on the right (instead of a "bad moon on the rise") or Michael rowing his boat ashore to get a noodle ("Hallelujah!").

Connecticut Audubon Society at Milford Point ★★/Free

This is a place to stroll along a boardwalk and climb up a 40-foot tower for a beautiful view of Long Island Sound and the lower Housatonic River—there's no kite-flying, swimming, or picnicking here. Inside, kids can spy on creatures in an ocean tank, draw pictures of wildlife, and peer through telescopes at seabirds. (This is one of the top ten coastal birding sites in the east.) You can even register for a canoe trip (two and a half or three and a half hours) or one of many family programs. *1 Milford Point Rd., Milford; (203) 878-7440.*

Lighthouse Point Park ★★/$$

In summer, carloads of cooler-toting families head for this 82-acre site along Long Island Sound for a day of playing on the beach, hiking on nature trails, cooking burgers on the grill, and riding the historic carousel in the waterside pavilion. In winter, the park hosts a popular holiday lights display. *Lighthouse Rd., New Haven; (203) 946-8005.*

FamilyFun MUST-SEE The Maritime Aquarium at Norwalk ★★★★/$

This aquarium delivers a triple whammy. Here you can see dozens of species of sea life, embark on a marine-life discovery cruise, and view a cool movie in the IMAX theater—one of the only theaters of its kind in Connecticut. The aquarium is housed in an old iron foundry, in the oyster capital of the northeast. Highlights include a pair of playful otters, a 110,000-gallon shark tank where you can view sharp-toothed specimens up to nine feet long, the seal pool where gregarious harbor seals are fed three times daily, and a touch tank where kids can handle clams and spider crabs. On cruises, aboard the *Oceanic*, you and your

MERRY CAROUSELS

NEW ENGLAND is blessed with vintage carousels that transport young passengers to another time. Here's a selection of family favorites; to learn more about the historic amusements, visit the New England Carousel Museum (see page 362). Carousel hours are seasonal, so call before you go.

Bushnell Park Carousel. Take a spin on a 1914 Stein and Goldstein merry-go-round, located in a pavilion with wraparound stained-glass windows. *Bushnell Park, Hartford, Connecticut; (860) 585-5411.*

Charles I.D. Looff Carousel. Travel back to 1895 on a brilliantly restored carousel. Ride on dogs, lions, and horses created by famed designer Charles I.D. Looff. *Slater Memorial Park, Armistice Blvd., Pawtucket, Rhode Island; (401) 728-7420.*

Crescent Park Looff Carousel. The last remnant of a Narragansett Bay amusement park, this carousel features 66 hand-carved horses and figures. It's housed in a pavilion with a stained-glass cupola. *Bullocks Point Ave., Riverside, Rhode Island; (401) 435-7518 or (401) 433-2828.*

Fall River Carousel. Trot on over to the modern Victorian pavilion for a ride on gorgeously restored horses and chariots originally carved by the Philadelphia Toboggan Company. *Battleship Cove, Fall River, Massachusetts; (508) 324-4300.*

Flying Horse Carousel. Little kids can ride this carousel (circa 1879), whose 20 horses are attached to a center frame instead of the floor. As a result, they "fly" during the ride. *Bay Street, Watch Hill, Westerly, Rhode Island; (401) 596-7761.*

Flying Horses Carousel. One of the best reasons to bring kids to Martha's Vineyard is this 1876 carousel, where children can still try to grab the elusive brass ring. *Circuit Ave. at Lake Ave., Oak Bluffs, Massachusetts; (508) 693-9481.*

Holyoke Merry-Go-Round. This restored 1929 carousel boasts 48 hand-carved steeds, two chariots, and 800 lights. *Heritage State Park, Holyoke, Massachusetts; (413) 536-9420.*

Lighthouse Point Park. After you ride on the 1911 carousel, you can swim, hike, and picnic at this 82-acre park along Long Island Sound. *Two Lighthouse Rd., New Haven, Connecticut; (203) 946-8005 or (203) 946-8750.*

kids will spend two and a half hours collecting and examining sea life in Long Island Sound. Reserve tickets in advance. *10 N. Water St., Norwalk; (203) 852-0700;* www.maritime aquarium.org

Schooner Sound Learning
★★★/$$

This nonprofit organization has been introducing families to the wonders of Long Island Sound for 25 years. Join the crew of the 91-foot, gaff-rigged *Quinnipiack* for a three-hour sailing adventure led by enthusiastic educators. While aboard the wooden schooner, you'll learn about the ecology and history of the sound. Call for a schedule. *60 S. Water St., New Haven; (203) 865-1737.*

Sheffield Island
Lighthouse ★★/$$

Get a taste of life as a lighthouse keeper by touring this structure, in service from 1868 to 1902. To reach the lighthouse, board the *Seaport Islander* for a 30-minute trip to Sheffield Island. During your 90-minute island visit, you can hunt for sea glass, enjoy a picnic, and walk along nature trails. Island clambakes —featuring lobster, steamers, and watermelon—are also available. *The ferry runs from May to September and leaves Hope Dock in front of the gazebo, at the intersection of Washington Street and North Water Street in South Norwalk. Call (203) 838-9444.*

Silverman's Farm
★★★/$$

One of the first farms you'll reach after leaving New York, Silverman's is a great spot to pick fresh fruit, pet animals, shop for fresh-baked pastries and pies, and enjoy a glass of cider. Depending on the season, you can gather peaches, apples, and pumpkins, take a haunted hayride, and see the cider press in action. The barnyard features emus, buffalo, pigs, llamas, and exotic French rabbits, some of which you can feed. *451 Sport Hill Rd., Easton; (203) 261-3306;* www.silvermansfarm.com

Sleeping Giant State Park
★★/$$

This park gets its name from its hilly crests, which resemble a sleeping giant. Here, families can hike on 32 miles of trails, pack a picnic, and fish in the Mill River, which is stocked with trout in spring. *200 Mt. Carmel Ave., Hamden; (203) 789-7498.*

SoundWaters ★★★/$$

Similar in mission to Schooner Sound Learning, this nonprofit organization invites families to board a steel-hulled, three-masted schooner for ecology sails. During your three-hour trip, you'll help hoist sails, trawl for creatures, and examine lobsters, flounder, horseshoe crabs, and jellyfish. You'll also add a sea chantey or two to your repertoire. Offered June to October. *1281 Cove Rd., Stamford; (203) 323-1978.*

BUNKING DOWN

Club Hotel at Doubletree
★★/$$

Geared to business travelers during the week, this hotel offers nice weekend rates for families. Kids will like the indoor pool and the treats at the on-site Au Bon Pain Bakery. If Mom or Dad needs to work during the trip, you're all set. The main floor contains spiffy personal offices equipped with chairs, desks, and dataports that you can use during your stay. *789 Connecticut Ave., Norwalk; (203) 853-3477; www. doubletree.com*

Howard Johnson Lodge
★★/$

What more could a kid want? This 165-unit hotel has a playground, indoor and outdoor pools, an on-site miniature-golf course—and the staff provides free activity booklets. For added convenience, rooms come with refrigerators. Located on Route 1 just off I-95, it's a quick drive to kid-pleasing restaurants, including Chili's, Dakota's, and Knickerbockers in the Connecticut Post Mall. *1052 Boston Post Rd., Milford; (800) I-GO-HOJO.*

Hyatt Regency Greenwich
★★★/$$$-$$$$

Here's a chance to stay in a tropical getaway without leaving the country. Step into the lobby—with its four-story atrium, fish-filled pools, and abundance of foliage—and you feel as if you've stumbled upon a fantasy island. In the midst of this lushness is Winfield's, a kid-friendly restaurant whose children's menu features Big Fat Wizard Waffles, Alphabet Soup, and Mountains of Ice Cream. Family packages entitle you to a night in one of 374 renovated rooms, use of the fitness facility (including an indoor pool), and a $25 dining voucher at Winfield's. For an extra fee, the hotel also offers Kidventures, planned activities for kids, including tennis lessons, nature walks, marine studies programs, and outings at the ballpark. *1800 E. Putnam Ave., Old Greenwich; (800) 233-1234; (203) 637-1234; www. hyatt.com*

Stamford Marriott
★★/$$-$$$

Another beautiful corporate hotel, it offers appealing weekend rates to families. Located across the street from the Stamford Town Center shopping complex, the Marriott has an indoor/outdoor pool, kids' menu in the dining room, and cable television in its 500 attractively furnished guest rooms. *Two Stamford Forum, Stamford; (203) 357-9555.*

Westport Inn ★★/$$

The best feature of this hotel is the beautiful indoor pool, which is surrounded by trees and located in a sunlit atrium. Families can opt for contemporary poolside rooms or rooms with a more traditional, country motif. The on-site restaurant serves children's meals. *1595 Post Rd. East, Westport; (800) 446-8997; (203) 259-5236.*

GOOD EATS

Abate ★★/$$

This family restaurant is a nice place to try Italian specialties in popular Wooster Square. The extensive menu includes white clam pizza, spaghetti and meatballs, and sausage calzones. Half portions are available for children. If you have room, split a creamy serving of toasted almond mousse. Mamma mia, is it good! *129 Wooster St., New Haven; (203) 776-4334.*

The Brewhouse
★★/$$

After you've visited Stepping Stones or the Maritime Aquarium, satisfy your appetite at this colossal brew pub, with a festive, upbeat atmosphere. Here, you can watch the brewing process while the kids dip into classics (burgers and grilled cheese) and color pictures. Their meal also includes a chocolate-chip cookie for dessert. The main menu features the usual pub fare, from fish-and-chips and nachos to grilled salmon and burgers. *13 Marshall St., S. Norwalk; (203) 853-9110.*

Chick's Drive-in
★★/$$

Since 1950, seafood lovers have come to this roadside eatery for whole-belly fried clams, split hot dogs, onion rings, and some first-class people-watching. There's no carhop service here—just go to the counter, take a number, pick a table, and watch the swooping seagulls. *183 Beach St., W. Haven; (203) 934-4510.*

Jimmies of Savin Rock
★★★/$$

You know a place is family-friendly when a sign at the entrance says "Always Bring the Children." In 1925, this West Haven institution started serving hot dogs to patrons who'd come to Savin Rock to play at the beachside amusement park. The park perished, but Jimmies grew into an excellent seafood restaurant, appreciated for both its location and its fare. Jimmies sits on a three- and-a-half-mile promenade where families can walk, swim, skate, and fly kites along the beach by Long Island

FamilyFun ACTIVITY

Keep a Trip Journal

On a journey to a new spot, pretend that your family is recording a great expedition, in the spirit of Lewis and Clark, and imagine that you've discovered the place. Have people take turns recording their feelings, plus the weather and wildlife sightings.

HOLD THE KETCHUP

Although ketchup and mustard are taboo at Louis' Lunch, there are three acceptable condiments available at "the birthplace of the burger": cheese, tomato, and onion.

Sound. The kids' menu features hamburgers, BLTs, and more. *5 Rock St., W. Haven; (203) 934-3212.*

Louis' Lunch ★/$

This tiny eatery made a huge impact on the country's obsession with fast food. It was here, in 1900, that Louis Lassen invented the hamburger sandwich (a customer asked for a meal he could eat on the run, and Lassen placed a broiled beef patty between two slices of bread). Today you can eat burgers cooked on the original grill—but don't dare ask for French fries or ketchup. Louis' is for purists. On the downside, the

place has little ambience, and the staff can be brusque; however, it does provide the kids with an edible history lesson. *261–263 Crown St., New Haven; (203) 562-5507.*

New York Ray's
★★★/$$

Families are transported to "New Yawk" for a pizza feast at this themed restaurant, which is decorated like the interior of a subway car. There's even a creepy-looking fare collector in a token booth. The atmosphere is casual and fun, and the pizzas are exceptional. You can order the Hell's Kitchen (lotsa hot peppers), Da' Works (with everything), and Tri-boro (with chicken, sausage, and broccoli), or create your own custom pizza. There are wrap sandwiches, pasta, and seafood dishes, too. *325 Westport Ave., Norwalk; (203) 846-9729.*

Pepe's Pizzeria
★★/$

According to a New Haven legend, in 1900 Frank Pepe introduced the first "tomato pie" to America at this very site. Still drawing crowds after all these years, Pepe's signature is thin-crusted pizza pies with customized toppings baked in the original brick ovens. Lines form early, but it's worth the wait. *157 Wooster St., New Haven; (203) 865-5762.*

Silvermine Tavern
★★★/$$$
Located by a waterfall in a wooded setting, this charming tavern dishes out Yankee pot roast, Cobb chicken salad, and crab cakes. Kids can dig into such specialties as The Turtle (PB&J), The Raccoon (fried chicken nuggets), and The Duck (pasta). All kids' meals include a clown ice cream surprise, plus there are balloons. The Sunday brunch is terrific. In warm weather, the best seats are outside by the waterfall. *194 Perry Ave., Norwalk; (203) 847-4558.*

SOUVENIR HUNTING

Stew Leonard's
With talking cows, singing farm animals, and lots of bells and whistles, Stew Leonard's is part theme park, part mega-market. You can pet animals outside in the small zoo, too. *100 Westport Ave., Norwalk; (203) 847-7213. (In Danbury, visit the store on Federal Rd.; 203/790-8030.)*

Wanda's Sugar Shack
Where would kids be without Wanda? She greets them when they enter, leaves baskets for them by the door to store their treats, and tempts them with chocolate-dipped Oreos. *8 Harbor Walk, Milford; (203) 878-9967.*

Northwest Connecticut is for lovers—nature lovers, that is. Oh, and there are a couple of terrific amusement parks here, as well.

Northwest Connecticut

LOCATED IN THE foothills of Massachusetts' Berkshires, the Litchfield Hills are a 1,000 square-mile nature lover's paradise. Here, you can spy on beavers at their lodge, swim in crystal clear lakes and ponds, camp under enormous evergreens, or pull out your fishing poles and catch some trout.

Though these pursuits may seem tame for some 21st-century children, they're just the ticket for families who want to leave contemporary concerns behind and escape to a landscape defined by white church steeples, sparkling lakes and rivers, and gently rolling hills. In the Litchfield Hills, modern-day commercialization is barely visible. Along beautiful Route 7 in Kent, you can even drive over the covered Bull's Bridge, where one of George Washington's horses fell into the raging Housatonic River in 1781.

(According to Washington's records, it cost $215 to fish out the animal.)

It's no wonder that celebrities such as Meryl Streep, Kevin Bacon, and Michael J. Fox have decided to raise their families here. The area is so photogenic, it might well be a movie set and is also sophisticated, with antiques shops, gourmet restau-

THE FamilyFun LIST

MUST-SEE MUST-SEE

Lake Compounce (page 364)

Quassy Amusement Park (page 365)

White Memorial Foundation and Conservation Center (page 366)

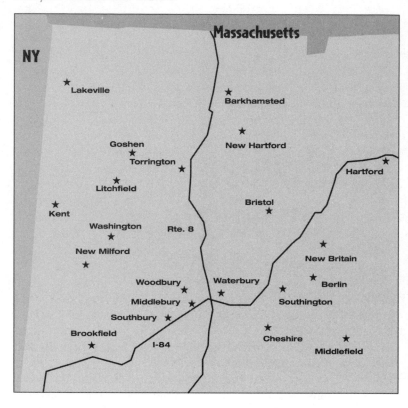

rants, and country inns suited to cultured tastes.

Packed with beautiful forests and parks, the Litchfield Hills are an awesome place to camp, and you can get a list of public and private campgrounds from the Litchfield Hills Visitors Bureau (860/567-4506; www.litchfieldhills.com). If chain hotels are more your preference, you can find them in the area's commercial hub, Torrington (or in neighboring Waterbury or Danbury), and take day trips to the area's small villages.

Though the region's pleasures tend toward the low-key and old-fashioned, things are not all quiet on the northwest front. Connecticut's two major theme parks—Quassy Amusement Park in Woodbury and Lake Compounce on the Bristol/Southington line—are both in the Litchfield Hills area, and they're two of the best reasons for families to visit this section of the state. Both abut gorgeous lakes, so kids can ride wacky roller coasters and cool off at the beach in one delicious afternoon.

You'll also find a fair share of cultural offerings in and around the Litchfield Hills. Merry-go-round fans can see a glorious collection of hand-carved creatures at Bristol's New England Carousel Museum. Kids can discover how much some of their old toys are worth at Cheshire's Barker Character, Comic and Cartoon Museum. You'll want to make time for Timexpo, an interactive museum in Waterbury. We also suggest that you call Torrington's Warner Theater. Located in the center of town, this Art Deco beauty frequently offers family-oriented plays (*68 Main St.; 860/489-7180*).

At the American Clock & Watch Museum (*100 Maple St., Bristol; 860/583-6070*) your family can learn about famed clockmaker Seth Thomas, who began making timepieces in the hamlet of Thomaston in 1813. Show up at noon and hear a chorus of antique grandfather clocks ring in the new hour.

CULTURAL ADVENTURES

Barker Character, Comic and Cartoon Museum
★/Free

Billed as a museum of memories, this roadside attraction holds more than 50,000 antique toys and kiddie collectibles. Displays include every-

thing from Roy Rogers metal lunch boxes and Mickey Mouse memorabilia to Snoopy dolls and Happy Meal boxes. (Your kids may be shocked to learn that a box in mint condition could fetch as much as $400!) Though you can't touch most of the items, kids will have fun watching cartoons in the on-site theater and posing with the cartoon cutouts that dot the lawn. There are special family events, including appearances by noted animators. *1188 Highland Ave. (Rte. 10), Cheshire; (800) 995-2357.*

The Institute for American Indian Studies
★★/$

Located in a wooded setting off the beaten path, the museum invites children to embark on a treasure hunt in the exhibit halls and search for items such as a fish vertebrae bracelet and painted deerskin cape. On your self-guided tour, you can visit a simulated archaeological site and an Algonquian village with wigwams. You also can hike on several

FamilyFun TIP

Do the Twist

Pipe cleaners and twist ties have saved many a parent's sanity on long car trips. Kids can quietly fashion these building tools into an endless array of designs — from stick figures to animals to houses with furniture.

trails. For an orientation to Native culture, ask the staff to play the 11-minute introductory film. If you can, try to time your visit with one of the special children's workshops. Topics may include everything from fashioning stone tools to crafting bark containers. In summer, the museum runs Native-themed day camps for kids ages 7 to 12; most sessions last five days. At press time, plans were underway to open a hands-on area for children. *38 Curtis Rd., Washington; (860) 868-0518.*

New England Carousel Museum
★★/$

Fans of carousels should gallop on over to this museum for a fascinating look at the history and mystery of merry-go-rounds. Here, you'll see dozens of exquisite hand-carved horses, from glitzy Coney Island steeds to classy Philadelphia fillies. Each has a special story told by volunteers who tailor tours to your child's interest level. During your visit, you'll learn how horses are carved. You'll also get to see a rare menagerie of carousel cuties, including a plump pig. With the exception of a working kiddie carousel for children ages 4 to 6, you can't ride the carousels here. You can, however, make themed crafts projects during your stay. *95 Riverside Ave., Rte. 72, Bristol; (860) 585-5411.*

Timexpo Museum
★★★/$

In this museum, Connecticut-based Timex invites families to have some hands-on fun while time-traveling back to the company's earliest days. Designed by the folks who created the Crayola Factory in Easton, Pennsylvania, this spot mixes history, archaeology, and navigation while tackling the topic of time. You'll learn about Timex's roots as the Waterbury Clock Company in the 1850s. You'll see more than 1,200

FamilyFun READER'S TIP

Road Scholars

As we were planning our family vacation to Steamboat Springs, Colorado, last summer, my husband and I realized that our boys, Nicholas, 7, and Jason 12, weren't as excited about the trip as we were. So my husband devised a fun pre-vacation research project. Each of the boys received questions appropriate for their age two weeks before our trip. They were allowed to choose as many questions to work on as they wished (What's the tallest mountain in Colorado? What states will we cross to get from Wisconsin to Colorado? What kind of animals live in Colorado and not Wisconsin?), and for each question answered, they received $4 of vacation money.

Diane Rush, Thiensville, Wisconsin

unusual clocks and watches, including the fabulously popular dollar pocket watch, which was a favorite of Mark Twain's. You'll also view the famous torture tests, which featured spokesman John Cameron Swayze and aired on television in the 1960s (Timex watches "take a licking and keep on ticking. . . ."). Along the way, kids can design their own watches, assemble a broken clock via computer, and play with gears. They can even enter a time tunnel, where they'll learn ancient ways of telling time and see how early (and contemporary) travelers have navigated the high seas in simple reed boats. *175 Union St., Waterbury; (203) 755-8463; www.timexpo.com*

JUST FOR FUN

Action Wildlife Foundation
★★/$

You're sure to get a glimpse of wildlife at this nonprofit organization, where 156 animals from around the world roam on 113 country acres. You'll see Russian boars, belted Galloways (also known as Oreo cookie cows), bison, water buffalo, and ibex. You can pet animals in a specially designated area and, on select weekends, can go for a hayride. The wildlife center maintains a museum of mounted animals, featuring species that are rarely seen in the wild. *337 Torrington Rd., Goshen; (860) 491-3701.*

Farmington Canal Linear Park
★★/Free

If you're in the mood for a walk or bike ride, check out this three-mile-long rail trail (these are recreational trails on old train rail beds). The trail is alongside the Farmington Canal, which was hand-dug by Irish immigrants. Back in the 1800s, the canal was the longest in New England, stretching 83 miles from New Haven to Northampton, Massachusetts. It even was used to transport the *Amistad* slaves to Farmington. Today, only one of the original 25 or so locks—Lock 12—remains. You can see it during a visit to Lock 12 Historic Park, which abuts the recreational path. The historic park also includes picnic areas and a blacksmith shop outfitted with old farm tools, including a cornstalk chopper and an apple press. *Cornwall Avenue near Willow St.; (203) 272-2743.*

Farmington River Tubing
★★/$$

On a hot summer day, you and your family can beat the heat by tubing down the Farmington River on a two-and-a-half-mile white-water journey. Each rider (you must be at least 10 years old, four feet five inches tall, and know how to swim) gets a bright-colored tube and flotation gear, then sets off on a splash-happy adventure. One of the longest thrill rides anywhere, the journey takes you through Satan's Kingdom,

363

the ultimate natural water park. You'll hear shrieks of joy as you drift through the forest and over three sets of rapids. At the end, a shuttle returns you to the entrance, where die-hard riders can tube again. *Satan's Kingdom State Recreation Area, Rte. 44, New Hartford; (860) 693-6465.*

Golf Quest Family Sports Center
★★/$
At this safe, well-run facility, chances are everyone will find something to do. You can putt on an 18-hole miniature-golf course, ride bumper boats past a spraying fountain, and

---

Training Slopes

Mount Southington is a reasonably priced, good place to learn to ski before venturing on to bigger slopes in Vermont and New Hampshire. The mountain has 14 trails — one-third for beginners, one-third for intermediate, one-third for advanced skiers. Family facilities include Penguin, Snow Fox, and Polar Bear children's programs for kids ages 4 through 12, plus a Ski Threes program for 3-year-olds and their parents. Winter fun only. *396 Mount Vernon Rd., Southington; (860) 628-0954; www.mountsouthington.com*

---

swing away in baseball and softball batting cages. The miniature-golf course features a replica of Merlin's castle. The golf practice range has 72 covered tee stations, plus a short game area with a 3,000-square-foot putting green. *125 Jude La., Southington; (860) 621-3663.* (Another fun miniature-golf course is **Safari Golf**, *2340 Berlin Tpke., Berlin; 860/828-9800;* with waterfalls and life-size jungle animals.) www.golfquestranges.com

Kent Falls State Park
★★/Free
On sunny days, families hightail it to this beautiful park with its 200-foot-high waterfall. You can hike alongside the falls, picnic on the vast lawn, and fish in the cool, clear water. *Rte. 7, Kent; (860) 927-3238.* **NOTE:** Great swimming spots in the area include **Torrington's Burr Pond** *(Rte. 8; 860/677-1819)* and **Litchfield's Mount Tom State Park** *(Rte. 202).*

Lake Compounce
FamilyFun ★★★★/$$$
MUST-SEE   If you're visiting Connecticut in summer, this park is a must. Featuring dozens of rides on 325 lakeside acres, Lake Compounce is one of New England's biggest theme parks—and one of the best. Since 1840, this playland, nestled in the hills along twinkling Lake Compounce, has entertained families and notables. In fact, Harry Houdini and Orson Welles once

worked here as a magician and a juggler, respectively. In the early days, the chief amusement was a hand-cranked "pleasure wheel," a precursor to the Ferris wheel. My, how things have changed. Thanks to a $35 million investment by Kenny-wood Entertainment (the folks who run Hershey Park in Pennsylvania), Lake Compounce is a New England gem. The Victorian-themed attraction is clean and the range of rides accommodates every age group, the park's size is manageable, and there are plenty of beautiful spots to relax. (The best: the porch outside the Art Deco Starlite Ballroom.) Boulder Dash is the signature ride. The world's first mountainside coaster and one of the fastest coasters in the East, it flies past boulders and trees on a wavy, milelong course by Lake Compounce. *Exit 31 off I-84, Bristol/Southington; (860) 583-3631.*

Lee's Riding Stable ★★/$$$

About 100 horses and ponies reside at this horse farm, and you can meet some of them on an hour-long trail ride in the country. The rides are geared to visitors ages 7 and up; kids ages 3 to 7 can saddle up for pony rides instead. In summer, it's best to call in advance, as the stables get busy. *Off of Rte. 118, Rte. 63, Litchfield; (860) 567-0785.*

Quassy Amusement Park ★★/$$

Combine the spirit of a kiddie carnival with the beauty of a lakeside beach, and you get the picture at this sweet amusement park. Located on Lake Quassapaug and run by the Frantzis family since 1908, the park is geared to children. It's not in the same league as Lake Compounce, but that's the point. The owners' goal is to provide a clean, fun, and inexpensive place to entertain young children. The 26 rides include a carousel with a hippocampus (half horse, half sea horse), the Little Dipper Coaster, and the Big Flush (glide on a raft down a 35-foot tube). Families can also hang out on the beach, ride paddleboats on the lake, or enjoy a picnic in a shady grove. Everyone from Michael J. Fox to Dustin Hoffman has taken their kids here—in summer, it's a local ritual. On Friday night, you can give the kids a bunch of quarters and let them go for it—rides, hot dogs, and cotton candy cost just 25 cents. *Rte. 64, Middlebury; (800) FOR-PARK; www.quassy.com*

White Memorial Foundation and Conservation Center
★★★/$

If yours is a family of nature lovers, this place is a must. The foundation maintains a 4,000-acre wildlife sanctuary that includes campgrounds, public boat launches, a bird-watching observatory, picnic facilities, and 35 miles of nature trails for hiking, cross-country skiing, and horseback riding. The jewel in the crown is the nature museum, filled with interactive exhibits that teach kids about wildlife, plants, rocks, and minerals. In the light-filled Children's Corner, decorated with hand-painted wildlife murals, kids can read nature books, play with puzzles, and watch birds outside the big window. They'll also like examining a working honeybee hive, climbing into a cave to view fluorescent minerals, and viewing a beaver lodge. If you visit only one nature center in Connecticut, make it this one. *80 Whitehall Rd., Litchfield; (860) 567-0857.*

BUNKING DOWN

The Heritage
★★/$$$

This resort offers an overnight Family Fun Package complete with discount coupons, a country breakfast buffet, free in-room movies with popcorn and soda, and use of the fitness facilities. Located on the grounds of the former estate of Danish piano comedian Victor Borge, the Heritage features 163 guest rooms and an on-site restaurant. You'll also find a full range of recreational offerings, from mountain bikes and croquet to tennis courts and indoor and outdoor pools. *Heritage Village, Southbury; (800) 932-3466; (203) 264-8200.*

Homestead Inn
★/$$

If you've enjoyed the bed-and-breakfast experience and want to share it with your kids, try this inn; it has freestanding motel units suitable for families. Furnished with country antiques, these rooms are air-conditioned and have televisions. The living room in the main inn is stocked with puzzles, blocks, and toys for young guests. Located in a quiet town at the edge of the main green, this isn't the place for nonstop action. Instead, it offers a nice alternative to a chain hotel, in an area known for its historic significance. *5 Elm St., New Milford; (860) 354-4080.*

Inn at Iron Masters
★★/$$

It can be difficult to find family lodging in the northwest corner's historic villages, so this pretty motel is a find. Children and dogs are welcome here. The guest rooms are good-sized and have a separate area for TV viewing. Colorful gardens surround the attractive outdoor pool, and the café off the lobby serves a generous, complimentary continental breakfast. The Appalachian Trail is just down the road, and the friendly staff can direct you to biking and ski trails. *229 Main St., Lakeville; (860) 435-9844.*

Interlaken Inn
★★★/$$$

Located on Lake Wononskopomuc on 30 country acres, this laid-back resort is perfect for a family reunion, or for those who want to hang out and enjoy on-site activities. You may choose from among several types of accommodations at this casual retreat. In the main building, you'll find rooms with two queen beds. Town-house suites feature full kitchens, a fireplace, and lofted bedrooms. During your stay, you can swim in the outdoor pool, take a complimentary pontoon boat ride, canoe on the lake, borrow a bike, or play tennis. The on-site restaurants feature children's menus. *74 Interlaken Rd., Lakeville; (860) 435-9878.*

GOOD EATS

DiLeo's ★★/$$

It seems everybody in Torrington is here on a Saturday night, and it's easy to see why. The vast menu includes everything from colossal burgers and meatball subs to fresh sea scallops and chicken parmigiana. Everyone in the family will be able to find something to their liking. Kids have their own menu and can color pictures in the comfortable booths. *545 Winsted Rd., Torrington; (860) 496-7330.*

El Sombrero
★★/$$

You'll tip your sombrero to this festive cantina, which treats the younger set to Mexican favorites. In addition to a kids' activity menu, El Sombrero dishes up balloons, crayons, and a general sense of merriment. For added fun, arrive after 6 P.M. Wednesday through Sunday and eat to the toe-tapping rhythms of a mariachi band. *Oak Hill Mall, Rte. 10, Southington; (860) 621-9474.*

Skiing Lite

Powder Ridge Ski Area, an affordable place to learn the sport, is a local favorite and also has snowboard and ski trails, plus tubing. The area has eight lifts, including three double chairlifts. There's something for all levels of skiers and snowmaking on all trails. Group ski and snowboard lessons are available for kids 6 and up; private lessons for younger children can be arranged. Summer fun, too. *99 Powder Hill, Middlefield; (860) 349-3454; www.powderridgect.com*

The Log House Restaurant
★★/$$

Fans of Lincoln Logs will love this large log cabin, which dishes out home-cooked meals all day long. The breakfasts are particularly hearty, with pancakes, home fries, and sausage portions large enough to satisfy Paul Bunyan. The kids' menu at this roadside eatery includes chicken strips, hot dogs, and child-size pancakes. The friendly waitresses provide crayons, too. *U.S. 44, Barkhamsted; (860) 379-8937.*

Maggie McFly's ★★★/$$

From the German World War II fighter plane hanging from the ceiling to the model train chugging along a track around the bar to the something-for-everyone menu, this family-oriented saloon offers a feast for the eyes and the tummy. The extensive menu runs from burgers and gourmet pizza to ribs and giant salads. The kids' menu is the goofi-est anywhere: "Liver and onions with Brussels sprouts, $19.75. Yuck! Only kidding." All joking aside, kids can feast on Jurassic Dinosaur Claws (chicken fingers), foot-long hot dogs, bacon cheeseburgers, and, for dessert, a scoop of dirt (chocolate pudding with Oreos and gummy worms). There's a video game room and free balloons, too. *6 Woodside Ave., Middlebury; (203) 577-2205.*

Vita's Italian Market & Deli
★★/$-$$

Inspired by his Mom's delicious Italian cooking, Nick Vita opened a family-oriented deli that serves scrumptious fare at reasonable prices. Kids can split meals with parents or choose kids' menu items such as pasta bambini, fried mozzarella, and junior sandwiches. Order your fare at the counter, find a table by the window, and enjoy. *562 Farmington Ave., Bristol; (860) 582-0440.*

FamilyFun TIP

Cool It

Whether you use a cooler, an insulated bag or box, or Tupperware, here are some ideas for keeping snacks cool without messy, melting ice: Add frozen juice boxes; make sandwiches on frozen bread; pack some frozen grapes; include a smoothie frozen in a tightly sealed container; use sealed ice packs.

SOUVENIR HUNTING

Avery's Beverages

Since 1904, this company has delicious, hand-brewed soft drinks in scrumptious flavors using 100 percent cane sugar. Sample white birch beer, red cream soda, and black cherry pop in a friendly shop that will make you feel as if you've stepped into a time warp. During brewing season (most of the summer), the staff will be happy to take you on an informal tour of the small plant. Wish you could enjoy some of your favorite flavors back home? Good news: soda is packaged in old-fashioned glass bottles and sold by the case. Hours vary, so call ahead. *520 Corbin Ave., New Britain; (860) 224-0830.*

The Connecticut Store

Homegrown pride is on display at this novel shop, which bills itself as the state's oldest department store and the only one dedicated to selling items made in Connecticut. Here, you'll find all of the state's claims to fame, from Wiffle balls and Pez products to locally made dolls and ice cream. *120–140 Bank St., Waterbury; (800) 4-SHOP-CT.*

Mother Earth Gallery and Mining Company

At this nature-oriented gallery, junior geologists can dig for buried treasure in a re-created mine, complete with cobwebs and stalactites. On your five-minute expedition, you may find amethyst, geodes, pyrite, and calcite. The activity is pricey, but you get to keep any stones you find, and staff members will be happy to share fun facts about the treasures. *806 Federal Rd., Brookfield; (203) 775-6272.*

Susan Wakeen Doll Factory

Internationally honored dollmaker (and Litchfield resident) Susan Wakeen has a knack for creating amazingly lifelike, cherubic dolls. Dozens of baby dolls are asleep in bassinets, while toddler-age creations are all dressed up for tea. Best of all, you can design—and purchase—your very own doll. Choose the vinyl head, wig, and outfit, and the staff will assemble your doll on the spot. Though far from inexpensive, the price is not unreasonable for an heirloom that your kids can one day hand down to their kids. *425 Bantam Rd., Litchfield; (860) 567-0007.*

The highlight of a hayride at Creamery Brook Bison is when the buffalo surround your wagon, looking for munchies.

Hartford and Northeast Connecticut

VISIT HARTFORD'S OLD State House on a Saturday, and you'll insist the place is run by a bunch of animals. There's a dastardly tiger lurking in the halls, a prim fox that enjoys chatting with a mountain goat, and a lobster that's known to break out into a silly dance (see page 373). They're all part of a puppet show, "Legend of the Charter Oak" (see "An O.K. Oak," page 373). The Old State House also is home to Mr. Steward's Museum of Curiosities, containing dozens of mounted animals. Elsewhere in the city, you can embark on a treasure hunt at the nation's oldest public art museum, dress up lifesize paper dolls at the Connecticut Historical Society, and see the Victorian home of Mark Twain, the city's most famous resident.

Indeed, there's much more to Hartford than its nickname, the Insurance City, would have you believe. (Yes, Hartford is headquarters for many insurance companies.) Thanks to a resuscitated riverfront, families can stroll along walkways

THE **FamilyFun** LIST

MUST-SEE
MUST-SEE

Creamery Brook Bison (page 375)

Dinosaur State Park (page 375)

"Legend of the Charter Oak"
   at the Old State House
   (page 373)

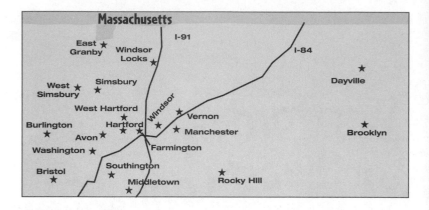

Massachusetts
I-91
I-84
East Granby ★
Windsor Locks ★
Dayville ★
West Simsbury ★
Simsbury ★
Windsor
West Hartford
Burlington ★
Hartford ★
Vernon ★
Avon ★
Manchester ★
Brooklyn ★
Washington ★
Farmington
Bristol ★
Southington ★
Middletown ★
Rocky Hill ★

and pedestrian bridges, enjoy a picnic by the Connecticut River, ride a historic carousel at the nation's first public park, and take in many a festival (including the kid-pleasing Mark Twain Days, a Victorian-themed celebration held in summer).

To the south of Hartford, in Rocky Hill, is Dinosaur State Park, marked by literally hundreds of dinosaur tracks. To the west, you can enjoy a canoeing adventure along the pretty Farmington River. Head east, for a scenic drive to Connecticut's rural "quiet corner," and watch buffalo roam in a pristine pasture. Greater Hartford is so compact that you can pack a lot into one day; it's entirely possible to spend the morning in the city perusing Egyptian art, and then hiking in the afternoon, where you'll be the only folks on the trail in a natural paradise.

Although not the place to experience quaint New England charm, the Buckland Hills section of Manchester is chain city, ideal if you want to go to the movies, eat at Chili's or Bugaboo Creek Steak House, and stay at the Marriott.

CULTURAL ADVENTURES

Connecticut Historical Society
★★★/$

Much more entertaining than its name suggests, this place has lots of hands-on exhibits that make history lessons fun. In Tours and Detours Through Early Connecticut, kids can sit in on a multimedia show about the Revolutionary War, try making Native American moccasins, and dress up in colonial breeches and bodices. In the Hands-on History gallery, children can build a stone wall, learn to set a Victorian table, discover the story behind unusual Colonial-era baby names (such as Preserved Fish), and even dress humongous paper dolls in costumes. At the circus exhibit, families can try on more than 60 colorful costumes and star in their own performance. You'll also learn that Connecticut is the birthplace of such offbeat inventions as the Wiffle ball, Pez dispenser, and Frisbee. On the first Saturday and Sunday of every month, admission is free. The society offers many weekend workshops for families, from sampler embroidery to genealogy training. *One Elizabeth St., Hartford; (860) 236-5621;* www.chs.org

Mark Twain House ★★/$

Mark Twain lived in this Victorian brick gingerbread house. From 1874 to 1891, Twain wrote *The Adventures of Tom Sawyer* and *The Adventures of Huckleberry Finn* during his Hartford years. The hour-long tour of the Tiffany decorated mansion is a bit dry for kids, although they may enjoy seeing the rooms that belonged to Twain's children. On Wednesdays in summer, the staff offers hands-on activities for families, including Victorian crafts and scavenger hunts. *351 Farmington Ave., Hartford; (860) 247-0998.*

Old New-Gate Prison and Copper Mine ★★/$$

You'll enjoy doing time at this historic prison, which ceased operation in 1827. Among its inmates were horse thieves, murderers, and British sympathizers during the American Revolution. On this self-guided tour, families can climb down into the dungeon of America's first copper mine, where prisoners once toiled to pay their debt to society. After you examine the chilly cells (wear a sweater), you can learn more about the prison's history in the reception area. *115 Newgate Rd., East Granby; (860) 653-3563 (May to October); (860) 566-3005 (November to April).*

MUST-SEE FamilyFun Old State House ★★★/$

MUST-SEE The nation's oldest statehouse goes the extra mile to welcome families, so you'll want to make it your first stop in Hartford. If your

An O.K. Oak

Connecticut's Charter Oak is pictured on its state quarter, but what is its significance to the state? In 1687, a representative of the British government demanded the return of Connecticut's charter. The paper lay on a table in the middle of the fierce debate when the room suddenly went dark. When light was restored, the charter had disappeared. Captain Joseph Wadsworth had taken and hidden it in the safest place he knew—the large white oak on the property.

kids aren't squeamish, you'll want to tour Mr. Steward's Hartford Museum, a collection of curiosities replicating the one Joseph Steward, a local painter and self-promoter, maintained in 1796. The original list of oddities includes everything from two-headed pigs and two-headed calves to a Bengal tiger and a mountain goat. The only fake item is the severed head of King Charles I—it's made of wax. Several of the mounted animals are the inspiration for "Legend of the Charter Oak." This half-hour puppet show, presented at 11:30 Saturday morning, interprets Connecticut's beloved legend (see "An O.K. Oak" on page 373) for families. At the end of the show, visitors are given a Connecticut quarter depicting the Charter Oak, along with a written copy of the legend. *800 Main St., Hartford; (860) 522-6766.*

Science Center of Connecticut
★★/$

You'll get a big bang for your buck at this attraction, a combination science center, natural history museum, planetarium, and small zoo, with something for kids of all ages. You can enjoy computer adventures at Planet Cyber, or step into the world's largest walk-in kaleidoscope. Take aim at humongous bubbles with a bubble blaster, or forecast the weather in the television studio. The resident animals include ferrets, chinchillas, copperheads, iguanas, crocodiles, a 25-year-old owl, bobcats, mountain lions, and a blue-tongued skink. *950 Trout Brook Dr., W. Hartford; (860) 231-282; www.sciencecenterct.org*

Wadsworth Atheneum
★★★/$

This cultural jewel, America's oldest continuously operated public art museum, boasts 50,000 works and a way to lure kids into looking at them: they can track down some of the masterpieces with the help of treasure-hunt game cards. Your junior detective, for example, may be challenged to "find the felines." **HINT:** The blue-headed lion and Egyptian lioness goddess are lurking in the first-floor galleries. Kids who complete the hunt get a small prize—and a big sense of accomplishment. The museum periodically runs family programs as well. Visit before noon on Saturday for free admission. *600 Main St., Hartford; (860) 278-2670.*

MARK TWAIN ONCE predicted that since his birth coincided with the appearance of Halley's Comet, his death would come when the astronomical event occurred again. Twain's prophecy came true—87 years later.

JUST FOR FUN

Bushnell Park★★/Free

At the nation's first public park, children can ride on a magnificent carousel, climb on a playscape, and cool off in the fountains. The Stein and Goldstein carousel was hand-carved in 1914, and its steeds circle to the tunes of a 1925 Wurlitzer. *One block west of Main St. at Gold and Jewell Sts.; 860/232-6710.*

Creamery Brook

FamilyFun Bison ★★★/$

Climb aboard the tractor-drawn wagon, grab a seat on a hay bale, and get ready for a big surprise. Just ahead is a herd of shaggy, bearded buffalo, grazing in a setting so picturesque, you'll swear you've stumbled onto the set of *Dances with Wolves.* Longtime dairy farmers Austin and Deborah Tanner have transformed their 100-acre property into a bison ranch—and love showing off their herd to families. The excitement reaches a crescendo when the blue-tongued beasts surround the wagon for snacks, giving kids a close-up look at the brood and its babies. After the 40-minute ride, you can slurp ice cream at the dairy bar (try Buffalo Chips—chocolate with chocolate-covered almonds), and meet Thunderbolt, a bison too acclimated to humans to live with the herd. This big fellow will eat right out of your hand. The gift shop sells farm-raised bison meat, as well as all manner of buffalo-imprinted products. You can take wagon rides on weekends, July through September. *19 Purvis Rd., Brooklyn; (860) 779-0837; www.creamerybrookbison.com*

Dinosaur State Park

FamilyFun ★★★/$

This place is absolutely dino-mite. You'll get goose bumps when you walk into the geodesic-domed facility and see 500 gargantuan tracks—the largest such display in North America. The footprints are preserved on a 200-million-year-old sandstone trackway, discovered by accident during a 1966 construction project. Sound and light effects, and awesome dioramas of life in the Jurassic and Triassic periods, make the great hall all the more spellbinding. At interactive exhibits, you can become a footprint detective by trying to match tracks with the appropriate animal. Best of all, out back in the crafts area, you can make a plaster cast of a dinosaur footprint, a very messy but fun activity. (**NOTE:** To do this you must bring cooking oil, rags, ten pounds of plaster of paris, and a five-gallon plastic bucket—the Website offers details.) The park offers special family programs, two and a half miles of hiking trails, a 300-foot-long swamp boardwalk, and a ten-acre Arboretum of Evolution containing plants that date back to the Age

375

of Dinosaurs. The excellent gift shop sells dinosaur figurines, rocks, sticker books, and more. *400 West St., Rocky Hill; (860) 529-8423; www. dinosaurstatepark.org*

Farmington Miniature Golf & Ice Cream Parlor ★★★/$

For 35 years, children have come to this sweet little course, where the village includes a tiny church and a light-house with a rotating light. The snack bar serves everything from cookie-dough sundaes to traveling tacos (crushed-up Fritos mixed with chili sour cream and cheese—served and eaten right out of the bag). *Rte. 4, 1048 Farmington Ave., Farmington; (860) 677-0118.*

Flamig Farm ★★★/$

Meet a barnyard of furry and feathery friends at this joyful, family-run farm. For $1, you can buy a big cup of grain and treat the llamas, ponies, goats, sheep, and horses to a snack. On weekends, your little ones can enjoy pony rides. The 93-year-old farm also offers horse-drawn hayrides, tractor rides, and sleigh rides. The small country store serves up cold bottles of locally brewed Avery soda (try the birch beer). Some activities are seasonal. *7 Shingle Mill Rd., W. Simsbury; (860) 658-5070; www.flamigfarm.com*

Huck Finn Adventures ★★★/$$$$

Named for the free-spirited boy in Mark Twain's beloved stories, Huck Finn Adventures specializes in helping families plan scenic canoe trips down the Farmington River. The river is so gentle and shallow that most families don't want or need guides. Instead, owner John Kulick supplies instruction, wide-bottom canoes, safety equipment, and maps—and sends you on your way. After your three-, five,- or nine-mile trip, the company shuttle returns you to the put-in. Wear your bathing suit so you can lounge on the sandy beaches along the river. Bring a picnic to enjoy at a premier lunch spot: beneath the boughs of the Pinchot Sycamore, whose 26-foot circumference reportedly makes it the largest tree east of the Mississippi. Children ages 9 and up may be game for the guided Lost Park River Tour, where paddlers don a headlamp and explore the fascinating tunnel system beneath the city of Hartford. *For information, call (860) 693-0385.*

International Skating Center of Connecticut ★★★/$

At this world-class facility, you just might see Olympic skating stars perfecting their moves on the ice. Nestled in the rolling hills of Simsbury, the center is open to the

Connecticut residents are lucky to have the musical talents of a **state troubadour**. The honorary position is awarded biannually.

public on weekends. You can rent skates; call for hours. *1375 Hopmeadow St., Simsbury; (860) 651-5400.*

Jonathan's Dream
★★/Free

This 25,000-square-foot playground isn't just a diversion, it's an attraction. Featuring playscapes with towers, climb-on automobiles and boats, a kid-size village, a sandy play area, and lots of swings and slides, this is a great place to let kids cut loose after sight-seeing in Hartford. But it's special for another reason, too: by using ramps, rubber surfacing, and specially designed swings, the majority of the playground can accommodate children in wheelchairs and walkers. Adjacent to the Jewish Community Center. *335 Bloomfield Ave., W. Hartford; (860) 243-8315.*

Northwest Park and Nature Center **★★/Free**

This spot is such a hidden gem that some *area* families don't even know

it exists. The park has 12 miles of wooded trails, including a Braille trail. It's also home to an animal barn containing rabbits, goats, sheep, roosters, and a resident ox. The nature center includes a kids' room where children can read nature books and piece together puzzles. A tobacco museum offers insights into the history of one of the area's oldest trades, cultivating shade-grown tobacco. *145 Lang Rd., Windsor; (860) 285-1886.*

Sessions Woods Wildlife Management Area
★/Free

At this 455-acre retreat, you can head down several hiking trails geared specifically to families. Along the way, keep an eye out for rabbits, flying squirrels, and bats. A favorite with kids is the Beaver Pond Trail, a three-mile loop that leads to a beaver dam and a waterfall. *Rte. 69, Furmington; (860) 675-8130.*

Talcott Mountain State Park
★★/Free

For a more ambitious hike, head one and a half miles up the mountain to 165-foot-high Heublein Tower. Climb to the top for an amazing view of four states. Considered the Farmington Valley's best hike, the trip takes about two hours round-trip—including frequent stops, with kids in tow. Initially, the trail is a bit steep, but most active kids will do just fine. *Rte. 185, Simsbury; (860) 677-0662 or (860) 566-2305.*

FamilyFun GAME

Geography

Start with A to Z anyplace in the world: Kansas, say. The next person has to think of a place that begins with the last letter of Kansas, such as South Africa. Whoever goes next needs a place that starts with A. It has to be a real place—and no using a map!

BUNKING DOWN

Hilton Hartford
★★/$$

At this renovated, downtown hotel, attached to the Hartford Civic Center, families are within an easy walk of several city attractions. The Hilton features an indoor pool, Nintendo (for a fee), and children's menus in the dining room. Special packages are often available. *315 Trumbull St., Hartford; (800) HILTONS; (860) 728-5151;* www.hilton.com

Holiday Inn Express Hotel & Suites ★★/$$

If you're exploring Connecticut's rural Quiet Corner or want a place to stay halfway between Hartford and Providence, this is a good bet. The hotel has an indoor pool and serves a complimentary continental breakfast in the attractive lobby. Choose from standard rooms and suites with refrigerators, microwaves,

sinks, and pullout sofas. *16 Tracy Rd., Dayville; (800) HOLIDAY; (860) 779-3200;* www.basshotels.com/holiday-inn/

Homewood Suites Hotel
★★★/$$

This appealing, all-suites hotel in the scenic Farmington Valley pampers families with spacious quarters. Each suite has separate living and sleeping areas, a fully equipped kitchen (stocked with cookware and utensils), two TV sets, and a VCR. There's an indoor pool, a courtyard with barbecue grills, and a generous complimentary continental breakfast served in the gorgeous lobby. The hotel shuttle operator will gladly transport you to sites within five miles of the property (such as the Westfarms Mall). *2 Farm Glen Blvd., Farmington; (800) CALL-HOME; (860) 321-0000.*

Quality Inn
★★/$

Just nine miles from Hartford and three miles from the Buckland Hills shopping area, this is a clean, affordable spot for families who want a standard room. There's an outdoor pool, complimentary continental breakfast, and a kids' menu in the dining room. Best of all, the inn is next to Connecticut Golf Land, a family entertainment complex that's open from April to October. *51 Hartford Tpke., Rte. 83, Vernon; (800) 235-INNS.*

GOOD EATS

Barbs Pizza ★★/$

Though Barbs can top your pie with chicken, clams, roasted spinach, pineapple, and more, kids most often go for the plain cheese, and servers can supply crayons and paper to make the cooked-to-order time go faster. *35 Park Ave., W. Hartford; (860) 232-3569.*

Bissell Tavern ★★/$-$$

What a nice place to enjoy pub fare on the Connecticut River. Located in the state's oldest town, this family-oriented restaurant is low-key and unpretentious, making it an ideal spot to unwind. In summer, you can dine outside on the patio and watch boats go by. Fare includes fish-and-chips, teriyaki chicken, and burgers, with a kids' menu featuring PB&J, junior burgers, and ribs with fries. *1530 Palisado Ave., Windsor; (860) 285-0878.*

Bugaboo Creek Steak House ★★★/$$$

A talking moose greets your family at this fun, faux Canadian Rockies retreat. Kids get crayons and their own menu, but they'll be more interested in looking at the animated bears, raccoons, and flapping fish that come to life during the meal. The hearty menu includes steak, ribs, and salmon; Kid's Grub features macaroni and cheese, burgers, a baby sirloin, and a free ice-cream treat. *1442 Pleasant Valley Rd., Manchester; (860) 644-6100.*

First & Last Tavern ★★★/$$

Since 1936, this cozy, brick-walled restaurant has attracted politicos and families, who love the tasty spaghetti and meatballs, pizza, and warm atmosphere. Slide into a big booth, snack on fresh focaccia, and treat yourself to a cherry-topped dessert pizza. Kids can order child-size portions of adult pasta entrées. *939 Maple Ave., Hartford; (860) 956-6000. (First & Last has two other locations: in Avon, 26 W. Main St., 860/676-2000; and Middletown, 220 Main St., 860/347-2220.)*

Hank's Restaurant/ Alice's Kitchen ★★/$$

From hearty bowls of soup to generous plates of chicken cordon bleu, Hank's has been dishing out comfort food for more than 25 years. *416 Providence Rd./Rte. 6, Brooklyn; (860) 774-6071.*

Harry's Pizza ★★/$

This popular pizza parlor dishes out scrumptious, thin-crust pies in a sophisticated, comfortable setting. If you like it hot, try yours with jalapeños and sausage. *1003 Farmington Ave., W. Hartford; (860) 231-7166.*

A Map of His Own

Whenever our family sets out on a road trip, my husband and I trace out the planned route for our 11-year-old son, David, and our 8-year-old daughter, Caytlin. Using AAA maps, I cut out the portion that pertains to our trip and glue it to a piece of cardboard. My husband highlights the roadways with a marker, then we cover the map with a sheet of clear Con-Tact paper. Besides being a big hit with the kids, the map is a ready reference for the driver. Although long stints in the car can be hard on kids (and adults), we have learned that when everyone is interested in following the route, the trip can be a special time spent together as a family.

Annette Payne, Santa Barbara, California

Rainforest Cafe ★★★/$$

This is one restaurant that's sure to be louder than your kids. In this re-created rain forest, thunder rolls and Congo drums beat, robotic monkeys whoop it up, and elephants squirt water from their trunks (in fact, the noise level and realistic beasts may frighten small children). Between the shooting stars, live cockatoos, and enormous aquariums packed with tropical fish, you'll have no trouble keeping kids entertained. The huge menu features colossal portions of themed sandwiches, burgers, pasta dishes, salads, and juice drinks. The food is good, not great—but it's the atmosphere and entertainment that lure families. To avoid enormously long waits (when school's out, a two-hour wait isn't unheard of), make reservations well in advance. *Westfarms Mall, Farmington; (860) 521-2002; www.rainforestcafe.com*

Randy's Wooster Street Pizza ★★★/$

This pizzeria provides an evening of race car-inspired fun. Kids will go into overdrive as they peruse the walls covered with Hot Wheels posters, watch NASCAR races on TV monitors, and drive on virtual speedways in the video game room. You and your kids can slip into red-and-white-vinyl booths or nosh in a converted school bus or Volkswagen van. The menu is as fun as the atmosphere, with such innovative pizzas as Skippy Dare (topped with provolone, peanut butter, and bacon) and This Spud's for You (topped with smashed potatoes, cheese, ham, and garlic), plus calzones, grinders, pasta dishes, and six special meals for kids ages 12 and under. *1131-T Tolland Tpke., Manchester; (860) 649-1166. (There's a second location—777 Queen St., Southington; 860/276-8600.)*

Rein's New York Deli ★★/$$

At Rein's, it's considered a rite of passage when kids try their first half-sour pickle. To mark the occasion, the staff takes your child's picture and hangs it on the wall with the other Pickle Pusses. The menu here is pure New York–style deli; kids can nosh on bagels with peanut butter or kosher hot dogs and can even try a chocolate egg cream. *435 Hartford Tpke., Vernon; (860) 875-1344.*

Romano's Macaroni Grill ★★★/$$

This themed restaurant takes your family to an aromatic Italian village, where the staff is extremely friendly and the food is excellent. Kids will enjoy drawing on the paper tablecloths, digging into the fresh hot loaves of bread, and completing puzzles in the free, colorful, activity booklet. *170 Slater St., Manchester; (860) 648-8819.*

Shady Glen ★★/$

This restaurant is straight out of the 1950s. The waiters wear crisp paper hats, the waitresses wear dresses with ladylike white collars, and the atmosphere is as wholesome as a vanilla milk shake. No menus here. All the standards—from hot dogs and hamburgers to tuna salad and sundaes with homemade ice cream—are posted on the wall. Try the "big cheeseburger," a juicy number topped with Shady Glen's signature fried cheese. *Two locations: 840 E. Middle Tpke., Manchester (860/649-4245), and 360 W. Middle Tpke., Manchester (860/643-0511).*

SOUVENIR HUNTING

West Hartford Center

This jamming center proves that malls haven't cornered the market on family fun. Split a pizza at Harry's, then peruse the specialty shops along LaSalle and Farmington Avenues: kid favorites include **The Toy Chest** *(975 Farmington Ave.; 860/233-5559)* and the **Three Dog Bakery** *(967 Farmington Ave.; 860/232-6299)*, which dishes up Pup Tarts and Ciao Wow Pizza for the family pet.

The only beluga whales to be found in New England are part of the Alaskan Coast exhibit at Mystic Aquarium.

Southeast Connecticut

STRETCHING 400 MILES FROM New Hampshire to Long Island Sound, the Connecticut River seems to tempt families with four little words: come out and play. Though the river isn't ideal for swimming, it's perfect for watery adventures in the Connecticut River Valley, a picturesque area that extends from Cromwell, south of Hartford, to Old Saybrook. For starters, you can cross the river on the nation's second-oldest ferry (the trip is just five minutes, but a kick), board a riverboat for an old-fashioned cruise past the wedding-cake-shaped Goodspeed Opera House, and even explore an eccentric actor's stone castle. Along the way, you'll see wildlife, sweet historic villages, and gently rolling hills so beautiful, the Nature Conservancy calls the Connecticut River Valley "one of the last great places on earth." If you visit in August or September, you may even take in a country fair. (The Durham Fair is the state's biggest agricultural fair and one of the best; it's always held the last full weekend in September. For a complete list of fairs, log on to www.ctfairs.org)

THE FamilyFun LIST
MUST-SEE · MUST-SEE

Mashantucket Pequot Museum & Research Center (page 386)

Mystic Aquarium and the Institute for Exploration (page 392)

Mystic Seaport (page 387)

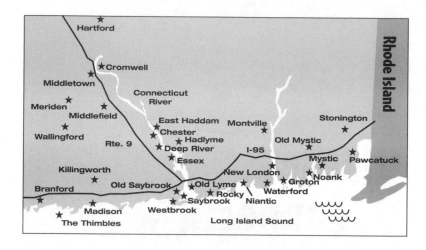

The southeast corner of the state is also blessed with the 253-mile shoreline along Long Island Sound. Although much of the shoreline is private, this area has a number of public beaches where children can build sand castles and splash in relatively calm waves. You can laze all day at New London's Ocean Beach Park, Madison's Hammonassett State Beach, or Niantic's Rocky Neck State Park. Through Project Oceanology, you can board a research boat and become a marine scientist for a day. Other choices include exploring the Thimble Islands (tiny wonderlands with thumb-size beaches) and taking a family kayak trip.

Mystic is the cultural hub for families visiting the region. The picturesque seaside village has been a shipbuilding center since the 1600s, and maritime history, marine science, and Native American culture are the key themes here. Fans of Julia Roberts may recognize the area from her 1988 film *Mystic Pizza*. You can even enjoy a slice of pie (and check out cast photos) at the restaurant that inspired the film. The one-time whaling port features several top attractions: the Mystic Aquarium, Mystic Seaport, and the Mashantucket Pequot Museum. To avoid becoming overtired, it's best to visit no more than one of these powerhouse attractions a day. (On-site restaurants at each attraction make long visits easier.) The area also has a marvelous children's museum, a nuclear submarine to tour, and scenic hiking trails.

As is true in other parts of the state, the towns themselves are attractions, and you'll want to make time to walk. Mystic has some fine sea captain's homes, with widow's walks and other interesting architectural features. It also features a bascule drawbridge that opens every 15 minutes for summer boat traffic. In the village of Essex, you can amble past historic taverns, well-tended Colonial homes, and antiques stores. You also can visit with the ducks at the Connecticut River Museum. Stonington's Water Street ends in a point, where kids can climb on the rocks and watch seagulls dive for their dinner.

Because summer is peak season, it can get crowded and pricey. The popularity of the region's casinos, Foxwoods and Mohegan Sun, makes the Mystic area particularly expensive. Expect to pay about $170 a night (at press time) for a standard room at a chain hotel (without a pool, in some cases), and there may be a two-night minimum. For more reasonable prices, stay in nearby Groton or Waterford. You'll find even better rates 20 miles away in Cromwell.

CULTURAL ADVENTURES

Children's Museum of Southeastern Connecticut
★★/$

This place has dozens of interactive exhibits, both indoors and out, that will keep young children busy for as long as their imaginations wander. Toddlers will enjoy Nursery Rhyme Land and Kidsville, a kid-size town complete with post office, fire station, and grocery store. There's also an art table, puppet theater, discovery gardens, a real yellow submarine, and a lobster boat where kids can haul up the day's catch. *409 Main St., Niantic; (860) 691-1111.*

Florence Griswold Museum
★★/$

Widely regarded as the center of American Impressionism, this fine-arts museum is an unlikely but definite kid pleaser. Like the woman for whom it's named, the museum encourages visitors to explore the artist within. (Florence Griswold fostered the prestigious Lyme Art Colony at the turn of the 20th century.) The museum's education center hosts Impromptu Encounters, family-oriented crafts workshops, on Sundays from 1 to 5 P.M. (April to December). Kid-oriented events include everything from storytelling to kite-making. You're also encouraged to bring a picnic and art supplies, plant yourselves on the lush lawn, and paint the landscape that so inspired some of our best artists. *96 Lyme St., Old Lyme; (860) 434-5542.*

Gillette Castle
★★★/$

A century ago, Hartford native William Gillette found fame and fortune portraying Sherlock Holmes on the stage. These days, he's also known for his other dramatic production: an intriguing, 24-room fieldstone castle atop a hill overlooking the Connecticut River. Kids love to explore this enormous home, which underscores Gillette's eccentric personality. You'll find secret passages, hidden mirrors and rooms, and a dining table on tracks, which Gillette used to trap his dinner guests into staying until after dessert had been served. Outside, a train encircles the property. Save time for a hike on the estate's scenic trails. *67 River Rd., E. Haddam; (860) 526-2336.*

Kidcity Children's Museum
★★★/$

Located in a historic home with colorful, hand-painted walls and large sun-filled windows, this excellent museum has lots of nooks and crannies for kids to explore. They can sail on a clipper ship, drive a Volkswagen, create comic book characters, and star in a video. They also can shop on a mini Main Street, try out instruments, and have many more hands-on adventures. Creativity pervades the atmosphere here, encouraging kids to cut loose. *119 Washington St., Middletown; (860) 347-0495.*

 ## Mashantucket Pequot Museum & Research Center
★★★★/$

One of America's best new museums, this is an absolute must for families who are interested in Native American culture. The $193 million museum is funded largely by profits from the nearby casinos. It uses

HAMMONASETT BEACH STATE PARK

WITH TWO MILES of white sand lining Long Island Sound, **Connecticut's largest public beach** is a haven for nature lovers. This 1,100-acre coastal paradise offers a half-mile-long boardwalk, a nature center (with a butterfly garden and seasonal children's activities), recreational trails for walking and bicycling, camping, picnicking, and boating (bring your own boat). You'll also find concession stands, fields for kite flying and ball games, changing rooms, flush toilets, and picnic shelters. *Route 1, Madison; (203) 245-2785.*

amazing new technology to illustrate the life and times of the Mashantucket Pequot Tribal Nation, which extends back thousands of years. The Pequot Village alone is worth the price of admission. As you wander through the re-created, 16th-century community—featuring 51 amazingly lifelike figures—you smell the campfire, hear the river running and birds calling, and see smoke drifting from the sweat lodge. A lifelike, multisensory diorama depicts the drama of a caribou hunt, and interactive computer stations make it fun to learn about native culture. For a panoramic view of southern Connecticut, take a ride to the top of the 18-story observation tower. Families can watch a variety of films at the facility, including the powerful, 30-minute movie *The Witness*, which vividly chronicles the 1637 Pequot massacre at Mystic. You can even sample Native American cuisine at the on-site restaurant, and buy moccasins, children's books, and locally made jewelry at the outstanding gift shop. *The museum is located on the Mashantucket Pequots' reservation, at 110 Pequot Trail (off Rte. 214), Mashantucket; (860) 396-6800.*

Mystic Seaport
FamilyFun ★★★★/$

Connecticut's top attraction and the nation's leading maritime museum, Mystic Seaport

SAILOR SPEAK

Aren't sure what some of those boat terms are that everyone keeps bandying about? Here are a few of the more common ones.

BOW: the front of the boat

STERN: the back of the boat

PORT: the left side of the boat (when facing the bow)

STARBOARD: the right side of the boat (when facing the bow)

WINDWARD: the direction toward the wind

LEEWARD: the direction away from the wind

GALLEY: the kitchen area of a boat

HEAD: the marine version of the toilet

houses the largest collection of boats and maritime photography in the world. With its tall ships, trade shops, and historic homes, this 19th-century village is a splendid place to teach children about the mystery and history of the sea. There's even an on-site children's museum, where kids can don a sailor's cap, swab the decks, and see what it's like sleeping in a boat-style bunk. Children can also climb aboard the *Charles W. Morgan*, the only wooden whaling ship that's still afloat, and sail down the Mystic River on the coal-fired steamship *Sabino*. In the workshop, master craftsmen still build ships.

Thimble Island Cruise

The 25 tiny islands off the coast of Stony Creek will delight tots during a 45-minute tour aboard the *Sea Mist*, a renovated excursion boat. Named for the thimbleberries that once grew rampantly on these granite hideaways, the Thimbles recall the scenery along Maine's craggy coast. Everyone from Captain Kidd to Tom Thumb has lived on these stony islets, which are all privately owned and boast some of the priciest summer cottages in the area. Offered from May to October, the tour goes by quickly for kids. They enjoy the entertaining narrative, and the chance to sit on the top deck and search for the place where the infamous pirate buried his booty. *Stony Creek, Branford; (203) 488-8905. (Other tours include Connecticut Sea Ventures; 203/397-3921, and cruises aboard the Volsunga IV; 203/488-9978 or 203/481-3345.)*

In fact, a replica of the freedom schooner *Amistad* was recently built here. For a real watery adventure, you can rent a sailboat or motorboat and cruise around the river. Family programs include crafts workshops, vintage games on the green, and storytelling. For meals, you can go casual at the Schaefer Spouter Tavern or treat yourselves to fancier fare at the Seamen's Inne Restaurant, which has a children's menu. *Rte. 27, Mystic; (888) 9-SEAPORT; (860) 572-5315.*

Science Center of Eastern Connecticut
★★★/$

Although a bit off the beaten track, this museum is well worth the trip. Its more than 100 hands-on exhibits offer something for everyone. Your kids can get a feel for creatures in the marine touch tank, meet live reptiles, experiment with lasers, and more. With advance notice, you can register for special programs, including the wildly popular Lego Logo classes, in which kids ages 8 and up build merry-go-rounds and other structures and power them via computer. Other classes focus on papermaking and telescope building. Younger children have their own special area, where they can play with puzzles and puppets. The center's garden is a pretty place for a walk. *33 Gallows La., New London; (860) 442-0391.*

Submarine Force Museum/ Historic Ship *Nautilus*
★★/Free

Even those who are not particularly interested in military history tend to enjoy this museum, located in Groton, America's "submarine capital." Here, you can explore the *Nautilus*, the world's first nuclear-powered submarine and the first ship to pass beneath the North Pole. As you duck under door frames and peek into the cramped crew's quarters, you'll get a new appreciation for those who spend weeks at a time aboard these tight vessels. The Navy staff is more than gracious, so if you have questions ("How does all the food fit on the sub?"), feel free to ask. Inside the expanded museum building, kids can learn about the history of submarines, from Bushnell's *Turtle*, the first sub used in the Revolutionary War, to the current Seawolf class of subs. Though some of the exhibits are a bit technical, you'll have fun peering through the periscopes and watching for watercraft on the Thames River. *Crystal Lake Rd., off Rte. 12, Groton; (800) 343-0079; (860) 448-0893.*

JUST FOR FUN

Allegra Farm
★★/$-$$$$

With a little advance planning, you can hire a costumed driver to squire your family around Connecticut's back roads in an antique, horse-drawn carriage. Many of the carriages at this farm were used in the film *Amistad*, and families can view them in the post-and-beam barn. On your self-guided tour, you'll see calèche models (also known as royal carriages), enclosed coaches known as broughams, and antique milk trucks, and trolleys. Proprietors John Allegra and Kate Keeney also invite you to meet the resident horses and sheep. In addition to the customized carriage rides (which you are encouraged to arrange several weeks ahead of time), your family can enjoy pony rides in the summer. Nostalgic sleigh rides, complete with lap robes and hand muffs, are featured in the winter. *Rte. 82, E. Haddam; (860) 873-9658.*

Amy's Udder Joy, Exotic Animal Farm and Nature Center ★/$

This place is about as kid friendly as they come, thanks to owner Amy O'Toole. A Mom, and a wildlife rehabilitator, she has opened her home and yard to more than 100 animals representing 54 species—and is happy to share the animals with you and your kids. This small, but diverse park features everything from wallabies and alligators to a llama (Rebel) and African aoudad sheep. Amy is big on touching, so you can stroke the baby chicks and feed the goats. You also can handle cobra eggs, possum jaws, bee combs, and Madagascar hissing cockroaches. The park isn't fancy, but it's a treasure, especially for younger kids. There are kid-size picnic tables and toys for children to play with, too. *27 North Rd., Cromwell; (860) 635-3924.*

B.F. Clyde's Cider Mill ★★/Free

Nestled along Mystic's wooded back roads, this mill is a great spot to wet your whistle with sweet apple cider- and get a firsthand look at how it's made. For four generations, the Miner family has run the nation's only existing steam-powered cider mill, and the only mill in the state with its own pasteurization system. The Miners are happy to show you how they process up to 50 tons of apples a week. Afterward, buy cookies and pie in the general store. Then step onto the wide porch and enjoy your snacks outdoors. Open from July to December. *129 N. Stonington Rd., Old Mystic; (860) 536-3354.*

Denison Pequotsepos Nature Center ★★★/$

Escape the frenzy of downtown Mystic at this natural gem, which has seven miles of hiking trails through meadows, woodlands, and wetlands. Inside, you can meet live frogs, turtles, crayfish, snakes, and owls in a marvelous natural history museum, which highlights each of the three habitats. Don't miss the wonderful exhibit on the night sky: you crawl into a dark theater and take in the sounds and sights that come alive when the sun goes down. Birdwatchers can spot more than 150 species on the center's 125-acre private preserve. Throughout the year, the center offers special programs for families. (One, for example, trains you and your kids as animal-track-

ing detectives.) *109 Pequotsepos Rd., Mystic; (860) 536-1216.*

Devil's Hopyard State Park ★★★/Free

Legend has it that the devil hopped from ledge to ledge at this popular 860-acre park, leaving his footprints in the form of potholes at the base of the waterfall. On a sunny day, pack a picnic, pull on your hiking shoes, and hoof it to the falls for a waterside lunch. *Three miles north of the junction of CT 82 and CT 156, E. Haddam; (860) 424-3200.* **NOTE:** Another popular hiking spot is **Chatfield Hollow State Park**, *Rte. 80, Killingworth; (860) 566-2304.*

Essex Steam Train and Riverboat ★★★/$$

All aboard this authentic, coal-fired steam train, which bellows black smoke and blasts its whistle. Conductors in full regalia enjoy welcoming kids on the half-hour excursion through the countryside, and on theme days, they pull out all the stops. There's a Trick-or-Treat Train, an Easter Train, a Thomas Train pulled by the beloved storybook engine, and Santa's North Pole Express, featuring Santa, Mrs. Claus, and the elves. If you're up to it, extend your outing to a half day by signing on for the hour-long steamboat cruise that follows the train ride. (You're welcome to do one leg of the journey and not the other.) The Essex Depot sells terrific train souvenirs, including kids' conductor caps and, of course, Thomas the Tank Engine books. *Railroad Ave., Essex; (860) 767-0103;* www.valleyrr.com

Ferry Landing State Park
★★/Free

If you crave a break from the traffic along I-95, head to this small, riverside park. Pack a lunch and dine at picnic tables or inside the gazebo. Stroll along the Connecticut River on a wide boardwalk that's perfect for strollers and wheelchairs. Along the way, stop to watch the pleasure boats, go fishing, or soak up views of a salt marsh. This is as close as you can come to the river without renting a boat. To get here, take exit 70 off I-95 in Old Lyme, head right, and take your first right onto Ferry Road. The park is across from the Department of Environmental Protection Marine headquarters. *Ferry Rd., Old Lyme.*

Hubbard Park ★★/Free

For a relaxing outing, stop by this 1,800-acre park, famous for its April Daffodil Festival (when more than half a million flowers welcome spring). The park has playground equipment, a concert pavilion, and tennis courts. Kids can even feed the ducks and fish in the pond, marked by a sign with a curious message: "Fishing for Children." Hiking trails lead to Castle Craig, a replica of an ancient stone castle, which you can climb to enjoy sweeping views of the hilly landscape. *West Main St., Meriden; (203) 630-4259.*

Lyman Orchards ★★★/Free

You'll thoroughly enjoy the fruits of your labor at this beautiful series of orchards, owned by the Lyman family for eight generations. Depending on the season, you can pick your own strawberries, raspberries, apples, pears, blueberries, and bright orange pumpkins (there's a fee for what you pick). The Apple Barrel Farm Store sells pastries, cookies, and delicious caramel dip to make your fresh apples even sweeter. Special events include an Easter Apple Hunt, Strawberry Jamboree, and Autumn Harvest Days. *Rtes. 147 and 157, Middlefield; (860) 349-1793 or (860) 349-1566 (24-hour hotline);* www.lymanorchards.com

A Five-Minute Float

A trip on the **Chester-Hadlyme Ferry** only lasts a few minutes, but it's a fun, scenic way to get you and your car from one side of the Connecticut River to the other. The *Selden III* is the second-oldest continually operating ferry in the nation. As you float across the river, you'll see the range of hills known as the Seven Sisters (one of which is topped by Gillette Castle), and maybe even an eagle, too. *Rte. 148, in either Chester or Hadlyme; (860) 526-2743.*

Maple Breeze Park ★★/$

Need a break from sight-seeing in Mystic? It's a breeze at this small family amusement park near the Rhode Island border. Kids can chill out on two 350-foot-long water slides, play miniature golf, or ride in bumper boats and go-carts. *Rte. 2, Pawcatuck; (860) 599-1232.*

Mystic Aquarium and Institute for Exploration
★★★★/$$

Thanks to a $50 million expansion, this is one of the most provocative aquariums in the country. Your family can easily spend an entire day exploring the deep and getting acquainted with the more than 4,000 specimens (representing 200 species) who make their home here. A good place to start is with Dr. Robert E. Ballard, the explorer who discovered the *Titanic*. His Challenge of the Deep exhibit invites you

aboard the research vessel *Discovery* for a seven-minute video descent to the bottom of the sea. In a dark hall filled with special effects, you'll hear actual audio from the moment Dr. Ballard discovered the *Titanic*. And at the Immersion Theater, you can observe a Monterey Bay sanctuary in real time.

In the aquarium's Alaskan Coast area, you'll find kids stationed, nose-to-glass, in front of giant tanks with underwater viewing areas. Inside the tanks, beluga whales and gargantuan sea lions cavort virtually nonstop, almost as if they're playing to the crowd. A new sea lion show is very popular, as are animal encounters with belugas and penguins (fee). *55 Coogan Blvd., Mystic; (860) 572-5955.*

Ocean Beach Park
★★/Free

When the going gets hot, water-loving families go to this park, which has a beautiful beach and boardwalk, an Olympic-size swimming pool, a carousel, picnic groves, a paintball shooting gallery, and musical entertainment on the weekends. The park is a bit tired-looking in places, but a new management group is working on renovations to restore it to its original grandeur. Located at the edge of Long Island Sound, the sugary-sand beach is protected by Fishers Island, so the waters are fairly calm for young ones. There's a bathhouse and a number of snack bars on the premises. *1225 Ocean Ave., New London; (800) 510-SAND; (860) 447-3031.*

Prime Climb ★★/$-$$

Kid-friendly instructors will help your family reach new heights at the region's largest climbing gym. Prime Climb boasts more than 14,000-square feet of climbing walls, some up to 40 feet high. It also features a fun form of encouragement: wall murals of Homer and Bart Simpson trying to scale the moon. Families can go "bouldering" and climb horizontally across a wall without special equipment, or go vertical by signing on for a Try a Climb program, which includes climbing shoes, equipment, and instruction. Either way, you'll get a foothold on this popular sport. *340 Silversmith Park, Bldg. 28, Wallingford; (203) 265-7880;* www.primeclimb.com

Project Oceanology ★★★/$$

Would-be marine scientists will love the chance to join professionals on expeditions sponsored by this non-profit research institute. From mid-February to March, you can sign on for a two-and-a-half-hour seal-watching adventure aboard the floating classroom, Enviro-lab. After a 20-minute slide program, you'll sail into Fisher's Island Sound and spot pods of seals lounging on the rocks. (In winter, the seals migrate from Maine to the warmer waters of

ROLLIN' ON THE RIVER

For more than 20 years, the Deep River Navigation Company has blended history and scenery on fun boat trips aboard several different vessels. Families especially enjoy the hour-long lighthouse cruises on the *Aunt Polly*, a two-deck excursion boat that departs from Saybrook Point. Another favorite is the hour-long riverboat cruise that follows an excursion aboard the Essex Steam Train (see page 390). You may want to bring binoculars for a better view of the wildlife you're likely to spot on these tours. Snacks are sold on the boats. For a complete list of tours and departure points, call (860) 526-4954.

Connecticut.) In the summer, join researchers on a hands-on adventure aboard Enviro-lab. You'll be able to pull up trawl nets along Long Island Sound and record and examine the contents of your catch: lobsters, crabs, and other sea life. You'll also view plankton under a microscope and conduct marine-science experiments.

Another option is a Project Oceanology tour to the historic New London Ledge Lighthouse. On this adventure, you can climb to the top of the tower that's guided ships since 1909. *Avery Point, 1084 Shennecosset Rd., Groton; (800) 364-8472; (860) 445-9007.*

BUNKING DOWN

Beachplum Hotel
★★/$

This well-run property is clean, comfortable, and affordable. Standard motel rooms have refrigerators and cable TV, while efficiencies contain small kitchens.

If you're in the area for a week, consider renting a cottage with a cozy sun porch. These little hideaways are beautifully decorated and have full kitchen facilities.

There's a heated outdoor pool on property, and it's just a five-minute stroll to the beach. **NOTE:** Make your reservations well in advance, since they tend to book up a year ahead. *1935 Boston Post Rd., Westbrook; (860) 399-9345.*

Sojourner Inn
★★/$$$

Set back from the road on a quiet stretch of Route 184, this lodge has one-bedroom suites that are fifty percent larger than standard hotel rooms. There's a spacious living room, a bedroom separated by a door, cable television, a fully equipped kitchen, and complimentary breakfast. *Route 184, Groton, (800) 697-8483; (860)-445-1986.*

The Water Purse
Talk about wash and wear!

Here's how to craft a thoroughly waterproof and easy-to-make drawstring purse from an onion bag, and it's more than just a fashion statement. Secured to your clothing with a plastic clip, it's invaluable for carrying quarters for the pool's soda machine, holding interesting river rocks, or hauling your goggles and earplugs to the beach.

To make one, simply weave a length of plastic twine (or other waterproof material) around the onion bag's opening to serve as a drawstring. About halfway around the bag, weave the twine through the loop of a plastic clip, like the kind commonly sold as key chains.

Griswold Inn
★★★/$$$

Since 1776, this inn has been an institution in the lovely village of Essex, which has been lauded by author Norman Crampton as one of the 100 best small towns in America. The appealing quarters are decorated in colonial furnishings and include a variety of suites, both in and around the main inn.

Though the rooms themselves have no televisions, you'll find a TV set and board games in a common area in the Hayden House. Continental breakfast is included in the rates, and there are children's menus available in the historic dining room.

Since there's no swimming pool, video games, or organized activities, the "Gris" is best for families who want a vacation that takes them back in time to Revolutionary War Days. *36 Main St., Essex; (860) 767-1776.*

Howard Johnson Inn at Mystic
★★/$$

One of Mystic's better values, this chain motel just across the street from Olde Mystik Village has an indoor pool, two Crayola-themed Kids Rooms (with themed decor, kid-size furniture, an easel with crayons and chalk, and a VCR), and complimentary loaner videos and books at the front desk.

Year-round packages include breakfast at Friendly's (across the parking lot), admission to top attrac-

tions, a Crayola Kids Pack, a regional discount card, and more. *253 Greenmanville Ave., Mystic; (860) 536-2654, (800) GO-HOJO; www. funtraveler.com*

Mystic Hilton
★★/$$$

This property, across from the Mystic Aquarium, has a small table where kids can draw and color while parents check in. There's an indoor pool and children's movies on weekend nights, as well as occasional magicians and face painters. *20 Coogan Blvd., Mystic; (860) 572-0731; www.hilton.com*

Mystic Marriott Hotel and Spa
★★★/$$$-$$$$

For a deluxe weekend getaway, this high-end hotel fits the bill with a beautiful indoor pool, a stylish restaurant with a gourmet kids' menu (filet mignon with fries, anyone?), an on-site Elizabeth Arden Red Door Space (clinicians will even give little girls a manicure while Mom is getting one), and periodic family packages that include admission to Mystic Aquarium and Mystic Seaport. *625 North Road, Groton; (860) 446-2600 or (866) 449-7390; www.mysticmarriott.com*

Sandpiper Motor Inn
★★/$$

This motel isn't fancy, but it's clean, close to the beach (the front desk will provide guest passes), and family-friendly. Located on a four-and-a-half-acre lot with a pool, it offers plenty of space for kids to roam. In summer, there's a two-night minimum; weekly rates are available, too. Continental breakfast is included in the room rate. *1750 Boston Post Rd. (Rte. 1), Old Saybrook; (800) 323-7973; (860) 399-7973.*

Water's Edge Resort and Country Club
★★★/$$$

Located directly on the shore, this destination resort is one of the area's prettiest vacation spots. Loaded with activities for kids, the Water's Edge has standard hotel rooms, suites, and villas that can accommodate large and small families. Kids can spend their days playing on the beautiful private beach, swimming in the pool, trying out a paddleboat,

---

FamilyFun TIP

A Beachside Shower

Everybody loves spending a fun-packed day at the shore until it's time to climb back in the car, still sticky and sandy, for the ride home. Here's a quick way for your backseat travelers to freshen up before hitting the road. Fill two or three clean plastic milk jugs with water and leave them in the car while you swim. When you're ready to leave, the water will be warm enough for a soothing rinse.

---

or joining organized activities, such as crafts classes, family swims, and candy hunts. The acclaimed waterfront dining room has a kids' menu. *1525 Boston Post Rd. (Rte. 1), Westbrook; (800) 222-5901; (860) 399-5901.*

GOOD EATS

Abbott's Lobster in the Rough/ Costello's Clam Shack
★★★/$$

Though Abbott's is crowded with tour bus and casino patrons, it's still worth a visit, especially in midafternoon, when it's less busy. Why so popular? The location is terrific. Nestled in a 300-year-old fishing village, the restaurant is the perfect place to watch the boats and take in views of Fishers Island Sound. Sit at picnic tables along the water's edge and dine on succulent lobsters (or peanut-butter-and jelly, if you'd rather). An even better bet for kids is neighboring **Costello's** *(860/572-2779)*, a classic seaside shack where clams, hot dogs, and chowder are served on the outdoor upper deck. *117 Pearl St., Noank; (860) 536-7719.*

Go Fish ★★★/$$$

If parents crave a fancier meal in a kid-friendly yet arty atmosphere, this is the place. While Mom and Dad dine on sushi and Asian-inspired fish dishes, kids can have pasta, chicken tenders, pizza, and

PB&J. In between bites, kids can color pretty pictures of mermaids. It works for everyone. *Olde Mystick Village, Mystic; (860) 536-2662.*

It's Only Natural
★★★/$$

The kids' menu here features scrumptious PB&J made with smooth peanut butter and organic jam on pita bread (served with apple slices), organic Os (like SpaghettiOs), and pita pizza, plus banana cake, juice spritzers, and fun fruit smoothies. The atmosphere is as creative as the cuisine, with funky mobiles and artwork hanging on the ceiling and walls. A special kids' area is outfitted with a miniature red sofa, puzzles, books, and toys for young guests to enjoy. Parents won't believe that delicacies like the Maryland crab cakes are made with tempeh. *386 Main St., Main Street Market, Middletown; (860) 346-9210.*

Lenny & Joe's Fish Tale Drive-In Menu
★★★★/$$

Order from a menu at the counter, pick a table inside or out, and have fun for a good cause while you wait for your meal. Choices include everything from fried clams and jumbo onion rings to cheeseburgers and chicken teriyaki. For $1— with all proceeds going to charity—you can hop on a wooden horse and ride the restaurant's 1880s-style merry-go-round. After dinner, head to the on-site ice-cream stand, for a kiddie cone, taffy, or fresh popcorn. There's not much in the way of scenery, but that doesn't seem to spoil the fun. *1301 Boston Post Rd. (Rte. 1), Madison; (203) 245-7289.*

Mystic Pizza
★★★/$-$$

If you're a Julia Roberts fan, chances are you've already seen this place in her 1988 film *Mystic Pizza.* Run by the Zepelos family since 1973, this is an appealing, kid-friendly restaurant. The pizza is excellent, the prices are reasonable, and the service is friendly. If your kids don't want pizza, they can order fish-and-chips, chicken tenders, hamburgers, and more off the children's menu. The kids can color while you wait for your food; the grown-ups can look at the movie stills. *56 W. Main St., Mystic; (860) 536-3700 or (860) 536-3737. (A second restaurant, Mystic Pizza II, is located at the rotary of Rtes. 2 and 184 in North Stonington; 860/388-2218.)*

Pat's Kountry Kitchen
★★/$$

This is a friendly, affordable place where families can enjoy a hearth-cooked meal. Here, you'll find everything from chicken potpie and Dagwood sandwiches (thinly sliced steak with melted cheese) to a kids' menu featuring Fido (hot dog with fries) and Mighty Mouse (grilled cheese with fries). In keeping with its country theme, the restaurant is decorated with teddy bears, miniature carousels, and other Americana. A shop across the street sells many of the items. *70 Mill Rock Rd., Old Saybrook; (860) 388-4784.*

Pizzaworks
★★★/$-$$

This historic freight depot delivers a kid-pleasing combo: awesome trains and pizza. Where else can you order exceptional pasta dishes and thin-crust pies (kids love the Hawaiian with pineapple and Canadian bacon), plus climb upstairs to see a wondrous train layout? Designed by the witty Steve Cryan, the River City display features a train chugging by businesses including Hoffa Cement and Ted Kennedy's Driving School. You'll have so much fun examining the intricately crafted miniature village, before you know it, your pizza might get cold. *455 Boston Post Rd. (Rte. 1), Old Saybrook; (860) 388-2218.* Other locations throughout the state.

Randall's Ordinary
★★★★/$$$$

There's nothing ordinary about this 17th-century tavern, which was once part of Connecticut's Underground Railroad. (Ask the staff to lift the trapdoor in the kitchen, so you can see the secret hiding place.) Hearty meals are cooked before your eyes

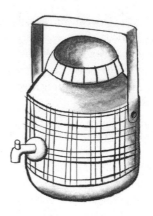

over an open hearth with a crackling fire. Depending on the time of day, you'll feast on home-cooked corn cakes, smoked turkey, and fish dishes. (**TIP:** To save money, come for breakfast.) After your repast, walk out back and visit donkeys Cricket and Billy, oxen Red and Rusty, and the 1,200-pound pig, Big Daddy. Located on 250 acres, Randall's Ordinary also has guest rooms, including an extremely cool silo suite (that's right, it's in a silo) with a Jacuzzi. Kids can entertain themselves by playing horseshoes, croquet, and volleyball. *Rte. 2, N. Stonington; (860) 599-4540.*

Sea Swirl ★★/$

One of the best clam shacks along this stretch of Route 1, Sea Swirl serves rolls stuffed with tender whole-belly fried clams, homemade corn chowder, ten-inch-long hot dogs, and fish-and-chips. Eat outside at a picnic table, and finish off the feast with soft-serve ice cream cones.

Junction of Rtes. 1 and 27, Mystic; (860) 536-3452. (Nearby, the Cove Fish Market, Old Stonington Rd., Mystic; 860/536-0061, has a similar menu and covered seating area.)

SOUVENIR HUNTING

Great American Trading Company

Bring your fun money to this outlet, which sells factory seconds on board games manufactured by the Great American Trading Company of York, Pennsylvania. You'll also find thousands of other fun toys and novelties, including yo-yos, Thomas the Tank Engine memorabilia, costumes, party items, and a selection of marbles that will thrill even the most avid collector. *39 Main St., Deep River; (860) 663-2625.*

Nature's Art

This retail entertainment venue sells fossils and nature-themed toys, but it's the hands-on activities (which run from $1 to $10) that attract kids. Here, you can pan for faux gold, dig for dinosaur bones at a re-created paleontological site, make sand art

creations, and visit a fossil gallery. *1650 Route 85, Montville; (860) 443-GEMS.*

Olde Mistick Village

This 18th-century-style shopping center has more than 60 shops, many of which will amuse kids (the **Toy Soldier, Mystic Kite Shop, Raining Cats and Dogs**). There are three ponds where you can feed the ducks and geese, a movie theater, and that dependable family restaurant, Newport Creamery (see page 321 for details). *Coogan Boulevard at Rte. 27, I-95, exit 90; (860) 536-4941.*

R. J. Julia Independent Booksellers

At a time when other independent bookstores are finding it difficult to survive, this place is so popular, it's practically an attraction in itself. Keep an eye out for famous authors as you and your kids browse through the vast collection, which includes an exceptional children's section. For a sweet treat, stop by the café. Children's authors frequently give readings, so call for a schedule. *768 Boston Post Rd., Madison; (203) 245-3959.*

Index

Also from FamilyFun

FAMILYFUN MAGAZINE: a creative guide to all the great things families can do together. Call 800-289-4849 for a subscription.

FAMILYFUN.COM: visit us at www.familyfun.com and search our extensive archives for games, crafts, recipes, and holiday projects.

FAMILYFUN COOKBOOK: a collection of more than 250 irresistible recipes for you and your kids, from healthy snacks to birthday cakes to dinners everyone in the family can enjoy (Disney Editions, 256 pages; $24.95).

FAMILYFUN CRAFTS: a step-by-step guide to more than 500 of the best crafts and activities to do with your kids (Disney Editions, 256 pages; $24.95).

FAMILYFUN PARTIES: a complete party planner featuring 100 celebrations for birthdays, holidays, and every day (Disney Editions, 224 pages; $24.95).

FAMILYFUN COOKIES FOR CHRISTMAS: a batch of 50 recipes for creative holiday treats (Disney Editions, 64 pages; $9.95).

FAMILYFUN TRICKS AND TREATS: a collection of wickedly easy crafts, costumes, party plans, and recipes for Halloween (Disney Editions, 98 pages; $14.95).

FAMILYFUN BOREDOM BUSTERS: a collection of 365 activities, from instant fun and after-school crafts to kitchen projects and learning games (Disney Editions, 224 pages; $24.95).

FAMILYFUN HOMEMADE HOLIDAYS: A collection of 150 holiday activities, from festive

 decorations and family traditions to holiday recipes and gifts kids can make. (Disney Editions; 96 pages; $14.95).